C000062914

THIS BOOK IS DEDICATED
TO THE MEMORY OF:
PATRICK MACK, JERRY
WILLIAMS, MIKE NICOLOSI,
DAVE "INSURGENT" RUBINSTEIN,
DAVE PARSONS, ANDY "APATHY"
BRYAN, FRENCHIE THE SKIN,
CHUCK VALLE, RAY "RAYBEEZ"
BARBERI, CARL 'MOSHER'
DIMOLA, BIG CHARLIE HANKINS,
LEON ROSS, JAVIER "SOB"
CARPIO, LAZAR, JOE FISH,
IRA OSTRELL, ADAM YAUCH,
DAVID SKILLKIN, BLUE,
JOHN NORDQUIST, AND ALL
THOSE WHO ARE NO LONGER
WITH US THAT HELPED
BUILD THE NYHC SCENE.

NYHC
NEW YORK HARDCORE, 1980–1990
BY TONY RETTMAN

Copyright © 2014 Tony Rettman
Fourth printing, published in 2020 by

Bazillion Points
New York, New York
www.bazillionpoints.com

Produced for Bazillion Points by Ian Christe
Cover layout and design by Bazillion Points

Photographs © Ken Salerno, Frank White, Gary Tse Tse Fly, John Kelly, Joe Foy, Greg Licht, Randy Underwood, Dave Brady, Jordan Cooper, Jamie Davis, Justine Demetrick, Adam Tanner, Chris Tsakis, Chris Minicucci, Dirk Behlau

"On My Own Authority" © Freddy Cricien 2014

Bazillion Points thanks Magnus Henriksson, Polly Watson, Dianna Dilworth, VIVI, Fox, Tesco Vee, Ken Salerno, Freddy Cricien, Danielle, and everyone who pulled together to support this book.

Library of Congress Control Number: 2020938785
Library of Congress Cataloging-in-Publication Data is available upon request.

ISBN 978-1-935950-12-7

Printed in China

All rights reserved. No part of this publication may be reproduced or transmitted in any form or by any means, electronic or mechanical, including photocopy, recording, or any information storage and retrieval system, without prior permission in writing from the publisher.

TABLE OF CONTENTS

Freddy Cricien fronts Agnostic Front in a pre-Madball moment, August 1988. **FRANK WHITE**

ON MY OWN AUTHORITY
BY FREDDY CRICIEN

When I was five years old, in 1980, my family moved from New Jersey to South Florida. My eldest brother, Roger, decided to stay behind. He had discovered this underground music scene that was starting to "make noise" in lower Manhattan. He became a "punk rocker"—but that would soon change. My life, too, would be altered by that noise within a few years.

My brother found a home in that scene. He shaved his punker Mohawk and proclaimed himself a NYHC skin—which is what the rough-around-the-edges bunch were doing at that time. His shaved head wasn't politically driven or a racially motivated statement in any way—my bro was a Cuban immigrant, after all—it was a rebellion. He was a bass player, and played in a couple bands before he was asked to sing for an outfit that used to go by the name Zoo Crew. They became Agnostic Front, Roger took the gig, and the rest is . . . well, if you don't know, you soon will! And if you don't even then, read more books like this one.

When I eventually got into the NYHC scene myself, I embraced it wholeheartedly. I got a chance to sing with AF at Great Gildersleeves in 1982, as a seven-year-old. That sparked my newfound interest. Eventually my brother encouraged me to start my own band. I released my first music, a seven-inch titled *Ball of Destruction*, in 1989, a year before the cutoff point of this book. My band was christened Madball, because that was my nickname at the time. For better or worse, the name stuck and so did my passion for this lifestyle.

I can't begin to speak as an authority on any other individual's perspective of this subculture we call hardcore, hardcore punk, and—my preference—NYHC. Everyone's experience is different. Everyone is initiated in different ways at different times. One thing I can say with certainty: There is no music scene, genre, culture, or movement like hardcore, and the New York faction is especially unique. That is a biased comment, in favor of my own particular faction, but I feel it's a factual observation, by anybody's measure. I think few would argue New York's place.

I am skeptical of "period piece" books that only cover a part of hardcore history. I'd hate for people to have the impression that NYHC was some sort of fad that only lasted ten years—that couldn't be further from truth! In reality, I know I have no reason to worry. I don't have to be the protector of the NYHC scene, or the hardcore scene in general, for that matter. The scene is still just fine and can take care of itself!

Documents like this book are necessary. These years were formative ones. For those who lived it, you will be transported back in time and you can revel in the nostalgia. To those who didn't live it, go ahead and transport yourself to that period and be grateful that you've discovered this special scene. Read on and take everything in—but don't feel like you missed out! This book is a way to get caught up on history, and also a bridge to a whole world that is as relevant today as it's ever been. This book is a fun and informative read—enjoy it!

Thanks for your time.

Freddy "Madball" Cricien

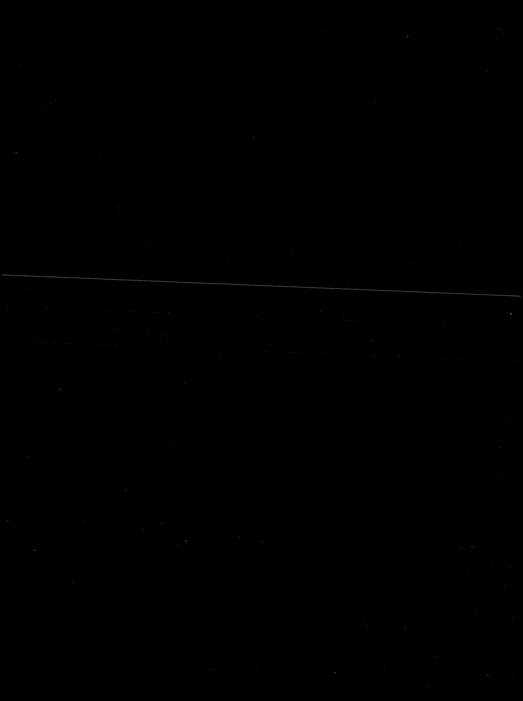

FRIDAY
JANUARY 1ST

STIMULATORS

CBGB

315 BOWERY (at Bleecker) 982-4052

1. THE STIMULATORS: LOUD FAST RULES!

"The Stimulators are definitely a rock band, as opposed to all that New York art (shit) rock and funk that pseudo-intellectuals rave about in clubs but can't remember when they exit." —Jack Rabid, Big Takeover *no. 1, June 1980*

DENISE MERCEDES (GUITARIST, THE STIMULATORS): There was no scene. We arrived after that Television and Ramones thing. At least in my world, that wasn't really happening. I don't even know if those people were still out playing. That wasn't our world. It seemed like there was a pause, and nothing was really happening.

STEVE WISHNIA (BASSIST, FALSE PROPHETS): As far as the first generation of punk in New York, that was really at a lull in 1980. Patti Smith Group broke up in '79, Television broke up in '78, Only the Talking Heads were successful. The Heartbreakers were playing maybe once a month. The Dictators had broken up. The Ramones thought they were going to break big with *Rocket to Russia* and *Road to Ruin*, and in a more just world they would have—but they didn't. Then they tried to be more commercial with *End of the Century* and that didn't happen.

REBECCA KORBET (VOCALIST, EVEN WORSE): Personally, I already felt a distance from people like the Ramones and Blondie and Television; they seemed quite old to me. At seventeen everyone seems old to you, don't they? A lot of those bands came from art school, or had been doing the clubs forever by the time we came along, so I didn't feel much of an affinity myself.

WENDY EAGER (EDITOR, *Guillotine* FANZINE): I was trying to get into punk, but punk had already transitioned into new wave. I was trying to find something that fit into the anger and the angst that I had at that time.

JESSE MALIN (Guitarist/vocalist, Heart Attack, D-Generation): When I was twelve, I put together a band with some other kids called Heart Attack. We played an audition at CBGB and failed. Later on, we found out the reason we didn't pass the audition was that the punk music we were playing had "happened" already. We were too late. The Clash was going funky, Blondie was going disco, and the Ramones were putting on striped shirts and trying to be power pop. So punk wasn't fully there. The stuff that was really going on in the clubs at the time was Spandau Ballet, Adam and the Ants, and Bow Wow Wow. Malcolm McLaren was playing with ducks. Rockabilly somehow was a new music. After the CBGB audition, someone said, "Hey kid! Why don't you check out some new sounds, like rockabilly?" We felt disillusioned, but we knew something was going on.

JACK RABID (Editor, *Big Takeover* fanzine; drummer, Even Worse): To me, it all comes down to that part in the *Please Kill Me* book [by Legs McNeil and Gillian McCain] where Seymour Stein throws the Dead Boys out of his office, and says, "I took a bet on punk rock and none of you sold any records." And that was that. No more Saints records. No more Rezillos records. No more Radio Birdman records. Pretty soon, he was signing Madonna.

SCREAMING MAD GEORGE (Vocalist, the Mad): I don't know that there was a void in the New York City music scene. The second generation of New York punks like the Stimulators and the Mad were given the opportunity to perform and shape what became the New York post-punk scene.

EDDIE SUTTON (Vocalist, Leeway): The whole original energy and attitude of punk rock came from New York in the mid-1970s. When Malcolm McLaren was out here managing the end of the New York Dolls, he took all that energy back to England and manufactured punk rock. So when American hardcore kicked in between '79 and '80, that's where punk came from again. But make no bones about it—punk rock is American. It's as American as hard apple cider.

VINNIE STIGMA (Guitarist, the Eliminators, Agnostic Front, Madball; vocalist, Stigma): The time we're talking about, we're talking the Stimulators. We're talking my band at the time, the Eliminators. We're talking Johnny Thunders, Vinnie Stigma, and Frankie Cadillac. Three guys who used to talk shit. Three goombas hangin' out on the corner, or talking over coffee. Talking about meatballs.

PAUL CRIPPLE (Guitarist, Reagan Youth): In all honesty, Denise Mercedes, the guitarist of the Stimulators, was the catalyst for New York hardcore. She set down the rules that governed NYHC. Play punk rock—but louder and faster. She does not get any credit. I saw her recently when her band, Judas Priestess—an all-girl Judas Priest cover band—opened for Pentagram. I told her, "You started New York hardcore!" She replied, "Right!"

DOUG HOLLAND (Guitarist, Apprehended, Kraut, Cro-Mags): I could tell you ten dudes off the top of my head who have thriving punk bands today because they went to see the Stimulators. I saw them one night at Max's Kansas City. There were all these cute little girls watching them, and I thought that was pretty fucking cool.

BOBBY STEELE (Guitarist, the Misfits; guitarist/vocalist, the Undead): The Stimulators; all you ever hear is one or two things by them. Their recordings are piss-poor representations of how great they were live. They were one of the best bands, and Dee Mercedes was one of the best guitar players ever in punk rock. Other guitar players were ripping off her licks. I'd go to see the Stimulators, and I'm watching Dee playing these intros for songs. Six months later, a Damned record would come out with the same intro. She never got the recognition she deserves. There weren't a lot of great lead guitar players in the punk scene. It always bugs me. She should have been something.

DENISE MERCEDES: I was very fortunate to have a friend who worked for the label that put out the first Damned album, *Damned Damned Damned*. We went down to CBGB to the first Damned show. Literally the second they started to play, my life changed. When I saw the Damned bust out, that was it. I went insane for punk rock. I felt this was what I wanted to be doing. I came from a place of listening to very accomplished musicians. Punk gave me the freedom where I didn't have to be Jimi Hendrix in order to get out there. I saw that creativity, all that looseness, and all that attitude.

I became friends with Rat Scabies, the drummer in the Damned. I was playing with somebody, and I held out the phone to him, saying, "Hey, listen to me play." A few months later, he got in touch with me and said, "Come to England. I'm not with the Damned anymore. I'm starting another band, and I want you to be the guitarist." So I went over there. We did some gigs. It didn't work out, but I met a lot of people who were big names in the British punk world.

I came back and started the Stimulators right away. I was just energized by all I had seen and felt. I guess you can say I just loved the total innocence of it.

People were just saying, "I want to play! I never touched an instrument in my life. I don't care!" That really stimulated me.

Basically, the band was initially me on guitar, a woman named Anne Gustavsson on bass, and Patrick Mack singing. He was my best friend. I miss him every day of my life. We found him at Max's Kansas City. We had a gig lined up at a place called Rock Bottom, on Eighth Street, but we didn't have a singer. We went to Max's, saw a guy who looked cute, and said, "Hey! Do you sing?" He goes, "No." I go, "Do you want to?" And he said yeah. Great, you know?

JACK RABID: I always got to Max's before the club opened. I'd line up so I could get one of the front tables. The first time I saw the Stimulators play there, all these punk rockers walked in. I'd seen maybe two of them at other gigs. But there were twenty-five of them. Who were these other twenty-three? Something was happening. I never saw these people at Dead Boys gigs!

Richard Hell used to scowl at me when I'd go by him in the stairwell of my old apartment at 437 East 12th, because I would be in my punk rock clothes. He'd look at me, like, "You're too late for that, Sonny Jim." That was the attitude: Punk rock was over. So to see twenty-five other kids walk in looking like punk rockers, it was like, "What the hell is this?" Then they ripped open the curtain and there were these two chicks, a wild-looking singer, and a little boy on drums.

DENISE MERCEDES: From our first gig, word spread like wildfire about the Stimulators. A very intense energy formed around us, which was nice. We had a very unique experience and people loved the music. We had two wild girls playing, and it was a real turning point that we had an eleven-year-old punk kid drummer. That meant every kid in New York City had to come and see this for themselves. I can honestly say we had hundreds of people showing up at gigs, many of them underage. That led the way to the all-ages shows, because so many people would come to see us and most of them couldn't get in.

SCREAMING MAD GEORGE: You can't ignore that twelve-year-old Harley Flanagan playing drums! He always stole the show.

BOBBY STEELE: I've known Harley since he was a kid. The first time I met him he put out his hand for a handshake and he had tar all over his hand. I spent the rest of the night trying to catch up with him to smear it on his face.

VINNIE STIGMA: I was at Harley Flanagan's twelfth birthday party. He was so small that he had to stand up to play the drums, because his foot couldn't reach the pedal. His twelfth birthday I'll never forget. I chased him around the bar of Max's all night long, because I'm a fun guy. He was twelve years old. He was a baby!

DARRYL JENIFER (Bassist, Bad Brains): The Stimulators were a very hot band with the chick on bass, the gay lead singer, Denise on guitar, and then there was this hyped-out kid on drums.

HARLEY FLANAGAN (Drummer, the Stimulators, M.O.I.; bassist and later vocalist, Cro-Mags): I was ten years old. I lived in Europe and Scandinavia at the time. I had been to London, and hung out with Rat Scabies from the Damned, and seen his band the White Cats play, and other punk bands. I was in my first punk band, Little Big Boss, in late '77. We toured once, played at a big anarchist festival, and at a big punk rock New Year's party, after midnight, so that was '78. Then we broke up. Then me and my mom moved back to NYC and the Lower East Side.

DENISE MERCEDES: Harley had been coming to rehearsals. He had been living in Europe and then came back to New York. I brought him to a few rehearsals and he was already drumming over there. I had him sit in a couple times during the Stimulators' rehearsals, and he very quickly learned songs like "Blind Ambition." He was the one who gave the force and the power to the song "Loud Fast Rules!". He took it from being an exciting song to an over-the-moon song. His energy was coming out, and with him on drums it was like, "Now it's right!"

We were on our way to Philadelphia, and Johnny Blitz from the Dead Boys was supposed to be drumming. He was a no-show. I couldn't reach him. Went to his house, ringing the bell. No answer. No nothing. I said, "Harley, guess what? You're going to be playing the show tonight." And that's how it all started.

JESSE MALIN: I went to see the Stimulators, and they had a kid who was the same age as me on drums. I had met him before, at the Clash concert at the Palladium. Seeing him play gave me the confidence to keep doing this.

JACK RABID: The Stimulators had a real high-energy attack. They never got it on record, except for their first single. But even that single didn't have the volume of the live gigs. It was a sheer-volume kind of thing; the guitars would just be screaming. They had pretty good equipment for those days. Almost all of the bands had crappy equipment. When they played at Max's, people kicked over the tables, and the kids started dancing, and Patrick threw himself

"NEED Stimulation?" bad brains — DJ "Jack rabid

STIMULATORS saturday

One Under JulY 5

one east FORty eighth street

into the crowd because he was a big Iggy Pop fan.

NICK MARDEN (Bassist, Even Worse, the Stimulators): Pat was a huge Iggy fan, but sometimes he was a little too much. There were times he was perfectly happy to dive off the stage into a nonexistent crowd. Once at Irving Plaza, he climbed up into the rigging, shimmied across, and dropped twelve feet out of the ceiling, right in front of the microphone, and then started the song.

JACK RABID: Three or four songs in, the first time seeing them, I was sold. I didn't know anything like that was happening in New York. This wasn't Poly-rock. This wasn't a bunch of people standing around clapping politely after songs. No one would dance to the Contortions, even though they were doing this heavy funk thing. All these kids were dancing. I was seventeen, I wanted to dance! So I started throwing myself around among these kids I didn't know.

JOHN WATSON: I was living in the Bronx when Russ 75 brought me down to Max's. I was amazed. I went by myself the next night and got hired as a busboy and bar-back. Then, one night, the Stimulators played. All the kids knocked down the tables and started doing a mixture of pogoing while slamming into each other. The Stimulators were the ones who kind of created this whole separate scene.

ROGER MIRET (Vocalist, Agnostic Front; bassist, the Psychos): The first time I ever saw Vinnie Stigma, he had a Mohawk at the Peppermint Lounge. He was in the center of the pit while the Stimulators were playing.

VINNIE STIGMA: The first time Roger saw me was at the Peppermint Lounge.

He was up in the balcony, and I was down in the pit. I was standing in the middle of the pit with my Mohawk, and that's his first image of me. He was like, "Who the hell is that guy?"

JAMES KONTRA (VOCALIST, AGNOSTIC FRONT, VIRUS): The kids around the Stimulators became the first prototype of hardcore punk rock for New York. We called ourselves hardcore, because we were different than the Johnny Thunders–looking people. We were younger and more energetic, and we weren't into heroin. No one did dope. We drank and smoked pot, but we didn't sniff anything—coke, dope, none of that shit.

UNCLE AL MORRIS (GUITARIST, THE ATTACK, MURPHY'S LAW, UNHOLY ALLIANCE): What differentiated punk from hardcore was heroin. To be considered punk in 1980, it seemed you had to emulate the junkies. I never did heroin; I thought it was real degenerate, so I drifted over to hardcore because it was not a heroin-based scene. To be hardcore meant you had to be healthy enough to rock the pit; junkies just nodded out in the corner. Punks got picked on and victimized by muggers and other junkies. We didn't buy dope, and if any of those types got in our faces, we'd crash their skulls in with a trash can.

JESSE MALIN: I never got into the drug thing, because it weirded me out. The generation before us had something to say, but they burnt out. I saw that and thought, "We're going to be in your face and have something to say. We're going to be energized and not be on fucking drugs, so we're not going away."

JOHNNY CARCO (BASSIST, THE MISGUIDED): We immediately set down rules for ourselves, regarding what would be acceptable and what wouldn't. Doing drugs was not acceptable. This mainly came about because our neighborhood in Queens was infested with angel dust, and kids who loved the Grateful Dead, the Doors, and southern rock. There were also the guido boys, who thought they were the real Italians. Both of those groups of peers were the enemy. They didn't like us, and we didn't like them. Back in those days, you could get threatened or beat up for wearing a Clash T-shirt, or having a differing opinion on just about anything.

RALPHIE G (VOCALIST, THE MOB): The transformation of the New York punk scene came with those of us who were the younger generation. Those from that first era who didn't die off, or get scared by what us kids started to do, joined in on the new thing we were doing and became part of our scene; or you might look at it like we took over theirs!

JACK RABID: With the Stimulators, we had a band that would play regularly.

The Heartbreakers would play their three-day weekend, and then you'd wait three or four months for another one. The Stimulators would play two or three shows a month. I remember before I left after seeing them the first time, the band told me, "We're playing Tier 3 next week." I said, "I'm there!" Just to have a regular thing to do like that was fantastic.

WENDY EAGER: The Stimulators simply did not have that attitude that the old punks had. They were grittier, and dirty sounding. They had more of a New York feel. So I think they're a band that really transitioned between punk and hardcore.

SEAN TAGGART (VOCALIST, SHOK; ARTIST (CRO-MAGS, CRUMBSUCKERS)): The Stimulators are definitely the bridging band for New York from punk to hardcore in the same way the Germs were the band from L.A. to do that.

JESSE MALIN: Harley Flanagan went over to Dublin in 1980 with the Stimulators, and he came back from Belfast with the Doc Martens and the shaved head.

DENISE MERCEDES: We had a wonderful opportunity to go to Ireland. We were there for a month. We went over with John Davis, who did a punk rock film in 1979 called *Shellshock Rock* which documented the Belfast and Northern Ireland punk scene. His perspective was that during the war going on for so long between the Catholics and the Protestants, the only thing he saw pulling people together was punk. We were the first American punk band to go to Ireland, and we found ourselves right smack in the middle of a war. We had no idea. It's not reality until you have machine guns pointed in your face and bricks thrown at you. I asked why all the clubs had chain-link fences around them, and they were like, "So the bombs bounce off them."

ROBBIE CRYPTCRASH (DRUMMER, CRYPTCRASHERS, AGNOSTIC FRONT, CAUSE FOR ALARM): When The Stimulators came back from Ireland, Harley was a skinhead. Everything about Harley after Ireland was different. Not better or worse, just different.

TODD YOUTH (BASSIST, AGNOSTIC FRONT, SKINHEAD YOUTH; GUITARIST, WARZONE, MURPHY'S LAW, D-GENERATION): Harley Flanagan played a really important role. Everybody hates on him now, but when Harley was fourteen or fifteen, he was the first guy to shave his head and get the first tattoo. I learned how to play hardcore music from Harley.

DAVE SCOTT (DRUMMER, ADRENALIN O.D.): The Stimulators weren't the only thing. Other than them, there were the Mad, the Violators, the Victims, and some others that were the last of the real punk bands playing back then.

BOBBY STEELE: One of the first bands on that early scene that impressed me—before anything was called hardcore—was this band called the Attack. That band never got anywhere, and had probably one of the worst heroin problems at that time. They found the guitar player dead of a heroin overdose and bloated in an abandoned building. The Attack never got any real recognition. One of the guys in that band, Jason, was later in Krieg Kopf. He came a long way.

UNCLE AL MORRIS: I was in the Attack. The Attack was a good band, but troubled with a heroin problem. Our bass player Zal died from an overdose, and our singer was wrestling with his problems. We were one of those bridge bands in the post-punk, not yet hardcore, era of '79 to '81, that looked back instead of forward.

STEVEN WISHNIA: Then there were the Offals. They did a punk version of Oscar the Grouch's "I Love Trash" from *Sesame Street*.

JACK RABID: When my band Even Worse couldn't get a gig with the Mad, or the Stimulators, or the Bad Brains, we did a couple of gigs with this band the Offals. They were pretty much the only band that was our age. They were all seventeen, eighteen, or nineteen. The Offals were definitely beginning musicians. We played two gigs with them at the U.K. Club, two weeks in a row, and we called it "Modesty Night at the U.K. Club." We believed in truth in advertising!

TOMMY RAT (VOCALIST, AGNOSTIC FRONT, WARZONE, LIFE'S BLOOD, TRIP 6, REJUVENATE): In 1980, I started going to shows in what was the New York City punk scene, and I saw that evolve into the hardcore scene in 1981. This was the true beginning of my life. The punk scene made me want to break away from this life I was living with my family and school. Everybody in Brooklyn was doing the same old shit, listening to disco or bad rock 'n' roll. I hopped onto the train, went to CBGB, and found an outlet where I truly belonged, with other like-minded individuals.

DONNA DAMAGE (VOCALIST, NO THANKS): Hardcore was a rebellion against the dinosaurs. It was a rebellion against the media. It was a rebellion against everything that was going on.

KEVIN CROWLEY (VOCALIST, THE ABUSED): Out of that scene came us—the subset of punk—the hardcore with that anger and raw energy. It was the antithesis of what commercial music was doing. There was definitely an evolution. If you listen to our music, it's not just punk. You can hear Black Sabbath overtones in there.

PAUL CRIPPLE: When I hear the term "mainstream punk" these days, I have to laugh. "Mainstream punk" is a bigger oxymoron than "jumbo shrimp." How can punk be mainstream? It's like saying "the *good* Nazis." Back then, punk meant you didn't care about the arena rock bullshit, you just wanted to play in front of stinky, crusty people—and it still means that today.

JESSE MALIN: Suddenly, all these kids in a certain age group met each other right on corners around the city. Some people had hung on from the punk rock days. Most of us were young kids coming from the boroughs. You'd see someone at a show, or at a record store, or on a street corner, and say, "Oh, those are those guys I met at the Stiv Bators gig," or, "There's that girl in the bondage pants and the Pony sneakers I saw the other week." We were craving something, all of us at the same time. We grew up watching Uncle Floyd on UHF. We heard the Ramones. We wanted to go further.

Suddenly, it felt like something was going on that us kids were truly a part of. We were making our own flyers. We had our own style of dancing and speaking. This was something that was our own. It started to grow and it had something to say.

DAVE SCOTT: Once the A7 club started up, I don't remember seeing the Stimulators that much anymore. That kind of faded. Then Patrick got sick, so they really weren't doing anything anymore. There were fewer Stimulators gigs, and the bands that were opening for them started to headline. Patrick eventually passed away in 1983, not too long after all that.

JESSE MALIN: I remember I went to see the Circle Jerks at Irving Plaza in the summer of 1981. The Stimulators opened, and it felt like what they were doing was already such an "older" thing. Pretty soon after that, the Stimulators kind of fizzled out.

PETER CROWLEY (TALENT BOOKER, MAX'S KANSAS CITY): The Stimulators, the Bad Brains, and the Mad are the ones that came before the great numbers of very similar bands that you would call hardcore. They made up a new generation of punk bands that brought the kids in. We didn't have any inkling then that they were starting a movement.

CLUB 57 57 57
AT IRVING PLACE & 15th ST.
FROM AMERICA

CIRCLE JERKS
STIMULATORS

The CIRCLE JERKS are one of the most energetic, agressive, new punk bands from L.A. No song longer than a minute and a half, most 30 seconds, the C.J.'s are a high energy,fun, suburban and one politically assault on the Suburban life('Group Sex','Beverly Hills-Century City).Teamed with New York's living legends, the STIMULATORS, whose huge following proves that LOUD,FAST, RULES,this is definitately not a sit down affair.

also **nekros**

JUNE ⑬
SATURDAY

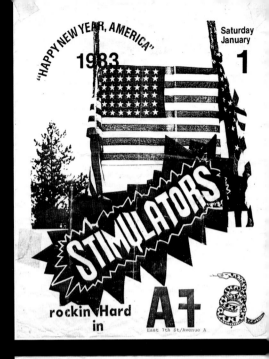

"HAPPY NEW YEAR, AMERICA"

1983

Saturday January **1**

STIMULATORS

rockin Hard in **A†**

East 7th St/Avenue A

STIMULATORS
FROM NEW YORK

LIVE! AT
ALDO'S
in Lyndhurst, New Jersey
MARIN AVENUE & ORIENT WAY

Thurs. Feb. 12

5$ CBGB · 315 · BOWERY
ROCK & ROLL MEMORIAL
FOR PATRICK MACK *FORMERLY OF THE STIMULATORS*

SHOW STARTS 8:00 SHARP!!

ANTIDOTE
ARTLESS
BEASTIE BOYS
COOTIES *THE DOBS*
DAVE ID
FALSE PROPHETS
FRONTLINE
ICE MEN
KHMER ROUGE
MOURNING NOISE
MORE?
MORE?

MURPHYS LAW
NO CONTROL
SONIC YOUTH
STIMULATORS
SWANS
THIS WAY TO GLORY
ULTRA VIOLENCE
THE UNDEAD
THE YOUNG AND
THE USELESS
MORE?

MONDAY! APRIL 11th

HARDCORE HALLOWEEN

WITH CHEETAH CHROME **AND** THE BLESSED

max's

LITTLE BORIS

max's
kansas city
213 PARK AVE. SOUTH AT 17TH STREET, NEW YORK.

max's kansas city

NEW YORK ROCK 'N' ROLL

213 PARK AVE. SOUTH AT 17th STREET

24 HR. SHOW INFORMATION: 777-7871

WED. AUG. 13	$5.00
PEPE VALENTINE &	
THE SQUIRRELS/STEW LANE &	
THE UNTOUCHABLES	
(guest — russ corey)	
THURS. AUG. 14	$5.00
TISH & SNOOKY	
THE MINX / THE SHADES	
FRI. AUG. 15	$5.00
CHEETAH CHROME/2-TIMERS	
SAT. AUG. 16	$6.00
JAYNE COUNTY / THE MAD	
SUN. AUG. 17	$3.00
X-DAVIS / EDDY DIXON &	
THE REDNECKS / COFFEE	
MON. AUG. 18	$3.00
THE VIOLATORS	
LEGIONAIRES DISEASE	
EDDIE ESTROGEN	
AND THE HORMONES	
TUES. AUG. 19	$4.00
THE END / THOM KHIDRIAN	
AND THE RHYTHM / FLINT	
WED. AUG. 20	$5.00
ELIOT MICHAELS' NEW YORK	
MINORS ALOUD (featuring alison east)	
HI-FI	
THURS. AUG. 21	$5.00
MAJOR THINKERS / KONGRESS	
FRI. AUG. 22	$5.00
NEON LEON	
and the original bondage babies	
JUSTIN TROUBLE	
SAT. AUG. 23	$5.00
SCIENCE / OZONE	

ROCK 'N' ROLL CLUB
T A ROCK DISCKO

CAMOUFLAGE

38-17 BELL BLVD, BAYSIDE   N.Y. 11361

RICHIE INVITES YOU TO A NIGHT

IN MEMORY OF

The ELIMINATORS   **SID**   Oct 29th DRESS TO KILL

Door Prizes   A GREAT

Dance   ROCK 'N' ROLL   DJ'S X-BOYS

upstairs at max's kansas city

Wed. Nov. 25	Thurs. Nov. 26

2. MAX'S KANSAS CITY: PUNK THURSDAYS

PETER CROWLEY: The person I'm aware of who first used the word *hardcore* was a journalist by the name of Pat Wadsley, who worked at the *SoHo Weekly News*. She wrote a review of the New York rock 'n' roll scene that read, "CBGB has mellowed with age. Hurrah is Macy's punk. Only Max's remains hardcore."

DENISE MERCEDES: Max's is interesting, because when we began playing there fairly regularly and became popular, hardcore slamming didn't exist. People were just jumping around—I guess they were pogoing. A lot of movement and a lot of energy came out from the audience. Tables and chairs were getting broken. Whenever the Stimulators played, Max's had to take out all the furniture. I always think that's a little badge of honor. "The Stimulators are coming! Get everything out of here!" That's a fond memory for me.

JACK RABID: The scene where I really thrived as a full-fledged member was those Max's Kansas City gigs.

VINNIE STIGMA: I used to play Max's Kansas City a lot with my band the Eliminators. I hung out at Max's and ran around with a leather jacket on with no shirt on underneath in the middle of the summer. It didn't matter! You had to have the leather jacket on! I was a punk rocker.

RICHIE BIRKENHEAD (VOCALIST, NUMSKULLS, UNDERDOG, INTO ANOTHER; GUITARIST, YOUTH OF TODAY): Back then, the clubs I used to go to were Max's, the Mudd Club, and the old Peppermint Lounge. I think Max's was the first to really have hardcore.

AL PIKE (BASSIST, REAGAN YOUTH; COEDITOR, *Straight Edge* FANZINE): Max's had this overpowering darkness. The walls were dark. Seats and tables were pushed to the side. A lot of the loud, fast people hung there.

KEITH BURKHARDT (VOCALIST, AGNOSTIC FRONT, CAUSE FOR ALARM): I came into the city from Nutley, New Jersey, and went to Max's Kansas City. Instead of being at the hole-in-the-wall pizzeria where I worked, now I was at Max's, where you could run into Mick Jagger or Andy Warhol. There were all these punks. It was a totally surreal scene.

JOHN JOSEPH (VOCALIST, BLOODCLOT, M.O.I., CRO-MAGS): I went to Max's in '77, and me and my boy got beat up. He stole some motherfucker's money off the bar downstairs on the ground floor. We were stoned on Tuinals. We were crazy and just living on the streets. Then I met this punk rock chick who became my first girlfriend. She was a little older than me, and she took me back to Max's. She was down with the whole punk shit and all that early stuff.

SEAN TAGGART: There were two versions of Max's. There was the Max's that was the artist hangout that was filled with downtown movers and shakers in the early '70s. The initial idea was for Max's to be like the Cedar Tavern, a place where artists hung out and drank. The Factory was right around the corner, so it was taken over by the Warhol crowd and became this celebrity fuckfest. That Max's closed in '74. Mickey Ruskin sold the place. He was a friend of my parents, because they were artists. When Max's reopened in '75 is when they started having punk rock, art rock, and all this weird shit—but I don't think it ever had the same pull as it did in the beginning.

DOUG HOLLAND: I used to go down to the Fourteenth Street Park and I would run into Bobby Snotz. He was Joe Punk Rock when I met him. I was listening to the Grateful Dead and Thin Lizzy and that wasn't in his groove, man. He was known for throwing a garbage can through Max's window. I remember going into Max's at fourteen years old and ordering a Heineken and I'd have to reach up to grab it from the bar! I never had problems. I always got served because I dressed right. Black engineer boots, black denim, black shirt, and black leather jacket. I had my hair done back like Joe Strummer.

JOHNNY CARCO: I remember seeing Rick Rubin's band the Pricks play Max's when there were video games and pinball games downstairs where the bar used to be. I'll never forget how the lead singer, Billy Syndome, jumped off the stage during a guitar solo. He ran downstairs and put a quarter in a pinball machine and started playing pinball. Then he ran back upstairs and jumped back onstage and finished the song. I think they were covering "Whole Lotta Love."

BOBBY STEELE: I was banned from Max's in '79 when I was still in the

Misfits. It was the end of the set, and we were just about to go into "Attitude." One of the bouncers came up on the stage with four glasses of water. He put them down next to me. We go into "Attitude," and tables and chairs are getting busted up and thrown around. It looked like a prison riot. So I wanted to douse people with some water. I picked up this glass of water and it was so cold and I was so sweaty, it was like K-Y Jelly. The glass went flying, hit a table, broke, and a big piece of it went into the arm of this guy. The guy went to the emergency room, and when they asked him what happened, he said he was stabbed. So, by law, if there's a stabbing, they have to report it to the police. I'm hanging out in the dressing room, we're partying, and two cops come in. They come up to me and ask if I'm in the band that played that night. I said yeah, and they arrested me for assault and battery. They cuffed me and took me out. The cop who arrested me ended up hiring my lawyer, because he didn't want to do the paperwork. A week later, I was smoking a joint with his partner in front of Max's.

DAVE SCOTT: At Max's, there was a combination of older drug addicts and this younger scene that was coming up that no one knew what to make of. I think the older people were not very impressed with us younger kids. They didn't want the infiltration.

DARRYL JENIFER: Max's was most likely the place where New York punk started. It felt more like drug rock as opposed to the punk rock that we embraced as youth in D.C. Our scene was fueled by the youth movement and culture: anti-Babylon and anti-Reagan. New York City was dope, Johnny Thunders, and the like.

PARRIS MAYHEW (GUITARIST, CRO-MAGS): It was a real odd place. In front there were motorcycles parked all the way down the block, because it was a Hells Angels hangout. Downstairs, it was all Hells Angels. Upstairs is where you went to see music. You walked up these old, moldy, worn-down wooden New York stairs—every step you stepped on felt like you were going *into* the steps.

RON RANCID (VOCALIST, THE NIHILISTICS): I have to give the most credit to Peter Crowley, who booked Max's Kansas City. We played there a lot, including the last three nights that Max's was open. People would scream, "Go back to Long Island, you hippies!" but he always put us on the bills.

DENISE MERCEDES: Peter Crowley was a true genius of his time for allowing us to do our thing.

JACK RABID: We got booked into Max's Kansas City thanks to the Bad Brains. After their set, they handed us their instruments and said, "Go up there and do it!" Peter Crowley was right there as soon as we got off the stage and asked, "Do you guys want to do your own gig? I'll book you." That was a quantum leap, to get a gig at Max's every month.

STEVE WISHNIA: Peter Crowley would give you a letter grade, and that was actually really good, because you knew where you stood. You'd play a Thursday night and he'd be like "A-minus. If you do another one like that, I'll give you a weekend"—or "You guys were fucking about a bit too much onstage, that's a B."

JACK RABID: Even Worse got B-pluses and A-minuses all the time.

PETER CROWLEY: I wasn't grading them in the way regular clubs would do. I wasn't worried about consulting the bartender to see who sold the most drinks or any of that stuff. Even at the end, when I should have been doing that, I didn't.

PAUL CRIPPLE: Since the drinking age was eighteen when I was a kid, and due to the fact that I looked older than fifteen—not to mention that my older sister would take me along with her hot friends—made it too easy for me to go to a venue like Max's and knock back beers at the age of fifteen! Then I'd hang by the jukebox and play songs and act like I was cool. But like all good things, Max's Kansas City was coming to an end.

PETER CROWLEY: As 1981 progressed and Max's went down the drain, the restaurant downstairs closed. The restaurant was the thing that allowed me to put anything on the stage, regardless of how much money it was going to make, because there was tons of money in the register by the end of dinner. Then we would open up at ten o'clock at night. It wasn't like CBGB, where you had to make money from the show. We didn't have that situation. But once the restaurant went under, I was pressured to try to make money upstairs, which was close to impossible. The owner was in love with the white lady and totally neglecting the club. Competition was terrible, and we didn't have a restaurant anymore. It was a mess—a terrible mess.

JESSE MALIN: Max's was crumbling in the last year. Peter Crowley would take me into the office and say, "Call your friends in Queens and book a few bills." So I'd get on the rotary phone and put on these bills, and he was very supportive of this new thing.

JOHN WATSON: Peter Crowley was absolutely essential in getting the early NYHC scene up and running. He booked the early shows, and then with my suggestion made it into "Punk Thursdays." Every week there were great shows featuring the early bands on the scene. He was really an amazing personality, and an unheralded player in the early growth of the NYHC scene.

PETER CROWLEY: We had a very young audience that didn't spend any money. Allowing them to play was an act of charity. The bartenders wanted to kill me. They would line up glasses of water on the bar before the doors opened, and then go and sit on the beer cooler, giving me dirty looks. Kids who were drunks were drinking out in the cars. There was no justifying the bands at Max's except as art.

JOHNNY CARCO: I saw the Bad Brains play in November 1981 during the final week of the club's existence, along with Billy Syndrome, Alex Totino, and Danny Reich. We started collecting money at the door at the top of the stairs as if we worked there. This happened because we were standing at the top of the stairs, and three new wave kids who were walking up the stairs sheepishly asked how much it was to get in. We looked at each other and said, "Five bucks." These kids gave us fifteen dollars. We took the money and gave them Max's buttons that were in a box on a table as a sort of entry stamp. We ran out laughing and went to a diner near Fourteenth Street and bought cheeseburger deluxes with the money. Danny and I just recently confessed to Peter Crowley about doing this some thirty years ago, so now my conscience is clean!

RON RANCID: We beat up the Beastie Boys at Max's Kansas City. They were sitting there telling us how they hated their parents and how much they loved the Nihilistics. Then Mommy and Daddy came with catered food and hot chocolate from some deli. When Mommy and Daddy left, we beat them up and took their dinner.

PAUL CRIPPLE: It has to be one of my favorite memories: going to Max's right before it was about to close down forever, not having to pay to get in, buying a quart of beer, and sparking up some herb with Jimmy G and Harley Flanagan while watching the Bad Brains, the Beastie Boys, Kraut, and Heart Attack. The original NYHC scene was as cool as cool could be. The Bad Brains allowed Reagan Youth to use their instruments so we could play a couple of songs the last night Max's was open. Like I said, cool as cool could be.

SUN. AUG 20th

CBGB
OMFUG
315 MAD · 315 MAD

MULTIMEDIA ROCK SHOW

THE MAD

with SCREAMIN' MAD GEORGE

3. THE MAD: I HATE MUSIC

ROGER MIRET: The Mad is a band you can't leave out. One of my favorite bands.

LOUIE RIVERA (VOCALIST, ANTIDOTE): Back then, it was very rare that you saw a Stimulators show that the Mad weren't also on the bill. Or a bill with the Stimulators, the Mad, and the Bad Brains all together. All three used to play together a lot.

BOBBY STEELE: The Mad! They were great. Screaming Mad George was a good boy. He didn't do the drugs. He didn't do the partying. There was something so wrong about them, but something that was so right at the same time.

JULIE H. ROSE (GUITARIST, THE MAD, THE CRAMPS): George was interesting in that he didn't drink or do drugs but surrounded himself with people who did. Someone called him the Japanese Andy Warhol, because he surrounded himself with so many weirdoes. In a way, George was a super-normal guy. He had a loft across from CB's and there were always a lot of people living and hanging out there.

SCREAMING MAD GEORGE: I was born in Osaka, Japan. When I graduated high school, I moved to the United States. First year I was living in Scarsdale, New York, working as a housekeeper at the Anderson residence. As a matter of fact, it was the home of Lindsey Anderson of Vatican Commandos and Kitty and the Kowalskis. Then I moved to Manhattan, renting a room at the corner of Fourteenth Street and Third Avenue. After one year, I moved to the corner of Bowery and Second Street. The band activity mainly started here. When I was in School of Visual Arts I met Julien Hechtlinger. At one point, I found out that she played ragtime blues guitar! So I started learning some techniques from her, and we started playing music together.

JULIE H. ROSE: One day, I was in the café at the School of Visual Arts, where both George and I went. I was sitting at a table behind him and heard him tell someone he was looking for a guitarist and thinking of starting a band, so I just turned around and starting talking with him.

SCREAMING MAD GEORGE: In 1977, punk rock was the hippest movement in NYC. So being in art school, my influences were everywhere. My first impression of punk was not too positive. The music seemed very simple, and the singers weren't really singing. The beat was just fast and short. I was very narrow-minded about music at that time. But when Julien took me to see the Dead Boys live at CBGB, that changed everything about my image of punk rock. The show was so full of energy and destructive performance—it was nasty, cool, and extreme fun! I became a Dead Boys fan immediately. When I asked Julien about forming a band, she wanted the band to be a punk band. After seeing the Dead Boys, I had no problem with that.

JULIE H. ROSE: I had never played electric guitar, but I didn't tell George that until I showed up at his place without one. He had an acoustic guitar, and I played some stuff. He said something like, "Oh, if you can play like that you can play punk rock." Originally, we were named Disgusting. George had lots of ideas. He was into special effects and stage shows and all that, but it never interested me. I loved Alice Cooper, but I really wasn't interested in his stage shows. I thought it was silly—but we had a good time with it all, just fooling around. I screen-printed the Disgusting T-shirts, which also had hand-stamped words on them, like "Shit Steak," a literal translation of some Japanese word. At one of our first CB's gigs, we all wore tampons around our necks with fake blood on them and generally acted "disgusting." It was just a goof. That it scared anyone was funny as hell.

SCREAMING MAD GEORGE: My paintings consisted of surreal situations influenced by Salvador Dalí, but for my band's debut I thought I'd need very extreme stage effects for the audience to remember us. I decided to make a plastic bag full of latex guts in red paint and tape it on my stomach, covered with latex skin in order to look like my belly was being ripped open. Also, I had a painted crucifix where Jesus's legs would spread open and fake shit came out. At the end of the set, I would pull out a red-paint-filled fake dick and use large scissors to perform a castration. Since my interest was more surreal than splatter, I didn't want to stay with "disgusting" as the concept.

PARRIS MAYHEW: I know it's stating the obvious, but in that early sea of people, there were a lot of creative individuals, like Screaming Mad George from the Mad. I went up to his apartment when I was a fifteen-year-old boy. I couldn't believe what I saw. The guy was a painter. The guy was an animator. The guy was a sculptor. He was a musician. He was a singer. He lived in this massive loft where he painted these massive paintings and made these humongous sculptures and then would take out a Super 8 projector and show animation on this huge screen. He would pick up a guitar, and then pick up a bass, and I was like, "Oh my God!" I wanted to be in a band with this guy!

ROBBIE CRYPTCRASH: Screaming Mad George would cut his head and meat would fall out. He'd cut his stomach and his intestines would fall out. He'd pull shit out of his pants and eat it. Okay, you saw that it was a plastic bag where he had mixed peanut butter and chocolate together, but that was one of the craziest shows that I have ever seen.

JULIE H. ROSE: George had a fake penis he would cut off. I wanted to do it myself, but he said, "Oh, that wouldn't be scary because it wouldn't be realistic." The last time I played with him, I finally got to wear—and cut off—the fake penis, and it was a blast. I was asking everyone for blow jobs. No takers.

SCREAMING MAD GEORGE: The Mad's first bass player, Rick, was a drug addict. One day, he started acting weird and tried to attack Julien. After that incident, we kicked him out. We called the band the Mad, but we didn't want a real madman in our band. By coincidence, a Japanese bass player named Hisashi Ikeda came to New York at the same time I was looking for new bass player. He joined the band, and we recorded a single, "Eyeball," in 1978. After several gigs with this lineup, our drummer Jun Nakanishi started feeling unpleasant about the violent performance of the Mad, and he wanted to quit. We had a roadie, David Hahn, who played the drums and knew the songs, so he became our new drummer. We recorded our second single, "Fried Egg," with this lineup in 1980, and I would say this was the period that the Mad got heavily into hardcore punk. Then a big incident happened. The Cramps wanted Julien for their guitarist, and she joined them. This caused the first breakup of the Mad.

JULIE H. ROSE: George and I were boyfriend and girlfriend, and then we weren't. About a year after that, I left the band for the Cramps. When I was done with that, I was going to start a band with Danny Zelonky, but that fell through. After a year of playing in a basement rehearsal studio, I figured if I had put that much effort into making art I would have had a decent career, so

I quit playing guitar. I was also a bit afraid I'd OD because I had drugs and music all mixed up together, and a bunch of people I knew did OD. There was a lot of cheap and good heroin in New York in 1980, and it was dangerous.

SCREAMING MAD GEORGE: The breakup changed me to have a different direction from hardcore punk. At that time, my interest in music shifted toward dark psychedelic new wave like Siouxsie and the Banshees, Bauhaus, PiL, and Magazine. Hisashi was interested in playing synthesizer, so I auditioned a new guitarist and bass player. I found Michael Manson as the guitarist, and Tetsu as the bass player. With my idea for a new performance, a girl name Ace joined the band as the mime performer. This lineup became the second period of the Mad. We performed with these members for a while. My visuals and performance were getting more involved, and I wanted to expand this musical performance from punk band to multimedia surreal theatrical music group. The Mad evolved into Irrational. I would say this was the end of the Mad.

JACK RABID: When the Mad played, it was always a big event, because they had films, they had dancers, and they had the whole extravaganza. They'd show these films that were utterly disgusting. They had one that was just a guy in a field who'd start plucking his eyes out and rip off his skin. I saw Johnny Thunders throw up watching one of those once. He was doing his usual "I'm the king of this scene" thing of standing up while everyone was sitting. So he's standing there watching it, but the guy was a junkie, so he had a weak stomach to begin with. He just threw up on the floor, and the whole Max's Kansas City laughed at him.

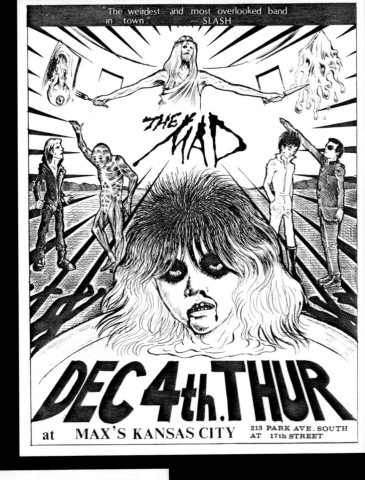

BAD BRAINS
MAX'S — DEC 11
WITH THE INFLUENCE AND THE BEASTIE BOYS

HR of the Bad Brains spits truth to the youth.
GARY TSE TSE FLY

BAD BRAINS
PLUS SPECIAL GUESTS
FROM VANCOUVER
THE SUBHUMANS

$3.00
BYOB
SATURDAY
MAY 30
171 A

ONLY N.Y. APPEA

BAD BRAINS
Direct From England 1st U.S. Tour
DISCHARGE
"Hear Nothing, See Nothing, Say Nothing"
285 W. BROADWAY (formerly Rock Lou
(½ Blk. South of Canal St. AA or E train to Canal)
For Info. Call. 226-7691
TWO SHOWS SAT. SEPT. 18th

MATINEE 5 pm
UNDER 18 WELCOME!
$8 Tickets ... Door.

EVENING SHOW — Door
$10, Tickets Avail at Door
advance tickets: Bleecker Bob's
Slip Disc Records, Valley Stream, L.I.

4. BAD BRAINS: THE BIG TAKEOVER

TIM SOMMER (RADIO HOST, WNYU *Noise the Show*; GUITARIST, EVEN WORSE): New York would have been a very different scene if the Bad Brains didn't come up from D.C. to play regularly, and eventually move here. I don't know what it would have been, but it would have been different. The Bad Brains were playing a different, very accomplished kind of music.

RALPHIE G: The visiting Bad Brains were definitely the band that kick-started what later became the NYHC scene.

DARRYL JENIFER: Our beliefs in PMA—positive mental attitude—led us to leave D.C. for fresher turf to conquer.

JACK FLANAGAN (GUITARIST, HEART ATTACK, THE MOB): I remember seeing an ad for Richard Lloyd from Television playing at CBGB on a Friday night early in 1981 with an opening band called the Bad Brains. I didn't know who they were, but I knew Richard Lloyd was a part of the punk scene, so I went. I came in from Queens with my high school friend Jose Gonzalez. We were very young and went to CBGB, and nobody checked our IDs. We got there pretty early because we were excited, so we were drinking and it got pretty wild. I saw the Bad Brains, lost my mind, and hung out with them after the set. I missed Richard Lloyd completely. After that, we would come home from high school, drink a quart of beer, smoke a little weed, and put on a Van Halen LP on 45 because it sounded like the Bad Brains. Luckily, we were able to get one of the Bad Brains *Pay to Cum* singles the second time we saw them.

TIM SOMMER: I got the Bad Brains *Pay to Cum* single as soon as it came out, and I knew immediately that was something completely different. That's a record that nothing was the same after, like "Blitzkrieg Bop" by the Ramones or "You Really Got Me" by the Kinks. It's in that league. "Pay to Cum" invented an entire genre of music in a minute and a half. I think that to this day, whether they know it or not, every band playing that style of music is imitating that 45.

LOUIE RIVERA: Dave Hahn—may he rest in peace—the drummer for the Mad, had a lot to do with the Bad Brains coming to New York. They always stayed with him when they came. Dave eventually became sort of their manager in New York.

DENISE MERCEDES: When the Bad Brains rolled into town from D.C., we met them at what I am positive was their first New York gig. Almost no people were there. I'd never seen anything like them. They were doing something we had never seen. We became very good friends, and since the Stimulators were popular, we got to expose them to the New York audience. It was our pleasure and our honor, because the moment that they hit, it was like a bomb going off. It was louder, it was faster. Our scene was mixed up with women and children and then comes this—the Bad Brains.

DARRYL JENIFER: We met the Stims through their singer, Nick Marden, and Dave Hahn, the drummer of the Mad. These folks were our hosts in New York City. They were showing us the ropes: how to eat Chinese food at Wo Hop, how to navigate the Lower East Side, and where to buy bum coats.

JACK FLANAGAN: Levels of success are dictated by one's own idea of success. Let's take it back to 1980. This is still rock 'n' roll record time, the worst time for popular music. There was still this "stick with me and you'll be a star" mentality to everything. I don't think the Stimulators gave a shit about that, and I know the Bad Brains didn't give a shit about that. That's the reason there was a connection between the Stimulators and the Bad Brains.

SEAN TAGGART: My very first show was a Speedies show at Max's Kansas City in '79. There was this girl I was hanging out with in high school that I considered the cool punk person in my school. I was telling her I saw the Speedies and she was disgusted and told me, "That's not punk!" The second show I went to was the Stimulators and the Bad Brains, and that really blew my mind. It was scary and liberating at the same time. I went out in the middle of the dance floor with my long hair and danced, and I didn't last very long.

JACK FLANAGAN: I found out about the Stimulators through going to see the Bad Brains. Once that happened, it started to gravitate to its own scene. The

Stimulators would bring them up from D.C. and give them a place to stay. It was the very beginning of this hardcore scene with the Bad Brains and the Stimulators.

SCREAMING MAD GEORGE: We were at the first show when the Bad Brains came to New York City from Washington, D.C. They were so incredible, and we all loved them instantly. We got to be such good friends that I let them stay in my loft located at the corner of Bowery and Second Street for about two months.

JULIE H. ROSE: I believe we met the Bad Brains just because we ran into them on the street or saw them wandering around. They were looking to crash in this old Yippie squat/hangout nearby. They'd come to New York to play at CBGB. They'd just come from D.C., and looked kind of fresh off the bus and lost. They wound up living at George's. We played with them a lot, double billed. We played a weekend of shows once in D.C. at Madam's Organ. Me and Gary Milller, Dr. Know from the Bad Brains, used to compete to see who could play faster. He won, but I wouldn't use any up strokes!

STEVEN WISHNIA: Bad Brains came up to New York in '79. Butch Lust, an Italian kid from Bensonhurst, told me about them. At that time, Bensonhurst was a hardcore white neighborhood. If you're black, you'd better be a big motherfucker to walk down there. He called me up and said, "Steve, you got to see this band. It's four black guys playing pure punk and they're fucking amazing." They were.

LOUIE RIVERA: One Sunday afternoon or something like that I was hanging out on the Lower East Side doing nothing. I ran into Harley Flanagan just around the corner from his mother's house. He asked me if I wanted to go with him up to Central Park. In the summer back then, they would have the Rock Against Racism shows up there. He was going up to see a band from D.C. called the Bad Brains. When I saw them that day, they gave me that total shock treatment vibe. I had never seen anything like that before. My life was changed from that point on.

PARRIS MAYHEW: I was out with my friend Paul Dordal at the Mudd Club. This song came on and the small hairs on the back of my neck started to stand up. "Holy shit! What the fuck is this?" At the time, I was listening to Van Halen, Rush, and Aerosmith. I saw these punk rockers standing there, and I walked up to them with my long hair and ripped jeans and said, "Excuse me, but who is this music?" One of them leaned forward and said, "Sex Pistols, dick!" I was like, "Uh, thank you?" The next Monday, I went up to the three punk rockers at my school and said "Hey, do any of you have a Sex Pistols record I can borrow?" They all smiled. They had a convert! A few days later, I went back and told them I loved the record. One of them said, "Well, if you like that, you should go see this band the Stimulators."

I saw an ad in the *Village Voice* for a double bill for the Bad Brains and the Stimulators and I went down to Max's Kansas City. At the club, I got to the top of the steps, and there was one of those old diner signs where you can stick letters to announce the lunch specials. It read bad brainz with a *z* and stimulatorz with a *z*, and it said they would play two sets. The Stimulators started playing and the guy at school was right: They were basically a Sex Pistols clone—even though the music was really the beginning of New York hardcore. Harley would step off the drum seat and shove the drumsticks up his nose, and that type of thing. They had a song called "M.A.C.H.I.N.E.," which Harley and I discussed many times covering in the Cro-Mags.

DENISE MERCEDES: We wrote "M.A.C.H.I.N.E." in '78 going into '79. I feel confident in saying it was one of the earliest of the thrash ideas on the East Coast. It was a song about alienation. "M.A.C.H.I.N.E. Is that all that's left for me?" Instead of being able to live in a more balanced way with nature, it's all about turning knobs. Have I been born to go to your office and play with your buttons?

PARRIS MAYHEW: After the Stimulators, then the Bad Brains came onstage, and it didn't make any sense to me at all, none whatsoever. They were just starting to grow their dreadlocks, so they had little nubs on their heads. They were wearing suits. Once I deciphered the Bad Brains code, I was a fan. For someone who was used to listening to something like Rush, it was too much coming at me all at once. Once I was able to decipher it, I recognized the musicality.

PAUL CRIPPLE: When you listen to "Stone Cold Crazy" by Queen, it's like the Bad Brains. Since that's what we were listening to as kids in Queens, it wasn't that far of a stretch for us to love them.

DARRYL JENIFER: When I first hit New York, I started looking for weed. Then I went to St. Marks and bought a slice of pizza. Then I sat on a stoop, ate my slice, and smoked a joint. I said to myself, "Damn, this is New York."

JAMES KONTRA: The Bad Brains played at a little club called Tier 3 the first time I saw them. Rose, Harley's mom, was bartending there. It was very cold.

It was February or some shit. We thought it was weird, because the Stimulators were opening for this band we never heard of. Harley was like, "You've got to see these guys, you'll bug out." Tier 3 was sort of a little room where if you put twenty fucking people on the dance floor, it's fucking packed. The Stimulators did a dope set, and we were like, "How can you top that?" Then the fucking Bad Brains went on. Dude, that was like, "Wow!" Shit was electric—un-fucking-real!

RALPHIE G: Before they came on, they had an introduction: "Quicker than the Dickies, faster than the Ramones, ladies and gentlemen: the Bad Brains!" That was enough for me. From that day on, I was hooked. It was also the beginning of a long-term friendship and mentorship.

RICHIE BIRKENHEAD: I was going to McBurney High School, and two friends asked me if I wanted to see the Bad Brains at Max's Kansas City. Someone taped me the *Pay to Cum* 7-inch, but I had no idea what they looked like or anything. It was so fast and so raw. I was a rockabilly guy at the time. I had a pompadour and I was wearing creepers and pink pegged slacks. My friends and I went down to Max's, and I was blown away.

JACK RABID: The Bad Brains used to play at least once a month, even when they still lived in D.C. We would show up every time they played. They played some of the worst clubs in New York, with some of the worst sound systems. It's funny because you couldn't really hear HR sing through these systems. You'd just hear this hum. Then they'd play CBGB after four or five of those shows, and I'd be like: "Oh! So that's what he sounds like!"

JESSE MALIN: We looked up to the Bad Brains because they could play better than anyone else.

GARY TSE TSE FLY (EDITOR, *Tse Tse Fly* FANZINE): Bad Brains are sort of the center of influences. Anybody from the Cro-Mags to Agnostic Front to the Mob and all the other main characters were indebted to the Bad Brains.

TODD YOUTH: The Bad Brains were our Led Zeppelin and our Beatles. That was a band I would fucking die for.

KEVIN CROWLEY: We were always striving for a tight sound. We rehearsed a lot and rented rehearsal space. It's not because we thought we were going to get famous. We just wanted to be the best band we could possibly be, and it all goes back to the Bad Brains. When we saw a band like that, and how tight they played, we wanted to be like those guys.

RALPHIE G: I think things started to snowball once the Bad Brains moved up to New York and made Jerry Williams' 171A their home.

JACK RABID: The Bad Brains were playing New York on such a regular basis, they were practically a local band. Their song "Banned in D.C." makes it pretty plain: It was hard for them to get gigs in D.C. There weren't a lot of venues, and they were having trouble getting bookings. Whereas there were numerous clubs in New York, and all of them were happy to book them. I moved in June 1981 to Eldridge Street, and they moved up from D.C. very soon after. Earl Hudson, drummer for the Bad Brains, was there at my apartment every day, and Gary was there most of the time. The other guys would stop by if they needed a bath or something.

DARRYL JENIFER: We were never banned anywhere—it's all made up to suit the situation. Think about it: If Bad Brains were really banned in D.C., we would have played in D.C. every night of the week upon this ban notification.

JESSE MALIN: It was really tough. Our gear kept getting ripped off, but then the Bad Brains would lend us their stuff and be like, "Get up here!" They were really into seeing this youth movement grow. I don't know where they thought it was going, but they really supported it.

MIKE JUDGE (VOCALIST AND DRUMMER, DEATH BEFORE DISHONOR, YOUTH OF TODAY; VOCALIST, JUDGE): I've always seen them as a New York band. I didn't know about their D.C. past until after seeing them. I saw them play at their rehearsal spot at 171A, and I also saw them play a squat on Avenue C. No fucking out-of-town band sets up a gig in a squat, you know? They were meant to come and save New York.

DREW STONE (VOCALIST, THE HIGH AND THE MIGHTY, ANTIDOTE; FILMMAKER): At the time, I thought they were a New York band, but the Bad Brains transcended all space and time. They were unbelievable, a magical band. Seeing them play back then was almost like a religious experience. That same energy and feeling I can only compare to the Grateful Dead, where it's just magic in the room and everybody's feeling it. I saw the Bad Brains many times. You get a little taste of that magic and you'd want more.

PAUL BEARER (VOCALIST, FATHEAD SUBURBIA, SHEER TERROR): I don't give a shit what the fuck Ian MacKaye or all these other jerk-offs say. The Bad Brains wouldn't have been shit if they didn't move to New York. No one would know who the fuck they were if they stayed in D.C. They would have been fuckin' unknown. That's the fuckin' truth.

LOUIE RIVERA: When the Bad Brains moved to New York and started to tour, they brought bands back with them. The Bad Brains brought Crucial Truth up to New York. They were originally from Florida. They loaded them in the van and the Crucial Truth guys were like, "Fuck it, let's go." They wound up in New York, and they never left either.

STEVE POSS (DRUMMER, CAVITY CREEPS; NYHC LEGEND): The people in D.C. would have eventually distanced themselves from the Bad Brains. They wouldn't have gone along with the pot and the Rasta stuff. They were probably happy to get rid of them.

EDDIE SUTTON: At my first Bad Brains show, Dr. Know pulled up and talked to people, and that was kind of a trip to me. I was coming from arena rock. I was into Van Halen, and here was this band that was within reach. I thought that was fucking cool. Seeing that taught me a lot as hardcore got bigger. I still run into kids that were influenced by me and Leeway, and I always give them the time of day. I talk to them on a one-on-one basis. I always wanted to be in a band, and when I saw that early, DIY ethic, I realized I could be a part of something.

DARRYL JENIFER: The Brains ran all scenes when it came to our brand of rock 'n' roll during this time. Bad Brains were truly ahead of our times with creative hard riffs, writing, and performing.

JOHN JOSEPH: There would be no scene if it wasn't for the Bad Brains. They built up the scene letting a lot of local bands open up for them, and that's when shit really started catching on. I would say they were an essential part to the evolution of this whole music scene. Every night they came onstage it was one thousand percent. They inspired us to start the Cro-Mags. Everybody wanted to be around them because they had an incredible energy. They were talking some revolutionary shit.

DON'T SHOW AND...
THIS COULD HAPPEN TO YOU!!!
SLAM!
FROM N.Y.
EVEN WORSE
LOST GEN.
← FROM BEAUTIFUL BPT.
C·I·A
SATURDAY, SEPT. 18

STAY NORMAL - COME TO...
THE BROTHERS
447 FIRST AVE. W. HAVEN
TEL: 933-9900 KIMBERLY AVE. EXIT OFF I-95

Celebrate
TIM SOMMER'S
And
JACK RABID'S
Twentieth
Birthday Bash

SATURDAY MARCH 27

WITH
THE MISFITS
KRAUT
EVEN WORSE
IRVING Plaza

DJ
Tim
Sommer

I'll be there!

EVEN WORSE
331 BOWERY
GREAT GILDERSLEEVES
with
MINOR THREAT
+ Artless

more
info:
call (212)
533
3940.

SUNDAY FEB. 20 MATINEE

5. EVEN WORSE: WE SUCK!

PETER CROWLEY: Even Worse came in on the idea that anybody can do it. "We're Even Worse than the rest of them and it doesn't matter"; that was their thing. There was an intellect working there and a smart sense of humor.

DARRYL JENIFER: Even Worse were really even worse than most, but had the heart of a lion. I loved them.

JACK RABID: The same night that I saw the Stimulators for the first time, I met Nick Marden, which was just as important as seeing the Stimulators, because Nick knew everything. He was only a year or two older than us, but he had already been living on Thirteenth Street for a year or two. He was Joan Baez's nephew. I still think the whole fricking scene revolved around him. He was a record collector. He was playing us things like the Viletones. I would read about these scenes in San Francisco and L.A in *Slash* and *Search & Destroy*. He said, "Oh, I got those records. Come over to my house," two seconds after I met the guy. "You want to hear the Dils? I have the Dils records." Actually, I do want to hear the Dils. Do you have the Avengers? "Yeah, I got the Avengers single, come over!" Before this, all these bands were just names. We never heard them. Nick Marden was a fountain of these things.

LOUIE RIVERA: Nick Marden was just this cool fuckin' kid who a lot of people knew. He was on the scene really deep. He was one of the kids who used to dress up in bondage gear. He'd have straps on his legs and stuff like that. He used to actually wear a kilt, too! He was a real unique individual. When I first saw Nick, I was like "Wow, that's pretty punk rock!" But he was a very approachable and gentle person.

JESSE MALIN: Nick Marden is an East Village guy who helped me out a lot. I went into his kitchen, and he had a sticker on his fridge that said love animals, don't eat them. I'm a vegetarian to this day after seeing that.

KITE HAWK (Bassist, the Eliminators, Killer Instinct, XKI, P.M.S.): Nick Marden used to make these amazing handmade buttons. I still have some on my leather jacket.

SEAN TAGGART: Nick Marden and his girlfriend at the time had this really cool dance where they would lock into one another and spin around the room. I remember being very taken by that very aggro way of showing affection.

ROBBIE CRYPTCRASH: The Cryptcrashers played one show only at CBGB. The only person who showed up was Nick Marden. We all stopped playing the minute we saw Nick sit down, and then we started playing again. That was the only show we ever played, and Nick is the only person who ever saw it.

JACK RABID: My friend Dave Stein kept scheming to get into various New York bands. He made inroads with the Whorelords and the Tearjerkers, but things never seemed to work out for him. Dave and I started talking to Nick, because Nick said he played the bass. Nothing happened for four months, because he lived in New York and we lived in New Jersey and were too busy going to shows and going to high school.

On April 29, 1980, Nick called me up and said, "The Stimulators don't have an opening act for their gig on Saturday at Tier 3. Why don't we play?" We couldn't do that; we'd never even played before! But the next day, we got into the Stimulators' practice space. They lent us their gear, but we had no songs. Nick said he could teach us "Rather See You Dead" by the Legionaire's Disease Band, because it was only two chords. We all knew "I Can't Stand My Baby" by the Rezillos. Well, we didn't know how to play it, but Nick figured it out. Dave then said he was fiddling around with two things that could be songs. They became "We Suck" and "Illusion Won Again." There were no words written, or bridges, or anything. John Pouridas was going to be the singer; he was a friend of Nick's that I didn't know very well. He just stood there the whole time and didn't say an entire word. Finally, Nick said, "You're supposed to be the singer, sing something. Just make something up." I said, "Just say what you think." He goes, "WE SUCK!" and that's how the song "We Suck" came about.

Two days later, we were in front of a sold-out crowd of three hundred people. Nick and Dave got scared and downed a bottle of tequila, so they were barely standing. All our two-minute songs went on for eight minutes. I was sober, and I was determined to fulfill my lifelong dream of being a drummer. It was like an accidental noise band, before Sonic Youth or any of those bands did anything like that. By then, we'd been hanging out for a year, so we knew everyone in the crowd. It was the most partisan crowd we ever played to. Tim Sommer always used to rave about the tape. We would have won *American Idol* that day! After we were done, people starting coming up and asking "When's your next gig?" So we decided to keep it up.

BOBBY STEELE: Even Worse . . . they sucked! Their whole thing was "We suck!" But they weren't as bad as they claimed to be. They had a lot more substance than some of these bands that thought they were great.

REBECCA KORBET: Back in the day, if you took yourself too seriously in that music scene, it could eat you alive. You had to be self-deprecating and have a decent sense of humor about life in general, or have a well-defined character of some sort to live in—like Von Lmo. You had to have that, unless you were a rich fuck who wasn't bothered with the difficulty of the downtown existence. In that instance, we didn't want to know you, frankly.

JACK RABID: We had a gig at the band shell in Tompkins Square Park one Saturday afternoon. John Pouridas didn't come, so we had no singer. Nick scanned the crowd, saw a guy, and said to him, "You look like Johnny Rotten! Come up here and be our singer!" So that's how John Berry joined. He was our singer from August to December of 1980. After that, he was in Young Aborigines with Michael Diamond and Adam Yauch, and later the Beastie Boys.

Nick got a somewhat devious offer to join the Stimulators after their bassist Anne quit. We were told he could play with both bands, then as soon as they decided he was in, they told us he no longer could! We were just defeated and deflated like the *Hindenburg*. We went from such an exciting precipice to nothing! It had really been Nick's band in a lot of ways. He was the guy in New York that everyone in the scene loved. So nothing happened with us for a few months.

By a stroke of great luck I met Rebecca, and she was exactly the sort of person we wanted to sing. She oozed wildness, like a young female Iggy Pop or something, and smarts and charisma. She was really daring in going after the things she wanted to do. She really was perfect. I don't think she gets enough credit for being pretty much the only female in any of the bands we played the most with, let alone being the focal point and main lyricist. I mean, there were girls all over the audience, really valued scene members. Why didn't more get up and play?

JACK FLANAGAN: Jack Rabid is a great guy. A few years ago we were talking about Even Worse, and he said something like, "When all the bands started playing really fast, we really didn't follow along with that, because man— that's a lot of work! It's really hard to do!" I loved that! He's being honest. "Yeah, I want to be in a band and all, but I'm not trying to sweat and hurt myself!" Now that's being genuine.

JACK RABID: Even Worse's last show was with Kraut and the Misfits in March of '82. There were 825 paid. I think a quarter of the crowd was there to see the show as a total package. We already played with Heart Attack at the Peppermint Lounge on a Sunday night in January of '82 and 450 people showed up. It seemed like it happened overnight. Punk rock hit New York in a way that the original punk rock thing didn't. Not until those first 1970s CBGB bands started putting out records was when they started to attract people. We were drawing people without records.

I put together one last version of Even Worse that lasted from 1982 to 1984, with Tim Sommer on bass and Sonic Youth's Thurston Moore on guitar. We released two singles that collectors now pay way too much for.

a.o.d.
and
even
Worse

(NEW LOOK EVEN WORSE)
please note: 12 string
guitar.

plus CHAPPAQUIDDICK + 5

First band: Chappaquiddick + 5 (from Nyack) (First Even Worse appearance in 6 months, featuring new vocalist Richard Butler + new guitarist Brian Jones) at Yoon's Anthony Club, 70 Main St., Stamford, Connecticut, Saturday, January 14, 1984, 10:00 P.M. That's all.

HEART ATTACK

JAN. 3

WITH

EVEN
WORSE

EVEN WORSE?

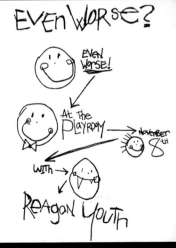

EVEN
WORSE!

AT THE
PLAYROOM → NOVEMBER 8th

WITH →

REAGON YOUTH

AT N.Y.T.E.
62 E 4th ST
BETW. 2nd
& BOWERY

BENEFIT FOR 171 A

BUY ADVANCED TICKETS AT THE RAT CAGE BELOW 171 A 11st AveA
$5 PER NIGHT
$10 FOR 3 NIGHTS OF MUSIC.

sunday NOV 29 11pm.
KONK
RICHARD hell
THE UNCALLED FOR

monday NOV 30 10pm
INFLUENCE
CRAZY HEARTS
JOHNSON & JOHNSON

tuesday DEC 1 10pm
BAD BRAINS
REAGAN YOUTH
BEASTIE BOYS
HEART ATTACK
THE MOB

Photo: *One of the birthplaces of NYHC: 171 A and Rat Cage Records*
COURTESY OF JOHN KELLY

the RAT CAGE
307 E. 9th ST
NYC 10013
*MIR
JUST EAST OF 2ND AVE

6. AVENUE A: 171A

JACK RABID: Right around the time I moved to Eldridge Street in the middle of May '81, it seemed like the scene was shifting to 171A and A7. They both became the places where Even Worse, the Stimulators, and the Bad Brains started to congregate.

JIMMY G (VOCALIST, CAVITY CREEPS, MURPHY'S LAW): One seventy-one Avenue A was down the block from A7, and, like A7, they also did shows, plus they sometimes showed movies. One seventy-one A was pretty much a community center run by a guy named Jerry Williams. In the basement of 171A was Rat Cage Records.

JOHN JOSEPH: Jerry was an integral part of the scene. He let the Bad Brains stay at his studio. He recorded them for free. He produced their record. He did everything. Plus he gave me all the knowledge on plant-based eating.

NICK MARDEN: Jerry Williams was from North Carolina, and his band Th' Cigaretz formed there. They sang songs about cancer and things like that, which was a slightly obtuse thing to be doing, but they decided to move to New York and build this little empire at 171 Avenue A.

JERRY WILLIAMS (OWNER, 171A; NYHC PRODUCER/ENGINEER): My band Th' Cigaretz moved to Bayshore, Long Island, from North Carolina in May of 1979. That September, we moved into Manhattan. Basically, we started crashing at the house of Holly George-Warren, a former editor at *Rolling Stone* who now does a lot of books. She got us our first gig in New York and then she put us up in her apartment on St. Marks Place. Holly found a rehearsal space at 171 Avenue A, and that's how things ended up there. Me and my compatriots started 171A in October of 1980.

JACK RABID: Jerry was such a nice guy. He was the friendliest fellow. He didn't care if you just walked in off the street at any hour of the day or night; he'd invite you in to come hang out in the booth with him.

JOHN JOSEPH: I'm from New York, and I knew I had to come back here at some point. I was down in D.C. after I went AWOL from the navy. For about a month, I stayed at both Henry Rollins' house and Ian MacKaye's house in Alexandria, Virginia. They let me crash there. Finally, Henry was like, "Yo, you've been eating my fuckin' food every day. It's time for you to go!" That's cool. I understand. The Undead were playing at the 9:30 Club in D.C. They gave me a ride back. I hopped out of the van, and the first person I ran into was Harley Flanagan, on Twelfth Street and Avenue A, where his mother lived. He was like, "Yo, I'm going to hang with the Bad Brains at their studio." I walked up to 171A, and right in the doorway was fuckin' HR, saying, "Yeah, mon, we knew we'd see you again." After that, they took me under their wing, and I moved into 171A.

NICK MARDEN: The Rat Cage record store started in the basement of 171A. That was Dave Parsons and Cathy Fitzsimmons from *Mouth of the Rat* from Florida. Their fanzine brought the current music down to Florida. Little scenes started happening down there, and then they came up here.

DAVE SCOTT: Dave Parsons came up from Florida in 1980. This was long before he had the record store, Rat Cage. He knew Jerry Williams from when he was in Th' Cigaretz down south. Rat Cage was one of those things where it was the right place at the right time. New York always had record stores, but never before an all-hardcore record store.

STEVEN WISHINIA: *Mouth of the Rat* was a great fanzine, really outspoken. He did this thing called "Rules for Rock Musicians." Things like, "Think of a band name that'll last. The Space Negroes is a name that's only funny for about ten seconds," or, "Never say you've gone into a hospital for exhaustion. Admit you're there to dry out." It was this really obsessive, forty-record-reviews-on-a-page-in-small-print thing, but it was smart and well written.

JACK RABID: We were reading *Mouth of the Rat* even when Dave was still down in Florida. He handwrote every single issue. I used to hang out with him a lot. One of the first times I met him was when the Clash did the Palladium. He found his way over to Nick Marden's house, where a lot of people found their entrance into our scene. He and I went to go see a Legionaire's Disease Band show together at Max's one time when he was up from Florida. The singer had his pants pulled down by the third or fourth song and I remember Dave turning to me and saying, "God, he's really small for a guy who's been rubbing it the whole show." He had so much fun hanging out with us, that he said, "Fuck it, I don't need South Florida anymore."

DAVE PARSONS (OWNER, RAT CAGE RECORDS; EDITOR, *Mouth of the Rat* FAN-ZINE): Once we got to New York, it was like Ian MacKaye once said, "Fuck man, this place sucks, man." It really did. We then met the people who hung out with the Stimulators and they were real. I started hanging out with them, but the fanzine ground to a halt. The guy who was helping me publish it got real discouraged with New York. He got mugged and went back to Florida. Things kind of gravitated to the 171A situation.

DONNA DAMAGE: Rat Cage started out at Cathy Fitzsimmons and Dave Parson's apartment on St. Marks Place between First and Second Avenues. That's where it all started. They used to take records out on the street and sell them off a blanket.

DAVE PARSONS: I had to make the rent and had this record collection. I decided to go up the street and sell it. We did really well, so instead of paying rent, we went out and bought more records and figured that if it kept going well, we could get a storefront by fall. So then we moved underneath 171A.

WENDY EAGER: Rat Cage was a hangout place. I remember going there one night and stapling issues of *Guillotine* before going to a show. It smelled like cat piss. You could show up there at eleven o'clock at night and hang out. They didn't have a massive amount of merchandise. The original one had a few boxes of 7-inches, some LPs, and some T-shirts. There were flyers. You got information and you got to know people.

LOUIE RIVERA: Dave—God bless him. He was never the type of dude who wouldn't let you hang out if you weren't buying something. If you had no place to go and it was cold out, he'd make some hot cocoa and invite you inside.

RALPHIE G: During the day, it wasn't unusual to find bands and close friends hanging, rehearsing, and recording at 171A. And you could find the records of all the bands right downstairs at Rat Cage! At night, A7 was abuzz with bands playing.

JOHN JOSEPH: Dave Parsons was great. He was into his own crazy, bugged-out shit, but he was a great dude who always had a spliff to smoke and new punk rock records to play. I always looked forward to going over there and hearing the new shit he got in. He was a cool human being, man. Dave was a very special and crazy kind of dude. And he was instrumental in putting out some of those first records.

JESSE MALIN: Dave moved out of that little hole-in-the-wall to Ninth Street, and everybody would hang out there and smoke weed. Then he went to a little skate place on Ninth and Second called Secret Spot Skates.

STEVE WISHNIA: Dave hung out in New York for a while after his store closed. Then he ended up moving to Switzerland, getting a sex change, and dying pretty young.

JERRY WILLIAMS: Sometime in early '81, one of the bands that was rehearsing at 171A got a gig at A7. That would constitute the first time I heard about A7. A guy named Rob was playing in a band called Eyewitness News and he got a gig there. That sort of formed a pipeline with a number of the bands that were rehearsing at 171A. Even before the hardcore bands started playing there, not much happened in that part of town in those days. Most people didn't go east of Avenue A without a really good reason.

EDDIE SUTTON: At that time, the Lower East Side was a war zone. It wasn't the gentrified neighborhood that it's been for the last twenty years. It was a fucking war zone, without question. It was worse than the worst neighborhoods you know in New York City today. It was a trip to be down there and go to those bars and A7 and shit like that. I wasn't even eighteen yet, and I was getting a peek into a world that most people will never see.

REBECCA KORBET: What people don't understand is how different downtown New York City was back then; it was like the Old West. Danger lurked at every corner. Failure was imminent, and the odds were often against you. You learned to be resilient, or you left, or you died—just like that.

DAVE SCOTT: There's no way to describe it. Back then, it was ridiculous. I remember playing a show on Avenue B with the False Prophets, and this guy was going down the street on his motorcycle. Someone just came out of the shadows with a two-by-four and hit the guy right in the head and knocked him off his bike. Without skipping a beat, he just got on the guy's motorcycle and took off. We had to go inside that night because someone was shooting outside. It was pretty bad.

SEAN TAGGART: I went to grade school on the Lower East Side, so I already knew about Puerto Rican kids preying on white kids down there. So when Parris Mayhew was taking me to A7, as soon as we got to First Avenue I stopped him and said, "Okay Parris, we're about to enter a really fucked-up neighborhood. Are you sure you want to go there?" I didn't want to go into this neighborhood. I was pissing my pants the entire trip. But once we got into A7, it was amazing.

PAUL BEARER: There were a lot of fucked-up crazy kids and it was a playground. You could see bands and get away with anything close to murder. It wasn't really our neighborhood, because you had a lot of Puerto Ricans here. If you went down the wrong block and did the wrong fucking thing, they didn't have a problem shanking you. So it was a playground down here, but you just had to watch how you played.

JIMMY G: My grandmother lived right down the block on Avenue D and Fourth St. Right across from A7 was where my grandfather and grandmother were laid out. I was born and raised in Astoria, but my father was from the Lower East Side and my mother comes from Brooklyn. How can you be intimidated when your grandmother lives two blocks away?

JERRY WILLIAMS: When 171A had a few showcase gigs and A7 opened up, it constituted young places to play along Avenue A. I guess the venue scored instantly because nothing else was happening down there. We had decent bands and a low cover charge, so it became a good place for kids to hang out.

ROGER MIRET: My cousin Chuchi, he was the first one to get really excited about punk. He was into the Clash and Blondie. I discovered the Exploited, the Business, Discharge, Blitz—that second generation of punk from Britain. I discovered this straight-up pirate radio station that was playing hardcore. I heard Urban Waste. I started going into the city, going to Rat Cage. Going to see Kraut, the Stimulators. Going to the Mudd Club, Max's Kansas City, and then it all went down to A7.

WENDY EAGER: I remember I was downtown and this guy Paul Dordal was handing out flyers for a show at A7. I started going to A7, and that's when it flowed from punk to hardcore.

DAVE SCOTT: Back then, you just go at a reasonable time and sign your name up to the list of bands. It's not like you're booked in advance, but we started making flyers for these shows.

JESSE MALIN: I came down to St. Marks a few times and bumped into

Stephan Ielpi from the False Prophets with his monkey-skull walking cane and Hitler moustache. He turned me onto this place A7. I went and saw the Bad Brains and the Subhumans for a dollar based on a flyer.

JACK RABID: Bad Brains and the Subhumans show in '81. I worked the door. It was two dollars. Jesse Malin suckered his way in for one dollar. I wasn't very talented as a doorman.

VINNIE STIGMA: I played at A7 with the Eliminators. The shows used to start at three in the morning. Three in the morning! These days, they get you out by ten o'clock. This is before all ages and all that. A7 was all ages, but it was an illegal all ages. I was the oldest guy in the joint!

DREW STONE: A7 was like the Madison Square Garden of New York hardcore. That's where Henry Rollins first took the mic for Black Flag. I remember Bad Brains playing on top of their amps because there wasn't enough room.

JERRY WILLIAMS: All credit has to go to Dave Gibson, who owned A7. Once he started having gigs, the crowds came because there was no alternative. All he had to do was open the club every weekend, and the people would come to him. A lot of Lower East Side bands wanted an opportunity to play. The club started booking itself. Bands were coming in, saying, "Can we play at 5 a.m.? We don't care."

RALPHIE G: Dave Gibson gets unnoticed and underrated when NYHC is discussed. He played a big part in giving bands a chance to play and letting us build a scene at his place.

CAROLYN LENGEL (VOCALIST, KILLER INSTINCT, XKI): Dave was an enigma to me. I don't know what he was getting out of running the club—he sure wasn't making any money. We didn't get paid much for playing, but he did pay us something. One night he scolded me for talking too much on stage. "You think you're Johnny Carson," he said. I'm sure he was right! He was rumored to be an ex-con, but as with most of the rumors about Dave, I never knew whether it was true. In any case, he was the center of the scene—a guy whose interest in promoting and supporting the music was the reason things held together as long as they did.

RAT CAGE &MR **PRESENTS:**

PARTY

LEFT BANK

DOORS OPEN 9PM

CAVITY CREEPS
GILLIGAN'S REVENGE
ANTI-DOTE MURPHY'S
BLOODCLOT! LAW
RING OF FIRE AND MORE

MOUNT VERNON

CONRAIL

WHITE PLAINS ROAD TURNS INTO 1ST ST.

LEFT BANK 20 E. 1ST.

241ST STREET & W.P.R.

JUNE 29 **5 BUX**
WEDNESDAY

DIRECTIONS: TAKE THE **2** TRAIN TO 241ST ST & WHITE PLAINS ROAD. WALK THE LAST 8 BLOCKS OR SO. LEFT BANK IS AN OLD BANK. IT WILL BE ON YOUR RIGHT AS YOU WALK NORTH. COME EARLY AND SKATE THE MANY SHREDDABLE SURFACES.

June 81   25¢   STIMS CLO

HARDCORE WEEKEND

VICE SQUAD

FRIDAY SEPT. 10
SOME GOOD CLEAN FUN

FALSE PROPHETS
&
MISGuided

FEATURING BECKI BONDAGE
"the new First Lady of Punk"
(PUNK LIVES!!)

THE FILMORE
2000 long beach road
island park, long island
(516) 432-8433

SAT. Sept 11
From England—
EMI recording artists

VICE SQUAD
with special guests

NIHILISTICS

SCREAMING MAD GEORGE presents
A NEW YEAR IN THE GRAVEYARD

SCREAMING MAD GEORGE'S
IRRATIONAL

FALSE PROPHETS

MIKEL BOARD'S
ARTLESS

AT CHARAS NEW ASSEMBLY 350 E 10th Info 982-0627

7. FALSE PROPHETS: GOOD CLEAN FUN

JACK RABID: Until the first time I saw the False Prophets, every gig I'd been to, I was the young man. Everyone else was twenty-six or twenty-seven. I kept thinking, "Boy! When I'm twenty-seven, I'll be in a band!" The New York punk scene was all people that were out of college. The False Prophets opened for Even Worse in November of 1980, I think it was their second gig ever, and I had a little inkling.

STEVE WISHNIA: The scene that the False Prophets came out of was not the original people. We were the kids and twenty-somethings who had gotten inspired by it, and we were still trying to do the loud, fast rock 'n' roll thing. Most people had moved on from it by that point, or weren't that into in the first place.

I was originally in a band called Disgraced with Butch Lust and Davey who was later in Ultra Violence. I put an ad in the *Voice* that read, "Sex Pistols, P-Funk, Patti Smith, and the Velvet Underground. Must be rebellious, romantic, and fun." I don't think anyone answered the ad. But the False Prophets formed soon after that. The first time we played out was a block party on Fifth Street across from the Ninth Precinct. We got the plug pulled on us after five songs.

DAVE SCOTT: False Prophets were a band that you either loved or hated: I loved them. They were more creative than the other bands. Because of that, people would call them arty. Their singer, Stephan, had a tendency to preach, which drove some people bat-shit crazy.

WENDY EAGER: Stephan had this very vaudevillian way of performing. He had props and stuff and was very sarcastic. They had that song "Good Clean

Fun," which was clearly a tongue-in-cheek song about slam dancing, and people would bash the shit out of each other to it. That always made me laugh.

STEVE WISHNIA: One of the few times I've ever been eighty-sixed from a club was after going to see the Misfits at the Ritz. They were advertising the show as "Just when you thought it was safe to go back to the Ritz, there's slam dancing!" There was a big sign at the entrance that said, SLAM DANCE AT YOUR OWN RISK! I had to editorialize that statement, so I took out my pen and starting writing, "All we want is good clean fun." I got as far as "All we" when this fucking gorilla taps me on the shoulder and says, "What are you? A fuckin' moron?" The guy is a foot taller and a hundred pounds heavier than me, so I just put the pen away. "Good Clean Fun" was our attempt to write a hardcore song and criticize the scene as well, and I think it worked out really well.

JOHNNY CARCO: They weren't afraid to break out of the short-hair macho stereotypical look, and they kind of caught a lot of shit.

ROB KABULA (BASSIST, CAUSE FOR ALARM, AGNOSTIC FRONT): I'd say the False Prophets were the NYHC version of the Dead Kennedys.

JACK FLANAGAN: I didn't really like False Prophets. The thing with them was their singer, Stephan. He'd come out in this long coat with these fingernails that were longer than I don't even fucking know and he had a walking stick. Time was moving quickly, and we wanted T-shirts and jeans. This was no longer about a punk rock thing. Stephan was always more punk rock than hardcore to me. There weren't that many bands around at the time, so you had to play with these folks. I remember a show at the Playroom when HR from the Bad Brains threw a garbage can at Stephan onstage. It was really easy not to like them. The music was changing, and they were so stuck in their own thing. Hardcore kids are the worst critics in the world and if they don't like you, you were fucked. The False Prophets were part of the scene, I guess, but it got harder and harder to appreciate their music as hardcore grew into this faster sound.

KITE HAWK: They were sort of an outcast band, but a lot of us still loved them. They were almost an avant-garde rock band. They were sort of like Crass, who didn't really fit into any scene, but their music was so abrasive, they had nowhere else to go but the punk scene. Like I said, I always went with my own instinct. If I liked a band, I didn't give a shit what others thought. I loved them.

STEVE WISHNIA: We fit in in some ways and in some ways we didn't. From 1979 to 1981 seemed like a wide-open period for music. Punk blew things open. We were drawing on reggae and other stuff. But at some point in the '80s you were either dance music like Madonna, or you were new wave like Duran Duran, or you were art noise like Sonic Youth or Swans. There wasn't much space for just rock 'n' roll. There started to be this buzz about the second wave of punk in New York by the summer of '81, and we just kind of got handicapped into it. We were trying to find our niche where we could still play high-intensity, loud, fast music and do other stuff while not being stuck in this hardcore bin. But there was really no place else we were going to fit in. All throughout the '80s in New York, we were stuck because we were *in* the hardcore scene, but not really *of* it.

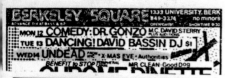

BERKELEY SQUARE 1333 UNIVERSITY, BERK 849-3374 · no minors
ADVANCE TIX AT BASS & BTO · OPEN DAILY 9:30 · SHOWTIME 9:30
MON 12 COMEDY: DR. GONZO M.C. DAVID STERRY PLUS AUDITIONS
TUE 13 DANCING! DAVID BASSIN DJ $1
WED 14 UNDEAD · X-MAS EVE · Authorities
BENEFIT to STOP MR CLEAN · Good Dog

Club 57
IRVING PLAZA

Fri., Sat. Apr. 24, 25
I.R.S. Recording Artists
DEAD KENNEDYS

Plus: Fri. **THE UNDEAD**
w/Bobby Steele Ex-Misfits
Sat. **SIC KIDZ**

Additional outlet: Metro Records, 252-02 Northern Blvd. Little Neck, L.I.

Fri. May 1
The Original Only N.Y.C. date (96 Tears)
? and The MYSTERIANS

Sat. May 2
SYL SYLVAIN and The **TEARDROPS**
WAYNE KRAMER

Fri. May 8 **BUSH TETRAS**
Sat. May 9 **THE PLIMSOULS**
Sat. May 23 **DELTA 5**

Doors open 10:00 PM Info 982·4863

---

77 WHITE **MUDD** 227-7777

FRI. JAN. 8 10:30/12:30

OUR DAUGHTERS WEDDING
THE UNDEAD

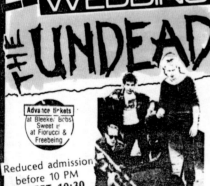

Advance tickets at Bleeker Bobs Sweet 16 at Fiorucci & Freebeing

Reduced admission before 10 PM
1ST SET 10:30

HARD CORE EXTRAVAGANZA!
Thurs. **17 DECEMBER**
JUST WHEN YOU THOUGHT IT WAS SAFE TO GO OUT
$5
THERE'S NOW SLAM DANCING!
MISFITS
UNDEAD
HEART ATTACK
RITZ

KEYSTONE FAMILY PRESENTS
KEYSTONE ConcertClub
ConcertClub Hotline 956-7898
Look for these symbols:
★ = FREE ☆ = $1 OFF

ConcertClub Cards available now! Call Hotline for Info.
Keystone ConcertClub Card is good for
ONE ADMISSION ONLY on free shows.

JACO PASTORIUS' WORD OF MOUTH
featuring Peter Erskine, Bobby Mintzer, Randy Brecker,
Othello Molineaux Wed 4/14 ☆ PA with
Dan Siegel · $8.50/$9.50

ANNOUNCES THIS WEEK
SLY & THE FAMILY STONE
Thurs 4/15 ★ PA 11 P.M.
Fri 4/16 ★ Berk 11 P.M.
Sat 4/17 ☆ SF 11 P.M. · $9.50/$11.00

Y&T (LAST BAY AREA DATE BEFORE EUROPEAN TOUR)
With Hi Fi and The Wolves Wed 4/21 ★ · $5.00/$6.00

Allen Holdsworth's IOU Thurs 4/22 ☆ SF
Fri 4/23 ☆ SF · Sat 4/24 ☆ Berk · $5.00/$6.00
NOTE NEW DATES—TICKETS HONORED AT VENUE.

THE PROFESSIONALS with The Undead
Thurs 4/22 ★ Berk · Fri 4/23 ☆ SF
Sat 4/24 ☆ PA · $5.50/$6.50

DWIGHT TWILLEY BAND
Thurs 4/22 ★ PA · Sat 4/24 ☆ SF · $5.50/$6.50

Announces **THE JERRY GARCIA BAND**
Sun 4/25, Mon 4/26 SF · $7.50 At Door Only

Back by Popular Demand **THE TWINKLE BROS.**
Sun 4/25 ★ · Wed 4/28 ★ SF
Thurs 4/29 ☆ Berk · $6.00/$7.00

PIGBAG
Sat.5/1 ☆ SF · $6.00/$7.00

CBGB and OMFUG
315 Bowery (at Bleecker) (212)982-4052
24 hour parking available
Wed. May 19
The Young Weasels (From Denver) ● **Network**
The Snapshots ● **Buster & The Big Ideas**

Thurs. May 20 HARDCORE NIGHT!
Stiff Recording Artists
THE UNDEAD
URBAN WASTE ● ANTIWARFARE
D. J. Dave Parsons

FRI. APRIL 23rd   8pm
dEAD KENNEDYS
NO ALTERNATIVE
SOLDIERS of FORTUNE
VETERENS MEMORIAL 8505
PARK Ave Old Redwood Hwy Cotati
the Show Of Spring
doa
tsol
no alternativ
crucifix
undead
SAT ARIL 24 8pm
OAKLAND AUDITORIUM
GOLD ROOM 10 10th STREET
LAKE MERIT BART EXIT

FRI MAY 7
DEAD KENNEDYS
with the **COOLS**
IN SACRAMENTO
BOX OFFICE OPENS 6pm
DOORS AT 7pm
SHOW STARTS 8pm
minors ok
INFO RRZ 415 957 9456

---

upstairs at
max's
kansas city

Wed. Aug 19, $5: Lyn Todd,
Media, Swingers

Thur. Aug 20, $5: Stimula-
tors, Undead, The Attack

Fri. Aug 21, $6: Heroes (ex-
heartbreakers), Knots

Sat. Aug 22, $6: Sic F*cks,
Necktie Party

Mon. Aug 24, $5: Mystery
Dates,   Poptronix

Tue. Aug 25, $5: The Sarah
Steele Television Show

Wed. Aug 26, $5: Afraid Of
The Dark, The Cooties,
Gentz

Thur. Aug 27, $5: Kraut
Heart Attack, Even Worse

Fri. Aug 28, $6: Cheap Per-
fume, Lisa & The Lost

Sat. Aug 29, $6: B-Girls, Ex-
Husbands
212 777-7871

8. THE UNDEAD: MY KINDA TOWN

JACK RABID: When Bobby Steele told me he had a new band after being kicked out of the Misfits, that's when I felt sure there was a new thing coming along for people in their late teens and early twenties.

DAVE SCOTT: When there was the transition from the old wave to the new wave of punk in New York, the Undead were one of the biggest bands at the time. They were really popular and drew a lot of people.

JOHNNY CARCO: They had great pop songs, and they probably looked the best out of all the NYHC bands. They just looked so great. They looked like rock stars.

BOBBY STEELE: In the summer of '78, I was in a band called the Scabs, which was very short-lived. After that, I was the manager for the Whorelords. They were having troubles with their guitar player, so they stuck me in that position. I think I did two shows at Max's with them, then I auditioned for the Misfits that fall.

Glenn Danzig and Jerry Only lived in New Jersey, so they just stayed at home. I moved into the city in late '78. I was living at Max's, practically. Glenn and Jerry would come in if it was a good show. They only went to Max's if Sid Vicious was there. Glenn was at home developing the band. Jerry, I don't know what he was doing. Glenn was the creative mind, and Jerry would be the one to have the money to do it.

DAVE SCOTT: The Misfits were more of a national band, even though they weren't that big at the time. They were on another plateau. They were just out for the Misfits. They wouldn't help anybody unless they had something they could do for them. That's why the only bands they would hang out with would be Black Flag or the Necros.

STEVEN LEWIS
INVITES YOU TO
**THE UNDEAD
FASHION SHOW**
HEAVY METAL TO WEAR!
TUESDAY OCTOBER 30, 10PM
DANCETERIA
30W 21ST
PRESENTING
**REBECCA DANENBERG
MICHAEL WYLDE
MARYANN KUCHERA
NATASHA**
FEATURING GUEST MODELS
FROM MEMBERS OF
BUTCH LUST
DE-A
POISON DOLLYS
RIXON
X-DAVIS
SPECIAL MUSIC PERFORMANCE BY
MAX
DJ. FREDDY BASTONE
SCARY ART SHOW
CURATED BY
MARGUERITE VAN COOK
JAMES ROMBERGER
SCARY STAGE DESIGN
BETH SEIDMAN, SEAN RANDOLPH,
ELIZABETH SEIDMAN
PERFORMANCES BY
THE UNDEAD (12AM)
ATTACK (1:00AM)
COMPLIMENTARY ADMISSION
FOR YOU AND YOUR GUEST

JAMES KONTRA: I was never that into the Misfits. I heard they were from wealthy families from Long Island, and I was dirt poor. I didn't relate to people who came from money and wore Halloween outfits with these thousand-dollar guitars. I was like, "Fuck you, I wish I had your fucking problems," you know? You play a gig in New York, fuck some hot chick, and then go to your daddy's mansion on Long Island. Let's switch fucking places! I wasn't a big fan.

BOBBY STEELE: When I got kicked out of the Misfits in the fall of '80, I remember sitting in my girlfriend's bedroom moping. "I just got fired from the Misfits; what do I do now? I know, I'll get back together with the Scabs and we'll actually do gigs." The Misfits would do a gig once every six months. I was getting frustrated; I wanted to play. I was free! That's when I started the Undead.

ROGER MIRET: Bobby was always around, hanging out at the squats we stayed at. He was real, and the Undead were playing shows every weekend.

STEVE WISHNIA: The Undead were the band we were closest to, because I had played with the drummer, Patrick Blanck, before. They were just a really good pop-rock band. Creative tension in the first lineup is what made them so good. Bobby is pretty much a straight pop-song writer, and Patrick and the bassist, Natz, were more musically adventurous and anarchistic.

PETER CROWLEY: The Undead were peculiarly Beatles-ish. They were the poppiest of the hardcore bands.

DAVE SCOTT: The Undead were one of the first bands that helped us out. Bobby Steele gave us shows in Long Island. He was one of the early people that helped us out a lot.

BOBBY STEELE: Glenn Danzig actually financed the first Undead recording, but he decided he didn't want to put it out after Tim Sommer did an article for *Sounds* where he wrote: "The Undead have accomplished more in six months than the Misfits have in five years." That's all it took. All of a sudden, this record that he said he loved, sucked.

After that, my goal was to be signed to Stiff Records. I didn't know how the hell I was going to do it, but I was going to do it. One night, we were hanging out at the Holiday on St. Marks Place. Someone said that Stiff Records was opening a new office in Manhattan, and they were having an opening party that night. I couldn't find our manager, but we needed to get into this party. We went out to get a cab, and there was a homeless guy named Ron outside that everybody knew. I said, "Ron, you're a manager for the night!" and I threw him into the back of the cab with us. We got to Stiff's office and I go to the guy out front, "I'm Bobby Steele, we're the Undead and this is our manager." It sounded official, so he let us in. We trashed the place!

After that, I would put Undead flyers up in front of their office and drive them nuts. We were doing an interview on a radio station, and they got a call-in from the promotion guy from Stiff Records. They put me on the phone with him, and he says, "You destroyed our office. You've been driving us crazy, we'd like to hear what you've got." We went down to meet with the president. I had a pet rat named Killer, and I took him with me. While we were playing the tape, Killer was taking shits all over the guy's office. They loved us, but they were wary because they hadn't done something like us in a while. This was when they were getting into the more new wave stuff. They came down and saw us open for the Misfits and they loved it. We signed the contract, and the word on the street was that the Undead were sellouts. This came from the very same people who signed record deals where their records sold vast amounts of records but didn't own the rights to their music. And I'm the sellout? I never got that.

JAMES KONTRA: Natz and Patrick from the Undead got sick and tired of Bobby Steele's egomaniacal quirks, so they left and let Bobby stay Undead by himself. So me and Natz were hanging out on the stoops on St. Marks Place, and he had a few riffs he wanted to show me. We went to that studio that Jesse had with the False Prophets. I put some lyrics on them, and Patrick Blanck stopped by and jumped on the drums. I really enjoyed screaming on the mic with those guys. We decided to call ourselves the Heretics; we later became Virus and put a record out on Rat Cage.

BOBBY STEELE: By 1983, I got really disgusted with the scene out here. I moved to San Francisco for a period and then down to Los Angeles. I was working on reforming the Undead with Olga de Volga from the Lewd, but it wasn't coming together. Olga got into a motorcycle accident and damaged her arm and was out of commission for a long period of time. That's when I came back and got a good lineup going with Brian Payne and Steve Zing. When I was working on our *Act Your Rage* LP, I sent it to every punk label and they all said it sucked. I got the last laugh. I sold six thousand copies on my own in two weeks. By the mid- to late '80s, my attitude was, "If you don't want to hear it, fine. I'm having fun," and that's still my attitude today.

RALLY: (NUREMBURG) '81

REAGAN YOUTH

THE POWER OF EVIL IS NO LONGER IN THE HANDS OF A CHILD

WITH
THE UNDEAD
HEART ATTACK
& KRAUT

AT A-7, FRI., SEPT. 25

ROCK AGAINST RENT

AUGUST 31ST   2:00–9:00PM

Tompkins Square Park (Ave A & 7th St)

WITH: ADJA

VIRUS × PARTNERS IN CONTROL with Joey Loerock ×

JOBS ROCKS × ANTIDOTE ×

BULLDOZER × STETSASONIC MC'S ×

URN CLIX × (NO PARTICULAR ORDER)

es by: ADAM PURPLE • ALI BABA • MARY BUMPURS.
Jackson • • FREE FOOD • FREE EXPRESSION • MORE •

UR NEIGHBORHOODS • END GENTRIFICATION • R.A.R.

BREAK THE SUBURBAN MOL

COME SEE

THE UNDEAD

BORSCHT

AND

THE DOUGH BOYS

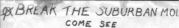

IN CONCERT ON
FRIDAY FEB. 25TH
AT 8:00 P.M. IN THE
CLARKSTOWN SOUTH AUDITORIUM

TICKETS
$4 IN ADVANCE
$5 AT THE DOOR

PURCHASE TICKETS
FROM ANY
MEMBER OF
THE CULTURAL
EVENTS CLUB
OR MR. ROSENSTOCK
IN RM. 312 OR IN
THE LOBBY DURING
THE 3 LUNCH
PERIODS. ALL
PROCEEDS GO TO
THE CULTURAL
EVENTS CLUB
THE UNDEAD APPEAR
COURTESY OF STIFF
RECORDS INC.

WHICH ONE IS THE REAL JUGHEAD

UNDEAD

CORPSICLES

THE UNJUST

@ CBGB's
315 BOWERY

THURS. JUNE 2ND
$4 ADMISSION

VIRUS

WORDCRAFT
JONATHAN LEAKE
AND
FILM "HERSTORY" BY LIZ

AT THE PYRAMID

TUESDAY AUG. 6TH
042

Beer = $1.

NIHILISTICS
DRUNK
DRIVING
CHARGE
+
MISGUIDED
ABUSED
2 LITTLE
DITTIES
BY "MURPHY'S
LAW"
JAN 22
8
PM
AT
PLUGG
140 W 24th ST.
N.Y.C.
SC9
Between
6th & 7th Ave.

Photos from top: *Nihilistics bring the love.* GARY TSE TSE FLY; *Chris T. on guitar and Mike Nicolosi wielding his black Hagstrom bass, circa 1979–1980.* COURTESY OF CHRIS TSAKIS

9. THE NIHILISTICS: KILL YOURSELF

ROGER MIRET: The Nihilistics were a great band with some crazy ideas. Who was that scary coming from Long Island? That band scared the shit out of me.

RON RANCID: A lot of people talk about growing up and living on the streets of New York. Try growing up on Long Island. Strip mall, cemetery, strip mall, cemetery, strip mall, cemetery. That's all there was on Long Island at that time. It is a very violent place. There were these guys who were termed the Northport Killers; they were some satanic group. They brought a human skull as a gift to us at a show at My Father's Place. I asked them where they got it from and they said they dug it up in a cemetery. That's what started me collecting human skulls.

GARY MESKIL (Bassist, Crumbsuckers, Pro-Pain): I think I was more intimated by anyone in the Nihilistics than by anyone that was from the New York City scene. I was always spooked out by them and afraid to go up and talk to them. But I thought they were great. You'd always hear stories about how one of them worked in a funeral parlor and stuff like that.

BOBBY STEELE: The Nihilistics were ahead of their time. They were heavy and they were pretty well hated for the image they put on, but they wanted to be hated!

CHRIS TSAKIS (Guitarist, the Nihilistics): I met Mike Nicolosi in junior high school. He was the heaviest kid in the school. He used to sit alone in the cafeteria. I ended up becoming friendly with him because I found out we had some things in common, like Monty Python, comic books, and cartoons. In junior high they offered a guitar class, which was something new. I decided I wanted to play guitar. Not too long after that I was in a cover band called

Cobra when I was fifteen, and we played the hits of the day. This would have been '76 or '77. By the time Cobra called it quits is when Mike and I discovered punk rock. Somewhere along the line, Mike made the decision to get a bass. We found ourselves in my mother's basement with a tape recorder and a microphone hung from the ceiling, and the two of us on either side of it. One of our first songs was "Grandmas Are Made for Kicking," about kicking your grandma down the stairs.

Mike had a pretty bleak outlook because his father had died recently as the result of a car accident. I remember him being a relatively upbeat, happy person who was overweight, then becoming really thin and really death-obsessed in the space of a summertime. We found out later he was a male bulemic.

RON RANCID: I would go to this place in Valley Stream called Legz. At that time, they were doing punk music on off nights. I physically bumped into Mike when he was coming out of the bathroom, and we started talking. Chris said that Mike wanted to form a band. I had a fourth-hand drum set that had parts of a *Sesame Street* drum set mixed in. That's where the Nihilistics started.

CHRIS TSAKIS: We went to the Salvation Army in Lindenhurst, and there was this book *Nausea* there by Jean-Paul Sartre, which I stole. Ron was driving his car, Mike was in the front seat, and I was in the backseat reading the book. I came across this word *nihilism* and I said, "Let's be the Nihilistics," based off the Stylistics.

RON RANCID: Our first show was outside during winter, in the parking lot adjacent to an American Legion Hall. We ran extension cords out the window. Halfway through the set, we got cut off. We all ended up getting locked up. Our first New York show was an audition at CBGB. You had to show up during the day. Hilly Kristal said, "You remind me of the Dead Boys, just way more animated and menacing." After he told us that, I pissed in their icemaker. That was the summer of 1980, I think.

SEAN TAGGART: There's this weird sense of pride of how broke everybody was in New York. I grew up in lower Manhattan. If you were from Astoria, I considered you to be from the suburbs. It was nice over there. If you were from any part of Queens and you had a backyard, you were from the fucking suburbs in my world.

CHRIS TSAKIS: There was definitely a snobbishness coming from these New York bands who thought Long Island was just about F. Scott Fitzgerald. They

Left to right: *Troy, Mike Nicolosi, and Ron Rancid of Nihilistics, backstage at CBGB, circa 1982.* COURTESY OF CHRIS TSAKIS

thought only wealthy people lived on Long Island. Lindenhurst was a blue-collar town. My dad was a mechanic. We did not grow up in great comfort. There was this perception that we were interlopers. When they heard we were from Long Island, they'd go, "Long Island? Fuck you guys!" But I think we proved early on that we could deliver the goods. Eventually, they had to accept us. We weren't going away.

RON RANCID: It was hard getting shows on Long Island, because country music was really popular. Long Island also had this tradition of cover bands. We tried to break into New York, but since we were coming from Long Island, it took so much time. Coming into the city from Long Island to play punk, we were like a band without a country.

PETER CROWLEY: I don't know why anyone would give them such a hard time. Hardly anybody was really from New York. Patti Smith was from New Jersey. The Ramones were from Queens. I guess that's almost New York, but it's certainly not the Lower East Side.

Their reputation is that they are some of the worst people on the planet, when in reality they are some of the nicest people on the planet. Don't tell them I said that.

WENDY EAGER: They had that whole shtick of being angry and pissed off, when they were really good guys. They weren't the most musically adept people, but it wasn't just about being musically adept; it was about the energy. The first time I saw them was at the Peppermint Lounge. I used to bring a tape recorder to shows. I was holding the tape recorder, and I don't remember if it was Mike or Ron, but one of them threw a beer can at me. They didn't do it intentionally, but it hit me in the head while I was recording. Back then, that stuff didn't bother me. I was just like, "Oh! This is so much fun!"

JOHNNY CARCO: Mike, the bass player, used to always give me and my band

shit. He would say, "You rich kids from Great Neck." Meanwhile, only one of the four of us was from Great Neck, and he wasn't a rich kid. I'll never forget the day Mike came to my neighborhood and hung out on my block in Glendale, Queens. I remember him looking at my apartment building in disgust, saying, "You live in this cell?" Then he apologized for giving me shit in the past. Then he went on to fuck with every idiot guido driving an IROC in my neighborhood.

JACK RABID: Nihilistics sent a tape to Tim Sommer and he liked it and played it on *Noise the Show* on WNYU. I was usually down at the station answering the phone while the show was going on, so I wouldn't have a chance to pay attention to what was being played. I would just tape it and listen to it when I got home. I remember when I went home and first heard them, I was thinking, "Wow, a band from Long Island sounds like that?" I got along with them right away, because they were droll motherfuckers. They were the most sarcastic, cynical, but funny people I ever met. Ron and Chris particularly were hilarious.

RON RANCID: I think people took issue with the Nihilistics at first because we were more real. We had nothing, coming from Long Island. I was an embalmer and a morgue attendant. Mike engraved tombstones. Chris was chronically unemployed, and Troy, our drummer, was totally fucked up.

CHRIS TSAKIS: I think the other reason we got pushed aside is because there was this idea at the time that you should be doing something that was socially relevant. I think of Minor Threat—that was a band with an agenda. We never really had an agenda. Our agenda was just saying, "You're going to die and rot in the mud." That wasn't the most wonderful message to be getting out to people. But there were some people who because they had a dark outlook took to us. Paul Bearer is someone who definitely took that ball and ran with it.

PAUL BEARER: I definitely thought I was the most miserable bastard on the planet until I met the Nihilistics. After that, I knew there were other people like me. They were dirgy and depressing sounding, and they just had me. They were dirty, nasty and angry. They were a great band, but they were socially retarded. They didn't like nobody, and they eventually turned on themselves. When they were done hating the audience, they'd turn to each other and go, "You!" They played that show with SS Decontrol and DYS at the Rock Hotel, and that was great! They played about four or five songs before Mike and Chris got into a fight onstage.

CHRIS TSAKIS: Ron and Mike quickly became best friends. They were thick as thieves. Mike's character changed, because Ron had this personality where he could get a hold of somebody and turn them into a partner in crime. There was pretty quickly a rift in the band that put Ron and Mike on one side and Troy the drummer and me on the other.

Mike would bring a warm case of beer and drink it before the show. He had to be thoroughly drunk to hit that stage. He was a belligerent drunk and took on this persona of a violent skinhead. He would flick cigarettes at people. He would spit on people. He would puke on people. That's what he enjoyed doing onstage.

VINNIE STIGMA: I loved when Mike used to throw up on the audience. I loved that. That was great.

CHRIS TSAKIS: There was a show at the Showplace that never happened. We were on the bill with the False Prophets. I was hanging out with Alex from the Misguided in the parking lot, and Mike said something to Stephan about his girlfriend, who was a black woman. I think he might have used the N-word. That's what I remember. Stephan came over and was getting in his face about it, and Mike was telling him off. I stepped in between the two of them to put it out and Mike ended up punching me in the face. After punching me, he said, "You're no Nihilistic." I was like, "Motherfucker, I named the band! I brought the band together! Who the fuck are *you*?"

After that, I just remember riding over the Manhattan Bridge into the city and it was raining. We were going to play a CBGB matinee and I was just thinking, "I'm not enjoying this. This is now like a chore." That was pretty much it.

RON RANCID: The band never really broke up officially. You can call it a hiatus. Ajax Lepinski came to the band after Chris. We always kept recording and keep doing it through the years.

CHRIS TSAKIS: Ron is still doing the Nihilistics. He was always the guy who was really good at schmoozing people and getting things together. He was always getting things done and he still is.

RON RANCID: A lot of these books and movies that have come out lately have their timeline off. There's a lot of revisionism. The first show Sheer Terror played, they opened up for us, and it's the same with Murphy's Law, and the same with Agnostic Front. Now, there's people who are into hanging plaques. I think they should just hang themselves.

CHRIS TSAKIS: Mike passed away a couple of years ago. He had some kind of cancer. From speaking to his wife, they thought he was going to beat it somehow. By the time I got around to seeing him, he couldn't communicate. I was trying to think of stuff to talk to him about and his wife said, "Why don't you talk about stuff from back in the day?" I mentioned CBGB, and he started twitching and his eyes stared rolling in his head. I think I started crying at that point. The stuff I've been through with this guy, and as long as I'd known him. It was too much. I saw Paul Bearer at Mike's funeral, and we both joked that we came just to make sure he was dead, y'know? "Why are you here?" "I just want to make sure the guy's dead!"

Clockwise from above: *Mike Nicolosi RIP.* GARY TSE TSE FLY; *Ron Rancid and Mike...; Chris T....; and Troy of Nihilistics, backstage at CBGB, circa 1982.* COURTESY OF CHRIS TSAKIS

The Most Brutal Uncompromising Band Ever

NIHILISTICS

New LP On BrainEater Records

Box J, Island Park, N.Y. 11558

NOW ON WEDNESDAY

NEW YORK'S ONLY HARDCORE RADIO

**FLIPPER
BLACK FLAG
UNDEAD
4-SKINS**

**CIRCLE JERKS
DAMNED
RUTS
EVEN WORSE**

NOISE THE SHOW

**MISFITS
D.O.A.
REJECTS
BAD BRAINS**

**SHAM 69
T.S.O.L.
TEEN IDLES
FLUX OF PINK INDIANS
...AND MUCH MOR.
TUES 7:30 - 89.1 WNYU**

REST...

WED..!

10. WNYU: NOISE THE SHOW

TIM SOMMER: I went to WNYU one day and told them there was a lot of amazing second-generation punk rock happening that they were not playing. There was English stuff like Cockney Rejects and Sham 69. There were bands from the West Coast like Circle Jerks and Bad Religion. And we had things in New York like Bad Brains. I wanted to do a show where, for a half hour every week, I just played pure punk rock. And they said okay. I went on the air in June of 1981.

JACK RABID: I met Tim Sommer in 1981, in front of a gig at Max's with the Undead and UXA. Lyle Hysen introduced me to him. I had been reading Tim's writing in *Trouser Press* for a couple of years, and I had a disdain for him. I said, "So, is this the Tim Sommer who wrote that Stiff Little Fingers review? The one where you put in a sentence that modern punk rock outfits like Cockney Rejects, the Stimulators, and Crass are too self-consciously punky to be taken seriously?" I called him on it and told him he didn't know what he was talking about! Those bands had nothing in common. He looked at me and said, "You're right, I don't know what I'm talking about." He thought the scene looked exciting and he wanted to know more.

LYLE HYSEN (DRUMMER, MISGUIDED; EDITOR, *Damaged Goods* FANZINE): Timmy Sommer worked at a record store in Little Neck called Scrooge. He contacted me because he was writing for *Sounds* magazine in the UK, and he wanted to learn more about the bands I was writing about in *Damaged Goods*. I introduced him to all the bands and to Jack Rabid. Then those two became besties. Tim wrote that article for *Sounds* about the New York hardcore scene, and then he and Jack did *Noise the Show* together.

JESSE MALIN: Suddenly, Tim Sommer was on the radio. His show was originally called *Oi! The Show* and then became *Noise the Show*. He started playing us on the radio. Next thing, we were opening for the Misfits.

TIM SOMMER: People immediately connected because there was no one else on the East Coast who was playing nothing but loud, fast punk rock on the radio. Nobody else was playing the Bad Brains or Stiff Little Fingers or Iron Cross or even the Stooges. Almost immediately, promoters started calling me, asking me to advertise shows. Very quickly, I noticed the show becoming something of a phenomenon.

JESSE MALIN: I would come home from school and ask, "Ma, did anyone call?" All of a sudden I was getting calls from Tim Sommer, asking if we wanted to open for the Misfits at the Ritz. My mom would taunt me when I'd ask if anyone called. She would mockingly say, "Yeah, Jello Biafra called." But one day he actually did call! He asked us to open for the Dead Kennedys. That meant so much.

JACK RABID: Tim's show became the focal point. He would announce a gig that wasn't even in the *Voice* and 150 people would come. After *Noise the Show* got established, everything changed. Except for shows with the Bad Brains or the Stimulators, hardcore shows usually only attracted thirty-five or fifty people. When *Noise the Show* started, all these suburban kids started coming in. That airplay had incredible power. The whole thing of reading magazines and asking older people what was what was completely thrown out. If Tim played a Reagan Youth demo on his show—it didn't matter they didn't have a record out. People heard it and said, "That's my thing!" A hundred and fifty people would come out.

JAMES KONTRA: Jack and Tim made it possible for a lot of new people to hear and feel real punk rock. They infected a lot of kids with the punk rock virus and were probably responsible for bands forming in a lot of places like New Jersey, Connecticut, and Pennsylvania, where hardcore would not exist if not for Jack and Tim's show—so big up to them.

CHRIS TSAKIS: We ended up sending a tape to Tim Sommer that was pretty much just us playing into a tape recorder. I remember being in my tiny little bedroom and hearing it on WNYU. It was such a thrill to hear your music coming out of the radio.

RICHIE BIRKENHEAD: I was into all manner of underground music at the time, but the thing that got me more and more into hardcore was *Noise the Show*. I used to listen to it constantly. I was never a guy who got so into a scene where I immersed myself so much that I excluded everything else, but that show did it for me.

KEITH BURKHARDT: I listened to *Noise the Show* religiously. That's where you got to know what was going on, and got to hear new music. We'd usually listen to it in the car driving into a show from Jersey. I have great memories of that.

MIKE JUDGE: I couldn't pick up the station on my house stereo, so I had to take this boom box and go down the street and stand in a field and fuck with the antenna until it would come in. I taped every single one of those shows. I would stand there holding this boom box out in a field; in my other hand, I had a notepad, and I would write down band names while trying to hold the boom box up and not lose the signal. I used to listen to that show like it was a religion. One of the first fucking memories I have of *Noise the Show* is hearing "Hate Breeders" by the Misfits. It's kind of corny, but you know that line in the song "They breed the hate right into your fucking bones"? I can still picture the moment I heard that line listening to that show. If I had to pick out a moment out of my whole period of growing up, that is probably one of my favorites. Sitting out in this field in the early evening, and hearing that line as I'm looking out over my fucking town full of jocks and shit, it all made sense. It put everything into perspective.

DAVE SCOTT: I listened to the show and taped it from the start. Every once in a while, I'll go through some old cassettes and find some old *Noise the Show* tapes. Having a radio show you could listen to on a regular basis once a week that told you what shows were coming up, what records were coming out, it was great. We needed that.

LYLE HYSEN: I was happy it was happening, and it was great exposure for bands, and a lot of people listened to the show. Tapes were made and traded and it definitely had an impact. But I really couldn't take Timmy screaming on the top of his lungs.

TIM SOMMER: For some reason, when it was time to back-announce, I just started screaming. I did not plan that; you can ask anyone who was there. I just kept it up, as it felt like a completely natural thing to do. I was just trying to match the energy of music.

DAVE SCOTT: I remember listening to the show in my room, and my mom would knock on the door asking about all the screaming going on behind the door. She hated it!

PAUL BEARER: *Noise The Show* was a great show. When he was yelling, it was great. But when he stopped yelling, it went downhill.

SPECIAL EVENT

'N.Y. THRASH NITE'

FRIDAY OCTOBER 22

Featuring 3 of the bands from the N.Y. Thrash tape:

KRAUT EVEN WORSE
and
ADRENALIN O.D.

New York Thrash is a 22 song album length tape on R.O.I.R. Cassettes with 11 of New York's best thrash groups. Available at Bleeker Bob's, Sounds, Freebeing, 99, Rat Cage, Metro and other stores that stock alternative music

ALSO APPEARING: The Young and Useless

IRVING Plaza

Doors open 10 PM

corner Irving Place/15th St

Jack Rabid and Tim Sommer at Irving Plaza 1981.
JOE FOY

TIM SOMMER: About three or four months into the show, I met Neil Cooper. He was starting an all-cassette label named ROIR. He approached me about doing a compilation of the New York City bands I was playing. Picking out the bands for the *New York Thrash* compilation was a very quick process. Basically, I chose any band I played on the show more than once, any band that had a decent sounding demo, and any band that played regularly. Some favors were thrown in. The compilation was put together by me, Neil, and David Hahn—the drummer for the Mad and the Bad Brains' manager in New York.

JACK RABID: The bands on the *New York Thrash* compilation; I guess it was the first NYHC scene, but we didn't think of ourselves strictly as a hardcore scene. "Hardcore" was just what they were calling it now. It's certainly not what people would consider NYHC later on. I wanted Reagan Youth and the Mob on there. Those were the two glaring omissions. Killer Instinct should have been on there, too.

JACK FLANAGAN: We probably weren't asked to be on *New York Thrash* because that was a very "city" record, and we were guys from Queens. And we had an attitude at the time. We weren't as open or friendly as we should have been. I don't know why the Mob wasn't asked; they certainly had my phone number.

MIKE JUDGE: We used to listen to that *New York Thrash* tape a lot because it was cool, but we did always wonder why the tape came out. I guess it's supposed to be New York's *Flex Your Head* or *This Is Boston Not L.A.*, but it doesn't have Agnostic Front or the Abused or Reagan Youth. Those bands are the heart and soul of New York to me, so I never knew why they weren't on that tape.

TIM SOMMER: The compilation came out in the fall of 1982, which means *Noise the Show* was already off the air by the time it came out. It's missing the next wave of bands like Agnostic Front, who must have been happening at the time; I'm not sure. Bands like Cause for Alarm and Agnostic Front had nothing to do with the bands I was playing or the scene I was supporting on the show. That's not a negative statement. It's just that by 1982 I was out of the hardcore scene. In retrospect, those bands were much better than the ones I was playing on the show.

JACK RABID: All the bands on that scene had a totally different concept on how to play punk rock. It wasn't as open-ended as the early CBGB scene, where you'd have a band like the Talking Heads play with the Ramones—but I think it's really obvious when you listen to the *New York Thrash* tape that none of those bands had the same approach.

DAVE SCOTT: Reagan Youth should have been on the original *New York Thrash* compilation. Some other bands were left off of there. The Mob is one of them. Urban Waste is another. A lot of bands had a lot more to do with the NYHC scene then some of the bands that were on there, like the Fiends.

JACK RABID: By 1982, I was out of the hardcore scene. The bands didn't dictate the audience. The audience started to dictate the bands, and I didn't like that. I respected Agnostic Front, the Cro-Mags, Urban Waste, Murphy's Law, and all the bands that came after. They are my friends. I'm still friends with Jimmy G. Doug Holland was my roommate. Vinnie Stigma will always be a good guy. I just didn't like their music that much. I just liked it better when there was no slam dancing, no Mohawks, and no idiots.

Eventually I couldn't tell the bands apart, other than knowing the people in the bands. For instance, Jimmy G went back to the '79 scene, so I knew who he was. But a lot of those bands sounded alike to me. It wasn't my thing. I tried not to be dismissive, because I could remember back to Richard Hell looking at me with this disdain. I was more dismissive on a critical level. I just didn't care for the music. I had nothing against them personally.

Above photos, from left: *Jack Flanagan (guitar) and Ralphie G (vocals) of the Mob come to crush at CBGB.* GREG LICHT

11. THE MOB: STEP FORWARD

ROGER MIRET: Heart Attack to me was one of the first New York hardcore bands. They were just fast and crazy.

TIM SOMMER: Heart Attack I fuckin' loved. They were probably my favorite band on the early NYHC scene.

STEVE POSS: People who were into the Stimulators ended up being the first wave of hardcore in New York, there's no doubt about it, but a lot of kids from Queens started coming in to see the Stimulators and started forming bands out there.

JESSE MALIN: I came from a broken home in middle-class Queens. My mom was working and single, and my dad took off. I would be left with this baby-sitter who liked rock music. I saw Kiss on TV, and that's what got me really into music. I was hyperactive and had all this aggressive energy at a young age. I was mad at my parents' breakup, and I was mad at the world. I was getting thrown out of school and getting bad grades. I wasn't a dumb kid; sometimes I'd even get into the special smart classes, but I'd always fuck that up. From Kiss I got into the Ramones. I found out the Ramones were from Queens and that was cool. I was trying to learn these hot licks by Jimmy Page, but now I was like, "Three chords? Cool! I can write a song now!" So I started to write my own songs and go see the Ramones. That's where Heart Attack started.

LYLE HYSEN: I was putting out my fanzine *Damaged Goods* out in Great Neck, Long Island, and somehow I met Jesse Malin. We were playing music together. I played keyboards in a very early version of Heart Attack. I was pretty much an Anglophile-type kid. I was more *Trouser Press* than *New York Rocker*, if you know what I mean. Jesse told me I should write more about the New York bands. I think he was the first one who took me to see the

Stimulators, the Bad Brains, and the False Prophets. There was no one before Malin. He was there from the beginning.

JOHNNY CARCO: At the time, I thought Heart Attack were the best hardcore band in New York City. They were tight, and had so much energy live. Jesse was a mini hardcore punk rock version of Angus Young. He played a Gibson SG like Angus, and actually played leads while spinning sideways on the floor of the stage the same exact way Angus Young did. He bit that move off of Angus, and he even darted around the stage like a frantic Angus Young. Then John Frawley was brooding, and held his Gibson EB-0 bass like it was a shotgun. He always had a pack of Lucky Strike cigarettes tucked and wrapped in his white T-shirt sleeve. They looked like a gang.

WENDY EAGER: The original lineup of Heart Attack had so much energy. It was amazing because Jesse was really young and he had so much savvy for such a young kid. I'm not surprised he is where he is today.

DOUG HOLLAND: I really liked Jesse's energy. He'd play that machine-gun kind of playing, and I thought it was pretty cool.

JESSE MALIN: The kids I was originally in the band with didn't want to commit to coming into the city all the time to play. So I put an ad in the *Village Voice* and got some people. I met this guy Jack Flanagan, and he turned me on to the Bad Brains.

RALPHIE G: I first met Jack Flanagan at Elmjack Little League at about twelve years old. We were both new to the Jackson Heights area and we became inseparable for years. Me, Jack, and another buddy took group guitar lessons.

Jack progressed much quicker than me and the other guy. So he continued, and we dropped out. Once Jack felt comfortable, he answered an ad he saw in a record store. I believe the ad said something like: "World's youngest punk band looking for guitar player." It was actually Heart Attack with Jesse Malin and some other kids from Whitestone, Queens.

JESSE MALIN: Jack was listening to the Ramones on the fast speed, 78 rpm. I didn't really want to play that fast.

STEVE POSS: Jack didn't want to do the stuff Jesse was doing, so he quit Heart Attack and formed the Mob with the three most un-hardcore people you would ever see.

PAUL BEARER: You had Jack with his Ronald McDonald Afro and Ralphie with his goofy dancing.

JOHNNY CARCO: The first show I saw of what later became known as NYHC was a show in Queens at a bar called the Shamus Pub. I think it was on Northern Boulevard in Jackson Heights. The bill was Heart Attack and the Mob. I remember the tension between the bands being really strong, which added to the drama of the night. The Mob and Heart Attack were rivals because Mob guitarist Jack Flanagan left playing Heart Attack and formed the Mob. John Frawley played bass in both bands at the time. It was a pretty serious vibe for back then.

JESSE MALIN: We put together a show in Queens, trying to bring hardcore out there. We did this flyer: "Punk comes to Queens!" The bill was Heart Attack, the Mob, and the Influence. It was two nights at the Shamus Pub on Northern Boulevard. Do you know what was going on in the city that same night? The Cramps and the Circle Jerks at the Peppermint Lounge, and Black Flag, Bad Brains, and UXA at Irving Plaza. So obviously we didn't get the draw we could have, and Shamus's was no longer interested in booking hardcore.

RALPHIE G: Jack rehearsed and played with Heart Attack for maybe a year, with Jose and I never far behind taunting Jack and them the whole way. The truth is, we were probably jealous and wanted to be doing it too. We convinced Jackie that Heart Attack wasn't where it was at, and it was time to put the Mob in action.

JOHNNY CARCO: Early on, the Mob were really fun. I loved the 1980 demo. We played it to death in the summer of 1980. Some of the songs on that demo made it to vinyl. Some that I really liked, like "Prisoner of Switzerland," one of my favorite early songs by them, didn't make it to vinyl. I always liked "Z.D.F. (Zombola Dust Fiend)." How could you not relate to that song when you grew up in Queens in the '80s? Queens, New York, was the capital of angel dust!

JACK FLANAGAN: We were genuine. We were four guys from Queens and we didn't hide it. Being genuine was a big piece of the puzzle. If you weren't genuine in the hardcore scene, it got noticed pretty quick. I don't think you would show up for a second show, you know what I mean?

RALPHIE G: The first show the Mob played was with the Bad Brains at a makeshift club on St. Marks Place called the B.C. Club. Later, this place became Coney Island High. I don't think we played very well, especially after hearing the Bad Brains, but we got a good response. I think the New York crowd was just finally glad to see some familiar faces and a hometown band representing hard.

TODD YOUTH: The Mob was the bridge band that was very influenced by the Bad Brains and came from the earlier scene. Jack was smart enough to put out a record and bring in the out-of-town bands to play. They're kind of unsung when it comes to NYHC.

JACK FLANAGAN: SS Decontrol was *the* straight-edge band from Boston. Minor Threat was *the* straight-edge band from D.C. And then here's the Mob, who has a song called "Z.D.F" about angel dust, and we're the band that brought SSD and Minor Threat to play their first shows in New York.

JESSE MALIN: The Mob were just faster than anybody and they were out there wrecking people. They were just regular guys from the suburbs coming out and killing it.

JACK FLANAGAN: The bands that were around early on didn't take the incentive to play with other bands. They were more concerned with their own band. The Mob started quickly. We rehearsed five days a week. We got good pretty quick. And once again we had the best teachers in the world, the Bad Brains. The reason we went to D.C. or Boston because it was natural. You had *Maximum Rocknroll*. You had fanzines and you would get scene reports. There was always a phone number there: "If you want to play, call Joey." I remember listening to the F.U.'s or Minor Threat or SOA and I liked this shit. There was always the show at A7 on Friday or Saturday and you'd have ten bands, all New York bands. For some reason, we thought it would be cool to go play other places and bring other bands to New York. No one else was making the effort. It snowballed from one cold call I made to Pete Stahl from Scream or someone in Boston. So the F.U.'s would come down to play A7, or Corrosion of Conformity would come to play. We didn't know each other. There were no contracts. We started very simple, and it snowballed into being something doable.

Our agenda was to have a good time. I think the bands from D.C. or Boston didn't feel intimated by the Mob because we obviously weren't going to beat them up. We just wanted to have good shows. We would always greet them with open arms, and let them use equipment and all of that. We weren't seen as a threat, so to speak. We were honest guys.

LOUIE RIVERA: I used to meet little Ralphie Boy and Jose at their work. It was this little book depository place up on Eighteenth Street in Chelsea. I'd meet them and get on the 7 train, and go all the fuck out the way to Queens and watch them dudes rehearse every night. They were jamming in Ralph's garage in the back of his mother's house. He was lucky. You were lucky if your mom even said, "Go make your noise in the garage," you know? We just had fun in that garage. They'd be practicing and we'd be bouncing off the walls.

But the beautiful thing was at the end of practice, Ralph would invite us in the house and we'd go upstairs and have an herb session. After the herb session, we'd be down in the kitchen and Ralphie would be feeding us. Before we went out the door, before we trekked back to fuckin' Manhattan, he'd make sure we had a belly full of food.

JACK FLANAGAN: When the Mob put out our first record. I think that was a turning point. That's when you started to see more organization. It wasn't just a hundred guys—mostly, guys by the way—who were doing this and having a good time. Now you thought you could possibly play somewhere else and make enough money for gas. That's pretty much when I saw most of the bands pop up and the organization come in. That was just around the start of '82.

RALPHIE G: In 1983, the Mob was at peak performance. We went into the studio with Jay Dublee, aka Jerry Williams, at the helm, and within a couple of days we walked out with what was our best work to date, the three-song "Step Forward" EP. That's HR from Bad Brains who introduces "Unity Lives On," saying, "Pay close attention, it might go by you."

JACK FLANAGAN: By '84, the Mob was the most popular NYHC band. Our shows were rammed once we had both EPs out. But, like most groups of an era like that, we usually don't get the credit. It's the next school that takes those elements and get the recognition. Listen, I don't care that I've done two interviews in twenty years regarding hardcore. I was there, I did it! I know what we did to get Boston bands to New York. I know what we did to get Urban Waste's record out. I know what I did to get other New York bands' records out to the rest of the country. All we wanted with the Mob was to have good shows and good records. We just wanted to be hard and tight and loud. We wanted people to have the best time. We wanted people to get fucked up. We just wanted to have a good time.

CBGB

THE MOB

ultra false
violence Phrofits
tue Jan 12

THE MOB

PLAYROOM
Sun. Oct. 18
9 St. Ave of Amer.

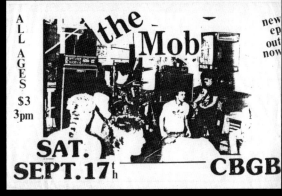

ALL AGES $3 3pm

the Mob

new ep out now

SAT. SEPT. 17th

CBGB

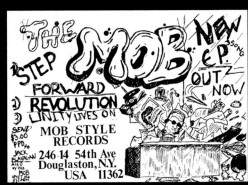

THE STEP M.O.B. NEW E.P. SONG OUT NOW

FORWARD
1) REVOLUTION
3) UNITY LIVES ON

SEND $3.00 PPD TO
JACK FLANAGAN ALSO BY THE MOB

MOB STYLE RECORDS
246-14 54th Ave
Douglaston, N.Y.
USA 11362

COMING IN SEPTEMBER

HEART ATTACK

3 SONG E.P. ON DAMAGED GOODS RECORDS

"YOU" "SHOTGUN" AND "GOD IS DEAD"

→ SEND $3.00 TO AMERICAS #1 KILLER!!!

Dr. R. C/O LYLE HYSEN
8 WYNGATE PL.
GREAT NECK, N.Y.

HEART ATTACK

MAN'S BEST FRIEND?

FEB. 25

HEART ATTACK WILL PLAY AT 11:00

WITH THE UNDEAD

CBGB
OMFUG

HEART ATTACK with URBAN WASTE + PORCELAIN GOD

AT NEGRIL
181 2nd Avenue
Btwn. 11 & 12th
WEDNESDAY MAY 4th
7:30 ALL AGES

REWARD
FOR INFORMATION LEADING TO THE APPREHENSION OF:

Jesus Christ

WANTED — FOR SEDITION, CRIMINAL ANARCHY, VAGRANCY, AND CONSPIRING TO OVERTHROW THE ESTABLISHED GOVERNMENT.

DRESSES POORLY, SAID TO BE A CARPENTER BY TRADE, ILL-NOURISHED, HAS VISIONARY IDEAS, ASSOCIATES WITH COMMON WORKING PEOPLE THE UNEMPLOYED AND BUMS. ALIEN — BELIEVED TO BE A JEW. ALIAS "PRINCE OF PEACE, SON OF MAN" "LIGHT OF THE WORLD" &c &c PROFESSIONAL AGITATOR RED BEARD, MARKS ON HANDS AND FEET THE RESULT OF INJURIES INFLICTED BY AN ANGRY MOB LED BY RESPECTABLE CITIZENS AND LEGAL AUTHORITIES.

128 W 45th
PEPPERMINT LOUNGE

HEART ATTACK AND FROM D.C. SCREAM

Sunday APRIL 25TH

LAST H.C. SUN AT PEPP...

TONITE!

RAT CAGE RECORDS
PRESENTS
• **SAT. NOV 20**
MATINEE STARTS AT 3:30
BEASTIE BOYS
REAGAN YOUTH
THE YOUNG AND THE USELESS
• **SUN NOV 21** •
MATINEE STARTS AT 3:30 PM
FROM PHOENIX ARIZONA
MEAT PUPPETS
BLOODCLOT!
FRONTLINE
CBGB
BOWERY AT BLEECKER ★MiR

REAGAN YOUTH

VOL 1

NEW AND IMPROVED

"oh, come now jim, it could never happen here...."

Top right: *Dave "Insurgent" Rubinstein exposes the evils of society.* RANDY UNDERWOOD

12. REAGAN YOUTH: I AM LIVING PROOF OF REAGAN'S LIES

RICHIE BIRKENHEAD: The band that I think best sonically summed up the Lower East Side in the early '80s is Reagan Youth. Their whole vibe was so uniquely NYHC; maybe more so than any other band.

JESSE MALIN: There would be certain people I would meet early on at something like a Stiv Bators gig, like these guys from a band called Pus from Forest Hills. They turned into Reagan Youth.

STEVE POSS: Reagan Youth grew up in my neighborhood. They all went to Forest Hills High School. I was three or four years younger than these guys, and I just started hanging around. My mother only let me hang out with them because she assumed they were good influences on me.

PAUL CRIPPLE: I had the worst acne out of anyone in my junior high, so that's where we got the name for our band Pus. A lot of our songs were childish in the beginning. The song that became "New Aryans" for Reagan Youth was originally called "Planet X." "It came from Planet X / It just wanted to have some sex." We were little kids, you know?

When I was fifteen, I started coming into the city with my sister, who was three years older than me. She would be like, "Come on! You've got to be cool! Fuck Little League! You have to know who the drummer for Led Zeppelin is!" My sister knew her music, and she imparted most of that to me.

My dad moved us from the Bronx to Queens, and I got to go to Forest Hills High School with all these Jewish kids. Dave Rubinstein was the only Jewish kid I knew who had all his relatives murdered by the Nazis—everyone on his mother's side, at least. Dave knew more about music than my sister. So I was like, "Fuck my sister, this guy knows some shit!"

In 1981, when Reagan took over as president, Dave was a little kid, so war and guns sounded cool. But a history teacher in our school, Mr. Gappleburg, set him straight, and said that we should be for the little guy. From there, Dave started writing lyrics that were very astute and had focus. We exposed the evils of society. We had a noble cause. That's where we changed over to Reagan Youth and somehow Dave became Dave Insurgent.

STEVE POSS: There was another teacher at their high school named Jack Depalma who was their physics teacher. He'd drive the band around. It's not like they had a ton of equipment. Two small amps and some guitars. So six of us would pile into his Dodge Dart. He ended up being asked to leave Forest Hills High School because they thought he was too friendly with the students. Not that he did anything creepy, but they weren't too thrilled with him driving students to after-hours rock clubs on his off time.

ARTHUR SMILIOS (GUITARIST/BASSIST, TOKEN ENTRY, UNDERDOG, GORILLA BISCUITS, WARZONE): Seeing Reagan Youth really impacted me. Dave Insurgent was a gifted front man. He threw himself completely into his performance. It was so primal, the way Iggy must have been in the beginning. Plus, Insurgent was so smart. His brain was fearsome.

STEVE POSS: Dave would go to the library and read books on politics and find out more about anarchy and political theories. That's pretty incredible for a kid.

WENDY EAGER: There was such a hatred of Reagan and Reaganomics. There was so much turmoil in the country at the time. So many people were disgusted with the conservative way the government was going. Reagan Youth had this perfect name and these great songs. They were the epitome of what NYHC was back then.

PAUL CRIPPLE: It was all about exposing the evils of society. Dave wanted each band member to know what was going on with America's political parties, as well as its history and the fact that his mother was the only member of her entire family to survive the Holocaust. He definitely wanted to take the side of the underdog, not rich, white, Anglo-Saxon Protestants who came to America and annihilated the native population while continuing, to this day, to refuse to pay their fair share of taxes to their king or the IRS.

MIKE JUDGE: Before I ever saw Reagan Youth, I met Dave Insurgent. He was at all my first shows. He had all these different-colored rubber bands in his hair to make dreadlocks, and he had this crazy-ass shiny shirt he'd always wear. On a sunny day, you could see him from a fucking mile away. He always stood out.

We went into the city; me and Paul Schraft and this guy Howard. We were headed to see the Bad Brains later that night at CB's, but we went in early to go to the record stores. My favorite was this store called Free Being, because there was this lady that worked there that had black hair with a white streak in it. If you had any interest in a record, she'd find it for you. She was awesome. So we're in there and Dave Insurgent is in there. We split and went to this little pizzeria. I remember this talk like it was yesterday. We were talking about the Bad Brains. Now, in my little mind, I loved the Bad Brains, but I couldn't get the reggae. To me, it killed the momentum. I'm feeling so much rage, and then this reggae happens, and I don't know what to do. I tell Dave that, and he starts telling me how the switch to reggae all makes sense to him. He was laying out some full-on Joe Strummer shit, man. He was like, "I understand you're full of rage, but you have to learn to hold it back."

I listened to the Bad Brains in a whole different light that night. When I finally saw Reagan Youth, I thought they were fucking great. He was one of the best showmen. He was intense. After that, I was like, "That guy is punk rock." His philosophy on music and how to use it as a tool was a big thing to me.

PAUL CRIPPLE: Our drummer Charlie "Tripper" Bonet looked a lot like Marky Ramone and played a lot like Tommy Ramone, so he was a perfect fit. But we had problems finding a bassist. When I first met Andy Apathy, he told me, "Why don't I join the band as a second guitarist instead of bass, and me and you could be like Jimmy Zero and Cheetah Chrome of the Dead Boys." It sounded cool, but it still wouldn't have solved our bassist problem. Eventually Andy traded his Gibson SG for a Rickenbacker bass, so finally he became a member of the band. Andy was already established on the punk scene in New York City. He had somehow gotten himself in John Holmstrom's *Punk* magazine, standing beside Joey Ramone and Debbie Harry in a picture where those two punk legends are supposedly getting married. Andy was credited as "Andy Zap, ring bearer."

STEVE POSS: Andy was a nut. Andy was a little older than us, and he was up to no good. Not like either Dave or Paul were saints, or had any right to judge him, but a couple of years' age difference when you're sixteen is a big thing.

PAUL CRIPPLE: Andy was already popular. When we were trying to get de-virginized, he was having threesomes. My sister told me this. He actually ate out my sister's best friend. He was far beyond the curve and he was mad cool, but he drove Dave crazy. Dave was like, "We have to get rid of him."

STEVE POSS: Dave never really wanted him in the band. He didn't like left-handed bass players. I remember him saying that.

PAUL CRIPPLE: I had to sit Andy down in a booth at Max's Kansas City and tell him. That really sucked. Then he went over to Dave and started screaming, "What gives you the right? What gives you the right?" Charlie left because he thought it was fucked up that we were firing Andy. We were in limbo for a little bit, and Dave said, "I guess we have to get Charlie back." I said, "No, let's just wait it out until we find a better drummer."

We were just sixteen-year-olds, and we were not musically astute until we replaced the rhythm section with Al Pike on bass and Steve Weissman on drums. But it must have looked adorable to a bunch of people watching these little kids playing songs that spoke out against racism and poked fun at Reagan for his bullshit political policy.

LYLE HYSEN: They were the best band on the scene. They could hold up to everything else that was going on in the country at the time. They were the band to beat, but they ended up just beating themselves later on.

KEN WAGNER (NYHC SCENESTER): Reagan Youth put out their *Youth Anthems for the New Order* album way too late. By the time it came out in 1984, that vibe had passed already. They missed their shot.

PAUL CRIPPLE: The reason it took so long for something to come out was that Dave had to have everything perfect. I remember Jello Biafra asking Dave, "When are you going to have something out?" Dave was like, "I have to take my time." Dave thought he had to get an A-triple-plus in hardcore. People stopped coming to see Reagan Youth around '84.

LYLE HYSEN: By the time they got that first 12-inch out in '84, it was over. It had this big foldout cover like a Crass record. The lyrics and the sentiment they had were already clichés on the hardcore scene.

WENDY EAGER: That band had so much going for them, but Dave got so fucked up on drugs. Then he got into this hippie-dippy thing where they'd play Led Zeppelin covers. They lost everybody.

BOBBY STEELE: The first version of Reagan Youth was great, before they became serious and into stupid politics. When they were satire, they were great.

The last days of Reagan Youth with the sadly departed Dave Insurgent. GARY TSE TSE FLY

They came out looking like bikers from the '50s with their hair greased back. Then they got sucked into all that San Francisco hippie bullshit and grew dreadlocks and they lost everything that they were.

DAVE SCOTT: Reagan Youth had so much internal turmoil. Even though they kept going, Dave got real into the drugged-out hippie stuff. They were a much different band than the original Reagan Youth. We ended up playing with them in Berkeley in 1986 and it was a completely different style. Dave was one of the best front men to come out of that scene. Him and HR are the two biggies.

PAUL CRIPPLE: With that song "It's a Beautiful Day" Dave was making fun of hippies and all their apathy. But then we got hooked up with the Rock Against Reagan tour and ended up staying out in San Francisco for two months. We ended up hanging out with the Yippies, and they're telling us about protesting the Vietnam War and we felt so stupid. They sold us acid at cost, and we were tripping every two or three days and eating huevos rancheros. We played the Republican convention in Dallas. I got arrested, but I didn't mind, because they gave me my own cubicle with my own toilet and my own phone. The food was good, and they had *Quincy* on the TV. There was only one other guy there. They let me out early, but I didn't want to leave, because the air conditioning was blasting. I ended up taking the bus home, and seeing all of

America on a bus ride. I traveled with fifteen black people eating pork and BBQ.

PETE KOLLER (GUITARIST, SICK OF IT ALL): Reagan Youth still had their niche in hardcore in the mid-'80s. I loved the Cro-Mags and Agnostic Front, but Reagan Youth were real. I guess they were the start of the crusty-punk thing in New York, but the delivery of what they did was so raw and mean sounding.

GARY TSE TSE FLY: When Reagan Youth played, everybody was in the pit. Jimmy G, Harley. They were really loved.

PAUL CRIPPLE: Fifteen people came to the last Reagan Youth gig with Dave. After the first song, half of them left. Everyone was like, "These losers are still around? No one cares about them anymore!" Anytime I play nowadays in front of fifteen people and they don't leave, I think, "Well, it's still better than the last gig I had with Dave."

WENDY EAGER: I always thought a band like Reagan Youth would be really huge, because Dave had amazing charisma. He could really take that audience with him. He had amazing energy. He knew how to control an audience and I thought it was really a shame that he got really screwed up on drugs and eventually died.

PAUL CRIPPLE: Dave would know where to cop coke at a store that was only selling it for the weekend. It was crazy! He would tell me, "They're going to change the spot." How did he know this? He was a super drug addict.

RON RANCID: I used to work for my uncle. He had a parking lot where prostitutes used to take johns. I'd stand across the street and make sure they came out. It cost two dollars to get in, and two dollars to get out. He closed that business. Got locked up or whatever. That left me to just watch prostitutes on the Lower East Side. I used to get fifty to one hundred dollars at the end of the night. At the end of one night, this one prostitute had no money to give me, and said, "How about I just give you a blow job?" I said, "I'm not interested in a blow job. I'm interested in my fucking money." It was right near the 2+2 Club. I ended up introducing Dave Insurgent to this prostitute, Tiffany Bresciani. They started dating after that.

PAUL CRIPPLE: With our second album, Dave was doing drugs like crazy and blew off three or four sessions. Finally, he came in and sang two versions of eleven songs in one night. Then he left and never showed up again. So I left a note on his door saying, "You better show up again, or I'm going to bash your fucking head open." I thought he was blowing off more sessions, but this drug dealer he owed money to caught up with him and beat him with a baseball bat. When I got a call that he was in the hospital, I was bewildered. I just figured he OD'd. Seeing him all beat up in the hospital bed with his mother in tears was the hardest thing I had to see in my life. His dad was acting all oblivious, saying things like, "See! I told you! He should have listened to me!" His mom was just crying, saying, "My son! My son!" I look back now, and I feel so stupid. Why did I assume that Dave just went off and got high? Why didn't I see something bad about to happen to him? What you hear on that record is the last time he was alive and singing. You're hearing the last thing he ever said before he was forever changed in a horrible way.

RON RANCID: Joel Rifkin worked in the warehouse of our label, Brain Eater Records. Everyone used to tease him. They'd put a sign on his back that said, kick me, and all that. I used to tell everybody, "Leave him alone. This guy's going to trip over the line one day. He looks nuts." So, the romantic triangle is that I introduced Dave and Tiffany, and then Joel Rifkin—who worked at our record label—ended up killing her in his spree of killing prostitutes. Then Dave ended up killing himself.

PAUL CRIPPLE: I know people hate the fact that I still do the band and that I'm the only original member, especially since Dave Insurgent was the main man in the band. I just want a better ending to the story than the way it actually ended, with the serial killer and the suicide and all that. I want to change that ending.

DOUG HOLLAND: He could have been the next musical Cesar Chavez. If he was famous, people would have thought it was some government conspiracy that he was killed.

PAUL CRIPPLE: I felt like Dave visited me once. I felt that whole Whoopi-Goldberg-turning-into-Patrick-Swayze thing for two seconds. Dave sent me a message and do you know what he said? "If you make a new record, it can't suck."

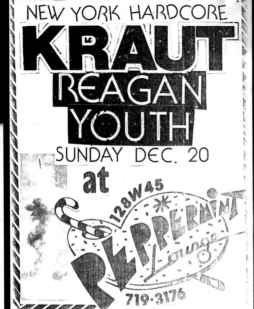

NEW YORK HARDCORE
KRAUT
REAGAN YOUTH
SUNDAY DEC. 20
at
128 W 45
PEPPERMINT Lounge
719-3176

KRA UT

CABBAGE RECORDS & ENIGMA RECORDS
CELEBRATE THE RELEASE OF
THE NEW ALBUM AND CASSETTE

"WHETTING THE
SCYTHE"
TUESDAY NOV 20, 1984
OPEN BAR 10PM—1AM, 3RD FLOOR
PERFORMANCE AT 1AM
DANCETERIA
30W 21ST
SPECIAL GUEST DJ: NANCY RAPAGHAN
COMP FOR TWO

KRAUT
WITH
BORSCHT
AND
CHAPPAQUIDDICK 5
AT
THE OFFICE NYACK, N.Y.
OCT. 22, 1983 10 P.M.
$3
VERY SCARY!
XMAS HALLOWEEN BASH $3
10 P.M.

KRAUT
an adjustment to society

KRAUT
HEART ATTACK
FIENDS
IRVING PLAZA
IRVING PLACE + 15 ST.
SAT. APRIL 17

INDEPEN-DANCE SLAM
July 4th
HADCORE MATINEE
KRAUT
HEART ATTACK
KHMER ROUGE
BOOM!

2+2 Club
2nd ave & Houston
STARTS AT 4:30 pm

L.E.S.R.M.A.S.
LOWER·EAST·SIDE·ROCK·MUSIC·APPRECIATION·SOC·
AND A7 PRESENTS
INDEPEND·DANCE·SLAM·MATINEE
AT 2+2 2ND AV. + HOUSTON ST.
JULY 4TH 2:00 PM
KRAUT
HEARTATTACK KHMER ROUGE $5
FREE BARBEQUE
DOORS OPEN 2:00 PM
BOOM!

13. KRAUT: KILL FOR CASH

JOHNNY CARCO: Kraut was and still is the pride of Astoria, Queens. They were one of the better bands in the sense that they had their shit together. I can't think of any other NYHC band in 1982 that released a full-length album but Kraut. They had a Clash-meets-Queens look about them. Doug Holland was solid on guitar and energetic, and he got enough of a Steve Jones guitar sound to cause a roar from his guitar. Johnny Feedback was like twelve years old, or at least he looked twelve, and he was a pretty good drummer. They had a cool black Kraut truck and they played a lot of shows. I saw them many times.

RALPHIE G: The first time we met Kraut was interesting. My garage on Eighty-Ninth and Astoria Boulevard in Jackson Heights had become the Mob headquarters, and it was well known in the neighborhood that we rehearsed and partied there just about every night. Rerun, one of the Mob moshers, went to high school with Johnny Feedback, the drummer from Kraut. Rerun told Johnny about the garage, and one day we heard banging on the garage door. Once the smoke cleared, we realized it was all four members of Kraut. We closed the door, they joined the party, and it was the start of a long friendship and rivalry.

DAVEY GUNNER (VOCALIST, KRAUT): The formation of Kraut happened in early '81. We didn't know it, but we were the start of something that was going to be big. It was really innocent. Doug was playing in another band at the time called Apprehended, but then he ended up starting up Kraut. It was Doug's band.

DOUG HOLLAND: Apprehended played two shows, one of them in the Queensbridge Projects. There was a very famous club there where they used to bus people in. You would meet at the end of the Fifty-Ninth Street Bridge. They had an old school bus, and they'd whisk you right over the bridge into Queens and drop you off. It was a beautiful club. I definitely felt mob drug money. The place was done in 1930s art deco, with lanterns over the tables. We played the gig, and the band wasn't working out. So I gave my resignation and started going to Max's. A really good friend of mine turned me on to punk. The four major bands that I first listened to were the Sex Pistols, then the Ramones, then the Clash, and Sham 69. I was really getting into this stuff after being a guy who listened to Atomic Rooster, Neil Young, ELP, and Pink Floyd. I had the cojones to push and get a band going.

Then I asked Jimmy G to sing. He was very interested in the music. It was a whole new thing for him. Jimmy went to public school like I did. One day he was like, "There's this little kid in my school, and he's wearing white T-shirts with 'Sham 69' and 'Sex Pistols' written on them in Magic Marker. He plays drums." That was Johnny Feedback. So we had a drummer. We had rehearsal booked a week in advance from seven to nine, but when I called Jimmy to remind him, he said, "That's tonight? Yo, the Stimulators are playing at Tier 3." At the last minute he said no, so it didn't work out with Jimmy.

DAVEY GUNNER: Me and Johnny had been good friends since we were five years old. We grew up on the same block together, so we got into punk rock together. Jimmy didn't want to be the singer of Kraut—he wasn't interested. So Johnny introduced me to Doug. I was singing for another band in Astoria. We didn't even have a name; it was just covers of Cream and Led Zeppelin songs. Doug gave me a copy of the lyrics and asked me if I wanted to try to sing one of his songs. That was it. It was like magic.

We're playing this angry, fast-paced music backed up by these lyrics. Ronald Reagan was president. We're feeling angst. Unbeknownst to us, while we're playing in that studio, there's a scene just starting to happen. It's all about timing. You can't chase the sound. You have to be there when it happens. It was just like they say in real estate: Timing, timing, timing. Location, location, location. Before you knew it, there was this scene going on simultaneously in places like Chicago and California and D.C. and Boston.

Looking back at it now, everything happened so fast. Doug is very precise about what he does, so he had his shit together. The songs were written, and for me to come in and fit like a glove at the first rehearsal, there was no hesitation. Donny Cowan, the bass player, worked in a recording studio, so we were able to record and mix some songs right away and get them out. We had our first single, "Kill For Cash," out right away.

MIKE JUDGE: The first New York band I really fell in love with was Kraut. This dude Paul Schraft had that first 7-inch, "Kill for Cash," and I dug that.

BOBBY STEELE: Doug used to ask me for advice. I just told him not to take no for an answer. Be persistent. And Kraut didn't take no for an answer. That's how they got that gig with the Clash and that opened up the doors for them. They were hot and tight. If they sucked, it wouldn't been what it was.

JESSE MALIN: I saw a poster for Kraut outside of A7, and I was like, "Who are these guys?" Someone said they opened for the Clash at Bond's. I was like, "Who'd they blow for that?"

DAVEY GUNNER: We played with the Clash on June 11, 1981. I can't forget that date. How could I? We got the biggest break of our life. The Clash were doing a week of shows at Bond's Casino in Times Square. Somebody duplicated the tickets. I still have my original ticket—five dollars! But instead of turning away the bootlegged tickets, the Clash did fourteen nights and honored all the tickets. They needed bands to open up for them, and we got our break. After that, Kraut just took off. We gave them some singles and some photos, and they just dug us. They liked the idea of this young punk band with an attitude from Queens. You look at these photos and we looked so innocent. Johnny had this bowl haircut that looked like a Ramones haircut.

DOUG HOLLAND: Mick Jones said we were the equivalent of the Ramones with a tinge of hard rock. I grew up on Thin Lizzy—give me a break!

DAVEY GUNNER: At one night of the shows, Doug and Donny were peppering the stage with paper airplanes they made out of our posters. There's a Clash live tape from one of those shows where, between songs, Joe Strummer picks up one of these flyers and goes, "This next song goes out to Johnny Feedback," and dedicates a song to him. I guess the name Johnny Feedback on the flyer stuck out to him.

DOUG HOLLAND: Our bass player, Donny, knew the girl who worked the ticket counter at Bond's. He was seeing her on the side. She got us in every night, and she told us, "Get me a demo and I'll get it to Mick Jones." Every day Donny would call this chick up and be like, "What did Mick say?" She'd say he was very busy, and she had to catch him at the right time and the right place. We got in free every night because of that chick, and we were allowed to stay in the club even while the cleanup crew was picking up bottles. We were sitting at a table at four thirty in the morning, and, all of a sudden, this cat comes out with a hat and short sleeves. He had a tattoo of a pair of dice on his arm, and I was like, "Rude Boy!" It was Kosmo Vinyl, the Clash's manager. So I said to my bass player, "Let's go over and talk to him. We put so much into this shit. If we burn it into the ground and get nothing out of it, that's just the way it is." But when I introduced myself, he was like, "Oh, right! Mick Jones says you're playing tomorrow night!" Which technically was tonight, because it was four o'clock in the morning and we were partying all night. Davey was in Cape Cod for a long weekend and we couldn't get to him, but we finally got to him and got him into the city. We couldn't believe that we did it.

JACK RABID: We were all jealous of Kraut for getting that Clash gig. We didn't think they deserved it. We had been playing for over a year, and here's this band and their first gig is playing for a couple of thousand people. But I have no issue with them because all they did was simply ask to play! They handed a tape to Kosmo Vinyl. They got lucky. Doug had been going to Stimulators gigs since 1980, so it wasn't like they were this band that just magically showed up and we knew nothing about them.

DAVEY GUNNER: Nineteen eighty-one was a huge year for us, and 1982 was even better. We put out the LP *An Adjustment to Society*, and we toured with Steve Jones. We used to play in Boston a lot, and we got this awesome gig there with the Professionals at the Channel. We met Steve Jones at the show and had a great show. Steve Jones didn't want to go back to England. He got friendly with Doug and he lived with Doug and Jack Rabid for a little while in their apartment on Eldridge Street. Doug ended up getting his own place, and Steve went along with him. He agreed to go on the road with us since Doug put him up. He hopped in the van with us and played all these dates with us.

MIKE JUDGE: Their LP *An Adjustment to Society* was fucking awesome. I loved it. This guy who was a freshman with me told me Kraut was playing a free show out in the park. We got there really early. I think it was some sort of pro-weed-smoking festival, because everyone was smoking weed out in public, carrying signs and shit. We sat through some of the craziest, weirdest music I had ever heard. We didn't see any punk rock guys, so we doubted that Kraut was really going to play. Then Kraut came onstage out of nowhere, and all these punks and skinheads came out of nowhere and start pitting up. Then I saw them at Irving Plaza at the *New York Thrash* show. They were my first love as far as New York bands go.

MIKE PERILLO (GUITARIST, SAVAGE CIRCLE; EDITOR, *Yet Another Rag* FANZINE): The first Savage Circle gig was at A7 opening for Kraut. I had put

Kraut stickers that I made myself all over my guitar case. One of the guys from the band laid some real Kraut stickers on me. To show you what a fucking goober I was at the time, it felt as if Eric Clapton gave me stickers. I was really into Kraut at the time. I couldn't believe I was up on that shitty A7 stage playing before this band that had an album out that I really liked.

DOUG HOLLAND: When the first album did well, our label, IRS, told us there was a little budget for us to shoot a video, which was all the rage. We knew someone who wanted to make a catalogue of their work, so they wrote a script for us, and the clip ended up on rotation on MTV. It was absurd. Then a few months later, IRS said they weren't doing too good, which didn't sound right to us. We were seeing the results of us playing, and how many records were going out. Then IRS Records folded. They invested all their money into the Bongos, and pushed them and not us. The Bongos weren't threatening and that's why they won. We found out later that people in charge of the safety of America didn't want another breakout of the 1960s, with all that protesting. They didn't want another youth revolution. So what they did was make a deal with these independent labels. They were told they wouldn't have to pay taxes if they closed. So IRS filed for bankruptcy. There were ten thousand Kraut albums in the warehouse, and they offered to sell us the albums for pennies on the dollar. So out of our own pockets from a few gigs, we got maybe twelve hundred dollars, and we went with our van and filled it up with albums. We shipped them to other independent distributors on our own. That's how we kept it going. The video was being played on MTV, but the kids couldn't get the album anymore. It was both a thumbs-up and a thumbs-down situation.

DAVEY GUNNER: If you look at the video today, it still holds water. It doesn't really look aged. It still looks really good.

DOUG HOLLAND: We eventually toured and played our way all the way back from California, driving an old Econoline van. The tour was okay. The guys in Kraut were like my brothers, but as soon as we got in the van and drove across the country, every one of those guys got a fucking ego.

DAVEY GUNNER: When we got back from California, we put out another record in '83, called *Whetting the Scythe*. After that, we got a gig with the Ramones at L'Amour East, the one on Queens Boulevard. That was a great show, because there were two thousand people in the place. After we played, one thousand people left. The Ramones took it personal. They thought we sabotaged the show. They accused of all this nonsense. It was just that they didn't have Dee Dee with them anymore, and they were going through changes. If you remember, there was a waning point for them. We were just more popular, and we were new and fresh. We blew them off the fucking stage.

DOUG HOLLAND: We tried to do a third album. We got more than three-fourths of it done, and truthfully, I didn't like the way it was coming out. The problem was bands like Guns N' Roses clogging up my head. Even TSOL were doing the hair-and-makeup thing.

DAVEY GUNNER: Chris Williamson at Rock Hotel was infatuated with Doug's guitar playing and wanted him to join the Cro-Mags. He was promising things like guitars, amps, and going on the road and playing big shows. Doug quit Kraut after a show we did with the Dead Kennedys at City Gardens in New Jersey. He was being pulled in different directions. It was a sad moment, since he started the band.

DOUG HOLLAND: Chris Williamson wanted to meet with me and the original Kraut bass player. We had a meeting, and Chris said he wanted to manage Kraut. We were like, "We did the dirty work. We got on MTV. We opened up for the Clash. Now you want to walk in and take fifty percent of everything we've created? What, are you crazy?" If we hadn't done anything before and you heard us, like Chas Chandler with Jimi Hendrix, then okay—you're recognizing talent. We laid it on the table and said he wasn't giving, he was just taking. He was basically trying to pull me apart and get me to join the Cro-Mags to destroy Kraut. So I had a meeting with the band, and I told them, "I give you seventy percent of the copyright." Who in their right mind in this day and age does things like that?

DAVEY GUNNER: We got Chris Smith from Battalion of Saints. He was looking for a change and he wanted to leave L.A. so he came here. He was great, and the band didn't miss a beat, until he tragically died in 1986.

Sometimes I think if Chris didn't pass away and we stayed together and we stuck around until 1987 or 1988, what would have happened is in 1991 we would have been playing with Nirvana. If Kraut would have been together, I believe we would have been swept up with that whole thing. When those bands were coming to New York, who was going to play with them? Kraut was going to play with them. By three or four years, we missed that whole wave. Nirvana reset the bar and put punk back on again, but since we weren't together, we didn't receive those prizes.

KRAUT

APPEARING
AT
THE

ROCK

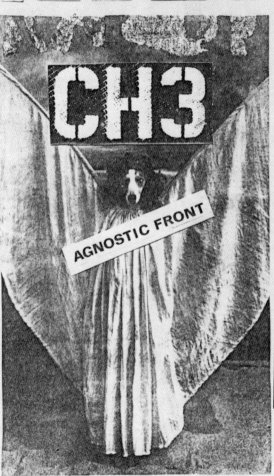

CH3

AGNOSTIC FRONT

HOTEL

113 JANE
STREET
at 8:00

113 JANE
STREET

SAT. JAN. 14

BIG
KEOVER

NUMBER TWELVE
VOLUME III — ISSUE II
WRITTEN, EDITED AND
PUBLISHED BY
JACK RABID

INVADES THE NEW YORK
AREA AGAIN !!

SATURDAY
SEPTEMBER 25
2 + 2 (AT ANNE'S)

THE EFFIGIES

HARDCORE PUNK
NEW YORK WORLD

KRAUT

FRIDAY
NOVEMBER 5

MDC

DAMAGED GOODS

OCT. 1981 · VOL. II · ISSUE SEVEN · **FREE #7**

BAD BRAINS

UNdead
SUBHUMANS   KRAUT
BLACK FLAG   EXPLOITED

ISSUE 3
AUGUST 1982

UNDEAD

GUILLOT

CHARGE

NEW YORK
HARDCORE

LOTINE

KILLERS INSTINCT

NIHILISTICS

FREE

M OuTH Of HE rAt Nº **2**
All rights REServed

A countdown
toward
disaster?

LITTLE
KE
NEROUSLY

Special
CLASH
Issue

new pain relief

**BOCA's
RATON**
BURNING

ComplEte
Why **Control**   *'the insect assault'*
says it all

It's lonely at the top   We promise you

NO DIS

...the Way
It Should Be

NO DISCO'S

VICTORY TOUR!

LOOKING
FOR
LAUGHS!!

This is what you w
This is what you g

"THEY DON'T MAKE 'EM LIKE THIS ANYMORE
LAUGH, ENTERTAINING, COLORFUL
AND FRESH."

how to

We wrote
the book
on it.   **DISCO SUCK**
Mac

14. THE ZINE SCENE: GIVE 'EM THE AXE!

DOUG HOLLAND: Do you know what Steve Jones from the Sex Pistols used to call Jack Rabid? Encyclopedia Punk.

JESSE MALIN: Jack Rabid started the *Big Takeover* as one piece of paper and now you can get it at Barnes and Noble. I always get a smile on my face when I see that in there.

JACK RABID: Soon after the first Even Worse show in April 1980, Dave Stein and I decided to start a fanzine. Dave's original idea was to do a David Johansen fanzine for some reason. I was like, "David Johansen? Wouldn't it be better if we did stuff about bands that don't get a lot of press?" So I think I was the catalyst regarding the idea of what we would cover.

The Big Takeover began as a fanzine about the Stimulators, but after two issues it was about the entire scene. We originally wanted to call the mag *The Cradle Robber*, after a Stimulators song. But I thought *The Big Takeover*, named after the Bad Brains song, was perfect for what we wanted to do: Take over and wipe off the face of the earth all the crap commercial rock bands we loathed, such as Styx, Foreigner, Kansas, Yes, and the Grateful Dead.

The first issue was in May of '80 and the second one was in the fall and then the early part of '81 we started doing it every month. If you look through those old issues, you'll see how surprised I am that all these great, new local bands start popping up as '81 goes along. I devoted an entire issue to the Bad Brains ROIR cassette. Another issue is totally dedicated to when *New York Rocker* and *Trouser Press* did multipage stories on our scene. It was so exciting to finally have recognition from these magazines that weren't even talking about the Bad Brains when they were at the absolute peak of their power.

After selling out two nights of shows at Max's Kansas City, there wouldn't be a peep. You'd think four black guys playing punk rock would draw some interest, but it didn't.

STEVE POSS: When *Big Takeover* started, it was a couple of pages stapled together with tiny print that was hard to read. Thirty years later, it's as big as the bible. It would take me a month on the toilet to read now.

GARY TSE TSE FLY: I was hanging out in the Village, and instead of buying all these British new wave fanzines, I bought a couple of local hardcore fanzines. I hadn't seen one show yet before I bought *Big City* and *Guillotine* at Bleecker Bob's. I just remember the fanzines looked really good. It seemed like everybody knew each other. There was a camaraderie flowing through the pages.

WENDY EAGER: In the fall of 1981, I went to England. I saw all these fanzines there, so when I got back home I started my own fanzine. I had a little, crappy Kodak 110 camera and a cheap tape recorder, and I started going to shows and taking pictures and interviewing bands. I asking questions to Butch Lust from Butch Lust and the Hypocrites, and he asked me what the name of my zine was. I hadn't really decided, but for some reason the word *guillotine* popped out of my mouth. I was a kid and it was something I was doing for fun. I had no idea what I was doing.

JACK RABID: Lyle Hysen's zine was one of the first, for sure, *Damaged Goods*. Lyle was a wonderful guy who was really enthusiastic about the music. Just the sort of guy you wanted to represent this scene. He was friendly, knowledgeable, and wanting to do something.

LYLE HYSEN: There was a fanzine called *Short News* that was done by Nancy Breslow. Me and Dave Motamed got that and thought, "We can do this! This is great!" The look and the aesthetic were very influential on us. So we started *Damaged Goods*. It wasn't like I made some major conscious decision to be that guy who does the fanzine, because "that guy" didn't really exist yet! I just wanted to write about the Dead Kennedys and Stiff Little Fingers. It was all good music to me. When I met the Stimulators, they were very supportive. I was so young and they were so nice. I remember Nick Marden was such a nice guy, inviting me over to his house to staple my fanzine. Now, was everyone being nice to me because I was the fanzine guy? Or are these people being nice just because they're nice? I don't know. All I know is Denise showed me how to do the halftones for the photos in my fanzines so they wouldn't come out too dark.

WENDY EAGER: Lyle was really helpful when I first started my zine. I had no idea what I was doing. He was the one who told me about doing halftones so your pictures didn't come out like blobs.

ROGER MIRET: Wendy did a great job with *Guillotine*. She was doing it in '81. You look at those old issues, and you see pictures of Agnostic Front with John Watson singing.

DOUG HOLLAND: Wendy was there for everything. There's no doubt about it. She was at every show, documenting it all.

MATT WARNKE (VOCALIST, BOLD): I always loved *Guillotine*. It was just chock-full of show reports from basically every show that happened in the city, with tons of crucial photos. *Guillotine* was basically a weekly chronicle of the New York scene, although it had a great open ear for out-of-town bands. I feel that the people who produced it were primarily concerned with good music and messages and didn't play favorites.

JEFF PERLIN (VOCALIST, RREAKDOWN): *Guillotine* was huge for me. Wendy had tons of record and show reviews, and did such a good job with that zine. It made me discover tons of new stuff, especially from outside of New York. She'd have really good interviews with touring bands like the Freeze, JFA, et cetera. So I'd learn about new stuff I could check out.

WENDY EAGER: When you do a zine, you are sort of the chronicler of your time. You see all the sides to it.

PAUL BEARER: Another good early zine was *Yet Another Rag*. The editor, Mike Perillo, lived in Co-op City in the Bronx, and his parents were deaf, but he never told me that in the beginning. I should have known something, because we'd go to his house at two in the morning and we'd be cranking the music. He'd be like, "Don't worry about it." One day I called and his dad picked up the phone, and was like, "Bleeeh!" You know like how a deaf person speaks? It scared the shit out of me and I just hung up.

MIKE PERILLO: I want to say I started *Yet Another Rag* in 1981. I only did four issues. When I started college I took a leave of absence. I did it at the time because I felt like I had something to say after we were all buying so many records and seeing so many bands. If we all sat down and wrote something, I thought we could put something pretty amusing together.

JACK RABID: You got so excited by doing a fanzine, but we didn't know how to do one. The only copy machine I'd ever seen at that point was the one in my dad's office, which shot out a copy a minute. We knew the one at the library was faster, so we used that one. That was about four copies a minute. You'd press the button and wait while the machine made these noises. I remember when we took the second issue down to the Unsloppy Copy Shop on Eighth Street, and they handed me a hundred copies in a couple of minutes. I just stared at them in disbelief. I said to them, "I can come back tomorrow." They said it would just be a couple of minutes. A couple of minutes? I'd never heard of such a thing!

MIKE PERILLO: Doing a zine was a lot of effort. If you wanted to put a fanzine together, you had to get all the photos halftoned so they would print properly. You had to type everything out and paste up everything. The thing looked like a twelve-page ransom note. I worked for a publishing company at the time, so I printed it there after hours.

JACK RABID: Along with *Noise the Show* on the radio, we did *Noise News*, which I published for Tim Sommer. We would send out a thousand copies of that, thanks to my job at the time. Little did they know!

MIKE BULLSHIT (VOCALIST, SFA, Go!; EDITOR, *Bullshit Monthly* FANZINE): My fanzine *Bullshit Monthly* was very news-oriented. I went around at every show to everyone to ask, "Hey, what's up with your band?" So my fanzine was filled with things about a band having a new demo, or where they were playing next Friday in Albany, or who needed a bassist or which band was recording or whatever. People really knew me and I knew them. The fanzine sold for between ten cents and thirty-five cents. I think a really expensive one was fifty cents.

JOHN BELLO (A&R, HAWKER RECORDS): *Bullshit Monthly* was kind of like a gossip column. I remember going to CB's, and Mike would be out there yelling, "Only a quarter! Only a quarter!" I knew I had to get it. Something about it was corny, but it was really good. It was the closest New York had to running to get the new *Maximum Rocknroll* at the record store.

CHRIS TSAKIS: *Flesh and Bones* was great. Jeff-O, the editor, was one of the most reticent people I ever met. For somebody who was a publisher, getting two words out of him was incredibly difficult. He had a very sardonic sense of humor and was one of the funniest people I ever met. He was such a tall guy, you couldn't miss him at a gig. As soon as he walked in, you were like, "Hey, Jeff-O's here."

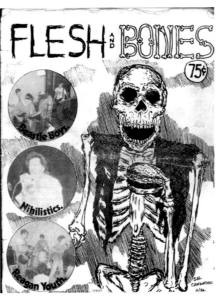

GARY TSE TSE FLY: I was just excited about the scene. I wanted my fanzine to be a zine that covered NYHC. California had *Maximum Rocknroll* and *Flipside*, which were concentrated on their scenes, so I wanted to do one that did that with NYHC. I didn't know how to start a band. I wanted to fill an outlet. I wanted to be a part. I never printed two hundred copies of any issue. My zine was just honestly the inability to hold in my euphoria on finding this scene.

MIKE PERILLO: I was in the band Savage Circle with Javi Savage, who used to do *Big City* fanzine. I used to think of Javi Savage as the punk rock version of Rupert Pupkin from *The King of Comedy*. He wouldn't take no for an answer. He saw big things, and I applaud him. Once I was out of the scene, I saw that he was still hanging on and doing the fanzine and doing compilations. But you have to ask why it didn't get any bigger than it did. Maybe it wasn't his fault. Maybe it was the scene, or he pissed people off along the way. He certainly tried to support the scene and you've got to love that. There weren't a lot of people doing what he was doing at the time.

JACK RABID: *Cheap Garbage for Snotty Teens* was another one. It was more wrapped up in the Beastie Boys scene. It was done by these girls we'd call the Minulators. They dressed like Siouxsie Sioux and went to all the Stimulators gigs. I think I was the only one who didn't sleep with any of them.

MIKE PERILLO: My grandmother died in Florida, and I had to go down with my mother to clear out her apartment. The Professionals were playing the Left

Bank in Mount Vernon, New York, the night my mother was scheduled to fly down. I had to lie to my mother and say I had work or something, because I wanted to catch the Professionals. I went down the next day. It was a blazing hot Saturday at Kennedy Airport. I was hanging out in the terminal, which was pretty much empty that early in the morning. This guy walks by, punk rock to the fucking hilt. He had the hair stiffed up, motorcycle jacket with stuff written on it, and combat boots. We started talking to him and he said his buddies had just opened for the Clash. We started talking about who we knew on the scene. I told him I did a fanzine, *Yet Another Rag*. He unzipped his leather jacket and pulled out a folded copy of my zine, and said, "I always carry this around with me." That blew my mind.

ROGER MIRET: I think *Schism* represented the late-'80s part of NYHC well.

MATT WARNKE: *Schism* was produced primarily by Alex Brown, with input from John Porcelly. It was obviously very well produced, with an insider's access. However, let's not forget that Alex had put out *Loveseat* fanzine when he was still living in Iowa. With his first love being graphic design and him being an accomplished artist, he set a very high standard.

ALEX BROWN (Guitarist, Side by Side, Gorilla Biscuits; coeditor, *Schism* fanzine): I got cracked on really hard during a road trip somewhere. I think it was Richie Birkenhead who was doing most of the needling, saying what a soft name *Loveseat* was for a fanzine. Raybeez from Warzone would always use that word. "Yo— schism, bo." It was a frequent refrain of his to refer to anything not cool or worthy of conflict. "Schism" was also one of the names that Jordan Cooper and Ray Cappo considered using for the record label they were starting, which became Revelation. I was living with Cappo at that point, so I must have pilfered it from them, but I remember taking it from Raybeez and him getting pissed about it, saying something about how that was his word or something. I felt like it was a continuation of *Loveseat*, inasmuch as it was my deal, but I probably should have started it as something new rather than just changing the name and keeping the numbers going. I think I thought it would look cooler the more numbers of issues I had—if that makes any sense.

WALTER SCHREIFELS (Guitarist, Gorilla Biscuits; guitarist/vocalist, Quicksand; bassist, Youth of Today, Project X, Warzone, Supertouch): *Schism* was such an awesome fanzine. It was the progenitor to *Vice* magazine, that snarky asshole thing. People got pissed, but it was awesome. The zine had narrow criteria, and there was a complete agenda—just like most Internet journalism is today, unfair and biased. *Schism* gave Verbal Assault a bad review because there was some issue between them and Youth of Today. When I was in Youth of Today, I would wear a Verbal Assault shirt onstage just to piss off Ray. It was politics, man; they had to be crushed. The reason why I remember the Verbal Assault jab is because I remember Alex telling me how bad he felt doing it. A lot of bands had to be crushed. But, you know, he wouldn't give Agnostic Front's record a bad review. Something that would really get his ass kicked, he wouldn't do that.

ALEX BROWN: *Schism* definitely became a different thing when Porcell came aboard. He brought a different sensibility and had a lot more connections than I did. He was also much more willing to let it rip, and not really care what people thought; either that, or he was just into ruffling people's feathers. He was definitely responsible for some of the cooler stuff we did with the zine and label.

JOHN PORCELLY (Guitarist, Violent Children, Youth of Today, Bold, Judge, Gorilla Biscuits, Shelter; vocalist, Project X; coeditor, *Schism* fanzine): Me and Al Brown, we hated anything that was soft. We were so into hardcore that if it wasn't super-fast with a guy screaming his lungs out, we didn't want to hear it. We talked a lot of shit that we shouldn't have, but whatever. We were young and dumb. Everyone navigates through their adolescence like that. It's just that we did a fanzine where that stuff was documented.

MINOR THREAT
DOUBLE-O
BAD BRAINS
One of the last few...
SATURDAY, MAY 15
Irving Plaza 15th Street & Irving Place, NYC

XXX

BOSTON
HARDCORE
WITH A CAST OF THOUSANDS
including: GANG GREEN / F.U.'s / JERRY'S KIDS / C.O.'s
AND D.Y.S.
A7
N.Y.C.
JUNE 11 FRI.
BE A TURKEY – JOIN THE CROWD

HE DAY THEY RETURNED...
THE FEW.
THE PROUD.
THE   PLUS
F.U.'S   D.Y.S.
Boston Mega-Hardcore
Thursday, July 8 at   Friday, July 9 a
ALDO'S / A7
Lyndhurst, NJ (201) 460-9824   N.Y.C.

DON'T MISS THIS...!
FROM Los Angeles!!!... New LP "Sound o Fury"!
YOUTH BRIGADE
RAISE YOUR VOICE, SING ALONG!
FROM WASHINGTON D.C....
VOID
FROM BOSTON...
JERRY'S KIDS
FROM HERE...
MURPHY'S LAW
ALL AGES
BE THERE!
TOMORROW NIGHT!
SUN.
AUG 21

GILDERSLEEVES

Bill Gilliamson presents
SS DECONTROL
Nihilistics
D.Y.S.
SAT. JAN 28
New York's Only
ROCK HOTEL
113 Jane St.
279-1995
Doors Open 9pm
Ad. $7

MISGUIDED PLUS FROM BOSTON: **F.U.'S**
JERRY'S KIDS / 3:00
JAN. 29 CBGB'S
SAT. MATINEE

PRODUCT OF OUR TIME

15. D.C. VS. NEW YORK VS. BOSTON: NO ONE RULES

Dear Lyle,

NY hardcore write-ups in major music mags make me sick. Pretty funny how D.C. bands are better, younger, and the scene in NY clones D.C., yet D.C. goes unnoticed. Oh well, breaks of life. D.C. crew will be up in NYC for Black Flag show at the Peppermint Lounge. We'll see how hardcore NY is, not too hard I don't think. —Henry D.C.

—Letter from Henry Rollins, printed in Damaged Goods *fanzine no. 7*

TODD YOUTH: I didn't realize it because I was in the middle of it all, but New York was really late in the game as far as hardcore goes, which is funny, since punk rock kind of started here.

TONY T-SHIRT (VOCALIST, ULTRA VIOLENCE): In '81 at Irving Plaza, the Necros opened up for the Circle Jerks. These chicks were telling me to watch out for the D.C. skins, but it was no connection to the skinheads from Europe. They were called that only because of their shaved heads. The D.C. skins sort of teamed up and took over the dance floor. I saw one of them throw a sucker punch at someone's head. Someone from the balcony shouted, "You know what D.C. stands for? Dicks and cunts!"

BOBBY STEELE: The first time I saw slam dancing was when I saw the Dead Kennedys at Irving Plaza. We opened for them the first night, and I went back to see their second show. I was out there pogoing to the Dead Kennedys, and all of a sudden these young guys started swinging around and everyone was terrorized. I was like, "Hey, this is my fuckin' turf," and I held my ground. Finally, they picked me up and put me on the stage with all the rest of the guys. They just thought I was as crazy as they were. That was Ian MacKaye and Henry Rollins.

DAVE SCOTT: The D.C. crew would come to those early, early shows in New York and show force. I remember Black Flag at Irving Plaza. Those D.C. people tore the New York dancers a new asshole on the dance floor. But that was the early scene. This wasn't the time of Agnostic Front or the Cro-Mags. It was college students, not super-hard kids. The people in Even Worse and False Prophets weren't necessarily brawlers.

STEVE WISHNIA: I think there was friction between the D.C. punks and the New York ones because the D.C. ones were these white, upper-middle-class kids. They looked at everyone in New York as effete art fags. I think they were envious of where we were, so they would be like, "Oh, do you think you're better than us? Well, then we're going to kick your asses!"

TOMMY RAT: The D.C. scene felt we were still in punk mode, while they had passed that stage a year earlier. When Black Flag first played New York City at the Peppermint Lounge in 1981, there were a lot of Adam Ant fans there getting high who gave the D.C. skins shit; they thought that was the nucleus of the scene.

JOHN JOSEPH: I got locked up, and then I joined the navy and then I went AWOL. I was in D.C. in 1980, before New York even knew what hardcore was. When the shit already made its way to D.C., it was still punk rock in New York. People were still pogoing at shows. We'd come up in vanloads to go to Circle Jerks and Black Flag shows. We'd be creepy-crawling on the dance floor, and people would be like, "What the fuck is this?"

JESSE MALIN: A lot of my friends who went to Stimulators shows would pogo or move side to side. But these guys from D.C. went out to the West Coast and got that creepy-crawl thing together. They moved real low down. They destroyed most of the people on that dance floor at Peppermint Lounge.

JACK RABID: When the D.C. people came up in March of '81 to see Black Flag at the Peppermint Lounge, they came up to our scene. We didn't know who they were, and they started slam dancing. Nobody in New York had ever seen slam dancing, so that turned into fights. That in turn fueled a lot of the animosity between the D.C. people and New York. They thought we were behind the times. They always came up with this gang mentality and I wasn't into that. If I wanted fighting, I would have stayed in junior high school. I hate being critical of people I ended up admiring, but I think they were really juvenile at the time. The D.C. people made common cause with the Boston people pretty quickly. The D.C. people and the Boston people both had a real gang mentality. Look at the cover of that first SS Decontrol record; a bunch of punks running in force. They were emphasizing their gang status. It might as well have been *West Side Story*.

SEAN TAGGART: I remember my friend coming back from that first Black Flag show at Irving Plaza like, "Holy shit! There were these guys with chains and spurs jumping into people's faces." He didn't know they were from D.C. He thought they came out here from L.A., because we had heard through the grapevine that they had a very violent scene.

DITO MONTIEL (GUITARIST, MAJOR CONFLICT): You would hear rumors about shows in California where there would be helicopters flying over hardcore shows. In my mind, I was picturing one hundred thousand people there, and I just had to get out there myself. In New York at the time, there were fifteen of us going crazy, but no one cared. New York was very behind it.

PARRIS MAYHEW: It took New York a little while to get over being punk rockers. Even in 1982, Bands like Kraut were more inspired by the Clash and the Sex Pistols than by the Dead Kennedys.

GARY TSE TSE FLY: I think it's true that NYHC started a little later than some of the scenes like D.C. or California. We had really good punk bands with the Dead Boys, the Plasmatics, and the Ramones. So there was no urgency to jump into this hardcore thing.

KEITH BURKHARDT: Other cities might have been more organized, but they didn't have as much stuff to distract them. They might have put more energy into their bands and had a better scene, but in New York, we had egg creams, bagels, and good coffee. When I lived on Norfolk Street, I used to walk over to Little Italy and get homemade ravioli. Good food was our main distraction. I think we could do good punk bands, but hardcore took us awhile.

DAVE SCOTT: The hardcore movement, since it started in California, was very much a suburban thing. That's probably why it took so long for people in New York to get it going. People thought New York had a more highbrow, intellectual kind of thing going on—and it did, with Sonic Youth and all that stuff. We were just kids. We were there for the energy and the camaraderie. We definitely had a different vibe than anywhere else, and that might have caused some people to react a certain way. You're not going to go to a punk show in Des Moines, Iowa, and see a drag queen slice someone with a knife on the dance floor, that's for sure.

RICHIE BIRKENHEAD: New York is a sovereign nation unto itself. A lot of the teen angst that spawned hardcore is uniquely suburban. But New York kids, even suburban New York kids, grow up very differently than other people around the country. New York is at the forefront of so many things, but hardcore was lagging.

PAUL DORDAL (NYHC SCENESTER): When Black Flag or the Circle Jerks or any out-of-town bands came, we really tried to welcome them or anyone else who came from out of town for the shows. I was living in my dad's house in Brooklyn and would tell them they could stay in my basement. A couple of them did. In the words of Jesus, "Whoever is not against us is for us." But I went down to D.C. once, and I felt a lot of animosity. Being from New York, I wondered what was up with that. We were always surprised that people from other cities would come and have this issue with us. In my perspective, it was about the music, and about the life we were living. If you were into the music, and you were living this life in your hometown, then come to us so we can share this life together. But there was this triangle of the Midwest, Boston, and D.C. that hated us. Frankly, we didn't have the big-name bands that they had. They had more hand than us, maybe.

KEN WAGNER: When Minor Threat would play New York, Ian MacKaye always had something to say about New York. He always had some dumbass remark. But then there were bands who came to New York from D.C., like Void, Double O, Scream, and Artificial Peace. They never had anything to say about New York. It was always Ian who had something to say, and it always brought the macho up in the New York guys.

JACK RABID: We got a lot of press from Tim Sommer in *Trouser Press* and *Sounds*. *New York Rocker* had Steve Graziano do a two-page spread. We were bands with no records. What I didn't know was that bands that were starting in D.C. and Boston and Detroit were all looking at this press, too, and they were getting angry.

KEITH BURKHARDT: A couple bands might have said things in fanzines. That got back to New York, and we might have given them some attitude, or danced a little bit harder at their shows—but maybe more of it might be myth. I was more concerned with some of the street gangs in the East Village. There was one point where the word was out that anyone who looked like a skinhead had a target on their back. That bothered me more.

SEAN TAGGART: Since we live in this media center, everyone found out about us. In a sense, that's not fair, but that's how it is. The people who had problems with that should have problems with the British press, not the people in the bands. Try living in New York—it's not that easy.

JACK RABID: It wasn't our fault! We didn't ask Steve Graziano to come around and interview us. I was just having a good time. Those guys in D.C. started to put out records because they had money and we didn't. I had my own apartment on Eldridge Street. I had to pay rent. I had to pay for my own food and Scotch tape. They were living with their parents, rehearsing in their basements for free. So every time they would play, they could put the money in a kitty, and that's how the Dischord Records label started in D.C. I'm not saying there's anything wrong with that; we just didn't have that option.

TODD YOUTH: The kids from New York, we were like these crazy fucking street rats. Meanwhile, the kids from Boston and D.C. were really well off. Also, everyone in every hardcore scene was trying to act all crazy and violent, but the kids from New York really were! You were getting chased down the street by gangs of Puerto Ricans that wanted to fucking kill you. You were seeing dead bodies carried out of abandoned buildings. It was real.

RICHIE BIRKENHEAD: The ethos of our scene was very different. New York was like, "Beer! Let's get fucked up! Let's fight! Let's fuck!" I don't mean this in a bad way at all. In the same way the Beatles were more cerebral than the Stones, New York was not the most cerebral hardcore scene. It was more oriented toward the raw energy and fun. D.C. was to a fault too smarty-pants.

BOBBY STEELE: New York had this reputation that we were all junkies. We didn't come here from Boston from our parents' house, you know? You come to A7 in the middle of the night, of course we're unconscious! Come back when we're not stoned! Come here at like 6 p.m. and we'll kick your asses!

MIKE JUDGE: The Boston bands were more straigtlaced type of guys—very jock types. In the early '80s, in New York, we were a bunch of misguided kids. We were going to hell with ourselves. Thirteen- or fourteen-year-olds nodding out on park benches. Crazy shit! So maybe they did kick our asses. I don't know! Maybe we were all too fucked up to know!

LYLE HYSEN: I remember when people were like, "Boston's coming and they're going to mosh all over you!" I was like "Boston? Really? Have you ever heard the Dogmatics?" That stuff cracked me up; the whole "hard" thing.

TODD YOUTH: Boston shows were always bad here. There was a show with Jerry's Kids and the F.U.'s when I was thirteen and I was small. Me and Eric Casanova were standing next to each other on the dance floor at CBGB and it was packed. As soon as Jerry's Kids started playing, this Boston dude with a mustache—just this big, jock frat guy—turned around and cracked me in the face. That was it; that set everything off. Me and my friends just fucking went *nuts*.

JACK FLANAGAN: There was this sophomoric competition between the New York bands and the outside bands. They were greeted with open arms, but they had to deliver. They would bring down six of their own guys and those guys had to dance hard. As much as it was supposed to be a good show, it was a proving ground. You couldn't get away with being some bullshit. It was the same thing for when the Mob went to D.C or Boston or Connecticut. We had to represent NYHC and play our hardest and the fans who were with us had to dance their hardest. People needed to see and realize that we were serious about this.

Also, you're talking about people who were twenty-one years old. That was a great edge! It was pure adrenaline. It wasn't maniacal. It was just "Let's rage." If you went down to D.C., you had to rage, and the same thing went for the bands that came up here. If you did it, everything was cool. Even if you didn't, it was just like, "You suck."

TODD YOUTH: I remember Jimmy G spray-painted a warning outside of A7 at an SSD show: "Out-of-town bands, remember where you are."

JIMMY G: I remember SS Decontrol showing up with ski masks on, trying to take over the pit. The whole place was just a pile of bodies. Back then, hardcore wasn't such a big thing that you could start a label and make a lot of loot. If you had a 7-inch that you pressed five hundred copies of, you were a big man. If you actually sold the five hundred copies, you were a *real* big man! There were always challenges going on between us and D.C. and Boston.

JACK FLANAGAN: When the Mob brought SS Decontrol down from Boston, it was basically Boston versus New York on the dance floor. That's when moshing really started to take off. People were getting hurt. That's almost how you gauged how good a show was, which in hindsight is completely retarded. When we played, the Boston guys tried to disrupt our show, and the same thing happened when SS Decontrol played. It was pretty warlike, but at the end of it when everyone walked out of there at six in the morning, with steam coming from their heads, they walked away saying, "That was pretty cool." I don't want to say there was a respect for one another, because it wasn't about getting or giving respect, but in hindsight—which is always 20/20—I say it was a great time; no harm, no foul. There were tensions, but they just stemmed from the same thing as if you went to a different high school than someone else.

RON RANCID: We played with DYS, and these guys from Boston took the lug nuts off of my tires so I would crash and die. I wish they had succeeded, to be honest with you.

MIKE JUDGE: When the first Judge record came out in 1988, it turned out Choke from Slapshot was really pissed about a line about Boston in the song "New York Crew." I didn't get why. The line was written in a broader perspective of telling what happened. It didn't say anybody won a fight or anything. I was trying to mention the Boston and New York rivalry. He took it the wrong way and it went from there. It wasn't until he took that line from "New York Crew" and blew it out of proportion that it seemed anybody was going to get hurt.

PETE KOLLER: I remember we were asked to play Boston, and I guess people still wanted to keep up this New York versus Boston hardcore rivalry. We were one of the first bands who didn't give a shit about that. We knew about the older guys and what they did, and we were just like, "Well, that's great for them." We went up there and played with Wrecking Crew at Green Street Station. There were a few older Boston guys there who wanted trouble, and there were a few older guys who came up from New York who wanted trouble. Then there were four hundred kids who were like, "What are these old guys talking about?" No one cared!

AGNOSTIC FRONT

UNITED BLOOD e.p.

HEART ATTACK

GOD IS DEAD

THE MOB

STEP FORWARD

NIHILISTICS

16. DIY VINYL: CRUCIAL CHANGES

TODD YOUTH: Nobody had the money to make records or start labels in New York; people were more concerned with how they were going to eat tomorrow.

JACK RABID: In some sense, that New York scene of '79 to '81 had more in common with what was going on in San Francisco at the time. The Avengers broke up having thirty songs, and only releasing three of them in their existence—and they were huge in their town. For most of us it was down to being too late for the first scene that happened at CBGB, and too early for the second scene, of Agnostic Front, Cro-Mags, and Youth of Today. There was no way for us to release records back then, and if you couldn't release records, then your scene was just some pleasant footnote for all the people who experienced it.

WENDY EAGER: During that period a lot of bands didn't get recognition because they weren't recorded. Bands like the Psychos and Killer Instinct had just as much to say and just as much influence, but because there are no recordings of them, people don't realize that. We didn't have a big label in New York.

JACK FLANAGAN: *Loud Fast Rules!* by the Stimulators in 1982 is the quintessential, cornerstone New York hardcore record. That changed things as far as putting records out on your own, and that song was pretty bitchin', man. It was a start.

DENISE MERCEDES: We did it with zilch money, because no one had a job or anything. Our manager, Donald Murk, funded it, God bless him. It was a total DIY recording experience. We didn't know what the heck we were doing. I think one of the songs ends with Harley going, "Do over!" Then we got Xerox paper and glue, and we sat there folding album covers. We had no distribution. I think some went to local record stores. They made their way here and there across America, but from what I'm told it's probably the rarest of punk rock records. A thousand were pressed. We had to get it done—it had to happen, and we made it happen. Somewhere on the cover it says, "Against all odds" and that's it. Don't wait for the moneybags, just do it.

In those days, it was hard to be a band. There was no clear path, we learned as we went. We took a lot of risks. We did it in a dangerous time in a dangerous place, the Lower East Side. With no money at all.

BOBBY STEELE: One of the big things was there was no support. If a band starts to succeed in New York, it's like crabs in a barrel. They try to pull you back in. In L.A., if any band was doing well, everybody got behind them and pushed them up. A band like the Circle Jerks were the pride of their town. In New York, if you got a decent record deal, no one came to see you anymore because you were a sellout. It was a dog-eat-dog scene.

DREW STONE: The main thing with New York at that time was there was no leader. D.C had Ian MacKaye doing the Dischord label. Boston had Al Barile doing X-Claim. San Francisco had Jello with Alternative Tentacles. Los Angeles was Greg Ginn and SST. Corey Rusk had Touch & Go in the Midwest. New York didn't have that. New York had a big mess of people hanging out in front of A7 drinking forty-ounces.

JESSE MALIN: NYHC was this totally *Honeymooners* working-class-guy type of thing. No one in New York had a van. Only one guy had a van—Roger from Agnostic Front—and he lived in it! We didn't have a lot of money! Bands from L.A. had albums and great equipment, and they could rehearse in a basement or a garage. Bad Religion came out with a full album. All these bands debuting with full albums. All of us could barely get a 7-inch out. Reagan Youth's record didn't come out at the time it was supposed to come out. The Undead didn't come out at the time it should have come out. We're just trying to buy beer. We didn't come from rich families. It was really tough. We played with TSOL out in Hoboken and they showed up in two vans with beautiful drum sets and Marshalls. We could barely pay for the batteries in the distortion box. You got on the train with your guitar and that was it.

RON RANCID: The Nihilistics really didn't know anything. We approached a few labels and they told us to drop dead. That's when we realized we had to do this ourselves. We printed a thousand copies and they were gone almost immediately. The end result was we stopped pressing them at about ten thousand.

STEVE WISHNIA: Stephan went to SVA but dropped out. But there was an older guy, a professor there who really liked him. He put up six hundred dollars for the False Prophets to record and the rest we put up from working or gigs. We got a producer to do it, this guy Joe Babbabian who was a rockabilly producer. Our first 7-inch came out in the summer of '81, and the second one, "Good Clean Fun," came out spring '82. We got the money to record our LP from Stephan's uncle, who won the trifecta at Aqueduct and gave Stephan the winning ticket for fifteen hundred dollars.

TIM SOMMER: If you're part of the scene, you really don't care what the records sound like. But let's say you're not part of the scene, and all you've got are the records to judge these bands. If you live in Canada and put on a record by False Prophets, you probably wouldn't play it again. It sounded like crap and there's nothing to hang onto. I think that's how the rest of the country felt. No one thought it was important to go make good records. An exception was Kraut—Kraut wanted to make good-sounding records.

JACK RABID: I remember sitting down with Kraut and peppering them with questions. "How did you do that?" "How did you put out a record?" The Bad Brains single had been distributed by blind men or something. If you were lucky enough to find a copy, it was without a sleeve. They were a band with tremendous demand. They were selling so many concert tickets, yet no one could put out their record at the time.

The Kraut singles were very eye-opening to me. You can just *do* this? It's hard to explain to people now, because there are a billion independent labels. It was really involved to put out a record. Not only paying for the recording, which was a lot of money, but arranging for mastering and plating. It was six-step process that people don't know how to do anymore.

LYLE HYSEN: I guess the big thing was that I put out the Heart Attack single *God Is Dead*. It wasn't a very fun experience. They recorded with my neighbor because he was the only guy we knew who knew anything about recording. The record didn't sound as great as the band actually sounded. It took months for it to come out. I had no idea what I was doing. I'd say it finally came out by the fall of '81. By the time it came out, Malin and everybody in the band hated it. That was it. They didn't want to repress it. Three hundred of them were gone.

JESSE MALIN: Six months seemed like sixty years back then! We thought we were ruining our momentum! But in the long view, it was worth it. I don't want to be the guy to say it, but people say the first NYHC 7-inch was *God Is Dead*.

SEAN TAGGART: Broke New Yorkers don't get guitar lessons when we're ten, so we don't have any money to put out records. We don't drive, so we can't tour. But most importantly, we really don't fucking give a shit. We don't need someone in Athens, Georgia, to give us applause to know we're the best. I fucking know, because everyone in New York knows it and that's really all that matters. We created it, we rock it. Case closed.

JACK FLANAGAN: We didn't have the mind-set that we wanted to start a record label. We were a part of the hardcore scene and we just wanted the best for it. Urban Waste were starting, and they were hot as shit. Kenny Ahrens was an insane front man. We knew it cost six hundred dollars to do, and they didn't have that much money. We had sold some Mob records by then and did have the money, so we said, "Why don't you put out your record with us? It'll be the cool thing to do."

JOHN KELLY (GUITARIST, URBAN WASTE, MAJOR CONFLICT): Overall, we were irresponsible kids, but we were responsible in that we knew we wanted to put out a record. We saved our pennies for the studio, and the one person who did guide us through getting the record out was Jack Flanagan.

JACK FLANAGAN: Also, there's Agnostic Front's first 7-inch, *United Blood*. I didn't put it out, but I bought five hundred of them from Vinnie Stigma and got them to distributors. So we helped out Agnostic Front as well. We saw the value in getting the records out.

DON FURY (OWNER, FURY STUDIOS): I walked into the club Great Gildersleeves one afternoon in 1982 or '83. It was a couple blocks uptown from CBGB on Bowery. Agnostic Front was playing to about thirty kids. I'd never heard or seen anything like it. Some kids were bloody, and the energy from the band blew me away. I usually get involved right away. I stayed for the show and let Vinnie Stigma know I wanted to work with the band. Vinnie lived right up the street from me. He said the band was ready to record. Not long after, Agnostic Front came in to record the *United Blood* EP on four-track tape. There were probably some live sessions I'd done with other punk HC bands before that, but *United Blood* was the true beginning of New York hardcore at the studio. The prototype. That record was recorded in a few hours.

TODD YOUTH: I remember me, Roger Miret, and Vinnie picking up the covers for *United Blood* in a big roll. We had to hand-cut them, fold them, and tape them together. Then you put the 7-inch in and then the insert. It felt like it took forever.

VINNIE STIGMA: We folded the covers of the records in my apartment. I did it with the wife of Jock Blyth from GBH! He married one of our girls, and she was the one who helped us. We still talk about it to this day.

ROGER MIRET: We knew that's what we had to do. We did a show, and we pressed them up and then sold them individually on corners. If you were a punk rocker coming down St. Marks Place, I would approach you and say, "Hey! Do you want to buy my record?"

KEVIN CROWLEY: In our minds, it didn't seem like you had to reach a certain level to have earned the right to make a 7-inch. It just seemed like the natural progression. You played some gigs, you sold your cassettes, you made your T-shirt, and then you did a 7-inch. The records weren't rated in the same realm as where other people put them. We never thought we were going to be famous. It was a rite of passage. The scene was a small group of people. Everybody was looking for something because there wasn't that much of that music around, so we were hungry.

JACK FLANAGAN: We paid the deposit on our second EP, "Step Forward," but we needed two hundred dollars more to get the finished records. We didn't have the dough. The gentleman who bought the first Mob 7-inch and the Urban Waste 7-inch from me for Important Distribution in Jamaica, Queens, kept asking if I had the new Mob record yet. I told him we didn't have the money to get it from the plant. He offered to give us the money right away if we would give Important the record two weeks before anyone else. I was like, "Fuckin' A! I don't give a shit!" That's when I realized something was up here. Usually, we got the records from the plant, we gave some to Dave at Rat Cage, and he gave us fifty bucks a month later. Now we had someone giving us money up front for those records. That's when I realized something was going on.

Photos clockwise from top right: *Kids on the LES* RANDY UNDERWOOD; *Hang session at the entrance of A7 including Harley Flanagan (2nd to left) NYHC scenester Blue (picking his nose) and Rob Kabula (2nd to right)* RANDY UNDERWOOD; *Future Death Before Dishonor and Supertouch vocalist Mark Ryan flips the bird while hanging with the Nutley, New Jersey, Crew* RANDY UNDERWOOD; *The doorway to NYHC's first regular live venue, A7* JOHN KELLY

17. EAST VILLAGE NIGHTS: A7 AND 2+2

KEITH BURKHARDT: I remember being at Irving Plaza with the Nutley, New Jersey, crew. I remember Harley Flanagan was there, and some people he was with were going after kids who looked like posers. They were eyeballing me until Harley came up and said to leave me alone, because by that point I was going to every show that was happening. After the show, Jimmy G came up to me and my friends and said, "You should come to A7. That's where everybody hangs out after these shows." It took us hours to find it, actually. Basically, you had the Park Inn, Ray's Pizza, and a little red light on the door of A7, and that's how we found the club. I guess I could say it was just a dump. And you know what? It might have been just a dump, but it was an amazing place to experience. To me, it was a magical time. I threw away any intentions to go to school or to do anything traditional and immediately moved into the city a couple months after that.

CAROLYN LENGEL: A normal night would start at midnight. You would start by drinking quarts of beer on the street by Tompkins Square Park.

DONNA DAMAGE: It was total mayhem, a free-for-all party every weekend on the corner of St. Marks and Avenue A, and in Tompkins Square Park. People used to shoot up on the benches in the park, and just sell heroin on the street or in these buildings. There would be a blue door and a brown door; one was coke, the other was heroin. There'd be big lines of people around the block to get their drugs. One the corner of Eleventh and B, they'd be selling works. It was like total anarchy down there. The cops didn't want anything to do with what was going down. That's how A7 was able to flourish. There was no police presence. The East Village and the Lower East Side was the mecca of the first wave of NYHC. That's where it all came together and I don't think it would have been possible without A7.

DREW STONE: A band would play and then when the next band would set up, everybody would pour out of A7 and go across the street to Tompkins Square Park for twenty minutes. As soon as you'd hear the next band start to play, you'd make your way back inside. This was a constant cycle.

RUSS IGLAY (GUITARIST, CHILD ABUSE; BASSIST, MURPHY'S LAW, UNDERDOG): We'd have a fire going in a garbage can in Tompkins Square Park in the winter. Somebody would have a boom box. We would drink beers and hang out. It was like when you have a party in your room with your stereo on, but it was in the park on Avenue A and Eighth Street. It was a huge party all the time every night; especially in the summer. But in the winter, it was the same thing except we'd just bundle up. You'd get to wear your cool clothes; your leather jacket or your trench coat. The Park Inn was across the street, and that was our headquarters. Lucy's was over there too.

DAVE SCOTT: There were rapes in the park, and it was the center of the lower New York drug scene. When you're a kid, you don't realize how vulnerable you really are. There were nights that I was walking around by myself in those areas. Thinking back on it, I was an idiot.

MIKE JUDGE: I remember having to go into the park and getting to a certain part and noticing that none of the lights worked. Billy Psycho was sitting on a bench, and he was like, "White guys don't go past that bench. You won't come back out of the dark, Jersey!"

ALEX KINON (GUITARIST, CAUSE FOR ALARM, AGNOSTIC FRONT, SKINHEAD YOUTH): I had knives pulled on me in the park. I think I remember being shot at. Vinnie Stigma was right there, and he had a garbage can lid he was using as a shield while charging at where the shots were coming from.

DREW STONE: Here's a quick A7 story: I grew up in the Bronx, and when I was in the High and the Mighty, the first time we played A7 was in 1983. We'd come down and I had a van and there was a lot of waiting at A7. You'd show up at eleven o'clock but you'd be sitting, waiting to play until three or four in the morning. Back then the Lower East Side was like downtown Beirut. It was graffiti-ridden, crime-ridden, ugly, dirty, scary, and had a lot of junkies around, so we stuck together. No one wandered very far from the van. We were all teenagers. So as we're all huddled in the van, waiting to play, this punk girl was crossing Avenue A with a beer in her hand, and a cab fucking hits her and she goes up on the hood, cartwheels over the windshield, over the roof, hits the pavement, and her forty smashes on the ground. The cab took off, and she staggered up on her feet and just walked over to Tompkins Square Park. We were like, "Holy shit! We ain't in Kansas anymore."

STEVEN WISHNIA: Stephan was dating this older woman who lived in the neighborhood and she took him for a drink there. The band that was on was pretty lame, so he talked to Dave Gibson, the owner, and he said, "Hey I've got a band, can we play here?" We became sort of the unofficial house band because we played every three weeks. That was great; that was some of the best times I ever had playing music in my life.

BOBBY STEELE: I was banned from Max's, I was banned from CBGB. I was banned from pretty much everywhere else because the Misfits slandered me, so I thought I'd start my own scene. I lived on Fourth Street between Avenues A and B and someone told me about A7. We walked in and there were these four or five black guys playing jazz. I looked around and no one was there. I brought a tape that I just recorded in the rehearsal space on a boom box. Dave listened to about five seconds of it and asked, "How does January 31 sound?" And that was the beginning of everything. The first Undead show was at A7. That was the show that put it on the map. There were shows going on there before, but it was bands like the False Prophets—these bands that if their girlfriends showed up it was a good turnout.

DONNA DAMAGE: I discovered A7 from an Undead flyer posted by Washington Square Park. I showed up and met the people and budding musicians I'd later play with. Many of these folks I am still friends with to this day.

STEVE WISHNIA: We opened up for DOA at A7. They went on at six in the morning and they said that was the latest they ever went on. At that point, it was a punk club, not a strict hardcore club. You'd have Elliott Sharp on a Thursday night, and us on a Saturday night. One weekend would be the Undead, and then an oddball pop band like Desi Desi Desi.

NICK MARDEN: All the misfits ended up there one way or another. Whether it was hanging out in the park or whatever. There was the night DOA were playing A7 and then they went over to 171A and did a set and then they went back over to A7 and did another set and the crowd just went followed them back and forth.

JIMMY G: Most after-hours clubs were basically just drug dens with no windows and this place was more than that. There was an eclectic mix of people and music. A7 was more of a music scene than most after-hours clubs. Most after-hours places don't want noise or music because it'll bring police, but on

Enter the early scene—with Harley Flanagan and John Watson on hand. JOHN KELLY

the Lower East Side back then, the police didn't give a shit, because there was no money to be made down there. Most of the fancier clubs wouldn't book hardcore bands, because no one really knew what it was yet. To them, hardcore was pretty much an unknown form of punk that wasn't as well-dressed as the previous punks! People didn't want us, so Dave started to have bands. There was already a reggae scene going on at A7 at the time. Jazz bands played there, too. Musicians gathered there. Dave would let anyone who played any form of music play there, and that's how the club grew.

JACK RABID: The first show I ever saw at A7 was Mofungo. I think the second show I saw there was the band Jerry Williams played in, Hi Sheriffs of Blue. So, the first few shows I saw there weren't punk or hardcore at all.

PAUL DORDAL: A7 was the central place to see bands because there were five or six bands a night. I was half in the bag most of the time, and didn't know who was playing, but I remember a New Jersey band named Genocide. They came and played, and we heard they were talking bad about Jews. I'm Puerto Rican first of all, so I'd love to dispel this idea that I was some sort of fascist skinhead. We would have black guys hang out with us and all sorts of immigrant New Yorkers. So Genocide played, and we heard they spit on some girl we knew and called her a filthy Jew, so we fought them all the way to their van and told them they would never play New York again. There was this feeling of righteous violence. Some of it was stupid, some of it was senseless, but there were times when we felt righteous in our violence.

JAMES KONTRA: Panhandling wasn't my thing. So we'd go to a head shop and buy the stuff they cut cocaine with—it was called procaine. It looked just like cocaine and it froze your mouth and the whole thing. You could buy a whole jar for five bucks. We'd bag it into coke baggies and sell them. All of a sudden, this black dude comes up to me and Bloodclot, John Joseph, in front of A7. He says, "I met some girls at the Pyramid who said they got some coke from you and they're zooted, they're flying. Can I get an ounce?" I'm like, "Yeah! For you? Eight hundred dollars." So I dumped what we had into a bag and gave it to him. He was like, "That's a healthy ounce!" Next thing you know, he comes back ten or fifteen minutes later. John Joseph and I went to Stromboli's and bought beers, we bought pizza, we were partying! Dave, the black guy who owned A7, came back with the guy. The guy says, "Yo, motherfucker! Do you know who I am? You sold me bullshit, give me back my fucking money!" I was like, "Nigga, fuck you! You went inside with my shit and you come back out twenty minutes later? I don't know what the fuck I gave you, get the fuck out of here!" The guy pulled out a knife, so we pulled off our bike chains from around our waists and beat him fucking stupid. We got eighty-sixed for a good seven or eight months, because that guy knew Dave.

KEVIN CROWLEY: I used to give haircuts to people in the bathroom. I walked around with a backpack with clippers, and I would just cut people's hair. The big thing was to find someone who it was their first time there and they had long hair, and I'd shave them bald. I'd tell them, "I'm just going to take a little off," and then shave them bald.

CAROLYN LENGEL: You'd have someone get you on the guest list, or you'd whine at Victor, the doorman, until he'd let you in. Then you would hang around inside until dawn.

ALEX KINON: I remember going into Midtown to see the Dead Kennedys play. I forget where it was. We came back to A7 afterwards and my friend Kim was working the door. You couldn't just walk into A7; you had to ring a bell to be let in. She pushed open the door and Jello Biafra was standing there, and she just goes, "Okay, ten bucks." I was like, "Nah nah nah, let the guy in."

DONNA DAMAGE: You had Doug Holland bartending. You had Steve Jones nodding out in a corner. The bar ran along the back, with Leroy or Victor manning the door, lots of ganja and reggae on a bad PA system, the house equipment was always broken. Dead Space Records, the folks responsible for funding the No Thanks 7-inch, were the house coke dealers. I also remember a pizza box replaced the house drumhead for a while.

RALPHIE G: Dave hired Doug Holland to work the bar and Jimmy G and Ray Beans, aka Raybeez, to work the door.

DOUG HOLLAND: I was basically the manager of the A7 club. Every day I had to go to the bars and the liquor shops and get a list of what liquor and beer I'd need for the night. So that was another part of my job while the boss stayed up until 11 a.m. for reasons unknown.

JIMMY G: I started working there as a DJ and bouncer because Doug became the bartender. I was fifteen and I was flipping records and flipping people out the door! Every now and then, the cops would come to the door and raid the fuckin' place. They'd take all the booze and money and leave. It was sort of a blessing in disguise, because the cops would feel sorry for me and throw me a hundred dollars. It would take me two weeks of working at A7 to make that much money!

JESSE MALIN: The equipment was nailed to the wall. There were no advertisements in the *Village Voice*. If you wanted to play, you saw Dave. You came down, there was a sign on the wall written with marker. You never knew who was going to be playing on the bill.

MIKE JUDGE: The first time Death Before Dishonor played in New York at A7 it was with me singing. We got there and actually left to go see the Necros, and when we got back we were still able to play our set. We played at five in the morning. I remember being done playing and walking out into daylight. That's just how A7 was.

JACK RABID: I remember the Effigies having a gig at A7, and they waited around until three in the morning to play. Eventually, they just got pissed off and left. They were a touring act with records out who were sitting there having to wait while all these two-bit bands who barely existed were having their sets.

DEAN ISLAY (DRUMMER, CHILD ABUSE, MURPHY'S LAW, UNDERDOG): Child Abuse played A7 once with JFA, and then there was another show with a bunch of New York bands. By that point, I think I was about twelve or thirteen. I remember I took a nap. I couldn't stay awake until we played. I was in the back room of A7 falling asleep on a pile of coats and then someone woke me up to play.

ERNIE PARADA (DRUMMER, GILLIGAN'S REVENGE, TOKEN ENTRY, UNDERDOG): The second hardcore gig of my life, I was playing. That gig was at A7 and I think we were playing with Murphy's Law and Bad Posture. A big crowd at that time was thirty people, and that would be almost the entire scene in attendance! Doors at A7 opened at like 2 a.m. I was all of maybe fourteen or fifteen years old. Eddie Sutton—later of Leeway—sang a lightning-fast cover of "Paranoid" with us.

EDDIE SUTTON: Before Leeway, I was doing Grandmaster Flash songs at a local bar for free beer and shit like that. That was my first attempt at performing in front of a live audience, singing "Paranoid" with Gilligan's Revenge at A7.

PITO MONTIEL: We went to Johnny Waste's place in the Ravenswood projects and Billy Phillips showed me how to play two-finger chords, the most basic stuff, and the next Saturday we played the A7 club. We pushed all our equipment there in a shopping cart and got off the subway at Eighth Street and walked down St. Marks Place.

TODD YOUTH: I learned how to play music in that back room. One night I'd be in there and the band didn't have a drummer so I'd play drums. That band Virus, their first show they didn't have a guitar player yet, so I played guitar. My first gig with Murphy's Law was in 1982 or '83. I played drums because Guzzy, their drummer, didn't show up. There would be a reggae night once a week. All the dreads in the neighborhood would show up and jam, so I learned how to play reggae just sitting in with those guys.

WENDY EAGER: Hardcore always had a dear part of my heart, because I was younger and the kids were younger and punk was such an older thing. The bands I saw at A7 were completely different, and it wasn't just the music. Hardcore is more than music. It's a way of life and a way of thinking. The music is just one part of the whole, because it was the entire scene that made it something special and something different.

DAVE SCOTT: It was very much like your own social club. It was more than a music club. It was sort of like the way a biker gang would have their hangout. In New Jersey, they weren't used to seeing punk rockers. We'd get our asses beat or get chased through the mall or have jocks kick the shit out of us. But in New York, there were so many of us, nobody fucked with us. That was probably the first time I experienced that fraternal brotherhood of the scene. If anyone messed with anyone in the scene, they'd get their ass whooped.

CAROLYN LENGEL: When the bands would finally stop, you'd go eat pierogies at Leshko's on Avenue A.

VINNIE STIGMA: We'd get out from A7 being in there all night with our hands all dirty. Then we'd go across the street and eat at Leshko's and have breakfast and then go home.

RALPHIE G: Hardcore got so big and out of control that, for a short time, Dave rented a larger loft space called 2+2, where we did some bigger shows.

DONNA DAMAGE: A7 opened an annex on Houston and Second Avenue in the summer of 1982. The Bad Brains were supposed to play there one night, and HR didn't show up, so Maggie McDermott and I got up and sang for them. That was fun.

JIMMY G: The funny thing about the A7 annex place was before Dave took it over it was this after-hours club with the bar in the freight elevator. So if it got raided, they'd just send the elevator down and the cops would come up, and it would just be people hanging out in a room!

LOUIE RIVERA: Dave expanded his thing and opened up 2+2. I worked the door there. What I loved about that place was how raw it was. You had to be careful, man. You had an elevator shaft right in the middle of the floor. There was an element of danger in that building!

JIMMY G: Everyone likes to go on about CB's, but CB's didn't support the scene like Dave at A7 did. He was the first to put on the shows. CB's had already had its history at that point with the Dead Boys and Blondie and the Talking Heads, and they didn't have time for us then. Hardcore is worldwide now, and we're still doing it, and I say thanks to A7.

RUSS ISLAY: I would say A7 stopped having shows sometime in '83. That's just around when I joined Murphy's Law. I know I didn't play there ever in a band, and we all know Murphy's Law played there plenty of times.

MERYL HURWICH (GUITARIST, XKI): When A7 closed, it was like someone cut out the heart of New York City punk. I don't think it ever was the same after that. Of course, we had CBGB to play at, but to me nothing was ever as good as A7 had been. I remember people feeling like they had no home! Anyone could play at A7, and I mean anyone; that was the whole point of punk in New York City for a while.

Photo: *Harley Flanagan and Jimmy G, flanked by two Jersey punks, running wild in the East Village, 1980s*
RANDY UNDERWOOD

Night of Noise
HARDCORE – HEAVYMETAL
AT THE
Eclipse
Damage Rose
and
Urban Waste

THURS JAN 6, 1983
93-77 Queens Blvd

THE MOB
$2.00 ADM
SHOW STARTS AT 3:00 P.M.
URBAN WASTE
MINOR THREAT
AT
CBGB's
SAT DEC 18

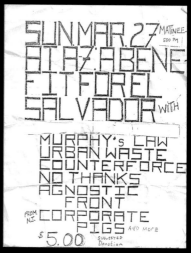

SUN MAR.27 MATINEE
5:00 PM
AT A7. ABENE
FIT FOR EL
SALVADOR WITH

MURPHY's LAW
URBAN WASTE
COUNTERFORCE
NO THANKS
AGNOSTIC
FRONT
FROM N.J. CORPORATE
PIGS AND MORE
$5.00 SUGGESTED Donation

Photo: *Urban Waste vocalist Kenny Ahrens at CBGB's.* GREG LICHT

18. URBAN WASTE AND MAJOR CONFLICT: HOW DO YOU FEEL?

EDDIE SUTTON: When I was fourteen, I moved from Suffolk County out on the island back to where I was born, which was Astoria, Queens. Coming back to Astoria after being in Suffolk County was like being put into a jungle.

TIM CHUNKS: I grew up in Queens and that's where I got turned onto the music, so for me, Queens was a huge, huge part of it. Reagan Youth was from Queens. Murphy's Law was from Queens. The guy who played bass in the Mob worked in the 7-Eleven up the street from my house. You felt where you lived was churning out all this fantastic music. I couldn't help but take pride.

JOE SONGCO (DRUMMER, OUTBURST): I had the good fortune geography-wise of growing up in Astoria. I grew up on the same street as A. J. Novello, who formed the Unruled—who became Leeway. We were thirteen or fourteen years old and hanging out in the park. He would bring tapes of the Zero Boys and the Dead Kennedys. He bought all the records and we borrowed them and recorded them. Kraut and Murphy's Law were in the neighborhood. New York Hoods, too. On any given summer night, you'd have a park bench with guys from New York Hoods, Doug and Davey from Kraut, and Eddie from Leeway sitting on it. Looking back, I'm like, "Wow, there's members of three huge bands sitting on that one park bench!"

GARY TSE TSE FLY: Astoria and Jackson Heights; I don't know what the hell they feed them out there, but they ruled the NYHC scene with Major Conflict and Urban Waste. Jackson Heights and Astoria were two working-class neighborhoods that were producing a whole lot of bands and hardcore kids.

KEN WAGNER: I always say, to this day, "No Queens, no NYHC."

BILLY PHILLIPS (VOCALIST, URBAN WASTE, MAJOR CONFLICT): When the boys from Queens went out to a show, we filled a whole train car or two! In my eyes, Astoria was responsible for keeping hardcore going.

ROGER MIRET: If it wasn't for Urban Waste, I wouldn't have got into this stuff. I heard them on the radio and that made me want to go into the city and find A7. That's when I met everybody.

KEN WAGNER: I got into it all from Doug Holland, who lived next door to me. It was both Doug Holland and Billy Phillips, the original singer for Urban Waste. There was a courtyard with two buildings next to each other. Doug would be blasting music from the fourth-floor apartment, and I could hear it. I was ten or eleven years old. I thought, "What the hell is this guy playing?" He influenced so many people to get into it.

BILLY PHILLIPS: We owe Doug Holland from Kraut a lot of thanks for his Queens hardcore involvement. He was my lifelong neighbor and took me to his rehearsals and then to my first show at A7 Club.

JOHN KELLY: Doug told us who to talk to, where to go—that type of thing—as far as going to shows, and then playing our own shows. I was seeing all the punk rock bands. We went down to Max's. I saw the Stimulators with Harley playing drums and I thought he was the best drummer in the world. After that, Heart Attack and Reagan Youth, to me, were the first hardcore bands in New York. Not long after that, in the spring of 1981, my friend John Dancy came to my apartment and asked if I wanted to start a band. I didn't know how to play guitar at the time. I went to lessons for a year, learned some chords, and started writing songs. The music teacher taught me the D chord and told me to write a song, so I took the D chord and ran it up and down the neck, and I wrote my first song, "Mutiny."

We didn't have a name for the band, and we had Doug Holland over and we started writing names on paper. We had the word *urban* and we had the word *waste* there, and a whole bunch of words like *awesome* and *energy*. Doug was like, "How about Urban Waste? You guys are a bunch of wastes!"

WENDY EAGER: Urban Waste were average New York kids who put this band together and wrote about themselves. They were kids who had a rough life and they represented what NYHC was about: social misfits who found this scene and took something from it.

JOHN KELLY: We used to practice in my bedroom because we couldn't afford a studio. We were raised by our mothers, who were all working hard just to keep food on the table. They couldn't buy us a drum set or a guitar—that just wasn't in the picture. Somehow, we managed to get a guitar and there was the start of Urban Waste's equipment. We used a garbage can lid for a cymbal, I plugged my guitar into a stereo receiver, and I think Billy just screamed. We didn't need anything big. We practiced in that bedroom for probably two years. Our first show was on February 5, 1982, at A7, and Jack Flanagan from the Mob helped us put out our 7-inch a few months after that.

PAUL BEARER: When Urban Waste first came out they were fucking hot shit, but a year or so later, everyone saw them get fucked up on drugs. I remember I saw them at CB's and I walked out, it was so bad.

JOHN KELLY: More and more people were getting turned on to us after our 7-inch came out. We probably gave away half our records, just trying to get a new person to listen to us. But we stopped writing new songs. We started getting into drugs and women. In the beginning of Urban Waste, drugs weren't prominent. I would drink beer or smoke pot. That led to psychedelics, cocaine, which led to going out partying and not really putting the time into the music. It was crazy. There was a lot of mescaline going on—microdots. People started coming to shows with windowpane and Snoopy acid. It turned more into a drug party than a show. Andy Apathy the bass player and Kenny quit, and then shit got real. I had quit school for Urban Waste. Instead of me and Dancy getting other members to replace them, we just joined Dito in Major Conflict.

DITO MONTIEL: I know this will sound like some funny shit, but here's how I got into hardcore. My friend had a record player in his basement, and we used to play a Blue Öyster Cult record on 45-rpm speed, turn out the lights out, and beat the shit out of one another. Our parents used to shave our heads in the summer because it was cheap way of keeping cool. When I wasn't in school in the summer, I was a foot messenger in Manhattan. So the first day I went to work as a foot messenger, I had a shaved head and a black eye. This guy Joe who worked there was really good friends with Jimmy from Murphy's Law. He said, "Hey! Are you into hardcore?" I said no way, I thought he was hitting on me or something. He asked me why I had a black eye and a shaved head. So I told him my mother shaved my head, and I told him how we'd play records on 45 and beat the shit out of each other in my friends' basement. He said, "Oh my god, you got to come down to this club! That's exactly what they do down there!"

I heard that the Circle Jerks were playing at Irving Plaza. I talked all my friends into going with me by saying, "Listen, this guy told me that's there's a fucking club where they play all the music really fast and they put the lights out and they beat the shit out of each other." They all said, "GET THE FUCK OUT OF HERE!" Only half my friends wanted to go, because they thought it was just going to full of fucking weirdoes. I got like seven people to come down with me, and we were the most non-punk crew in history. I basically brought a bunch of guidos who were just psychos. My friends kept leaving as the night went on. By the time the Circle Jerks played, only my friends Lucia, Gratiano, and Tommy Burns were left. The Circle Jerks went on, and the place went fucking nuts. I couldn't fucking believe it. We just started jumping on-stage and punching everybody we could in the face. That's what we thought went down. Of course, later on we found out what we were doing wasn't cool.

BILLY PHILLIPS: I first met Dito at an Urban Waste concert in the Ravenswood Houses in Queens. Johnny Kelly's mom got us the housing project's meeting hall. As I started singing "Skank," I skanked my way into the crowd and bumped into Dito. He made a fist! I said, "Shit, man, you're all right!"

JOE SONGCO: Every Halloween, we'd go out and look for trouble. We had eggs and shaving cream and decided to go on the other side of Ditmars Boulevard. Dito and his boys were driving around with fire extinguishers filled with piss and ammonia, looking to spray kids. We were by St. John's Prep and Dito got out of the car with the fire extinguisher, and we just broke out trying to run back to our neighborhood. It wasn't fair, because they had a car and we were on foot. We all split up and me and this kid Rob got caught in a dead-end alleyway. Dito said, "Just turn around." I wasn't going to fuck around, so I just turned around and he sprayed me all over my back with this piss and ammonia. I had an army jacket on and it just absorbed it and it stunk

Urban Waste reach out and take what they can get from the CBGB's stage.
PHOTOS CLOCKWISE FROM LEFT BY GREG LICHT, GREG LICHT, JOHN KELLY

forever. He punched my friend Rob in the nose, and then he was like, "Don't fuck around in my neighborhood! Don't come around here no more! I got you fuckers!" Rob was standing there holding his face saying, "I think he broke my nose." My thing was—where'd they get a fire extinguisher?

DITO MONTIEL: Major Conflict was an actual inner-city hardcore band. We had real problems. The furthest we ever went to play was Long Island, and I don't even know how the fuck we got there. We had no fucking money. We were just a disaster, with people having hang-ups with whatever bad things you get into as a teenager. We couldn't get it together. None of us dared think we were going to make money off of this, and I don't even think it was because we were idealistic. We just wouldn't give ourselves that much credit. At the same time, we were fifteen-year-old kids doing something. We didn't just go to see people play, we also played or did a fanzine or made T-shirts. It was a very involved thing, and that was what really interested me as a kid. You weren't just saving your money to go see the Who. You got to go onstage and make a whole bunch of noise. I could have gotten into making fucking volcanoes. It just happened to be hardcore.

JOHN KELLY: Dito was a hard worker; he got Major Conflict going.

DITO MONTIEL: We started talking to Dave from Rat Cage about recording with Jerry Williams. Of course, we were too much of a disaster to get it together.

Javi from Big City wanted us to be on his label, but we were a fucking mess. Somehow this guy from Queens put us in a studio on Forty-Second Street in Manhattan. We had one afternoon to record everything. The night before, everybody got really fucked up on bad drugs. So in 1983 we had a thousand copies of the 7-inch pressed, and one of the guys in our band had a nervous breakdown and threw them all out his window. I think seven hundred of them got broken.

BILLY PHILLIPS: I started Major Conflict with Dito. Me and Dito first practiced in his bedroom. To have a band, you have to be loyal, dedicated, and honest. If you break any of these codes you're finished. Me and Dito missed practices and were constantly starting late, sometimes by hours. I gave up on the band.

DITO MONTIEL: In all honesty, I didn't really like playing music. I just liked the chaos. I just loved being there. I did love Bad Brains and Reagan Youth, but most of the time, it was just about being there for me. Nobody had any big aspirations. The one thing that'll stick with me my whole life is that I've never thought once in my life, "Oh shit, I can't do that"—and it's because of hardcore. I had friends in high school who were into Yes, and they sat at home perfecting playing fucking "Roundabout." By the time they were fucking thirty, they maybe had done their first show at a wedding and no one gave a shit. It was a total waste of time. I thought there was something special about thinking, "We suck so much that we can't play other people's songs, so let's just make up our own and say things we believe in."

Photos clockwise from top: *Urban Waste bassist Andy Apathy—R.I.P.* GREG LICHT; Johnny, Freddy, and Kenny in Urban Waste JOHN KELLY

Kevin Crowley of The Abused sports the classic NYHC look of 1983. GREG LICHT

19. THE ABUSED: DRUG FREE YOUTH

ROBBIE CRYPTCRASH: There weren't a bunch of straight-edge folks in New York. What was it? "Peace, love, and beer."

BOBBY STEELE: The whole straight-edge thing, I just read that as being scared of drugs and girls. When they overcame that fear, I'm sure they sang a different tune.

PAUL DORDAL: We were all drunks and druggies; the straight edge wasn't a New York thing. That came along down from Boston or D.C. We would kind of laugh at those guys when they came in, you know, "Why do this and not party?"

KEVIN CROWLEY: I think you could count the straight-edge kids in New York at the time on one hand. There was me, Al Pike, Abbie Mahler who did *Straight Edge* fanzine, and Charlie Bonet, who played drums for us and Reagan Youth. Being straight-edge certainly didn't gain us any additional popularity on the scene, that's for sure. We were the outcasts within the outcasts.

MIKE JUDGE: I didn't go straight-edge because I heard it in a song. I went straight-edge without knowing it, after I got my ass kicked really badly at CBGB at a UK Subs show. I was way fucking loaded. When I came to and got my head together, I promised myself I wouldn't get into a situation again where I couldn't defend myself. I wanted to be the guy doing the rag-dolling. But at that time, there were guys in New York with names like "Willy No Edge." There wasn't a lot of us who weren't drinking and doing drugs, and I was getting my balls busted for it. But then Kevin Crowley from the Abused had a jacket that had "Drug Free Youth" stenciled on the back. Then they had the song of the same name on their *Loud and Clear* EP in 1983, and that was fucking awesome.

KEVIN CROWLEY: I had already dabbled in many a thing by that age, but to see kids starting to shoot up, that was a total "Oh, shit!" moment. I couldn't stand that. A lot of my friends were turning into junkies. You were surrounded by it, and it was very prevalent back then on the Lower East Side. Heroin was a really big thing. For me, it was a control issue. When you're fifteen years old, what can you control in your life? I liked the idea of not having anything control me. Nothing was going to get in my way.

ROB KABULA: When Kevin Crowley started the Abused, they were definitely on the straight-edge tip.

KEVIN CROWLEY: I was a fixture on the scene back then, always hanging out with Harley. Raf Astor, the guitarist, and Dave Colon, the bass player of the Abused, approached me at A7 and asked me if I ever sang in a band before. I said no. I think they asked me because they needed a schmoozer and someone who hung out. We rehearsed and rehearsed. I started hyping the shit out of the band. I made a flyer that said "Coming Soon" before we even played any gigs. They all thought I was going to choke at the first show. Thankfully, we sounded good, but we certainly were setting ourselves up for disaster.

ROB KABULA: Look at all those Abused flyers. Kevin was a great artist. Those flyers were amazing. I think that's what really gained them attention.

KEVIN CROWLEY: First and foremost, I was the singer for the Abused—it just happened that I could also draw. Because of the technique I was using, the flyers were really labor-intensive to produce, which is why there are only twelve of them. Actually, I did thirteen but never released one. There was definitely a conscious effort to give the band a distinctive look. Up until that point, not much effort was put into creating visually captivating show flyers. I wanted to make people remember us.

MIKE JUDGE: Sound-wise, *Loud and Clear* is fucking awesome. Sonically, it's one of the best records to come out of New York, especially for the time period.

KEN WAGNER: The thing about the Abused was Kevin's voice. It was different than other singers' on the scene at the time. Then there was Kevin's persona onstage. He was a tall guy—a skinhead with construction gloves on. He was hard before everyone else was hard.

KEVIN CROWLEY: Where did I get the idea to wear construction gloves? I was a total comic book nerd, and if you look at every drawing I ever did, everybody was wearing gloves. That comes from superheroes always wearing gloves. I drew all these muscle-bound guys for our flyers, and I was probably 150 pounds soaking wet. The funny thing is that from those flyers, people perceived me as this huge, muscular guy. I learned that how you project yourself is how people are going to perceive you.

Another reason I started wearing them was that I was getting into a lot of fights and I was bruising my hands up too much. I started wearing the gloves to protect my hands. I wasn't a guy who liked to fight. It's not like it was my calling. I just felt like I had to stick up for what we were doing. I was wearing them, and then Jimmy G started wearing them. Then I graduated up to welding gloves. I used to wear them on the dance floor.

I remember Dave, the owner of A7, putting me on probation for wearing them. He always wanted me to take them off when I was in the club. He'd ask, "Why are you wearing these gloves here? You want to hit people, don't you?"

MIKE JUDGE: The first time I saw Kevin Crowley from the Abused, he was wearing construction gloves. Then Jimmy G was wearing them on the dance floor, with a chain around his waist. John Watson always wore the gloves with a chain around his waist; so did Raybeez from Warzone. I never knew what that meant or why they did it, but I was like, "Fuck it! I'll do it!"

KEVIN CROWLEY: When we went to record the 7-inch, we borrowed some Marshall amps from this guy Frank Sathio in Long Island. We drove up to get them, and we actually drove back from Long Island down to High Five Studios in that huge, huge blizzard of '82. The amps were hanging out of the trunk. We're lucky they didn't fall out or get damaged. But it took so long for the 7-inch to come out and to get any traction. I think we were already slowing down a little bit, too. We never really broke up or had any kind of falling-out. It was just a succession of things. We lost our rehearsal space. Then Raf ended up going to Guitar Institute of Technology to learn guitar. Dave was in the carpenters' union. Brian was getting very into martial arts. I ended up working, and got my own apartment. My focus shifted to day-to-day life. Our ending was very anticlimactic, compared to those of other bands of the day.

MIKE JUDGE: I remember talking to Kevin Crowley about that song "Drug Free Youth." He told me he wrote that song for himself, to keep himself in check; it was like him screaming at himself. I had never thought of a song like that up until then, but I ended up doing a lot of that myself in Judge. I don't have the prettiest background. My family doesn't have the greatest past. At an early age, I was going down the same road pretty quick myself. One of the first things I ever got in trouble for was bringing booze to a seventh-grade dance. I got it in there, and halfway through the dance, I couldn't fucking walk. They called my parents, but I never got in trouble because they couldn't get my dad on the phone. He was home drunk—in the same state. My dad worked all day and drank all night until he bought a bar: Then he was never around. I was definitely a fuckup, and it was in my blood to self-destruct. The only way not to self-destruct was to yell about it to myself. So a lot of the things you hear in Judge where people thought I was being militant and telling people how to live; it was basically me trying to tell myself how to live. And it all came from that talk with Kevin.

KEVIN CROWLEY: Yes, I was the person who first drew the NYHC symbol. The hardcore scene was pretty territorial. New York, Boston, D.C.—it was almost the way people are with sports teams. Don't get me wrong, I was a huge fan of the music coming out of those other cities, but New York City was my hometown! In a way, the NYHC logo was a declaration of our scene, a statement. The truth is, I never imagined it would catch on like it did.

A few years ago, I saw some kids with the NYHC logo on their clothes. I asked them about hardcore, and then I said something like, "You know, I made up that logo." They gave me this look that just said, "Whatever! Fuck you, old man!"

THE ABUSED with THE NIHILISTICS AND THE MIS-GUIDED
??? MYSTERY VICTIM ???
SAT. JAN. 22nd AT the PLUG.
SUPPORT N.Y. HARDCORE
Adm. $5

THE ABUSED WITH T.S.O.L. AND THE MOB
RONNY ROTTEN.
SUN MARCH 20TH AT
Great Gildersleves

THE ABUSED WITH AGNOSTIC FRONT
D.F.Y.
SAT. MATINEE AT CBGB's ON Dec. 4th
NHXYDY

THE ABUSED with SQUIRM AND ULTRA-VIOLENCE
MR. SOFTY
Doors open at 10:00 Adm. 15-$$/$$00
Late Night Show!!
if you're not there, you're soft!
Tue. July 20th AT ZAPPA'S
For MORE INFO. Ask 359-9275

THE ABUSED PLUS REAGAN YOUTH!!!
KURT WAY HERE.
SAT. MATINEE at CBGB's ON Aug. 7
BLOW YOUR BRAINS OUT!

THE ABUSED
COMING SOON

THE ABUSED with CAUSE FOR ALARM
SAT. JAN. 29 AT A-7
SUPPORT N.Y. HARDCORE!!

ABUSED MOB, SQUIRM PLUS. D.C. THRASHERS
DOUBLE-O
FAITH and SCREAM
FRI. JULY 23
AT A-7
the new
A-7
29 Ave. 2 Houston st

THE ABUSED with special guest
GOV'T. ISSUE
FROM D.C.
N.Y.P.D.
SAT. MATINEE AT CBGB's ON FEB. 12 REIGN
POLICE

MISGUIDED FALSE PROPHETS
SAT. MATINEE AT CBGB'S
OCT. 30TH DOORS OPEN 4:30

USE YOUR BRAIN: DEC. 31st
NEW YEAR'S EVE
FALSE PROPHETS   REAGAN YOUTH
SADISTIC
EXPLOITS   ENGLISH
                  CUNTZ
MISGUIDED   Ultimatum
DOORS OPEN AT 9:00
1st BAND ON 10:00 SHARP!   PLUS
                            SPECIAL
                            SURPRISES
3 FLOORS OF FUN!   Plugg   ONLY
                   CLUB $5
                   140 WEST
                   24th St.
ALSO FILMS, FOOD, BEVERAGES AND D.J. MAL

MISGUIDED FROM D.C. MARGINAL MAN (EX. ARTIFICIAL PEACE)
TRIBAL HOUNDS
APRIL 9TH SATURDAY MATINEE 3:00 PM
CBGB'S 315 BOWERY $3
"MAN'S BEST FRIEND"

MISGUIDED
BRINGING IT DOWN...

MISGUIDED
PLUS FROM NORTHERN CALIFORNIA:
FANG
CRUCIFIX
MAY 7TH
SATURDAY MATINEE AT CBGB'S
3:00 - $3

MISGUIDED   JULY 29TH
ADRENALIN O.D.   THURSDAY 11:00
              ALDO'S
              LYNDHURST
              NEW JERSEY!

20. THE MISGUIDED: DEFY STANDARDS

JACK FLANAGAN: The Misguided is a great example of how things were growing. In some ways, they were like the Mob in that they were some guys from Queens who came into the city and saw Heart Attack and started their own band. That's a band that was created by the scene. They were on the outside, embraced it, and became a band.

WENDY EAGER: I loved the Misguided. They never got enough recognition.

JOHNNY CARCO: John Rizzo and I became friends during the summer of '79. He was delivering the afternoon *New York Post* on my street in Glendale, Queens, on Sixty-Sixth Street and Myrtle Ave. I delivered the *Daily News* in the morning. He was kinda standoffish. He had a Clash button, and he wore white suspenders and jeans. This was not the normal look in Queens in 1979. He almost looked ready to fight, delivering the papers. I said something about the Clash; then we started talking music as he was delivering papers, and we became friends.

RALPHIE G: John Rizzo and Johnny Carco joined me at Thomas Edison High School. They were a year behind me, and before they came I was the only punk rocker in the school. As soon as I saw the leather jackets with Ramones and Clash buttons, we were buds!

JOHNNY CARCO: We were seriously bent on starting a band. We had no idea how to do this, but we were determined to do so and we felt like we had to do anything to make it happen. I remember John bought a guitar and tried to learn how to play "White Riot" by the Clash. Then, soon after buying the guitar, he told me, "I met the guitarist for our band. He was on Myrtle Avenue in Ridgewood today and had on a black leather jacket with a Jam button." So now we had our guitarist, Alex Totino.

LYLE HYSEN: To me, the whole hardcore thing in the beginning was "Why not?" I really embraced that. "Of course we should all do a fanzine! Why not?" I liked all these other bands and I'm excited, so why not start a band? I was in the Misguided. We weren't very good, but we tried hard. I think that's a motto we can still live by.

JOHNNY CARCO: We met with Lyle to check him out at a Dead Boys show at a place called the Playroom on Sixth Ave and Ninth Street. The only thing I knew of Lyle at that time was that he had a fanzine called *Damaged Goods*. We went to that Dead Boys show and it was a fun night, I always liked seeing the Dead Boys.

The first rehearsal was hilarious. I just sat there with my bass in the guitar case on my lap, because I couldn't play yet. John Rizzo tried to play guitar and sing, and Alex played guitar and tried his best to direct John Rizzo how to play the songs on guitar. After this train wreck of a rehearsal, I think Lyle said something like, "Alex, you should teach Carco how to play these songs on bass, and Rizzo should be the lead singer and not play guitar, and we'll try this again in a few weeks." It wasn't as grim as it sounds. We were all enthused and happy and felt like we were actually moving forward. I remember we had such a blind ambition and nothing could get in our way.

RON RANCID: I'll give them a lot of credit, but a band like the Misguided were musically horrible in my opinion. But the musicality didn't matter. The whole thing was you got up there, you picked up an instrument, you made noise, and you had your say. That's what mattered to me.

JOHNNY CARCO: The Misguided were together from July '80 till July of '84. A lot went down in the NYHC in that time. When we started doing gigs in 1981, the early NYHC was very accepting. We were welcomed with open arms by most of the other bands and kids. There were only a handful of bands then: Reagan Youth, Heart Attack, the Mob, Kraut, the Influence, False Prophets, Undead, et cetera. Later on, when we wanted to stretch out musically and play a song longer than one minute, and that wasn't a thrash song, a lot of people in that scene were turned off by what we were trying to do.

LYLE HYSEN: By 1982, I had had enough. You couldn't watch the bands anymore. All these cement heads started coming to the shows and they were getting violent, and it wasn't any fun.

JOHNNY CARCO: We just didn't want to play thrash music anymore. We wanted to play songs. We started covering Stooges songs, like "Loose" from

Fun House. We started to write songs that were closer to being three minutes long. So by 1983, after playing together for a couple of years, we wanted to grow musically. Our heads were way ahead of our ability at the time, and that brought us to an abrupt end. The last thing we did was a demo that Brian Baker from Minor Threat recorded in D.C.

LYLE HYSEN: By 1983 we said, "Okay, we're going to grow out our hair." We loved '60s garage, so then we thought, "If you think we're bad at playing hardcore, wait until you hear us play some '60s garage!" We played a CBGB hardcore matinee, and we opened with "1-2-5" by the mid-1960s band the Haunted. John Rizzo wore a tuxedo. My boy's up front in a tuxedo, and I'm wearing a paisley shirt behind the drums. What is more FUCK OFF at a hardcore matinee than coming out dressed like Brian Ferry from Roxy Music, and opening up with a Haunted cover?

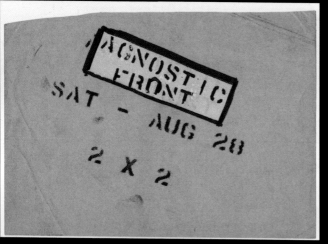

Agnostic Front hitting its stride with third and final singer, Roger Miret.
RANDY UNDERWOOD

21. AGNOSTIC FRONT: UNITED BLOOD

JAMES KONTRA: Vinnie Stigma was always around. He was from Little Italy and he was a good guitar player. He played in the Eliminators; they were punk rock.

RALPHIE G: Vinnie Stigma and I are cousins and we have always been very close. He had been playing in glam bands and punk bands.

VINNIE STIGMA: Before the Eliminators, I played in a band called Black Angus. They were my band with Frankie and Sally and Vinnie—all the Italian boys from the neighborhood. Johnny Sacomaro, an older guy than me, showed me the way. Black Angus was forty years ago. I just found this little flyer I had for one of our shows. That was a milestone to me.

After the neighborhood band, I was in a transition band called Future Shock, a new age kind of rock band. We had keyboards and it was trippy. That wasn't me, but I just wanted to be in a band. I owned a studio at the time, and they were my friends. We were just jamming. The studio folded on me in 1975. It was a beautiful studio. I had my dog in there, a German shepherd. We lived there together. From there, I was a punk rocker, and that's when I really came into it.

KITE. HAWK: The Eliminators was the first band I played with in the city. I became friends with Vinnie Stigma and I told him I wanted to play bass, and he said, "Come on," and he taught me all the songs. It was more old-school melodic punk than the hardcore which he went on to become the godfather of.

STEVE POSS: I tried out to be the singer for the Eliminators, but I froze at the microphone. If I didn't freeze then, who knows? Maybe I would have been the singer of a hardcore band. One time they all came out dressed up as droogs from *A Clockwork Orange*—it might have been for Halloween.

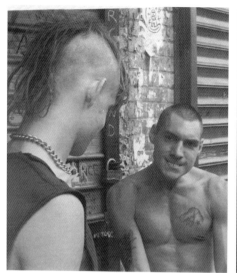

Left: Early Agnostic front drummer *Robbie Cryptcrash hangs with Vinnie Stigma*; *Roger Miret takes a dive while early A.F. vocalist John Watson looks ready to pummel.* RANDY UNDERWOOD

JESSE MALIN: I met Vinnie Stigma when he was in the Eliminators. He had spiky hair and a dog chain around his neck. He bought the Heart Attack *God Is Dead* single from me; then the next week he shaved his head and made the change.

RALPHIE G: Vinnie saw where the scene was heading, and he made a lot of new friends in the hardcore scene. He wanted to do something different, and, like a lot of us, he envisioned a band in his head.

VINNIE STIGMA: The Eliminators came to an end because the guys weren't committed the way I am. The thing was, I'm from New York City, and the rest of the guys were from Queens. Not that it matters, but the scene was here in New York City on Eighth Street. St. Marks Place. Everybody flocked to St. Marks Place, and then we moved from St. Marks Place to Avenue A. When the hardcore kids started coming there, I started Agnostic Front and NYHC.

Being I was so committed to this movement, I didn't want a name like the Beatles or Blondie or the Cars. I wanted a statement. I wanted to say "fuck you" to society. So I came up with a concept instead of a name. *Agnostic* means to be in doubt, and *Front* was a point a view. I know it goes under a religious epithet, but it means more than that.

ROGER MIRET: The first time I saw Agnostic Front was in Astoria, Queens. It was this great big show. Everyone was playing: Reagan Youth, Murphy's Law, Cause for Alarm, and Urban Waste. This show was straight up in the projects. John Watson was the singer of Agnostic Front, Diego Casalins was on bass, Robbie Cryptcrash on drums, and Vinnie Stigma was on guitar. They looked hard as fuck. They'd start a song, and halfway through the song—which isn't saying much, since the songs were like twenty seconds long—at that ten-second mark, the mic went down, and John Watson would be in the pit. Then Diego would drop his bass and go into the pit, leaving just Vinnie standing there with Robbie Cryptcrash. They just kept going like that the whole set. I was like, "Are these guys ever going to finish a song? This is awful."

JESSE MALIN: Agnostic Front went through a lot of singers, but they were on a mission and people really connected to them.

VINNIE STIGMA: With the beginning of Agnostic Front, I had a lot of guys here and there, but not troupers. I had Raybeez from Warzone in the band on drums. I brought him into the scene because no one would talk to him. He was crazy. But you know me, Vinnie. I talk to everybody! Raybeez was a crazy guy with a triple Mohawk. He'd cut his pants up with scissors and stuff. Everyone thought this guy was a nut. But I love everybody, and he ended up being one of the heroes of our scene.

JOHN WATSON (Vocalist, Agnostic Front): I knew Vinnie from Max's and A7. He was a little bit older and hung out with some of the older punks. One night as I was coming out of A7, he asked me if I wanted to start a band. I told him that I played a little bass. He just laughed and said that he wanted to see if I could sing. When we first went into the studio, it was myself, Vinnie

on guitar, Diego on bass, and Raybeez on drums. I remember the day like it was yesterday. They put together a song, and I wrote some lyrics. We wound up recording, and it was absolute magic, technically speaking. Right away, we knew we had created something special. We all started moshing on the spot. Raybeez was awesome, but he couldn't play very well. But I wanted him because he was my good friend, and he had such enthusiasm.

CAROLYN LENGEL: When John Watson was the singer of Agnostic Front? Oh my God, they were the worst band ever. Watson had no idea where the tune was, if there was one, or the beat, for that matter.

DREW STONE: I was at Agnostic Front's first show. They were originally called the Zoo Crew. Back then, you supported bands and you went to see them play. Agnostic Front was not good for a long time, but they worked hard.

KEITH BURKHARDT: Agnostic Front with John Watson—that was a scene band. We were just friends, and they'd play and we'd dance and sing along.

MIKE JUDGE: After seeing Agnostic Front at my first CB's matinee, they became a huge part of my life. Somehow, I knew that was the people's band. John Watson made this announcement they were heading to Philly to play with SSD and Minor Threat. They were leaving at a certain time, so if anyone wanted to caravan with them, they could. Steve Yu had his mom's car, so we asked him if he wanted to do it. We were pretty stoked for it. That was a huge day for me. Here's Agnostic Front—the people's band—and we were caravanning down to support them.

JOHN WATSON: I was changing, I started going to the Hare Krishna temple. The scene was changing as well. We started attracting a real rough crowd, a lot of skinheads. A lot of big jock types who would just beat kids up on the dance floor. A real ugly element got introduced, and the spirit that I loved from the early Max's and A7 shows seemed lost. It took a lot out of me at every show to schmooze with people I really didn't have much in common with. It all came to a head in South Carolina. We were on a little tour opening up for Corrosion of Conformity, and I had to drive all the way back in the rain. By the time I got back home I was burnt, broke, and hoarse.

JAMES KONTRA: Agnostic Front was really primitive, but what it lacked in complexity, it made up for in spirit. If Vinnie knew how to do anything, it was how to pass out stickers. He stuck those Agnostic Front stickers on whoever had a jacket. Before long, everybody you knew who had a leather jacket had an Agnostic Front sticker on it. Then there was this Minor Threat gig at CB's.

Roger Miret with Raybeez behind the drums at Great Gildersleeves. GREG LICHT

I was thrashing so hard because I was high on dust. After the gig, John Watson got arrested or some shit. Vinnie and Raybeez came up to me and said, "Do you want to join A.F.? John's going to be in jail for a minute."

STEVE POSS: Kontra was the last person you would expect to sing for Agnostic Front, because he was this anarchist and all that, but everybody was one big happy family back then. Everyone was friends. Everybody knew each other.

JAMES KONTRA: I was never one of those "Yo! Yo! Yo! Hardcore!" guys. What does being hardcore even mean? You want to be violent? Let's go to Coney Island and do a drive-by, and you'll see what violence is. I saw people get shot and stabbed, and it wasn't this cartoon violence. I was into more socially relevant shit musically. I liked Crass, Poison Girls, and Flux of Pink Indians. But nobody fucked with me, because I killed it on the dance floor. I'm a crazy person.

When I was in A.F., we had a gig at Great Gildersleeves. Like I said before, Vinnie is a marketing nigga. He is good at promotion. I get to GIldersleeves, and Vinnie hands me this stack of like two hundred stickers. I was sick of these stickers already. He was like, "James, anyone you don't see with an

Agnostic Front sticker on them, stick it on them." I said, "Vinnie, before I stick these things up your ass, bro, let me just tell you nice and polite: I'm done. I quit." That's when they got Roger to sing.

ROGER MIRET: I went to the barber on Astor Place and got my head shaved. I had a Mohawk, so I just shaved it off. I went to this show with army boots on, and I was in the pit. The next thing you know, Adam Mucci and Raybeez approached me to join Agnostic Front. They would never talk to me before. I'd just talked to Vinnie, at Psychos shows.

VINNIE STIGMA: Here's how it was: I didn't get you in Agnostic Front because you were a good musician; I got you in the band because you were part of the scene and I seen you in the pit. If you're not in the pit then I don't know you! That's how I got Roger. He used to come to CBGB and he was a nice guy. I'd seen him in the pit, and we'd mosh together. He'd push me, and I'd push him, and it was done mutually. There's a way of doing things. Even if I'm in the pit and I hit you by accident, who cares? We're moshin'! There was common courtesy. I found Roger to be a nice guy. So I came up to him and said, "You're in my band now." That's it. That was the end of that.

DREW STONE: None of those early New York bands had vision or focus. Roger Miret might have been the first New York guy to have it. When he joined Agnostic Front, he went out and got a van, and he booked shows out of town. They did it no matter what. If somebody wasn't pulling their weight, he got somebody else. Most bands started falling apart around that time, but Roger kept going no matter what—damn the torpedoes.

VINNIE STIGMA: Roger was more of the business guy. I was more the fun guy. Vinnie would be at the bar, and Roger would be in the office. So I got to give it to Roger. I did the concept and the creation, and he did the business.

TODD YOUTH: Within a couple months of being down on the Lower East Side, I was asked to join Agnostic Front. Adam Mucci was playing the bass for both A.F. and Murphy's Law at the time. The *United Blood* 7-inch hadn't come out yet, but they had recorded it. Agnostic Front gave Adam an ultimatum: Either Murphy's Law or A.F. He chose Murphy's Law. Roger heard me playing bass in an apartment on Second Street between A and B where Robbie Cryptcrash from Cause for Alarm and his wife lived. Roger lived there too, and I was over there one day and I started playing "N.I.B." from Black Sabbath. He was like, "Dude, you can play! You're really good!" That's when I joined Agnostic Front.

CAUSE FOR
ALARM

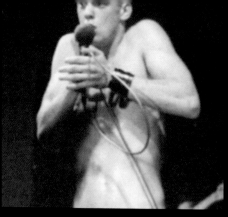

*Classic CFA lineup
featuring vocalist Keith
Burkhardt* PHOTOS BY
RANDY UNDERWOOD

22. CAUSE FOR ALARM: STAND AS ONE!

DREW STONE: I thought the Cause for Alarm 7-inch really captured what NYHC was at that time—that raw energy that was around.

ROB KABULA: I first started coming into the city from New Jersey with an old friend, Lou, who passed away. He died of a heroin overdose in Tompkins Square Park. Later on, I came in with Billy Milano. We all met up on the Lower East Side. Me and Billy started a joking-around band called Hinckley's Fan Club. Most of the people going to these shows were in a band or wanted to start a band. Billy Milano was the original vocalist, and Alex Kinon was playing guitar.

ROBBIE CRYPTCRASH: Alex Kinon and I met in Tompkins Square Park. He had a guitar and a little battery-powered Pignose amp. We sat around, either I had drumsticks or I played with my hands. We had a great time that night, sitting on a bench.

ALEX KINON: Across from A7 was Tompkins Square Park, and there was some punk rock guy sitting there playing his guitar. I thought I was better than this guy, so I started playing Sex Pistols songs. Kabula and Billy Milano noticed, and they asked me to come down and play with them in somebody's basement. At that time, Kabula was a guitar player and they had a bass player. Since I was a better guitar player, they threw out the bass player and moved Kabula over to bass. Then we became Cause for Alarm. We got rid of Billy and got Keith Burkhardt.

KEITH BURKHARDT: Alex Kinon was the driving force behind Cause for Alarm. Nobody was more dedicated to playing music than Alex. Lisa James was the one who named the band.

Alex Kinon and Robbie Cryptcrash with an unknown substance. RANDY UNDERWOOD

ROBBIE CRYPTCRASH: Hinckley's Fan Club were doing a gig out in New Jersey, but there were only one or two members left. They really needed people, and asked if I would help. It was Alex, me, and maybe Kabula. We played all of the Hinckley's Fan Club songs, and we felt like we needed to keep doing this. We threw out most of the Hinckley's Fan Club songs, and we changed the name to Cause for Alarm.

KEITH BURKHARDT: Alex had these songs like "Time to Try," then we wrote "United Races" together. We wrote "Parasite" together, too. Rob Kabula had written "Stand as One" as an old Hinckley's Fan Club song. We became a pretty popular band in our scene quickly, so we decided to make the dream. You know, "Let's put out a 7-inch!" That was kind of a big deal to us in 1983.

We were all really broke, so it wasn't really easy to get the money together. At the time, I was a foot messenger. I came from a pretty basic background. When I left New Jersey and moved to New York, I was on my own. It was tough just to pay rent.

We scraped up the money, though. I think Alex's father helped a little bit. We got together with Jerry Williams and went to High Rise Studios, which was a real studio. I was utterly clueless. I sang all those songs on that 7-inch with one take. I didn't know I was allowed to try a couple times! So I just nailed it every time. Now I go back and listen, and I'm like, "Damn, that sounds pretty controlled!" I didn't want to make a mistake!

My girlfriend Angelica drew up the original sleeve cover, and the rest of the guys didn't like it. It was something with a skull, and they didn't think it fit our image. I was in a gallery on Eighth Street where Alex Morris from Murphy's Law was doing an art show. He had this art he'd drawn on display, and I asked him there if we could use it. It was a drawing of two English police officers dragging a Northern Irish protester. He drew it from an actual photograph. My friend Billy printed up the covers at this stationery store in Nutley called Peerless. We stuck all those pictures together, put together the dedication list, and that was it. We printed up five hundred of them.

I became a Hare Krishna devotee before the 7-inch came out. Rob Kabula and to some extent Alex Kinon really didn't care. They just wanted to play music. They just thought I was nuts. If I wanted to talk about that Krishna stuff, it was fine. But I might have been being a bit fanatical, and that caused problems with the band. I wanted to write lyrics that were more Krishna-conscious at the time, but they weren't allowing me to do that. "In Search Of" was the first song I wrote thinking about Prabhupada, and pretty much going against this punk rock movement's bible. That song caused a lot of stress with the band and people who were associated with the band. Robbie Cryptcrash and his wife were not into this Krishna stuff at all, and it caused a great deal of tension. He was into M.D.C. and left-wing stuff, where it's all about politics and soup kitchens and all that. Robbie and I had our tensions in the band.

ROBBIE CRYPTCRASH: I can't describe religion mathematically, so this isn't something that can be won or lost. Believe in what you want. But you can't make a platform where you're preaching your beliefs. I think that was the issue. I was not okay with him doing that, but Keith kept saying, "Well, I want to say it!" That was okay, but not in our band.

KEITH BURKHARDT: I would be onstage, talking about stuff that looking back was not right. It wasn't my band—it wasn't the Keith Burkhardt Experience; but I would be up there talking about Krishna consciousness. There would be people on the side of the stage, screaming at the band members, "Do you hear what he's saying?" It was silly, but I guess it made things interesting.

ALEX KINON: I was just in a band to play music. I wasn't listening to what Keith was saying and I didn't care. But Robbie's wife, Michelle, this crazy anarchist girl, said, "Look at these lyrics! They're crazy!" She was really upset, and started pressuring Rob to get Keith out of the band. I remember Keith and Michelle yelling at each other back and forth over the contents of the lyrics.

It was like *Spinal Tap*. The wife of someone else in the band doesn't get along with someone else in the band, and that's it. So for whatever reason, we were forced to kick Keith out. It sucked for everybody except Michelle. She was happy.

ROB KABULA: I was living on Norfolk Street at Apartment X, and the band got the bright idea to move out to San Francisco. We thought we'd give it a try. D.R.I. had come out to New York, and they had lived there for a while. We figured we'd go out there and give it a try, and hang out there with them.

KEITH BURKHARDT: I was waiting on Twenty-Second Street to be picked up, with my bags packed, with my girlfriend Angelica sitting on the curb. The band never showed up. There were no cell phones then, so I just waited on the curb. Somehow, Rob Kabula got in touch with me. They had all gone out the night before, had a big night of partying, and decided they had to kick me out of the band because my views were slowing them down. It didn't really break my heart. Things were good with me in New York.

ROB KABULA: We took our band in the van and went to California. We got a rehearsal space in the beer vats with D.R.I., and we hung out with them.

ALEX KINON: D.R.I. and M.D.C were from San Francisco, and we were all friends back then. "Who am I? D.R.I. Who are we? M.D.C. Who are they? C.F.A." We lived in a vat that we shared with D.R.I. in a building where they used to brew beer. On the very top floor there would be parties. They were these big tubs where the mash went, and every floor had these vats. Each beer vat was turned into a rehearsal studio. It was a pretty cool place.

We found a singer there, some guy from Chicago that M.D.C. knew. I can see him in my mind, but I can't tell you his name. We just practiced with him but never did a show.

ROB KABULA: In those abandoned beer vats, they'd have these crazy parties. We would go to a soup kitchen every day to eat. It wasn't like a New York soup kitchen; it would be filled with punks and musicians.

KEITH BURKHARDT: About a month after they left New York, I moved out to L.A. I was living on the beach in this little studio apartment Angelica's dad kept for when he worked out there. We took a road trip up to San Francisco to visit Angelica's mom. I saw posters for the Dead Kennedys playing in the park. So I went to the show. Lo and behold, someone tapped me on the shoulder—it was Rob Kabula. They had found a singer in San Francisco, and it didn't really work out. They invited me to where they were practicing, and I had no ill feelings toward them. I was happy being a devotee. Alex knew that I was a little quirky, and that's the kind of guy you need singing. He said if I wanted to come back and sing, that I could do it. I said, "Sure."

ALEX KINON: We were living in the Mission, and our singer was sleeping on the floor in the kitchen. One day, Keith and Angelica showed up, and we practiced with Keith, and the writing was on the wall for this other guy. By the time we got back to the house, his stuff was out of there and he was gone. He ended up back in Chicago in a band called Life Sentence.

KEITH BURKHARDT: We wound up going back to New York. I remember playing this show at Johnny Stiff's club, Belfast, which was in a basement on Avenue A. That was the last show I played with the old C.F.A. The show was packed, and I remember singing and everything was in slow motion. I thought, "I'm not feeling this in my heart. This really isn't my path anymore." You can't be in punk rock and pretend. After that, I quit.

ROGER MIRET: C.F.A. went on tour, they went out to California, and when they came back they were kind of hippies. I wondered what the fuck happened to this band? After they went out there and stayed with M.D.C., it wasn't the Cause for Alarm we loved.

ROB KABULA: When we went out to San Francisco, the rest of the guys in the band got more liberal. When Keith left, we got Chris Charucki to sing. He was a total Deadhead, but he was a good guy.

KEITH BURKHARDT: I didn't know Chris that well, but he was funny. A class-clown type of guy. He went out to San Francisco and got very involved with M.D.C. and the hippie political thing. I remember seeing Chris after he came back to New York from San Francisco, and it was just a total transformation. This guy was all about politics. Before that, he was into partying.

ROB KABULA: We were out in San Francisco for about a year. We played in L.A. with Suicidal Tendencies, and we played shows in San Francisco. Then we got back to New York, and the Rock Hotel shows had just started on Jane Street. Agnostic Front was the big band, but they were having problems with their bass player, Todd Youth. He was too young. His father started showing up at rehearsals and grabbing Todd out of them.

TODD YOUTH: I was a runaway and I hadn't been going to school for a really long time. My parents were going to get in trouble for me being away. When I got put on probation, my parents made me quit the band.

ROB KABULA: When Vinnie asked me if I wanted to join, I was a free agent. Cause for Alarm wasn't happening for me anymore, so I joined Agnostic Front.

ALEX KINON: After Rob left, Robbie and I got a guy named Joe Orgera to play bass. He was just hanging out. He knew all the songs and he was great. He shaved his hair off and he fit right in. Then we started to get full of ourselves. The bass player and I felt like we were on a different musical level than Charucki's singing abilities, so we threw him out. I look back on it now, and it was a mistake. We wanted to push the band further, but we kicked out our brother for no good reason. It wasn't like he was lying, or on drugs, or anything. That sucked. We got this guy Zowie Ackerman as a singer, who was a metal kid from Queens. Later on, he was in Leeway, playing bass. Once we had Zowie, Joe and I started looking at Robbie and thinking he wasn't very good either, so we threw him out. We got some other drummer, and that's when it all fell apart. Shortly after Cause for Alarm broke up, I joined Agnostic Front too.

*Revamped CFA lineup
with Chris Charucki*
GARY TSE TSE FLY

THE ½ CROWN PUB
1 ATLANTIC AV. E. ROCKAWAY
after 8 (516) 887-3667 or
(516) 599-9453
FRI. NOV. 16 9:00 pm
An Evening of HARDCORE with
CAUSE FOR
ALARM
CRUMBSUCKERS &
PSYCHOS

FANG
C.F.A.
CAUSE FOR ALARM
MORTAL SIN
FATAL
RAGE
AT A-7 AVE A E.7TH ST
FRI. MAY
13. 11 PM

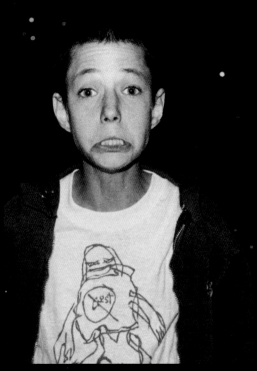

From top: *Cavity Creeps drummer and NYHC legend Steve Poss outside of Apartment X; Cavity Creeps "percussionist" Randy Underwood shows off some new body art.*
COURTESY OF RANDY UNDERWOOD

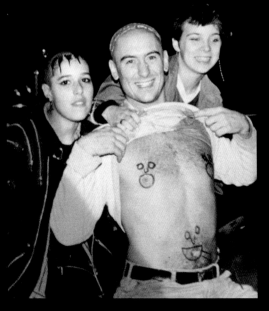

23. APARTMENT X: A PLACE TO CRAP AND MAKE COFFEE

MIKE JUDGE: I remember in 1982, someone had an apartment on Norfolk Street and they called it Apartment X. It was pretty much a crash pad. After gigs, everyone would go there.

KEITH BURKHARDT: I became friends with the old Agnostic Front singer John Watson. I was originally going to move in with him on Norfolk Street, but it was tight quarters. I found my own place with Tony T-Shirt. He drove into Nutley one night and picked me up. We picked up the *Village Voice* on Astor Place at something like three in the morning, and looked for apartments. We found what would become Apartment X that night. I think it was 186 or 188 Norfolk Street. This was probably in January of 1982.

TONY T-SHIRT: Apartment X was a windowless basement apartment. It lasted a couple of years. Big Charlie Hankins would be hanging out there. Frenchie, Agnostic Front's roadie, was staying there at one time.

ROBBIE CRYPTCRASH: So many people lived there and crashed at Apartment X. I lived there for three or four weeks. Rob Kabula lived there. Alex from Cause for Alarm lived there. We all lived there for at least a week or two. That was a crazy apartment.

ROGER MIRET: I got the lease for Apartment X from Keith C.F.A. After me, I gave the lease to Tony T-Shirt. We'd crash there and bands would crash there. When it came time to pay rent, it was kind of tough, because we had like fifty fucking people living there—including me, Steve Poss, Raybeez, Harley Flanagan, and Eric Casanova. I got fed up and moved into Robbie Cryptcrash's place. Then I lived in the band van and would just shower there. I ended up getting an apartment, but it got burned down.

STEVE POSS: I lived in Apartment X, but I certainly didn't have to. I didn't end up staying too long. All of a sudden it went from being fun to being crazy. There were hypodermic needles around. People were doing things secretly, and I realized it was best to leave.

ROGER MIRET: I needed a place to sleep. I didn't have the van then. When I got the A.F. van, I lived in the van with my dogs. I would park it in front of Tompkins Square Park and it felt safer than living in a squat. The apartment I had that burned down, some junkies started a fire on the sixth floor. Those squats were dangerous. People were going up and down from that apartment, shooting up.

JESSE MALIN: I didn't live in the squats. I moved into my rehearsal space that I shared with the False Prophets on Avenue B. I was living in a lawn chair, eating outdated yogurts. I went to a school in the city that was sort of a joke, but it satisfied my parents that I was attempting to have an education. Meanwhile, some administrators were running a male prostitution ring out of the school. I wasn't involved in that, but if I was I guess I could have bought some nicer guitars.

RUSS IGGAY: Apartment X, that's where Jimmy G and Raybeez took me to sleep. Some parts were curtained up. Everyone had their little spot. I remember waking up in Apartment X one day, hanging out listening to music, waiting for the Cause for Alarm 7-inch to be delivered. But we couldn't open it, because the band wasn't around. So we just waited around for the band to get there to open up the box so we could check it out.

ROBBIE CRYPTCRASH: We got our records delivered to Apartment X just before going on tour. We waited there for two or three days for those records. By this point, we were all living outside of Apartment X, because there were so many people living there. We figured that we had a van that everyone could fit inside—we all just started to sleep in the van. We still had a place with Apartment X to crap in the morning and make coffee.

STEVE POSS: D.R.I. were camping in a van in front of Apartment X when Cause for Alarm toured with them. There was a point where a lot of San Francisco bands were coming out here. Spike from D.R.I.'s sister was married to the guy in Pissed Youth, and they lived in a building on Third Street where the guitarist of the Cavity Creeps lived. So they were next-door neighbors. There was definitely a connection between the San Francisco and the New York scenes, because San Francisco was fucked up too. They were shooting speed and everything. When D.R.I. or Crucifix or M.D.C. came here and stayed, they really stayed! The San Francisco bands were friends with New York, and they were real friends.

ROBBIE CRYPTCRASH: There was a problem with the lady upstairs. We had pet rats in Apartment X, and she didn't like that fact, because the rats were going to get into the building. We'd tell her, "No, it's a pet," and she's like, "No, it's a rat!" So she put out rat poison. I don't remember who it was, but we found a couple of glass orange juice bottles and filled them up with water. Then we taped them together with some wire we found in the garbage and a dead nine-volt battery. The whole thing looked like it was some sort of bomb. The cops showed up and they were laughing. Yeah, that was Apartment X.

Roger Miret gives Cavity Creeps bass player Jenny a new 'do in Apartment X. RANDY UNDERWOOD

24. SKINHEAD YOUTH: SOCIETY'S VICTIMS

JOHN PORCELLY: New York City has an energy that you're not going to find anywhere else. People who have that passionate, driven mind-set, they gravitate to New York City. A lot of the key players in the New York hardcore scene weren't from New York. They were from New Jersey or way out in Queens. But there was this energy of the Lower East Side. It wasn't even just music. There was art, there was hip-hop. It was an underground energy. You couldn't match it anywhere else. Even being in that intense environment—you had to come into your own to survive that area.

MIKE JUDGE: Even though we were from New Jersey, it was hard for us to see shows there. You had to drive to them, you couldn't take a bus to the clubs in these towns. It was actually simpler for us to just take a bus into New York. One of the first bands I ever saw was Adrenalin O.D., from New Jersey, but even that was an Irving Plaza gig. After going to CBGB three or four times, and seeing the same group of people hanging out together, I wanted to hang out with those guys. Maybe I was just looking for something to replace my own family. It wasn't easy for us Jersey guys to be a part of it, though. There was definitely a clique going on, and they were standoffish. They would find out we were from Jersey, and they weren't exactly fucking thrilled.

RUSS IGLAY: Around the beginning of 1982 I started going into the city to see shows. I was still in Belmar, New Jersey, in high school. The first people I met were Jimmy G from Murphy's Law and Johnny Koncz, aka Johnny Feedback, from Kraut. I think it came from skateboarding, because I would bring my skateboard. After I met Jimmy and Johnny, I wouldn't go home after shows; I'd stay with them all weekend long. My routine was to come home from school on a Friday, change, get a bag with some clothes and shit, and take the train into the city and meet up with Jimmy or Johnny. Then I would take the very last train out of Penn Station on Sunday night, walk home, and go to school the next day. I feel very lucky to have found that back then. I was drawn there, and it became my second home. I never realized something so cool was going on.

MIKE JUDGE: After a while of us coming out and standing up for ourselves at the gigs, those New York guys eventually thought we were all right. Once Vinnie Stigma started talking to us, then Roger Miret was talking to us, and slowly we became a part of it. We were supporters. We were going everywhere. We were going to squats to see shows. We weren't afraid to go where the music was. We would road-trip to Philly or Boston to support New York bands. Then I'd find out that guys who were part of the New York crew were actually Jersey guys. All of a sudden, I'm going down to Nutley to hang out with a guy who I thought was from New York. I feel if everyone just got together and admitted they were from Jersey in the first place, it would have saved a whole lot of time and trouble.

JOHN KELLY: A lot of people I knew came from broken homes or lived on the street. Their parents were too strict, or they didn't want to live a rich Long Island lifestyle. Urban Waste's singer Kenny Ahrens is a fine example of that. He moved out of his parents' place in Farmingdale. He had opportunities, but he wanted to do his own thing. There was a lot of rebellion involved in starting our own little community.

VINNIE STIGMA: Frenchie was my first roadie. He lived in an abandoned building. People were saying he was this big crazy guy. Right away, I was like, "Crazy guy? In my neighborhood? I'm there!" When he first came around, I shaved his head with glass and soap in the street under a fire hydrant. It was right around the corner from where the radio show is where they do the *Black N' Blue Takeover*. That little pump is still there!

JAMES KONTRA: We were all street kids. I think we gravitated to the Lower East Side from different socioeconomic backgrounds and family structures for one main reason: We did not fit into our respective communities. I was with a girlfriend, and I was living in Brighton Beach and she lived in Coney Island. That was a whole different kind of ghetto. We were the only two punks in our high schools. I was a Russian immigrant on top of that! It was either, "Hey! Why don't you go back to fuckin' Russia?" or, "Just go away you fuckin' freak." There would be these guineas, these *Saturday Night Fever* type niggas, and they'd be like, "What's up with this every day being Halloween type of shit?" Real as cancer! For us, getting to Manhattan on a D train was a fucking adventure in itself. We didn't know what kind of fucking fight we were going to get into on the train. Walking down from Coney Island to Brighton Beach to get on the D train, a lot of the Puerto Rican gangs would jump us.

JESSE MALIN: On the trains, it was intense. There was no unity. This wasn't some big Lollapalooza festival where white people like rap music and industrial music. You couldn't be like, "I just like music." If you were into something, you lived and died for it. You'd get on the subway to get back to Queens, you'd have b-boys and regular people going to work, and you would be confronted by both about the way you looked. We were battling society in our own little way. I built up a lot of rage to write songs, and I spent it on the dance floor.

MIKE JUDGE: I always thought Steve Poss was a runaway. I could never wrap my head around him being so young and being at these shows. He was ten years old and watching the Bad Brains at a squat down on Avenue C. It would be one in the morning. We were all sticking together so we could get through Tompkins Square Park safely to get to Avenue C from Avenue A. Why was this little boy there, you know?

HOWIE ABRAMS (A&R, IN-EFFECT RECORDS): Early on, the undesirable things were unavoidable. The shows were in shitty places in sketchy neighborhoods, filled with sketchy kids doing sketchy things around you. It was a volatile, real-deal scene. There were kids who latched onto it, and then carried on in a certain manner. That's when it got weird. I think the kids who were true to themselves realized what was important was supporting the bands and the places that bands played. There was a community that was really unique and really special.

PAUL DORDAL: We were these Queens- and Brooklyn-based kids who came down to the city and were all from jacked-up families. We found our place on the Lower East Side because we were really looking to belong. I think one of the key pieces of the scene in the beginning is that it was a place to belong. It was not a place to show off and put on a Mohawk and throw on a black leather jacket and be a punk rocker for the weekend. You actually said, "I'm leaving Queens, I'm leaving the Upper East Side. This is where I really live."

ALEXA POLI-SCHEIBERT (NYHC SCENESTER): I was sitting in Tompkins Square Park playing Negative Approach on my boom box. Roger Miret came up to me and started quizzing me on music. It was kind of funny, like he was trying to see if I was serious. While Roger started talking to me, all of a sudden people started passing me beers and spliffs, and it just happened like that. It was pretty awesome, because these were my heroes, and they accepted me right away. It was such a cool feeling.

I was one of the few girls. There weren't very many of us. There was me, little Michelle, Cindy D., and Mo Brown. Big Kim was around, too, and so were the Scab girls. We were pretty fearsome. It was so much a dude thing, and I just kind of fell into it and became talked about. It became this thing, "Watch out for Alexa!" I did get into a lot of fights. But there really weren't many of us.

VINNIE STIGMA: I was never a punk rocker who ran away from home and was dirty. I could never see being dirty. I have to wash my hands a hundred times a day. I got the phobia. I had no reason to run away. I had a good family, and I believed in that idea. That's why I took a lot of people under my wing and took care of them. When bands came, I was there for them. I almost felt like it was obligation. I was being a hardcore diplomat—and being plain Italian. My mother used to cook for all of us. I was just telling Richie Krutch from Wisdom in Chains how my grandmother and my aunt used to come and say, "Vincent, open the door!" Their hands were full with bowls of pasta, the big Italian bowls! They'd just want me to give the bowls back—without even washing them, because they were afraid I might chip them. This is my neighborhood, and I fed everyone.

ALEXA POLI-SCHEIGERT: I never squatted, I just lived in shitty apartments. I did stay at the C Squat here and there, but I like a bath now and again. I lived in Tompkins Square Park for a summer, and there was this guy Gary who was pretty infamous who watched out for the girls in the park. One night, somebody fondled my friend Cass, and Gary beat the living shit out of them. One Halloween, we were in the park, and the Guardian Angels came and told us to turn our radio down. It turned into a fucking brawl. Tommy Carroll beat the living shit out of three of them at once. It was fucking hysterical, with kids swinging skateboards. We were all protecting one another. Everybody protected everybody.

JOHN PORCELLY: The Lower East Side was a jungle. It brought a lot of strong personalities out in people, and you had to be a strong personality to be down there. If you were a meek person, you weren't going to last there very long. Tons of people moved there, and two weeks later, they got their shoes stolen and went back to where they came from.

EDDIE SUTTON: I wasn't as much of a street kid like these other guys were. Even though I was a teenager hanging out on the Lower East Side and not coming home until the next day, I didn't have a criminal record until I was in my twenties. Nowadays, I have a heavier rap sheet than most of these thugs and hooligans. I'm not saying this to prove I'm a tough guy or anything; there's always someone bigger and badder than you.

PAUL BEARER: The kids who were living in squats or whatever, I don't know whether that was a choice they made or if they had issues at home. But not everybody who ended up in a squat has a bad-luck story. Sometimes people put themselves out on the streets because they thought it was the cool thing to do. I always loved my family and I always got along with them. It's not like we had anything, but living in an abandoned building was never an option for me. My mom is a great cook and I had a warm bed to go home to at night.

PETE KOLLER: Let me explain something: Everybody in Sick of It All came from good families. Mom and Dad stayed together. Everyone in the band had jobs as kids. But that scene just before us, that was hardcore. They all had mental problems and they all lived in the street. *That's* hardcore to me.

ROGER MIRET: We were speaking up against Reagan, just standing up for our rights. That element of danger back then doesn't exist today. You can mimic the sound and mimic the look, but that danger isn't there. If you go down to the Lower East Side now, I'm sure people who've read my lyrics wonder what the hell I was talking about. We were just kids trying everything. I'm able to tell you these stories, and some of my friends are not here to tell the stories. Some people got caught up in shit and things turned into bigger things. People started getting desperate and ended up in jail. Basically, we were a bunch of misfits and outcasts. We were a bunch of criminals in the street.

GARY TSE TSE FLY: There was no central authority, and all these kids were putting on shows and doing flyers and doing fanzines. I think that's anarchy. That's what anarchy is all about in the philosophical sense. At the same time, we lived in New York City in the early '80s, and it was a ruthless world. Those kids lived on the Lower East Side with the gangs and stuff, and it was truly survival of the fittest.

JESSE MALIN: Harley Flanagan did a lot for the scene. When I first met him, he had this slight dismissive attitude like I was just a punk rocker. He was down on the Lower East Side fighting these people every day, dealing with the Puerto Rican and black gangs who didn't understand punk. He was fighting in this ghetto while we went back to Queens. But we were fighting people too!

JOHN PORCELLY: I knew who Harley Flanagan was from the cover of that Stimulators single. I was out front of a matinee one time, and Ray Cappo nudged me and pointed out Harley. I looked down the street, and there was Harley Flanagan goose-stepping down the Bowery with that chick from the *Another State of Mind* movie, Manon. He was such a personality.

JOHN BELLO: One of the first shows I went to at CBGB, I had hair down to my shoulders. I was hanging out, and I didn't know anyone. This was 1981 or '82, so if you had long hair, forget it—people thought you were in AC/DC. A couple of skins were getting a little rough with me. Harley Flanagan came over put a stop to it, even though he didn't know who I was. He looked at me and said if there was any problem to come to him.

RUSSELL ISLAY: I was the outsider, a kid coming from Jersey on a skateboard, and Harley basically took me in. My life was different from city life, so he showed me the ropes. I feel fortunate that he did. Everything Harley did was cool. Kids always wanted to be Harley, but he was born into that. He was never fake. He never had to be fake, and I doubt he even thought about being fake. He lived that life. I could always go back here to Belmar, New Jersey. Harley didn't have that pleasure. He was a street kid, and he did what he could do to get by, even if it wasn't the best thing to be doing. He didn't want to be cool or show off, he did it because he needed to buy food, or find somewhere to sleep, or get new clothes. He was and still is the real deal. He never had to impress anyone. He just did what he did.

MIKE JUDGE: Todd Youth was a Jersey kid. When I met him, he was like, "I'm from Jersey." When I asked him where he lived, he said, "I live here on the streets. I ran away two months ago."

TODD YOUTH: I ran away from North Jersey. I had gotten into punk rock really early. I used to get *Rock Scene*, which was a New York–based magazine that was on all the newsstands. It would have Kiss and Aerosmith, the bands I liked as a kid, but there would always have something on the New York scene with Bob Gruen photos, or the New York Dolls, or the Dead Boys, the Heartbreakers, or the Ramones. I got hip to that, and I thought everybody looked so wild. The Sex Pistols, and their names—Johnny Rotten and Sid Vicious—and the way they looked and everything just really impressed me. All within a week or two, I bought the Ramones' *Leave Home*, and Iggy Pop's *TV Eye Live*. *TV Eye Live* was the first time I heard a curse on a record, and I that was a big deal. Around '80 or '81, there was some Saturday-evening TV exposé on slam dancing, and what's wrong with these kids. Everybody had shaved heads and combat boots, and it looked so fucking crazy. I just started buying hardcore records.

When it got really bad at home, finally I ran away and came to the Lower East Side. My first show was the Bad Brains at CBGB. I'll never forget walking in there as a twelve-year-old who came from a very unhappy home, and seeing people that looked as fucked up as I felt inside. I was like, "Ah! My people!" and that was it. A group of kids who hung out on the Lower East Side who were just basically on the street took me in. Me and Harley Flanagan became really good friends really fast. There was also this dude Eric Casanova, this other guy Little Chris, and we were the youngest, under fifteen or sixteen. We were also the craziest, because we didn't give a fuck. We did the most drugs and beat the most people up.

VINNIE STIGMA: Todd was twelve years old, and he used to run away to my house. I used to go, "Excuse me, let me call your mother." I'd tell her, "You don't have to send the cops, he's here." He just wanted to live on the scene, and my house was part of the scene. I took care of him. I made sure he was fed. I'd always ask, "Are you hungry?" I'm Italian and I'm crazy like that.

TODD YOUTH: I had a band with Raybeez shortly after I left A.F. called Skinhead Youth. Big Al from Cause for Alarm was on guitar, and Billy Psycho was on drums. In February or March of '84, we were playing our sound check for a matinee at CBGB. I saw my father come into CB's with two cops through that long hallway from the back. I threw my bass down and ran out the back door of CB's, down an alley, and I hid. Eventually, someone came and found me. The band started playing the show with this guy Larry playing bass. Halfway through the show they brought me back, and I played the second half of the set with a ski mask on. After that, we were all living in this apartment on Sixth Street. The cops and my father knocked on my door and got me, so I had to go back home for a while, but then I would just eventually bail again.

ANTIDOTE

THOU
SHALT
NOT
KILL

RIT CAGE PARTY
BENEFIT FOR RENT

ANTIDOTE
MURPHY'S LAW "BONGO MADNESS"
DOOR PRIZE !!!!!
SANTA CRUZ SKATEBOARD
YO CHECK IT OUT!
GILLIGAN'S REVENGE
CAVITY CREEPS
AND MORE.

OCT. 9 CBGB SUN. 3PM
MATINEE!

NO GOVT...NO BOSES...-NO PRES?...

ANTIDOTE

SOCIAL PLEASURE SOUND
presents

HARDCORE 83
with

ANTIDOTE FROM NEW YORK
AND

TMO

THOU
SHALT
NOT
KILL

Patrix
385-6577

SUN. NOV
13 TH
JUST #2.00

Above: *Rob Nunzio from Antidote showing everyone the "real deal"* GARY TSE TSE FLY

25. ANTIDOTE:
WAKE UP TO THE REAL DEAL

DAVE SCOTT: The Antidote *Thou Shalt Not Kill* EP from 1983 is brutally good. They were one of the heaviest bands on the New York scene. It's one of those perfect records; the sound on it is amazing, the takes on it are amazing, and the guitar playing is great on it. I loved that record.

ROBB NUNZIO (GUITAR, ANTIDOTE, M.O.I.): I had started several bands, including the Lust Scabs and Vas Deferens, with friends in Jackson Heights after graduating high school. I started to try out the early songs I had written. Antidote was formed after I had met the guys in the Bad Brains. I saw them open for the Clash at Bond's Casino, and I had to meet them. One of the guys in Vas Deferens knew they rehearsed at 171A on Avenue A. So I went down there and booked us a block of rehearsal time. The guy who ran the place was Jerry Williams. We got along well enough that he let me hang around while he was recording the Bad Brains' infamous ROIR cassette. I got to know HR and Dr. Know as friends, and they kind of took me under their wings.

One weekend, the Bad Brains were playing Trudy Heller's on Sixth Avenue and they invited us to get onstage and do some songs. Tommy Victor was in the audience and approached me after the show with some feedback. I wound up sharing an apartment with him on First Avenue and First Street, and we immersed ourselves in music. Tom taught me a lot of shit. He knew everyone on the downtown music scene because he was the soundman at CBGB for years and he played in a few bands before he later formed Prong. Arthur Googy from the Misfits was a good friend of mine from Jackson Heights. He and I and a couple other people were the only punks in the hood at that time, so I got him to play with me and Tom and that was the earliest lineup of Antidote.

DREW STONE: Nunzio from Antidote was in Tompkins Square Park smoking weed, and that's where I met him.

MATT WARNKE: *Thou Shalt Not Kill* is one of the singularly sickest, most perfect blasts of hardcore ever created. I don't believe the band itself ever achieved anything close to it live, or had a presence about them in the scene to match the recording.

LOUIE RIVERA: Antidote had a singer before me named T, he was this little graffiti kid. Antidote was doing a show at CBGB. They were working on a song called "Real Deal," and T didn't want to sing the song that night. I was backstage with them smoking weed. Bliss, the drummer, aka Arthur Googy after he left the Misfits, had the lyric sheet on him, and he said, "Louie, just go up there and sing this song." I did the song with them. About a week later, I was hanging out in front of Rat Cage Records one afternoon and saw Nunzio and Bliss coming down the street. We started smoking a spliff. Next thing you know, they're saying, "Things aren't working out with T, do you think you'd want to come rehearse with us?" After three or four months of me being in the unit, we were in High Five Studios recording the *Thou Shalt Not Kill* single.

ROBB NUNZIO: We went into the studio for the first time to record the songs that became *Thou Shalt Not Kill* with HR and Earl from the Bad Brains as our sound engineers. When I heard the recording of that session, I thought the whole thing sucked, so the whole thing wound up in the garbage can. We needed our regular soundman, Jerry Williams. Two months later, we went back into the studio to do it all again, and this time the result was great.

LOUIE RIVERA: Jerry Williams was on tour with M.D.C as a soundman. When we went in the first time to record, we were very unsatisfied with the results. Not even mastering would help the music. At the moment that we were bumming hardest about it, who did we see but this halo of light Jerry Williams coming down the street toward us with his gallon of water in his hands and his licorice root in his mouth. Bliss didn't hesitate. He said, "Fuck it, I'm calling the studio right now. I'm booking another twelve hours."

I remember when we were mastering the Jerry Williams recording, the engineer and Jerry told us if we went another notch louder on the volume, we would have problems with little kids with cheap styluses. Their needles would just slide across the vinyl. So told them to just tweak it to the point that the little kids with the cheap styluses wouldn't be bumming.

ROBB NUNZIO: As far as the guitar sound on the recording, I had this cheap, tiny little practice amp, a tiny box with a six-inch speaker and a click-on distortion button on the back. I think it was a Fox amp. Jerry positioned it on a bar stool with two sound-dampening walls on either side, then moved the whole setup into a long corridor outside of the actual studio. One mic was placed in front of the speaker, and another mic was placed on a stand at the opposite end of the corridor. That is how my wall-of-Marshall-stacks sound was created: With a cheap-ass six-inch speaker!

DREW STONE: I started a band called the High and the Mighty with a few guys I grew up with in the Bronx. They had no connection to hardcore. This is how it was back then: "I'm starting a band. Oh, you got a bass guitar? You're playing bass! Oh, you know a few Santana licks? You're playing lead guitar!" I wrote all the songs on acoustic guitar and immediately we started playing A7. We played with Antidote a few times. We played with them down in D.C. On the way back to New York, the drummer in Antidote and the singer in Antidote were fighting the whole way back; it almost came to blows. I was tight with Nunzio and I ended up being the singer for Antidote. I loved the band, and I loved the *Thou Shalt Not Kill* single.

I was embraced. It wasn't a bummer, but this was hitting 1984 and other things were permeating the scene at that point. We were moving away from the basic hardcore formula and we wanted to start doing other things. I joined Antidote as a hardcore band, but it started changing immediately. The drummer and bass player left, and they were replaced, and we eventually became a rock band.

ROBB NUNZIO: When I listen to *Thou Shalt Not Kill* now, I hear the impassioned plea of a struggling young man—or band—crying out for hope and togetherness of some sort in a world gone mad. Even though I wrote it a long time ago, it feels like it could have just been released yesterday in some ways. Though some of my opinions have grown since then, I still feel that a lot of the record's core message remains true in my heart.

A typical Sunday afternoon on the Bowery PHOTOS BY KEN SALERNO

26. CBGB MATINEE

ERNIE PARADA: CBGB wasn't doing hardcore in the beginning. They had an audition night on Mondays, and if they liked you and you drew a crowd, then you would get a gig. It wasn't until around late 1982 that they started with the matinees.

DON FURY: I had played in bands at CBGB for a few years and Carol Costa, my ex, was helping book the band. About 1979, she started work at CB's, helping Hilly Kristal manage the club and, later on, book the acts. By the early '80s, lots of hardcore punk was coming out. The bands needed a regular venue to support them. I knew CB's would be a good spot. I asked Carol to put the idea to Hilly. First he said no, but after a few tries he said okay—and the CBGB hardcore matinee was born.

VINNIE STIGMA: What do I remember about the CBGB matinees? First of all, I'm Italian, so I eat dinner at three o'clock on Sundays. I'm Nablidon, so we eat at three. If I was Sicilian, I'd eat at two o'clock. I used to go to CBGB with a full belly, and my grandmother gave me a glass of wine, so I was ready!

STEVE WISHNIA: CBGB were not really comfortable with punk as it started becoming hardcore. They thought it was too violent, and most of the crowd didn't drink as much.

KEVIN CROWLEY: The first time we played CBGB we ended up owing Hilly money because stuff got damaged. We passed a hat around, and everyone gave what they could. The hardcore stuff was on probation with Hilly at that point, but ultimately we ended up doing a bunch of the matinees.

MIKE JUDGE: We would get the *Village Voice* and to see who was playing. We saw there was a matinee going on during a Saturday afternoon at CBGB. The first time I went to a CB's matinee, I saw Agnostic Front, back when John Watson was the singer. After I saw that show, every Saturday, I was there. I had to be a part of that scene.

VINNIE STIGMA: On Sunday matinee shows, what I used to do with Agnostic Front is go do the sound check and then go home at eat. Hilly would be there. He was a man of few words. This is how it would go. This happened every time I ever played there:

Me: Hey Hilly, how are ya?

Hilly: Hey Vinnie, how ya doin'?

Me: All right. We're going to load in.

Hilly: All right.

Me: Coffee?

Hilly: Yeah, okay.

I used to bring back the pignoli cookies. Man, he loved them Italian cookies! I left the cookies there, did my sound check, and then he would disappear.

DREW STONE: This shit got too big for A7, and that's when it percolated over into Saturday and Sunday afternoons at CBGB. No one was fucking there then anyway, so Hilly scored.

RALPHIE G: Hardcore with the right bands could fill a club. The drinking part was another story. That's how the idea for the matinees came about. CBGB could still keep the nights for the older, drinking crowd, but still have a venue for hardcore without eating too much into the profits.

GARY TSE TSE FLY: We made it down to a matinee in 1984 when they were on Saturdays and they cost four dollars. Satan's Cheerleaders from Long Island, No Control, and Government Issue were playing. I remember that it was cold. This was the first time I saw a hardcore punk crowd. Just from a visual perspective, they just looked pretty pitiful. I think the squats were at their peak that winter. I remember a lot of kids were sniffing glue from bags, and people were drinking in the streets.

JOHN PORCELLY: You'd go into the bathroom of CBGB, and there would be people doing heroin in there. There were people sniffing glue in the bathroom. I thought the Ramones were kidding! The scene was so drugged out. It created this really dramatic and really violent scene.

At the first Agnostic Front show I went to there, Tony Ultra Violence and his girlfriend were watching everyone filing out. She's going, "Not him . . . not him . . . not him . . ." and then she pointed to me and said, "Not him." I

From left: *Vinnie Stigma belts one out with The Psychos.* GARY TSE TSE FLY; *Old-school CBGB crowd reaction at the Crumbsuckers' first show there.* GARY TSE TSE FLY

didn't know what that meant, but I never felt so glad to be "not him." Tony was sitting there with a bottle in his hand. Finally, she saw who she was looking for and goes, "HIM!" and Tony took this bottle and smashed it over the guy's head and cracked it open.

GARY TSE TSE FLY: My first impression was that the crowd was kind of shabby and looked cold and kind of miserable. Then we paid our four dollars and went inside and there was this amazing transformation. There was just this *energy.* No Control got on stage and maybe during the second song people started slam-dancing. There was a short break and Government Issue came on and then the place just exploded. I was hooked. I remember the physical need to get into the pit and move around. I had no idea what to do in the pit, and I probably looked like an idiot just pushing people. At my first show, I was this guy who doesn't know what he's doing. After that, I loved everything about it. The very next week I came again, and I don't think I missed a matinee for a year.

JOHN PORCELLY: My dad wouldn't let me go to New York City from Westchester for shows, because he thought New York City was sketchy, but he let me go to the Anthrax Club in Stamford and Stamford is a fuckin' ghetto! I think he just heard "Connecticut" and figured it was fine. I started to go to shows at the Anthrax, and I saw a million great bands. But when CBGB started to do matinees, that was a dream come true. I took the Metro North train down and went to one CBGB matinee, and I went every single weekend after that. I'd go to the Anthrax on Friday and Saturday no matter who was playing. Then

Sunday, I'd go to the CBGB matinee. Again, I wouldn't care who was playing. I'd go just to hang out and meet people. But it wasn't like you hung out at CBGB for the entire week. The rest of the week you wouldn't want to go there because it was just a bunch of crappy bands playing. The only thing exciting going on at CBGB was the Sunday matinees.

RAY CAPPO (DRUMMER, VIOLENT CHILDREN; VOCALIST, YOUTH OF TODAY, SHELTER, REFLEX FROM PAIN): CBGB became an escape from my world. You could see incredible bands for three dollars. It was almost like walking into a comic book, with superheroes and villains and characters that were bigger than life. That's what the New York scene was like. The characters on the scene were more colorful than the black and white people in my high school. There was no Raybeez or Vinnie Stigma or Harley Flanagan in my high school. When I went back to high school on a Monday morning and tried to explain the bands I saw, or how I saw one guy hit another guy over the head with a beer bottle, people would ask, "Where do you go where you see people hitting each other over the head with beer bottles?" The only place people would be seeing something like that is in a movie.

GARY MESKIL: The CBGB scene could be a bit intimidating at times. It was a complete contrast to my upbringing. I grew up in South Baldwin, Long Island, right on the water, in a suburban environment with lush, green grass and all the clichés that come along with it. To find myself in New York City down on the Bowery every weekend was pretty interesting. Kids who grow up in suburbia, they get bored of it, especially if you're of the artistic nature. I wanted something more edgy and exciting in my life.

JOHN PORCELLY: To me, it's like bees in the winter—they get together because it's them against the elements. People hated punk and thought punkers were nut cases. We got beat up. So there was this brotherhood, where everyone looked out for each other. We were all misfits and fucked up in our own ways. But we were accepted on a very base level.

RICHIE BIRKENHEAD: I went to a lot of CB's matinees. I'd say I almost went to every single one of them. Even if I didn't go inside, I went down there to see who was hanging out.

PETE KOLLER: I'm pretty sure the the first matinee we went to was the release party for Agnostic Front's *Victim in Pain* album in 1984. We took the 7 train to the E train, and then we got off by Bleecker Bob's Records. Right away I saw a big, sort of chubby dude with a shaved head and a huge eagle tattooed on the back of it. I never saw anything like this in my life. I thought, "Holy shit, this guy is going to kill us!" That was Billy Psycho—and he was super cool! He accepted us right away. As kids in high school who weren't accepted, and weren't into what everybody else in our school was into, that was what we needed. We weren't wearing Capezios and Cavaricci pants. We were outcasts where we came from, and we finally found our place. From that minute on, I thought hardcore was the greatest thing ever.

BRENDAN RAFFERTY (VOCALIST, SFA; BOUNCER, CBGB): When I first started hanging out there regularly, what struck me was the sense of family that all the hardcore kids had. Being the new kid, I had people walking up to me and introducing themselves and asking me a million questions and introducing me around to other people. "Hey, this is Brendan, he just started hanging out." It was very accepting, and as a young teenager who never felt he fit in anywhere, I finally found where I belonged and who I was.

There was a sense that no one mattered more than anyone else. That was a strong first impression that kind of turned my perceptions upside down in a good way. I remember sitting in the gutter and drinking a beer with some people I had just met, and they were completely cool and down-to-earth. When we all went back inside because the next band was about to start, much to my surprise, the people I had just met got up onstage. They were the next band. Bands and audience were the same people, and nobody was more important. That really made a deep impression.

JOHN JOSEPH: I started going to CBGB in the 1970s and I got to meet Hilly Kristal. At the other big venues, you had to have a record deal. CBGB only had one rule: You had to play your own music. Hilly inspired these kids to make music. He was a musician himself. He really inspired a whole scene by letting bands come in there and play. CBGB was our home. Hilly let people like me and Roger Miret and Harley Flanagan and Jimmy G have shows, and be able to have our scene. That's where the NYHC scene really took fuckin' flight and started really happening. We ran it, and we policed it.

CRAIG SETARI (BASSIST, NYC MAYHEM, STRAIGHT AHEAD, AGNOSTIC FRONT, YOUTH OF TODAY, SICK OF IT ALL): The first time I went to a matinee, this guy Big Charlie was there who went to school with my brother and Danny Lilker. He introduced me to everybody and he put me on his shoulders. I was immediately a friend of everybody. So I was lucky in that regard. He was the biggest and coolest guy in the room.

GARY TSE TSE FLY: Early on, Big Charlie was at every show. Granted, he was three hundred pounds and six foot five, so you couldn't miss him. He just loved hardcore. He would come to every show. He knew everyone.

MIKE BULLSHIT: He was like three hundred pounds of muscle. People ask about racism on the New York scene and I laugh. If you had said anything racist around him, he would have probably put you through the sidewalk.

CHRIS TSAKIS: I always loved playing CBGB. It was legendary, and had a fairly good sound system. The best thing was that it had a high stage. My least favorite thing was the jackasses who would want to dive off the stage and invariably pull out one of my cables. They always jumped on my side of the stage, because I think they were too intimated by Mike or Ron. Ron would pretty much kick anyone in the balls and shove them off the stage.

DAVE KOENIG (EDITOR, *In Memory Of . . .* FANZINE; COEDITOR, *Hardware* FANZINE): The *Guillotine* fanzine benefit show and the infamous riot that occurred afterwards is one of my most vivid memories of CBGB. Right when the band Straight Ahead finished, Big Charlie Hankins grabbed the mic and let everybody know that there was a big riot going on outside. "You guys all talk about unity! It's time to prove it, because those guys out there have bats!"

The show was packed, and there were a lot of people outside, too. I don't know what really started the big ruckus. Rumors abounded. The conclusion that everybody could basically agree on was that somebody started with one of the homeless guys living in the halfway house over CBGB. In turn, the people upstairs started throwing garbage, bricks, and piss-filled balloons out the windows on the crowd below. I was standing outside just when this began to happen. Just imagine about fifty people trying to run into CBGB at the same time through that crappy door. The guys with the bats were a group of skinheads who were just looking for an excuse to hit people. There was word that Mike from the Nihilistics got cut on the arm by a transvestite. After about ten minutes inside CBGB, I found my friend Pat from *Guillotine* zine who said he was getting a ride out of there. I asked if I could go with him, because I was worried I was going to get killed. We ran outside, and it was chaos; a mix of people throwing stuff, people fighting, and people standing there watching. Traffic was stopped. I don't know the kid, but somebody smacked this guy in the face with a skateboard, and the guy flew into a taxicab windshield. We ran across the street to where Pat's car was parked. I dove into the open window and just took in this crazy scene. We bolted out of there to the train station, not believing what we just went through.

BRENDAN RAFFERTY: As far as any problems getting in because of age, that was not a problem until late 1985, when New York state changed the drinking age from nineteen to twenty-one. Before the law changed, CBGB was allowed to let in all ages, with ID for nineteen to drink. When the law changed, CBGB was forced to change to sixteen to enter, twenty-one to drink. Cops were cracking down hard on clubs back then. It sucked, but I understood. Yes, I was denied entrance once when the law first changed and I didn't have ID. I think all the kids who bitched about the sixteen-plus policy were absolutely shortsighted idiots, though. They blamed CBGB for a New York State law. I guess it was easier for zine writers and straight-edge retards to bitch about CBGB than to bitch about the laws being set in Albany.

RUSS ISLAY: Karen at CBGB used to give my brother Dean shit for being too young. We'd take in the drums, then walk out with an empty bass drum and put Dean in the case, then walk back into CB's with Dean inside the case.

GAVIN VAN VLACK (GUITARIST, NY HOODS, SUBURBAN UPRISE, SIDE BY SIDE, ABSOLUTION, BURN, DIE 116): I remember there was this kid Yoko. He was like everybody's little brother. When I was in Absolution, we used to sneak him into CB's in the kick-drum case. He wasn't the first to do that, though. I think that Agnostic Front or the Psychos used to sneak little Chris in that way. I guess it's a hand-me-down rite of passage, literally.

MATTWARNKE: When Bold was called Crippled Youth, we played our first show at CBGB in June of 1986 with Rest In Pieces, Warzone, and Youth of Today. I was able to play because Karen called my parents to verify my age. Despite their strong Catholic beliefs, they lied for their son that day.

TOM O'HARA (Coeditor, *Combat Stance* fanzine): Between August of '86 and February of '87, when I actually turned sixteen, I tried to get into CBGB twice. The first time I was able to get in somehow. I don't think Karen Kristal was at the door. The next time I tried to go I got turned away. I stayed outside and listened to the entire matinee anyway. The time after that was early January, and I asked my dad to go with me and get me in. It was Token Entry opening up for Murphy's Law. I had to be there. I remember him telling Karen, "This is my son, he is fifteen, but he'll be sixteen soon. He has my permission to come here anytime he wants." From that point on, I was never carded by her again.

JOHN JOSEPH: In the '90s, when all the stupid fights started happening, that's when Hilly Kristal put the kibosh on that shit. For a while, Hilly didn't want no hardcore shows there because of all the idiots fighting. They were fighting each other! When we were out there in the early '80s, we were fighting off rednecks and jocks and whoever else fucked with us. It was never us fighting ourselves. We were fighting people who fucked with our friends. When these assholes started getting drunk and fighting each other at shows like tough guys, it was wack. Hilly was like, "I'm not having this shit at my club." Then there weren't any hardcore shows in the '90s. But do you know who were the first ones who got to go in there and play again? The fuckin' Cro-Mags. I said, "We'll police the shit," and it went fine.

MATT WARNKE: When we played our first CB's matinee, I was surprised how many people were in front of stage, singing the words. Our record wasn't even out yet! We had immediate kinship with people who had been around for a few years—the Death Before Dishonor guys like Mark Ryan and Mike Judge; and also people who were just coming up like ourselves, like Straight Ahead. We basically met almost everyone, and most people were incredibly cool and inclusive. I remember walking down Fourth Street after the matinee, and hearing, "Hey! Crippled Youth!" It was some of the Warzone women—as they were then known—toasting us from an apartment.

VINNIE STIGMA: One of the greatest things ever for me was having a full belly of macaroni and meatballs, standing in front of CBGB at a hardcore matinee, and seeing my grandfather's pigeons flying over. I was like, "Yeah! A full belly, hardcore music, and seeing my grandfather's on the roof flying his pigeons, and knowing this is my neighborhood." When someone from the neighborhood would pass by CBGB, they'd be like "Hey Vinnie!" I was the Italian kid who used to hang out in front of CBGB. That was my thing.

ARTHUR SMILIOS: CBGB was the most comfortable and lovable dump and I miss it. Its demise is pretty much a microcosm of the Lower East Side I knew, growing up. Gentrification and synthetic faux culture have replaced the organic grit that made the neighborhood—and city, for that matter—so special. The horror of the successive big-business fascists, Giuliani and Bloomberg, has made this place into New Disney City. You could never have had what we had in the 1980s. CBGB reeked of sweat, stale beer, cigarettes, blood, and general filth. It was the cathedral of punk and hardcore.

JOHN JOSEPH: God bless Hilly's soul. He really needs to get the real acknowledgment for really helping this scene by giving us a home. For all the people out there now who are just wearing the CBGB T-shirts, they don't know nothing. It's just a T-shirt to them. They think they're cool by wearing it. It has a much deeper meaning to me and the rest of us in New York. That was our spot, and it was essential to making the whole shit happen. I give major props to Hilly. His true story really needs to be told. What he did for the NYHC scene, that's what I hope motherfuckers really remember.

The classic Victim in Pain *line-up of Agnostic Front* PHOTOS BY GARY TSE TSE FLY

27. AGNOSTIC FRONT: VICTIM IN PAIN

PARRIS MAYHEW: Sometimes you see a painting on a wall, and it's a painting of a duck. You're like, "Wow! That's the best painting of a duck I've ever seen! This guy really knows how to paint a duck!" Then you meet the artist, but he says, "Yeah, but when I sat down, I started to draw a horse." I think what happened in New York with hardcore was people kept trying to draw this horse, and it took us a while, but we finally drew the best fuckin' duck anyone had ever seen! *Victim in Pain* is a fuckin' hell of a duck!

PETE KOLLER: If you listen to *Victim in Pain*, it's a great record. But if you're a musician—which I am not!—you will say, "These guys can't play! The guitar is out of tune!" When I heard that, I said, "I can do this. Vinnie Stigma can play guitar? Then I can too!"

ROGER MIRET: *Victim in Pain* was my biggest accomplishment. There was something magical with that record.

DON FURY: Agnostic Front was ready to record *Victim in Pain* but had no cash to do it. I said if they could pay to rent a sixteen-track tape deck for a week, I'd do the record at Spring Street for free. So that's what we did. Agnostic Front booked a benefit for the record at CBGB. They invited Balls, an art/punk band I was playing bass with, onto the matinee. We were worried about that, but by the second song kids were moshing and fighting. We figured we were fine.

JOHN PORCELLY: The second show I saw at CBGB was the famous Agnostic Front/Skinhead Youth/Death Before Dishonor show where Don Fury's band Balls opened. What a fucking show that was! Agnostic Front was incredible. Eighty percent of the crowd was skinheads. There was such a powerful scene. Raybeez was the singer of Skinhead Youth, and he was saying all this crazy crap. I was not in Westchester anymore.

VINNIE STIGMA: *Victim in Pain* was recorded in one take on sixteen tracks, and it was done in my neighborhood. Earlier that day, I was flying pigeons with my grandfather, and then I went to go play hardcore. That means so much to me that I recorded my first records in my neighborhood. We recorded *Victim in Pain* on April 16, the day after taxes. The whole thing was symbolic. Everything about *Victim in Pain* is symbolic.

DON FURY: We got the tape deck, set it up, and recorded *Victim in Pain* in three days. Roger sang the vocals right behind the door of the control room—and almost all the vocals on *Victim In Pain* are live. I spent four days mixing, then the tape deck had to go. It took a while for the record to be pressed. Rat Cage Records did the first release. Finally, the record went to be mastered for vinyl, and we went along. One sweltering summer day in midtown Manhattan, we all went to Frankford/Wayne Mastering Labs in midtown: skinheads Stigma and Roger—both covered in tats; Dave Rat Cage, wearing a dress; and me with pink hair and my two little kids in tow. New Yorkers don't usually pay attention to anything. Everybody stopped to look.

ROGER MIRET: *Victim in Pain* came out in 1984. I remember it was snowing. I was working, and I went to Rat Cage and bought a copy. To this day, I always buy my own records.

VINNIE STIGMA: I still live at the same address printed inside the gatefold sleeve. If the FBI wants me, they can come right to my door! I didn't do nothin' wrong anyway!

HOWIE ABRAMS: Album covers were a big deal for me, so to see certain covers under somebody's arm in Bleecker Bob's had an effect on me. There were a couple of New York bands whose artwork I noticed. One of the first was Agnostic Front's *Victim in Pain*. It's a pretty startling, striking album cover. When you first see it, you're confused: "Am I supposed to be offended by that? Is there a message I should be absorbing from this?"

MATT WARNKE: I went to Rat Cage Records when it was a store, because we got the address from an ad for *Victim in Pain* in *Maximum Rocknroll*. I remember walking in and being greeted by Dave Rat Cage in a dress. *Victim in Pain* was the record that initially made the biggest impact on us as far as defining and characterizing the New York sound. The production, the tones, the imperfection, the urgency, and the relevancy all transcended. I started loving rock 'n' roll at the age of nine—the Stones, the Doors, new wave, and punk—but this record was here and now. I will say the same about all of the early

hardcore: Minor Threat, Black Flag, Circle Jerks, and Dead Kennedys. But knowing Agnostic Front were a New York band, and just having the experience of walking in and buying their record from the source, made it feel more immediate. Also, just as California bands incorporate their living and breathing into their output, whether it's the Beach Boys or the Circle Jerks, there is some inexorable, just-out-of-reach, undefined, unspoken, yet understood element to regional sounds and bands. New York is perfectly captured on *Victim in Pain*.

ALEX BROWN: When I lived in Iowa, I had the first Agnostic Front LP, *Victim in Pain*, and I was fascinated by it. The Nazi imagery, the gatefold sleeve with that iconic image of tattooed tough guys rocking out, and even the Rat Cage logo and graphics had a New York City attitude. The music was amazing as well, a blur, a rapid-fire assault on the normalcy vibe, a cry for something different, something new, raw, and of the streets.

DAVE SCOTT: After *Victim in Pain* came out, there was so much shit being put upon Agnostic Front and the whole New York scene by Tim Yohannon at *Maximum Rocknroll*. Everyone assumed Agnostic Front were Nazi skinheads, and that all their shows were just violence, violence, and violence. I knew the guys in A.F.; I was the one who got them the initial interview for *Maximum Rocknroll* to clear the air. I kept telling Tim Yohannon they were not like that. Some people who went to their shows were pretty damn stupid, but the band didn't condone them. People were really buying into the bogeyman thing. I knew Roger, and he was a very sweet guy. For him to be portrayed as some crazy Nazi was ridiculous—he was Cuban!

ROB KABULA: I think Tim Yohannon had a different mind-set. He was an older guy, a hippie who latched onto punk and tried to steer it in his direction. He didn't like what he was hearing about New York. Who knows what happened? Maybe some California kid came out to New York, went to a show, got beat up, and ran back to Tim Yohannon and told him. But there were no Nazis in New York. If anything, it was out there in California. We went out there on our first tour and saw these really organized groups of skinheads who were into that stuff. Maybe he saw that and just projected that onto what he thought of New York.

DANNY LILKER (BASSIST, ANTHRAX, NUCLEAR ASSAULT, S.O.D.): New York is a coarse town. We weren't from San Francisco, where it's super PC, and everyone is trying to outdo each other with their righteousness and telling everyone else what to eat. New York is a rougher place. Sometimes things might have been more tolerated because we were not caught up in being as PC as possible.

GARY TSE TSE FLY: By 1984, in the hardcore scene, there were still people talking about anarchy, and getting the U.S. out of El Salvador. People on the New York scene were saying, "We don't have enough information about fucking El Salvador to write a whole album about it. I'm going to write a song about what I'm experiencing." People were living on the Lower East Side in squats and writing about that. There was a disconnection with what was going on in the rest of the country.

I certainly sympathized with the New York hardcore point of view. I came from a communist country. I was born in Russia. When I came to the U.S. in 1981, I couldn't get along until I found the hardcore scene. But I couldn't relate to someone calling America fascist. That idea was so removed from reality. In the first issue of my fanzine, I wrote, "You can't just yell, 'U.S.A. out of Nicaragua,' because Russia is just going to move in!" Maybe if I was born in America, I would have taken the more leftist side. But coming from a communist country, I couldn't grasp it. So I thought all the New York bands were realistic. Their heads weren't in the clouds. They wanted to sing about humanity. They wanted to talk about their friends and their struggles.

JOHN PORCELLY: As far as *Maximum Rocknroll* and Agnostic Front goes, I used to tell Tim Yohannon what great guys they were. He would never believe

Roger Miret KEN SALERNO

me. To say Agnostic Front were a bunch of Nazis in a skinhead gang was ridiculous. I was there, and no one united NYHC like Roger Miret. At all of those early shows, Roger would be up there saying, "Punks and skins unite! We're all misfits and we have to look out for each other!" *Maximum Rock-nroll* slammed *Victim in Pain* because of the cover—meanwhile, look at the lyrics! "United and strong / Blacks and whites / United and strong / Punks and skins!" They really got an unfair thing from *Maximum Rocknroll*—it was fucked up.

ROGER MIRET: The original photo that was supposed to be the cover of *Victim in Pain* was this picture of me with the mic on top of a bunch of people at a show. At the last minute I changed it, because I saw this war book. I saw that photo that became the cover, and I thought it was incredible. Dave Parsons thought it was great too. It was very controversial, but it was what we wanted. The true test was one day at Rat Cage Records when this Hasidic Jew came in. He was going through all the record bins. He saw *Victim in Pain*, picked it up, and looked at it. I was like, "Oh man, what is this guy going to say?" He went up to Dave and said, "This is great! Everybody should see this picture as a reminder of what happened." Meanwhile, everyone was pegging us as Nazi skinheads.

from top left: HR presides ...rains pit action at CBGB ... Frontline diver at CBGB ... The tradition continues ...'80s KEN SALERNO; *Original ...ront vocalist John Watson ...al at an MDC show at the ...unge.* RANDY UNDERWOOD

28. SKANK YOURSELF TO DEATH

WALTER SCHREIFELS: There was a certain amount of self-assuredness to New York that could be confused with machismo, but it's just that New York hardcore had way better mosh parts. No one else could have as good mosh parts as New York.

ALEXA POLI-SCHEIGERT: We had mosh breaks in New York, and it made the dancing harder. It was different. It wasn't just fast thrash like Boston.

WALTER SCHREIFELS: We just had more moshing going on. CBGB was like the Madison Square Garden of mosh. In New York, you didn't have to front a band. You could just mosh and get appreciation and respect.

RAY CAPPO: By the way, *mosh* was a word only used in New York. Anyone out of New York wouldn't know what you were talking about.

JACK FLANAGAN: The word *mosh* was first used by the Mob at a show with SS Decontrol and the Mob at A7. The Bad Brains used the word *mash* in the Jamaican term. When we played at A7, one of the Boston kids said—with his thick Boston accent—"Mash it up." Because of his accent, it sounded like "mosh." We have it on tape, but it's so low you can barely hear it. After this kid said this, I said, "Well, I guess we're going to have to 'mosh' it up"—just making fun of his accent. That's where "mosh it up" came from, my hand to God! It just stuck. Ralphie kept saying, "Mosh it up, man!" We would be like, "Ya gonna mosh?" "Oh yeah, it's gonna be a total mosh!" I'm trying to be as humble as possible, and people will contest it, but that's what I remember.

KEVIN CROWLEY: We used to go to McGrills in the Bronx, the place where break dancing first started. We'd go there as skinheads and hang out while these guys did rap. This is when break dancing was pseudo-fighting. They

Going for a dive during an Outcrowd set GREG LICHT

would kind of go up against each other. Nobody ever bothered us.

JIMMY G: In other parts of our neighborhood, guys were break-dancing against each other; we were moshing against each other. It was all about who had the most style, as opposed to today, where it's just picking up change and karate kicking. It was all about trying to keep dancing, while still blasting into someone from D.C. or Boston, and all about who had the hardest pit for their town's band. It was like supporting your city's hockey team or something.

JESSE MALIN: Some of our guys—like James Kontra—they hung pretty tough. That guy, you probably couldn't take down with an army.

JAMES KONTRA: The summer of 1981 was probably the most intense period of my life. I ran off from Brooklyn with my girlfriend Micki, and then she broke up with me for smoking pot. Then I met up with John Bloodclot. We ran into one another on the dance floor at Irving Plaza at a Bad Brains show. He had a shaved head. He was AWOL from the navy, and he had a chain around his neck with an iron cross on it. Me and John started bumping heads on the dance floor. He skanked pretty hard, as did I. We got into a little competition there. BANG! BANG! BANG! We almost went at it, and then Lisa, my girlfriend for five years, got in the middle and said, "John let me introduce you to James, and James let me introduce you to John. John's my friend from D.C., and James is the coolest dude here in New York, and you boys should be friends." So we just went off on the whole fucking dance floor, and started taking niggas out.

KEVIN CROWLEY: The pits could get crazy, but no one was sitting there waiting to do something to someone. If some jerk-off was standing on the sidelines punching people, that was the guy who ended up getting beat up.

MIKE JUDGE: Back then, it seemed that it was violent because it was physical, but it was still dancing.

RUSS ISLAY: Usually, everything went smoothly. There would be some fights on the dance floor, but they would get broken up pretty quickly. If you were an asshole who didn't go by the rules, you would get pushed out; I mean, pushed out to the point where you wouldn't want to come back again.

GARY TSE TSE FLY: In 1984, there was some misconception that people were getting beat up at shows in New York. There was all this back-and-forth going on in the letters section of *Maximum Rocknroll*. I wrote a letter that was published in *Maximum Rocknroll*, and I said, "Look, I'm a foreigner with spiky hair, and I go to the matinees every week and I never have a problem. If you're some college kid who shows up drunk and starts punching people because you think that's what happens here, you're going to get your ass kicked."

JOHN PORCELLY: The only warning I ever got was the very first time I went to CBGB. I think the Mob was playing. It was a small show, with not many people there. I didn't know how to mosh that well, and somebody punched me in the back of the head. I just thought it was an elbow or something, so I didn't even think about it. But then again, I got pounded in the back of the head. And again and again and again. I turned around, and there was Jimmy G with construction gloves on, and he cocked back his fist and looked at me. But I got it—it was a warning: "Hey, you don't know how it is here. You're dancing like a fucking madman." He didn't have to say anything; I just understood. It's not my home, it was his home, and he was warning me that I better chill out. I stepped back and watched and realized people weren't just running into each other—they were actually dancing. I respected Jimmy G for that. He could have kicked my ass!

DAVE SCOTT: One time at A7, some guy sucker punched me while I was on the dance floor. I went up to him. "What the fuck, dude? What's your problem?" And Jimmy G kept repeating, "You don't want to fuck with that guy." But he fuckin' hit me! Jimmy was like, "The dude is in one of the neighborhood drug gangs, and he has a machete in his back pocket." That was all he needed to say. You can be as tough as you want, but you're still a sixteen-year-old douche bag from suburbia. This other guy was in his own neighborhood.

MIKE JUDGE: The way John Watson did it and Diego did it and Jimmy did it and Harley did it, there was style. Today, it just looks like a big fucking fight to me. Guys like Diego had style, but he would crush you when he rammed into you. Jimmy had this thing where, out of nowhere, he'd bend down and go straight back.

KEVIN CROWLEY: Everybody did their own thing. John Watson from Agnostic Front always had really good flair when he was out in the pit. It was more about feeling the music and just the movement. It was just so cool to go apeshit until you couldn't breathe anymore. My style was flailing fists. You couldn't dance like that at a school dance—they'd arrest you!

JOHN PORCELLY: John Watson invented the circle pit, for God's sake! Seriously, he was one of the first people to mosh instead of slam, and his style is pretty much the blueprint for what became NYHC style of pitting.

JOHN WATSON: I've never personally claimed that, but I've heard others say that. I do know that I was very slim when I was younger. During one of our earlier Agnostic Front shows, I jumped into the pit. Back then, it was a frenetic pit of elbows and boots flying around, so I started doing a little skank around the outskirts. After a while, some other guys started following me around, and it just grew from there. After a while, Harley started scolding me, saying, "What is this circle shit now at every show?"

WALTER SCHREIFELS: One of the hardest dancers was Jay Surface from Krakdown. I remember going to a show at the Ritz and seeing Jason mosh, and thinking he was one of the scariest fucking dudes I'd ever seen in my life. Eventually I became friends with him and he's a really sweet guy. He's probably beaten the fucking shit out of people who don't feel the same way, but I think he embodied NYHC and that was cool.

JOHN PORCELLY: Jason Krakdown. If he was in the pit, you were leaving with bruises. He gets points for sheer brutality.

ALEXA POLI-SCHEIBERT: We danced harder and crazier. There was a lot of ballet to it. Carl the Mosher who just died, he was incredible. Harley was incredible. It was like ballet to me. It was amazing. You weren't just flailing your arms, which the metal kids did later on. We had style and it was unique. You see kids now and they can't do it. I go to shows now and see how they dance and they can't do it. What they're doing is an echo, but it's a weak one.

From top: *NYHC legends Billy Psycho and Tommy Carroll starting up the NYHC pit* GARY TSE TSE FLY;
Late '80s NYHC aggression KEN SALERNO

New York Krishna-core:
Shelter KEN SALERNO

NIRVANA presents:
"ROCK AGAINST MAYA"
(A FREE ROCK CONCERT
IN TOMPKINS SQ. PARK)
FEATURING
IN ORDER OF APPEARANCE:
VIRUS - M.O.I. 12-12:30
MURPHY'S LAW 12:30-1
CAUSE FOR ALARM 1-1:30
FRONT LINE 1:30-2
ANTIDOTE 2-2:30
SOVIET SEX 2:30-3
REAGAN YOUTH 3-3:30
THE MOB 3:30-4
KRAUT 4-4:30
AND SPECIAL GUESTS: FOOD FOR LIFE
SATURDAY-JUNE 18TH 12-5 P.M.
TOMPKINS SQ. PARK (AVE. A & ST. MARKS PL.)

29. HARE KRISHNA:
IN SEARCH OF...

STEVE POSS: The singer of Hi Sheriffs of Blue was the first guy to become Krishna. I remember he had a beard, and next he had a robe. I was like, "Holy shit!"

KEITH BURKHARDT: It came in through John Joseph. I think everybody can trace it back to him.

JOHN WATSON: One night outside of A7, I saw John Joseph crossing the street wearing flip-flops, shorts, and an Indian devotional–type shirt. Now, in 1983, no one wore flip-flops on Avenue A, *ever*. Bloodclot steps up and says, "Hey, I just got back from Hawaii, you want to hit a spliff?" I'm like, "Dude, you look like a freak! I heard you joined some cult!" He just laughed, and we went into Tompkins Square Park. After one or two hours of conversation, my whole life's paradigm went on a complete tangent. From that day on, I've never eaten meat again. I've traveled on a pilgrimage to India, and I raised my kids as Krishnas. That was some spliff—to say the least!

LOUIE RIVERA: Johnny Joseph used to hang out with this kid Tomas. Tomas was a beautiful kid. He just had a beautiful spirit. He was like a ray of light. He just had a really nice aura to him. Never had anything negative to say about anything. He'd go up and hug a tree. If he could stop the death of a mosquito, he would, you know what I mean? So him and Johnny Joseph, they planted the seed. John used to have the books in the studio. He used to go to the temple on Sundays. One Sunday, John invited me out to Brooklyn with him. Next thing I know, I'm in the temple eating free food, getting exposed, and getting my feet wet.

JOHN JOSEPH: I didn't bring nothing into the scene. I went to the temple be- cause shit fell apart between me and the Bad Brains. They wanted to just be around Rastas. They hooked up with this guy who would bring fucking tapes of Farrakhan into the van and play them. I put my life on the line for the Bad Brains, and then this motherfucker is coming in and playing these tapes of Farrakhan talking about how the white man is the devil. This guy tried to influence the Bad Brains to stop playing punk rock. I had to get away from that element. They went and toured the West Coast and left me behind. I needed to go on my own journey. I was already going to yoga centers, so I stopped smoking weed and got on this spiritual kick. When I came out of the temple, I wasn't trying to spread Hare Krishna to anybody. It was just something everybody wanted to know about, so I would tell them. They would be intrigued. Then it would be something like, "Yo, can you get me a book?" That's how it went down.

KEITH BURKHARDT: I was always a spiritual person, in the sense that I felt there has to be something bigger behind this whole creation. I wasn't a religious person. I couldn't connect to the Bible or the typical religious experiences you would have being raised in a Catholic family in New Jersey. I was used to Reverend O'Flaherty trying to scare everyone. I was always asking John Joseph to come see Cause for Alarm, but he was always in bed by nine o'clock at night. One night he came out to see us at A7. It was January or February. We went outside, smoked a joint, and we started talking about spiritual stuff. He started talking about Krishna consciousness. I was all ears. That was the first night I heard the name Krishna. He was very conscious of the fact that here we were in 1982, outside of A7, and he was talking about Hare Krishnas. Back then, it was seen as wacky and cultish.

He was talking in a very roundabout way, but John was always very articulate and very intelligent. He was very knowledgeable about Krishna consciousness, even back then. I wasn't shocked at all. A couple of days later, I got a copy of the book *The Science of Self-Realization*, and that made a really big impression on me. So I went to the temple in downtown Brooklyn with John, and that was wild. To me, that was as wild and awesome and liberating as going to A7 for the first time. Taking part in those big kirtans, eating the food, chanting, and listening to the spiritual masters blew my mind.

LOUIE RIVERA: Within six months or less than a year of me first going to a temple with John, we put together a show in Tompkins Square Park called the Rock Against Maya show. We gave out free food, and it was a pretty good lineup. I don't think we even got permission. You didn't have to go down to city hall and get a permit in 1982. You could do whatever the fuck you wanted in that park as long as the power was still on.

JOHN JOSEPH: Harley and I were living at 730 East Ninth and talking philosophy every day. He went vegetarian and started seeing it was deep.

KEITH BURKHARDT: We used to do a lot of programs at my house. In 1983, I was living on West Twenty-Second Street with this girl Angelica that I would eventually marry and have two kids with. She ended up going Krishna. Then Harley ended up there. This guy Rich Stig became a devotee, and slowly we had this little group of devotees.

JOHN PORCELLY: I was at CBGB when all the Hare Krishnas started giving out free food. I had no idea anyone in hardcore had any affiliation with Hare Krishna. I didn't even know what Hare Krishna was! All I knew was what I saw on TV, that it was a cult and all that. So it was weird to come into CBGB and see people in robes and shaved heads giving out vegetarian food.

STEVE POSS: Krishna saved a lot of peoples' lives. These were street kids. They gave out free dinner on Sunday nights to people who were hungry. Some people went to get free dinner and really got into it, and then some people went to get free dinner just to get a free dinner. My mother would kill me before she would let me become a Krishna. It wasn't my thing.

LOUIE RIVERA: Krishna was more accepted in the New York hardcore scene than in any other place at the time, simply because New York includes people from all walks of life. You're just going to have people who are more accepting. I would think people into punk would be more into an alternative frame of thought like that. The people in punk who weren't accepting of it just weren't doing the research. There's always fear of the unknown in all cultures.

KEITH BURKHARDT: Those were very magical times with me and John, Harley, Rich Stig, and John Watson going to that temple. John and I had the same guru. He was a really intelligent guy who would get your head spinning. It resonated with me, and that was the beginning of my spiritual life.

JOHN PORCELLY: When the first singer for the Cro-Mags, Eric Casanova, moved into the Krishna temple, I used to see him selling books on Broadway. Every time he offered me a book, I would buy it and read it. That was very strange; the Krishnas had this association with peace, love, and harmony, and then you had people from the Cro-Mags endorsing it. There were guys in that band who would hit you with a bike lock! But I was always into hearing people speak when they were talking about going above and beyond the idea of mundane living.

Much later on in the 1980s, a huge thing for me was getting a job at Prana Foods, the health food store on First Avenue. Little did I know that everyone there was a devotee. Vinnie from the Unsane worked there, and he was a Hare Krishna! He always was talking about not living your life materialistically, and that we are the soul, not the body. I thought he was the smartest guy I ever met! John Watson would come to Prana, and he was a deep guy. Bliss from Antidote would come in. I found myself surrounded by people who were able to present Krishna consciousness in a very intellectual yet real way, so it made sense to me. All of this eventually led to me becoming a devotee and joining Ray Cappo in Shelter in the 1990s.

JOHN JOSEPH: I wasn't going out trying to be like Shelter, wearing Krishna robes onstage. Like I've always said, Shelter would hit you with a flower, the Cro-Mags would hit you with a fuckin' baseball bat. The Cro-Mags was not Shelter. We didn't try to inject Hare Krishna like everybody tries to say.

Bassist Harley Flanagan at an early Cro-Mags gig at CBGB. Note Cavity Creeps tag on the P.A! GARY TSE TSE FLY

The Cro-Mags in 1987 PHOTOS BY KEN SALERNO

30. THE CRO-MAGS: EVERYBODY'S GONNA DIE

MIKE JUDGE: I remember seeing Cro-Mags as a tag all over the city for years. I knew Harley from the beginning. He was there from day one. But the band didn't take off until later in the '80s.

GAVIN VAN VLACK: At the time, you had to be down with the Cro-Mags. It was like if you weren't down with them, you weren't going to live long.

PETE KOLLER: The Cro-Mags is what really sucked you in. They were great, like Agnostic Front, but could play much better and they had a better sound—a powerful, mean sound.

PARRIS MAYHEW: One day I was at school, and I overheard this kid say he auditioned for the Mad. So I went out that night to Max's looking for Screaming Mad George and couldn't find him. I found him about a week later, playing bass for Butch Lust and the Hypocrites. After the gig I came up to him and said I heard the Mad was looking for a bass player. George said they already got somebody, so I said, "But I'm better than him!" We went over to George's house and jammed a little bit. He said he agreed with me! So I ended up playing bass for Irrational, which the Mad had transitioned into, for about a month. I played George the riff that would become "World Peace," and he told me to stop playing. "I write all the music," he said. So I quit.

While I was putting up flyers around Avenue A near 171A to start a new band, Paul Dordal and Harley came walking down the street. Harley saw the flyer and asked Paul why didn't he start a band with me. Paul's like, "I'm not good enough to play with Parris, he plays like Rush." Harley was like, "Oh yeah?"

Harley brought me down to 171A. I plugged into Denise Mercedes' amp and I played "World Peace," and probably "Do Unto Others" and "Life of My Own." Harley and Denise started talking about me like I wasn't in the room.

She was like "Where did you find this kid? I've seen him hanging out at our shows, but I didn't know he played!"

PAUL BEARER: Harley had so many fuckin' bands going on, like the Disco Smoothies. Cro-Mags was just a name for a while before they played.

MIKE JUDGE: I remember being outside of Apartment X and Harley had just come back from Canada. He was showing everyone his chest tattoo. He said he recorded a demo when he was out on the West Coast, with him playing everything. He said he was going to call it *Here's to the Ink in Ya*. He let us all hear it, and a lot of those songs I heard much later as Cro-Mags songs.

JOHN JOSEPH: The original Cro-Mags was Dave Hahn, who was the Bad Brains' manager, on drums. The guitar player was Dave Stein from Even Worse, and then me and Harley. We were all hanging out at 171A. Mugger came up with the name. Harley was actually going to try to do the band with Mugger, but that was all beer-drinking, stupid shit-talking. Nothing ever came of that.

I went and lived in ashrams in Puerto Rico and Hawaii for a little while, and when I came back I saw Harley in the park. He said, "We got the band back together." Harley wanted me back in the band, but Kevin Mayhew wanted Roger Miret to sing. Both of us had to audition.

STEVE POSS: I saw the Cro-Mags upstairs at 171A when it was Dave Hahn playing drums and Dave Stein playing guitar, but those were practices. Years later, I saw the Cro-Mags at CBGB, and it was a totally different version of the band.

PARRIS MAYHEW: The reason it took so long for things to come together for the Cro-Mags is because Harley would see some kid with a shaved head and think, "This kid is hard, this kid is tough. Let's bring him into the band." Then I would end up tolerating some horrible, talentless person for however long it took Harley to realize that the guy had no talent.

You know, underneath his façade and front and street thing, Harley below all that is a real artist. Even though he was trying to form this band of tough guys, he had very little tolerance for people who had genuine power; this parade of knuckleheads went by the wayside quickly. We had this guy Steve in the band. Harley dressed him up appropriately. He put boots on him, with a white shirt and suspenders and shorter pants, and dressed him up like a skinhead. Obviously, I was never a skinhead like that. He would make recommendations to me, but he would dress up the other recruits in the way he wanted. One day we went to a CBGB matinee, and this guy Steve was walking around like a tough guy and he mouthed off to Dito Montiel. Dito proceeded to annihilate this kid in a way I had never seen in my life. It was merciless. There was one point where this Steve guy crawled under a van, and Dito pulled him out by his ankles and continued to beat him. Harley just stood there and watched the whole thing; so did the other two hundred people who were there for the matinee. When Dito was done with him, the guy came up to Harley. Harley just turned his back on him and we never saw him again. There were quite a few people like that, so it took a long, long time to get a solid band together.

TODD YOUTH: A lot of people don't know that some early Cro-Mags rehearsals were Harley on drums, me on bass, Kevin on guitar, and Eric Casanova on vocals. Roger Miret tried out to sing at one point.

PARRIS MAYHEW: The first time we got up onstage Eric Casanova sang, Roger Miret played bass, I played guitar, and Harley played drums. That was the first Cro-Mags gig, if you want to call it that. I think we played five songs. After that, we thought, "Okay, Eric is our singer." Then we wanted to get rid of Eric because when he was sixteen years old, he got a twenty-four-year-old girl pregnant. He wanted to bring the baby on tour.

JOHN JOSEPH: I don't try to dis Eric, because he's had his problems over the years, but, c'mon man—he had songs like "Kill the Ayatollah." I was at the two shows that he sang for the Cro-Mags at CBGB. He didn't even know the words. Eric would be standing there not knowing what to do, and Harley would be screaming at him onstage. He kicked him in the ass. After the second show, they fired him.

PARRIS MAYHEW: We spent a lot of time writing songs. In the interim, we would look at other bands and wonder who we could steal. We stole Mackie Jayson from Frontline to play drums, and we stole John from Bloodclot! to sing.

JOHN JOSEPH: Bloodclot! was all the Bad Brains roadies: Jerry Williams, who did sound; Alvin Robertson, who was the tech for the guitars; myself; and this guy Teddy Horowitz. We called it Bloodclot! because when the Bad Brains first got into Rastafari, every time something went wrong onstage they were like, "Blood clot, fix the blood clot!" Blood clot this and blood clot that. So we thought it would be funny if we called the band Bloodclot!.

Flyers for John Joseph's pre-Cro-Mags band Bloodclot

GARY TSE TSE FLY: I remember coming into a CBGB matinee on a hot day. A band came on named Mode of Ignorance that I had never heard of. John Joseph was on vocals, Harley on drums, Nunzio from Antidote on guitar, and this guy everybody knew named Elroy on bass. That was the beginning of the Cro-Mags. You could see the future. John was and still is an awesome front man. He was doing that pacing-back-and-forth shit. Harley had this intensity. A few months later, Harley and John came in as the Cro-Mags. I had been telling people who didn't see M.O.I. how great they were, and when they were blown away by the Cro-Mags, I was like, "See? See? I told you bitches!"

MIKE JUDGE: M.O.I. are still one of the most incredible bands I saw back then.

PARRIS MAYHEW: The band was Todd Youth playing bass, Harley playing drums, and I was playing guitar. John was always hanging around, and I said, "John, why don't you grab the mic?" John started jumping off the drum riser and going off like the Tasmanian devil that he is. He was performing as if we were at the Ritz. John came into the band and immediately made his mark. He wrote the lyrics to "Malfunction" and "We Gotta Know." Great stuff.

TODD YOUTH: When John started singing for them is when they really started to gain some traction.

JOHN PORCELLY: Violent Children played with the Cro-Mags, and I can never forget that. I walked into CBGB for sound check, and there was Harley, dressed head to toe in black with his head shaved to the bone. He was the only one in the club. He was walking around the dance floor of CBGB wearing that old, weird acoustic bass. One hand was on the bass neck. In the other hand, he had this leg of a table with a big screw sticking out of it. Harley always had interesting weapons. It was always an eight ball in a sock, or a padlock in a handkerchief, or a table leg. When they played, it was just incredible. When they got to that point in the song "Hard Times" where they shout "Cro-Mags! Skinheads!" it made you want to be a skinhead.

TODD YOUTH: Their 1985 demo was just amazing. You just knew it was going to be as important as the Bad Brains ROIR cassette.

JOHN JOSEPH: Jerry Williams' brother worked at a studio on Park Avenue South, and Jerry hooked up the recording of that fucking demo for us. Me and Parris paid for it. I was working as a bike messenger. Parris' father owned a record label in Tennessee, and we got him to print up the cassettes.

JOHN PORCELLY: Harley told me, "Our demo tape is out. Go get it at Free Being Records, I just sold them a whole bunch." I didn't even walk, I fuckin' ran down to Free Being and bought that demo tape. It was the holy grail. You finally could hear all this stuff outside of a show. I like the sound of that Cro-Mags demo even more than the first record, *Age of Quarrel*. Mackie's drums are so up-front in the mix. Violent Children played with them again somewhere in Jersey, with Bedlam, at a weird place with no stage. I knew all the Cro-Mags songs this time, and it was great.

PETE KOLLER: I saw them once where there weren't that many people at the show, and there was no P.A., so John sang through a bullhorn. The shit was crazy! That's *hardcore*. You wouldn't see any other shit where someone would just be like, "No PA? Well, I guess I'll just scream through this bullhorn!" The sad thing is, if you didn't see it then, you'll never see it now. That was real.

GARY TSE TSE FLY: I think the Cro-Mags were the line in the sand. There was this change in the scene where everybody liked M.D.C. and the Dead Kennedys, and then they said, "We're going to support the local bands." They were huge innovators, lyrics-wise and appearance-wise. They were literally something new happening in NYHC.

DREW STONE: The New York scene was so fractured and dispersed that no one could get behind a band. It wasn't until the first wave subsided that people could get behind something like the Cro-Mags. When they finally did get it together, they became a rallying point. They were like an all-star band. I remember them playing "Show You No Mercy" at CB's and it was intense and violent and delivered with such conviction. They talked the talk and they walked the walk and it came through in their music. I remember really feeling it.

PARRIS MAYHEW: Eventually, we stole Doug Holland from Kraut to play second guitar.

DOUG HOLLAND: Kraut was a very influential band that started the post-punk genre, but then the Cro-Mags did the ultimate crunch and turned punk rock into hard metal. There were no bands doing that. We were the ones who broke that open.

JOHN JOSEPH: I had my personal experiences from life; being on the streets, being locked up, and being in abusive foster homes. I was fighting. I was shot and stabbed, and that's what came out. We sang about street justice and survival on the streets because that shit was for real. That shit was a way to express ourselves and get out that angst. It was real. It wasn't some hypothetical bullshit. That's the thing about the Cro-Mags. Harley and I were out there roughing it. That's why we called the first album *Age of Quarrel*! The age of quarrel means Kali Yuga, the iron age of quarrel and hypocrisy.

TIM CHUNKS: When the Cro-Mags *Age of Quarrel* record came out, it became apparent that it was going to be huge. This isn't Cro-Mags just playing CB's anymore. This wasn't a DIY thing. This was a record on a real record label. I remember thinking, "The Cro-Mags are going to play Madison Square Garden." They were one of the few bands I believed were going to support themselves off of their music. When that record came out, I thought those guys would never have to work again. And that record was scary! If you went to the store, picked that record up, and put it on, you either said, "This is crazy! This is way too scary for me," or you said, "I understand this frustration and this fear and I'm in it. I can relate to this."

WALTER SCHREIFELS: The Cro-Mags were such a great band, and they went into this other stratosphere very quickly. Hardcore was a place where you could get massively popular to a limited amount of people, and I think they naturally wanted to expand. The Cro-Mags were doing shit that was way cooler than anybody at that time. I'd say they were even better than Metallica at that time, so it was natural for them to want to take it to the next level and tour with Motörhead and play to great crowds.

DOUG HOLLAND: We played with Venom in Chicago, and the promoter made this poster with the big horns and the backwards star; very demonic. Before we went on, they announced us: "From New York City . . . skinheads gone metal mad . . . the Cro-Mags!" The lights went down, and all of a sudden I hear Harley yell, "My bass light is out." So we're on stage in the dark, and

Harley Flanagan, Cro-Mags
KEN SALERNO

there's all these headbangers along the front. All of a sudden, I started to hear chanting, and it got loud: "What the fuck? Skinheads suck!" The whole house started chanting it. I stood still behind my amplifier. Less than two minutes later, I hear Harley go, "All right, my light is on now." We went into "We Gotta Know," the lights came on, and in one chord we sold that whole audience. They were all headbanging to the music. They had never heard anything of that caliber, with that energy, and they dug it. They'd never seen slam dancing done like that before. There might have been fifteen die-hard Cro-Mags fans who had to show these people how to dance. That was a lot of fun, man. That night so many people came up to the band saying we gave them their money's worth. They didn't even want to stick around for Venom.

JOHN JOSEPH: Listen, we had a great time in the early run. Everybody was cool. But when the rock-star attitude started kicking in with those guys, that's when I realized I didn't sign on for this. I'm not in here trying to be no rock star. It's about keeping it real with the people who are coming to see your shows and having a good time. Not starting shit with people and trying to be some fake-ass rock star. That was when I was like, "Yo, that's it. I quit." I left right before they recorded *Best Wishes*.

Listen to *Age of Quarrel* and then listen to *Best Wishes*. That's not a fuckin' progression. That was a conscious choice to try to be some fake rock stars. There are no elements of Sabbath or the Bad Brains. That shit was straight-up sellout to be the next fuckin' Metallica. That's what those dudes thought they were. Between the attitudes and pissing off the punk rock people who got them there, they turned off everybody within one year's time. They had about a one-year career after I left the band.

PARRIS MAYHEW: Truthfully, as a band we were fractured. Harley and I would never recover from the rift that John manufactured between us. John saw our musical partnership as an obstacle to him dominating Harley. He had to divide and conquer. After all, *Age of Quarrel* was handed to John on a silver platter, most of the lyrics already written and vocal melodies. But when it came down to writing the second album, John was struggling. The music was simply more musical and he couldn't find a groove. Ultimately, his singing was conspicuously falling behind the band's progress. One day, after one of a dozen times John threatened to quit the band, we just stopped inviting him to rehearsals. He finally called me up and asked, "What's been going on with the band?" I said, "We have been playing all along and we have decide to go on without you." John simply said, "Okay, that's it then?" I said, "That's it." No fireworks, no fuck-yous. I was happy, and we recorded *Best Wishes* and never looked back.

It was a weird time. No unity. It's hard to crystallize that time in a sentence, because it seemed then that we were all on a launching pad, and all the guys were trying to push the others off before it took off. Of course in the end that behavior just sank the ship for all of us. It's sad and shameful to look back and see what we could have accomplished with our music if only they had cooperated.

THE CRO MAGS
CB JUNE 30th GB'S
THE MOB "AND MORE!"
HCXY

CRO·MAGS
SUNDAY MAT. JUNE 16TH

"HARD TIMES" AT CBGB'S OMFUG

CRO'S
BLEEKER
BOWERY

BENEFIT FOR CBGB'S
SUPPORT THE CBS THAT'S SUPPORTED US!
CRO-MAGS!
VIRUS · NEVERMORE
Malignant Tumor · NO REMORSE
ULTRAVIOLENCE · N.I.E.
HAPPY WORLD ·
HCXY

OVERKILL PRESENTS THE CRO-MAGS
SUNDAY MARCH 31 3PM
CRO-MAGS HCXY

SEAN '85

NO REMORSE · VIOLENT CHILDREN
AND THE UNWANTED (FROM CANADA)
At CBGB'S OMFUG
317 BOWERY

A BENEFIT FOR THE SQUATS
WITH

SCAB

REAGAN
YOUTH

Sacrilege
DOG
IRON ROCKERS

SAT. JAN. 12, 1985   8:00 TILL ??

19 WEST 21 STREET

ADMISSION: $4.00

FOR FREE

TRIP SIX

AND

NAUSEA

at midnight
show starts
Sat May 14th

AT Tin Pan Alley LOCATED ON 220 W. 49th St.

NAUSEA

AS OUR SHIPS SLOWLY
WAD OUR LIVES MAT LIKE WAX
WE TRY OUR HANDS UPON THE ROCK
AND ARE SENT TO THE FIRE

BUT YOURSELF... FREEDOM IS INTERNAL... LOOK INWARD.

WITH:
P.M.S. APPLE

CIRCLE CHAOS + MORE

CBGB OMFUG
315 Bowery (at Bleecker) (212)982-4657

SUNDAY
OCT. 26th
3:00 P.M.

31. PEACE PUNKS: FALLOUT OF OUR BEING

STEVE WISHNIA: When Reagan came in, it made the American punk scene way more political. People were complaining about being bored in the '70s, but when Reagan came in, it was like the temperature just dropped about twenty fucking degrees.

At some point, there was a split between what would be considered the peace punks—us, Reagan Youth, Heart Attack, No Thanks, A.P.P.L.E.—and the skinhead bands like Cro-Mags and Agnostic Front. Cause for Alarm straddled the gap. Chris Charucki was Stephan from False Prophets' best friend, and he roadied for us, but I felt pretty alienated by the skinhead contingent.

JESSE MALIN: During the Reagan era, we were all thinking we could get drafted and go to Central America. There was a nuclear arms race going on, and just a ton of things to sing about. After Heart Attack released our first 7-inch, *God Is Dead*, my friends and I got more into the politics and less into the partying. Heart Attack was always political in some way. We sang about the NRA in "Shotgun"; "Victim's Inquisition" was about the Holocaust. "The Last War" was about World War Three. But then we got to the third record, and we were singing about the Indians being exploited for their land. We were singing about rape and sexual abuse.

JOHNNY CARCO: Heart Attack completely changed after John Frawley quit. The sound became thin, and the tempos sped up and they got sloppy and shrill. The youthful fun was gone when the vegan-Crass-diet politics came. They became a complete bore. They lost me.

DANNY SAGE (GUITARIST, THE POSSESSED, HEART ATTACK, D-GENERATION): I was in Heart Attack for a while, but when it got too political I quit the band. I didn't want to write long manifestos that got stuffed into record sleeves. The reason I learned to play guitar was so I didn't have to do those kinds of things.

JESSE MALIN: We got real political toward the end. We got serious and went to a lot of demonstrations. Suddenly, my little group of people became a hierarchy of its own. We were fighting against the close-minded government, but we were telling people they couldn't be anarchists if they looked at porn. It went beyond telling people they weren't animal rights activists if they wore leather, and became, "You have Iggy Pop records? Well, he's sexist!" I went to St. Marks Place and sold all my rock records for money for Indian food.

LYLE HYSEN: Malin and that band got very political, and I had no patience for that. Their last 12-inch in 1984 had all these essays inside like a Crass record. That was all fine and good, but where were the tunes? Are there any songs on there as good as "Shotgun"? I just didn't understand why they had to tell the same one hundred people about how bad everything was.

JESSE MALIN: I was making a statement that the world was changing, and we were going to change with it. We were going to try to be as perfect as possible politically. We'd go out to Great Neck, Long Island, and stencil "Wealth Is a Ghetto" on a wall at a train station. We'd go down to SoHo and spray-paint a penis on some sexist shop window. We meant well. Then hardcore evolved into something more metal, more macho, and more mainstream. I liked it when it was more female-friendly and had more angst. It became a formula really quick—here's the skank part, and here's the thrash part—just real knuckleheaded, cement-head music. You had to look like this, dance like this, and sound like this. Once there was a guidebook, it lost something artistically. I gave up in 1984 and broke up the band. I felt the thing I was trying to get away from—that football mentality—had become what the hardcore matinees were now all about. The first Cro-Mags gig was the same bill as the last Heart Attack gig, and I think that says something.

ADAM NATHANSON (GUITARIST, LIFE'S BLOOD, MISTER SOFTY, BORN AGAINST): In 1986, I was at a CB's matinee, and the singer of the band playing said, "Yo, I was Washington Square Park the other day, and this guy was saying all this stuff about how America is fucked up, and he had a hammer and a sickle on his jacket. I'm not telling you what to do, but his name is Stephan and he's from the False Prophets. If you see him, you know what to do!" Everyone in the audience was like "Kill him! Kill him!" It was like a scene from *Frankenstein.*

DONNA DAMAGE: Skinhead kids liked to sneer "peace punk" at me; it wasn't meant as a compliment. The label didn't bother us at all, because I was really into peace. I was antiwar, and I was a vegetarian and all that stuff. Our band No Thanks was the first band to put a peace sign in our logo.

TODD YOUTH: The whole peace-punk political thing didn't have anything to do with our world. They were all really trying to be British peace punk bands and do the Crass-type thing. To me, it was just too much. I wasn't into that at all. In hindsight, maybe it was a reaction to the skinhead thing. Maybe the peace-punk thing was for the people who weren't tough enough to fight.

STEVE WISHNIA: Whatever I might say about the hardcore culture, at least it was one of the few places in America in the early '80s that was saying, "Fuck you, Ronald Reagan, and everything you stand for!" The 1980s converted the country to a place where everything is about money, and there's no respect for the working people. It's weird, because I was a red-diaper baby. My parents used to take me out to demonstrations when I was a kid. I'll never say you can't write a political song in the same way I'll never say you can't write a love song. Just don't make it a cliché! At that time, a lot of political music was a cliché. Whatever critical things I might say about hardcore, at least it brought that stuff into people's awareness. On the other hand, I didn't want pictures of Ronald Reagan on *my* album.

DONNA DAMAGE: I was a serious anarchist. All the lyrics I wrote were serious. I wasn't just saying things. We were living it. We'd go to all the marches, and I'd bring a lot of those politics to the shows, talking about Reagan and what was going on at the time in El Salvador and Nicaragua around 1983. We hated Reagan. We'd burn American flags onstage. We were totally radical in that sense. No Thanks were probably the first peace-punk band.

TODD YOUTH: To me, Sacrilege was the first New York peace-punk band, which is funny. One of the guys who started it was Adam Mucci, the bass player of Agnostic Front.

JAE MONROE (VOCALIST, A.P.P.L.E.): Adam Mucci was my first boyfriend. I was more into English punk stuff than American hardcore, and I think Adam got more into it when we were going out. Next thing you know, he went from being a total skinhead to looking like he was a member of Discharge.

ADAM MUCCI (BASSIST, AGNOSTIC FRONT, MURPHY'S LAW, SACRILEGE): I finished my tenure with Agnostic Front and Murphy's Law and I was ready to do something less hardcore, more English in style and sound. For me, style and sound seemed to go together. It was more of a philosophy than a sound, I thought, a style to go with the music.

VICTOR VENOM: We started Sacrilege in 1984. Adam was going through all these stages. He went from the skinhead thing to this 1982 British punk look, and that morphed into a total peace punk thing. Adam freaked out, sold all his stuff, and said he was moving to California. He took a sheet of acid, hopped on a Greyhound bus, and just left. I joined Reagan Youth and went on tour with them across America. When we got to San Francisco, Adam was out there living on rooftops. He wanted to come back to New York. When we both returned, we started Sacrilege and it progressed really fast. New York at the time was in a weird state. The skinhead thing was getting popular. When I got into the scene, it was more punk rock—hardcore punk, you know? There was nothing like us going. We weren't exactly accepted, Adam had been a skinhead in Agnostic Front, so we were tolerated, like a stepchild.

ADAM MUCCI: There was no niche for us, not hardcore, and not even what was perceived as punk. Our heroes were probably what was going on in Finland or England at the time. We had long, long spiked hair. We painted our leather jackets with logos and mottos; Discharge, Crass, and Flux of Pink Indians. We wore skinny jeans twenty years before they existed, made ourselves out of Levi's 501s. We made most of what we wore. The girls had such great looks. Roxie, Marta, and Fee used to groom us and spike our hair. We kept each other warm during the long, cold nights in unheated squats.

VICTOR VENOM (Guitarist, Reagan Youth, Sacrilege, Nausea): Clay Rice quit Sacrilege, so we got his friend Fish to sing. Adam Mucci was losing interest, and he joined Raging Slab. Then Tim Copeland and Clay moved back to Virginia Beach and that's the last I ever saw of them. Then it all fell apart and morphed into Nausea. We found out there was the UK Sacrilege and another one from Vancouver. That was one too many Sacrileges. I came up with the name Nausea. Adam was cool with it, but Tim didn't want to play in a band with a name like that. This was coming from a guy that wanted to be known as Vomit!

FREDDY ALVA (Editor, New Breed fanzine; show promoter, ABC No Rio; owner, Wardance Records; coowner Urban Style Records): Nausea was definitely a catalyst in 1985 for forging an alternative to the CBGB hardcore matinees. Their brand of highly politically charged punk had antecedents in NYC with documented groups like False Prophets and Reagan Youth, and the unknown ones like Sacrilege and Counterforce. But Nausea had a connection to the squatter movement that spoke to people who felt disconnected from the NYHC scene of the day.

*Peace punks A.P.P.L.E.
provoking a reaction*
GARY TSE TSE FLY

VICTOR VENOM: I took the good concepts of Sacrilege and used them for Nausea. This guy John Guzman; he must have been sixteen years old, and he was the biggest Sacrilege fan. He interviewed us for his fanzine, *Living Free*. When Sacrilege fell apart, I wasn't too thrilled with rejoining Reagan Youth. John was trying to start a band with Neil Robinson. John had the basics of four songs and I had four songs that I brought over from Sacrilege.

JOHN JOHN JESSE (BASSIST, NAUSEA): There needed to be a key punk band at that moment, so I knew it was my duty to make the best I could happen.

FREDDY ALVA: Within six months of Nausea's start, a separate scene had sprung up, called Squat or Rot, with their own venues and bands.

JAE MONROE: To me, the NYHC scene was already over by 1985, which is funny, since that's around when my band A.P.P.L.E. started. We filled a gap for whoever didn't want to follow along with the skinhead thing and all the fighting. People might have felt safer or more righteous being in a part of the anarcho-punk thing in New York, but we were just preaching to the converted. If anything, we gave an alternative to the people who didn't fit in with where NYHC was going.

VICTOR VENOM: When Sacrilege was around, we felt like we were alone in the wilderness. About six months after Nausea started, the whole Squat or Rot scene started. Not that we're taking credit for that, but there were a lot of people that were disenfranchised from the scene. A lot of them felt there was no place for them if they weren't a skinhead or a hardcore straight-edge person. They said, "Hey, we're not alone." Bands like Public Nuisance, A.P.P.L.E., Apostates, Insurgence, plus others all of a sudden came out of nowhere and started a scene outside of the hardcore scene.

Above photo: *Combat Records Crossover titans Nuclear Assault at CBGB in December 1985*
FRANK WHITE

32. HEAVY METAL: UNITED FORCES

PAUL BEARER: Me and my buddy Wayne were in front of CBGB, and there were some metal guys out there. We were like, "What are you long-haired cocksuckers doing here?" There was some argument, and we were going to fight them—we were going to beat them down. Billy Milano broke it up, and then he said to us, "You think old." What did that mean? Just because he liked it didn't mean we had to like it!

ALEX KINON: I remember being on Avenue A, and Billy Milano was sitting in a Camaro blasting Mötley Crüe. He was like, "One day, metal and hardcore are going to mix. Mark my words." He called it.

MICHAEL GIBBONS (GUITARIST, LEEWAY): The crossing of metal and hardcore in New York was the perfect storm. If you went out to Hermosa Beach in 1983 and had a metal band opening for the Circle Jerks, forget it. That wouldn't have worked at all. It would have been a bloodbath. But what happened in New York worked, and it spread throughout the country.

EDDIE SUTTON: Southern Californian bands at the time were either one style or the other. They had the old-style punk rock songwriting going on. But they didn't have the Reese's-peanut-butter-cup thing like the New York bands did. Out there either you grabbed a peanut butter sandwich and were metal, or you got a piece of chocolate and were punk rock. We were mixing the two, and they weren't.

MIKE BULLSHIT: There were a certain number of metal people coming into the scene around 1985 or so. If you were into metal, well, shit, you might as well be into hardcore, too.

ROB KABULA: When we got back from the first Agnostic Front tour we did by ourselves, that's when the metal stuff was beginning to happen in New York. Metalheads started coming to the shows. Record label people started checking it out. Industry people were starting to take note.

TODD YOUTH: Doug Holland was actually the first guy to play me metal. He played me Metallica's *Kill 'Em All* at that apartment he shared with Jack Rabid. I just wondered who these long-haired dudes were, trying to rip off Discharge.

EDDIE SUTTON: Sometime around 1984, *Kill 'Em All* came out. We didn't know this band was living on the roof of a rehearsal studio in Jamaica, Queens. All we knew was that when that record came out, anybody who was in a band or starting a band, whether it was hardcore or metal, said, "These are the fucking riffs I'd want in my band." *Everybody* wished they came up with that. We knew that was the direction Leeway wanted to go in.

STEVE POSS: When the metal guys came in, that's when it stopped from everybody knowing each other. It stopped being just one hundred people. It went to four hundred people, to even more. It just changed. I'm not saying it happened overnight; it took a couple of years, but one day it just felt different.

GARY TSE TSE FLY: The very first time I ever heard any metal influence come in was when Death Before Dishonor played at CBGB either in November or December of '84. Their singer, Mark Ryan, said from the stage, "Have you guys heard Metallica? They're pretty cool!" Half of CB's went "Booo!" and the other half went "Fuckin' A!" and then they did an Iron Maiden cover. I was pissed off.

MIKE JUDGE: I'd say 1984 was when the metal thing first came in. I wish I knew how it started. I'd love to go back and just change it. Our band Death Before Dishonor was listening to more metal, and we started bringing that into our band. That just seemed like the way things were going. We were listening to the first few Iron Maiden records, and we were turning into the jocks that we hated. We were listening to the music they played while they got naked in the locker room. It was a fucking weird thing. The last show we played at CB's with Agnostic Front, we actually did "Run to the Hills" as a cover. Right after that set, I left the band and left the hardcore scene for a couple years. I felt awful, like, "Goddamn, I helped this happen." Around that time, the guys from Anthrax started coming to CB's. We really tried to discourage them from coming to our shows. They already had their metal scene going on at L'Amour, so I was of the mind that those guys already had their club and scene, and they should just stay there.

LYLE HYSEN: I remember seeing Anthrax on TV. They used the word *mosh* and it totally broke my brain. How did that happen?

CRAIG SETARI: My brother originally got me into rock and metal. Then he ended up going to school with a guy named Danny Lilker, who brought over a bunch of hardcore records. Once Danny Lilker came around, things at my house went from Aerosmith records to Mob 7-inches.

DANNY LILKER: The thing that really struck us about hardcore, coming from the metal scene, was that there wasn't much ego involved. It wasn't like Overkill, with their big stage setups. There was nothing like a backstage pass. The hardcore attitude was really inspiring to us. At the same time, there was stuff that was amusing to us. Like how the dude who was the singer—usually the least musically talented dude—was always two beats behind. After a while, things like that made this stuff very endearing in a way. There wasn't a wall between the musicians and the crowd. It was all about coming up and stage diving. With metal, a lot of the kids who got into it wanted to be rock stars and fuck chicks. For us, we had to start playing music or we would have gone crazy; another thing similar to the hardcore bands. So we latched on to hardcore pretty naturally.

CHARLIE BENANTE (DRUMMER, ANTHRAX, S.O.D.)**:** At first, it was a little intimidating because we weren't so welcome down there. If it wasn't for people like Big Charlie or Billy Milano or Raybeez, we may have never made it out of there alive! They took us under their wing and said, "These guys are okay."

DANNY LILKER: The person who turned me onto NYHC was actually Scott Rosenfeld—better known as Scott Ian from Anthrax. He went down to a couple of CBGB matinees before I did. We were thrash metal dudes, trying to find all the fastest music we could. It was so exciting to find this whole, big new source of intense music. The realistic lyrics were really cool to us too. Metal bands wrote lyrics about anything that would just fit into the music; it was just cool to find music that had some focus.

GARY TSE TSE FLY: There were larger-than-life personalities in the hardcore scene who became involved in that crossover, which made it hard for others to just come out and say, "Metal sucks." These were good people who you respected, so them embracing metal made it hard for anyone to put up a resistance.

ROGER MIRET: There's so much similarity between the metal and the hardcore scenes that it had to happen. Whether you had long hair or a Mohawk, you were walking out of step with society. Both styles of music were loud and aggressive, the only difference was lyrically; I could never deal with the satanic thing.

EDDIE SUTTON: Around the time we started in '84 and '85, there were not that many metal-sounding bands. We were bringing something new to the table that everybody would start doing. Vinnie and Roger from A.F. were paying attention to us, and giving us the thumbs-up. Within a short period of time, they started working with Pete Steele and they collaborated on *Cause for Alarm*. I can definitely say that we were influencing the noted bands on the scene at the time. But I think it all came from being in the right place at the right time. I don't think we had any musical edge over anybody else.

GARY TSE TSE FLY: When Agnostic Front came out with the second album, *Cause for Alarm*, people thought it sounded too metal. They were called sellouts. If anything, they were getting more underground with that record. Those were the signs of the times—every older band either broke up or went metal.

HOWIE ABRAMS: I interviewed Agnostic Front for my fanzine, and they talked about their new album. Originally, the album was supposed to be called *A Growing Concern*. I was amped up, and the release date was announced, but it kept getting pushed back. I was just a kid, so I would be calling record stores asking about it. Finally I got it, and I took it home and I listened to it. I was really thrown off by the first listen. I listened to it a second time, and—no bullshit—I broke it. I felt betrayed almost. I just felt like we had bands like Exodus already, and I could just listen to them if I wanted. I can't say *Cause for Alarm* is one of my favorite albums, but now I accept it without the baggage.

TIM CHUNKS: When *Cause for Alarm* came out, it really felt like the metal thing was coming on strong. Agnostic Front went from *Victim in Pain* to this, and people didn't know what was going on.

ALEXA POLI-SCHEIGERT: I was living at Vinnie's house at the time they were writing *Cause for Alarm*. I walked in one day, and Vinnie was there with Peter Steele. This was a tiny fucking apartment, and Peter Steele was like seven and a half feet tall. They were sitting there writing songs, and I'm thinking, "Oh God, this sucks." I told Vinnie, "Please don't do this, these songs suck." But they did it. Some of it came out okay, but for the most part, I'm not that fond of that album.

VINNIE STIGMA: We did *Cause for Alarm* and got on Combat Records. That's when we became friends with Carnivore and bands like that. They became our brothers. Pete Steele helped me write some lyrics, and helped me with chord structure. I helped him write some songs, too. There was a mutual respect with the metal guys. NYHC accepted anyone. It didn't matter who, what, where, or when. There was straight edge, no edge, and people who just didn't care about it. If you were a metal guy—so what? You could play guitar better than me, that's all that meant.

ALEX KINON: I gave Agnostic Front a try and joined the band, and we made the second record. Since Kabula and I were in the band now, they were like, "Why don't we call the album *Cause for Alarm*?" after our old band. We weren't trying for a Cause for Alarm sound, though. We were hanging out with Pete Steele, so there was a metal influence happening there, and it shows.

ROGER MIRET: *Cause for Alarm* was a big record, even though to me it's a strange record. I know a lot of people who hated it from the get-go but love it now.

DANNY LILKER: When thrash metal kicked in, it wasn't hair metal like Winger. Thrash was something that was unpalatable to most people. It was fast, noisy music, and that's where the lines started to blur between metal and hardcore. Whether it had crazy lyrical content like Slayer or the socially relevant message of Agnostic Front, we were all underdogs and it was us against the world. Both hardcore and thrash metal were something that when most normal people heard it, they just went "Ick!" So that united us.

CHARLIE BENANTE: Metallica was playing L'Amour in Brooklyn, and me and Scott Ian took James Hetfield to the Sunday matinee at CBGB to see Broken Bones. Some people didn't like the fact there were these long-haired people at their show. But by the end of the day, James was in the pit on someone's shoulders, and that was it. Then the crossover thing really hit. A lot of the hardcore guys even started coming to L'Amour to see the bands there.

ERNIE PARADA: I remember playing CB's once, and there were a couple dudes with long hair in the pit, going nuts. Any hair at all in the pit was strange at that time. Long, long hair was really rare. I later found out it was the Metallica guys. Before you knew it, most hardcore bands had a taste of metal in them. It was fun when it was new. The first Token Entry album has some of that style. I played with the double bass drums and all. By the second album, *Jaybird*, I was over it, and it wasn't even really hitting its stride yet.

TOMMY CARROLL (Vocalist/drummer, NYC Mayhem; drummer, Youth of Today; vocalist, Straight Ahead, Irate): Back in the day, Craig Setari and I had a thrash band called Mayhem. I used to make our demos by taking my sister's cassettes and erasing them and putting our shit on there. Then I'd send them out to all the underground metal zines. I was really into the tape-trading shit. That whole thing was fucking awesome. You had the Metallica demo with Dave Mustaine playing, and then that band Death from Florida. It was a great, great scene. You'd be on the phone with these guys, and the long-distance bill was building up. I guess the Internet is a good thing, since it saves these new bands a lot of money on phone bills!

BILL WILSON (Owner, Blackout Records): I was a part of the crossover generation, that early group of kids who said, "Fuck this suburban shit," and decided to go down to CBGB. I went down there in my homemade Suicidal Tendencies shirt, and Big Charlie gave me the side eye. I remember seeing this guy walking around wielding the thighbone of a beast. His jacket was all safety-pinned, and he was walking down the street yelling at people.

TOMMY CARROLL: We were aware of Circle Jerks, GBH, and Discharge—the bands the metal bands liked. I went to CBGB and saw Adrenalin O.D. I liked the hardcore scene. There were so many restraints in heavy metal. These hardcore guys were jumping offstage and dancing around. I wanted to be a part of it. I was a young kid, and I was still searching for things. I wanted something more real, more pure.

DANNY LILKER: Lou and Pete Koller from Sick of It All came down as metalheads and got into all that shit. There was just a bunch of people getting into it simultaneously.

ARMAND MAJIDI (Vocalist/drummer, Rest in Pieces; drummer, Straight Ahead, Sick of It All): We were the first generation of metalheads converted into the hardcore scene. As a high school freshman, I had a few classes with a kid who was hanging out with Murphy's Law. I was always interested in whatever music was more extreme than Priest and Maiden and all the New Wave of British Heavy Metal bands. I wanted a more aggressive form of that music, which ended up being hardcore.

PETE KOLLER: My brother Lou and I always hung out together. We were into heavier music with Deep Purple and stuff like that, but always looking for something more extreme, heavy, and basic. Lou would bring home Motör-head records, and then GBH records, and then Exploited and Discharge. The first year of high school, we ran into Armand Majidi. He told us about a club in the city that always had hardcore punk shows—CBGB—and we all went down at the same time.

DANNY LILKER: John Connelly of Nuclear Assault and I worked up the nerve to go down to CBGB to a hardcore matinee. We thought all these skinheads were going to beat the shit out of us, which of course they didn't. If anything, it was the total opposite. The first people we met were Billy Milano and Billy Psycho. All those dudes were so welcoming. A mutual-respect thing ended up going on, which was cool. Firstly, we were glad we weren't going to get the shit pounded out of us by the skinheads. And it was cool to have this camaraderie with a new group of people.

GARY MESKIL: When I first got turned on to this underground music back in 1981, I immediately wanted to be involved in it. I think Scott Ian and Dan Lilker and those metal guys felt the same way. And since they were musicians, they were also consciously looking for broader influences to incorporate into their own style.

CHARLIE BENANTE: At least for me, it was about the love of music and not about the aesthetic. I definitely wasn't into the straight-edge culture or the skinhead culture. I just loved the music.

DANNY LILKER: Some people were dubious that us metal guys were just trying to be cool and hardcore, and truthfully there were some people who were. Some metal people only got into the circus elements of hardcore and embarrassed themselves in the mosh pit by doing some weird gyrations.

ALEXA POLI-SCHEIBERT: I wasn't too fond of the metal thing. I went to a couple of shows at L'Amour and got kicked out for fighting. These metal guys got in the pit and knocked me down on purpose because I was a girl. So I pulled their hair off. Around that time, I started getting groped a lot in the pit—a lot of people went down for that. Grab my tit and I'll fuck you up! These guys thought, "Oh, a free feel!" I don't think so. I will fuck you up! The metal people danced liked chickens. They weren't a part of what I wanted to be part of.

TIM CHUNKS (VOCALIST, TOKEN ENTRY): I remember seeing a show with Megadeth, the Bad Brains, and Voivod at the New Music Seminar show. It was an incredible night. Bad Brains opened with "Pay to Cum" and me and my friends went fuckin' ballistic. When Megadeth came on, I was like, "Fuck these guys!" I didn't want any part of it. They were unacceptable. But then

Voivod came on and they were fucking amazing. Megadeth was something I couldn't understand, but Voivod I could get behind. Megadeth still had some kind of rock 'n' roll vibe to them. Voivod had the raw vibe of hardcore.

GARY MESKIL: In hardcore music, there are a lot of purists. When the scene was all of a sudden infiltrated by outsiders, things got uncomfortable for some people. When metal guys started coming to the hardcore shows, a lot of fights popped up. It was all due to a lack of open-mindedness, if nothing else.

LUKE ABBEY (DRUMMER, LOUD & BOISTEROUS, GORILLA BISCUITS, WAR-ZONE, JUDGE): I was an angry, nonconformist kid. When I discovered the hardcore scene, it just suited me perfectly. I heard something in the music that I connected with intuitively. Once I began going to shows, I also found out how much fun, excitement, and friendship was there. I relished the fact that most people didn't appreciate it. I think that the reason the scene survived as it did for several years was because of how insular it was. Nobody seemed to either want nor expect any attention from anybody other than the people who were already going to shows.

CHARLIE BENANTE: I guess these guys wanted to keep what they had pure. They didn't want it exposed. I can understand that one hundred percent. People don't understand that music is supposed to break down boundaries and bring people together.

Some people came down on us and talked a lot of shit about us. There was this girl from Japan who did a drawing for an Anthrax shirt. It was a drawing of our "Not" man and she put the NYHC logo on him. The NYHC logo was a part of what he was wearing, and the drawing was copyrighted. People were saying we were trying to copyright the NYHC logo. They thought we were stealing the NYHC logo. It was so ridiculous. It's not like we were making profit off of it. How can you make a profit off of that? I didn't think it was fair, because people didn't know the truth about things.

STEVE POSS: Anthrax had nothing to do with NYHC. They can say they put the logo on their shirt to make it popular. They can go play Yankee Stadium with Metallica and tell that to everyone they play to there—but people who were a part of the hardcore scene were confused by what they did.

MICHAEL GIBBONS: When Leeway supported Overkill at the old Ritz in the late '80s, I remember Scott Ian approached Jimmy G and asked him was his gripe was with Anthrax. Jimmy was like, "My gripe is the logo I knew all my life is on a twenty-five-dollar T-shirt!" I talked to Scott afterwards and said,

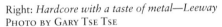

Right: *Hardcore with a taste of metal—Leeway*
PHOTO BY GARY TSE TSE

"Scott, listen, I'm a metal kid from Queens who loves hardcore, too, but I would drop this whole NYHC thing. It's not worth it." They were looking for street cred, but this was a band that could sell out the Beacon Theatre four nights in a row. Why did they care about people in hardcore?

EDDIE SUTTON: When Leeway blew up, people called me a rock star. I said they could call me a rock star when I got a five-figure check. "When I get that five-figure check, I will come directly to you and show it to you. Then you can call me a rock star." How can you be a rock star when you still have to work to make a living? I was accessible to anyone who wanted to talk to me.

DANNY LILKER: Imagine if there were Internet message boards back then? It would have been insane! Most of the people who were the biggest loudmouths were the ones who got into hardcore from metal six months earlier and were insecure about it. They didn't want anyone to know their pasts, so all of a sudden they became self-appointed scene judges. All they were doing was projecting. You'd see these people talking shit, and I'd say, "I remember you from L'Amour. You might be a skinhead now, but I know just who the fuck you are." I would watch people walk into Bleecker Bob's and trade in their Slayer records and buy Minor Threat records. I always thought—why can't you have both?

BILL WILSON: Like any other hardcore kid, when I decided to shave my head, I disavowed metal. I went through a denial period. Everybody wanted identity and everybody wanted to belong. As an adult, I laugh at the stupid shit we'd do to be "true to ourselves." We should have just done what we wanted. It's more punk to do what you want than to conform to somebody's standards.

GARY MESKIL: When Metallica went on their first arena tour with Metal Church, we heard they were spinning the Crumbsuckers every night in between bands. I was so happy to hear that. I think Kirk Hammett was turned onto the Crumbsuckers by Johnny Z at Megaforce. We had some pretty damn good guitar players in the band, so I think that's why Kirk appreciated the Crumbsuckers so much. He joined us onstage at a CBGB matinee and people still talk about it to this day.

DAVE WYNN (GUITARIST, CRUMBSUCKERS): We were told Kirk from Metallica was going to come down and join us on stage at CBGB, so we really thought long and hard trying to figure out on which song he should come in on.

GARY MESKIL: Back in those days, anyone who had any mainstream notoriety was deemed a rock star. When Kirk was onstage with us and we were having our moment, Tommy from Straight Ahead started causing a ruckus.

TOMMY CARROLL: When I saw Kirk Hammett come in with his big bouncers, it bothered me. I was there to see a hardcore show. I grabbed the mic and said, "Get this fuckin' rock star out of here!" Maybe I was wrong about that, but I was a fifteen-year-old kid. I honestly didn't think he heard it!

DAVE WYNNE: We figured the best place for Kirk to come in was at the end of "Hub Run." I would go into this solo and then just hand him the guitar. I was using our other guitarist Chuck Lenihan's guitar, which had a whammy bar on it. When I handed it to Kirk, he starting going crazy. All you could hear was "Whee whoo whoo." He was doing all these dive bombs, and I guess that's what set Tommy off. Shortly after that, I heard, "BRAANNGG!" I guess Tommy was giving Kirk a lot of shit and he had enough. I have to say Kirk held his own. I thought he was going to fight with the guitar on!

TOMMY CARROLL: Kirk made a face at me, and he took his guitar and jammed me in the chest with it, and then he made a motion like he was going to spit on me. I don't know if he actually spit, but then I spit on him. And then he definitely spit back! Then his two big bouncers grabbed me, and then Billy Milano said something on the mic. Then one of the guys from the Crumbsuckers said something like, "Looks like you bit off more than you could chew." I was a fifteen-year-old kid, I wasn't going to take on two six-foot-eight bouncers. I don't care how tough I thought I was.

GARY MESKIL: Billy Milano stepped in and put the kibosh on it immediately. He wasn't having it because Billy had brought Kirk down as his friend.

TOMMY CARROLL: Everybody was pissed off at me, but fuck this guy! If he wasn't a rock star, then why was he affected by what I said in the first place? But I don't want to rehash things. Like everything else in hardcore, it's made out to be more than it was.

GARY TSE TSE FLY: To this day, I felt like the scene changed for the worse with the emergence of the heavy metal influence and their fans getting into the scene. It was watering down; it was bringing big business into the scene. It was everything I was against.

DANNY LILKER: That whole thing followed Nuclear Assault, even when we went on our first tour of the UK. There were bands like Heresy and Concrete Sox over there that were very, very cynical about metal bands. They thought we were just trying to be cool, and wanting to make money off the hardcore scene. We came all the way there, played in some crusty squat, and sold our shirts for the equivalent of six dollars or something. I was just like, "Oh yeah, you got us! We're really trying to cash in!"

HOWIE ABRAMS: The crossover of the '80s was more influential musically than people realize. So many people at the time were so worried about whether metalheads and skinheads could get along on the dance floor, they didn't notice that the newcomers opened up a real stagnant hardcore scene. It infused some energy into the thing, and changed up the sound of New York.

CHARLIE BENANTE: The crossover of metal and hardcore in New York took totally different forms of music and brought them together, so that the next generation could actually learn from them. Maybe some people didn't get paid for it, and maybe some others did, but it all worked out in the end. Look how many great bands came out of that.

From top: *An early shot of Long Island's Crumbsuckers with Dave Brady on vocals; Chuck Lenihan of the Crumbsuckers.*
PHOTOS COURTESY DAVE BRADY

33. CRUMBSUCKERS: LIFE OF DREAMS

DANNY LILKER: There was this whole thing in New York where there were bands like Nuclear Assault and Carnivore and Whiplash coming from the metal scene and crossing over into hardcore. But then you had a hardcore band like the Crumbsuckers, who were already heavy and had the chugging guitars that were more like metal. Hardcore had the fast strumming style, but once you palm-mute the guitar, all of a sudden it sounds like metal.

PARRIS MAYHEW: The only New York hardcore band that ever really blew me away was the Crumbsuckers. They were the only band that ever made me nervous in terms of talent. Out of all the bands that were happening, I wasn't hearing anything that made me think the Cro-Mags would be overshadowed until I heard the Crumbsuckers. I really tried to be influenced by them, but they entered a realm that was so magical, I couldn't really fathom what they were doing.

JOHN KELLY: When the Crumbsuckers came in, those guys pretty much changed the face of hardcore. They were the birth of crossover as far as I'm concerned. I'm proud to say I was at their first show at CB's, and everyone was standing there with their jaws dropped open.

PARRIS MAYHEW: Every time I saw the Crumbsuckers, I couldn't believe how great they were. The only thing that working against them was that they didn't have a marketable image. They wore Bermuda shorts and Hawaiian shirts. I'm sure the rest of the New York hardcore scene looked at them as these Long Island boys, which they were.

GARY MESKIL: The first hardcore punk show I saw was the Misfits and the Necros at a Polish American hall. I was surprised at how intimate the music was. I had no preconceived notions, but I thought it would be some huge place and we'd be sitting down movie-theater style. As soon as the Necros hit the stage, the room broke into this crazy mosh pit. I was completely unprepared, but it was a lot of fun. That led to weekly trips to CBGB, A7, Gildersleeves, Danceteria, and Bond's. Wherever there was a good show going on, that's where you'd find me and a handful of friends from Baldwin, New York, supporting the scene.

I had this friend, Franco Capelli, that I used to eat lunch with in the high school cafeteria in 1981 or 1982. I knew he was a guitar player, but he was into Van Halen. I asked him if he had any major plans for the summer, because I wanted to start a band. We found a drummer who lived right down the block from me named Jason Bolognini; he was thirteen, but he was a really great drummer. Due to a joke we formulated in the high school cafeteria, we called it the Crumbsuckers. We became a Baldwin sensation in a very short time. We played Baldwin High School. Then we started to have lineup changes very early on. We got Dave Brady to sing. Dave was a major score for us because he was this really artistic guy in high school who knew a lot about the punk and hardcore scene.

DAVE BRADY (VOCALIST, CRUMBSUCKERS): When I brought Dave Wynn into the band with his chops, that's when things started taking off. Dave was very notorious around our school for his guitar playing. He played in bands that did Ozzy Osbourne covers. When I brought him over to punk, people were shocked.

DAVE WYNN: Dave convinced me to go for a Mohawk right before the first show I played with the Crumbsuckers. We played a little backyard party right around high school graduation. There was noise and people talking, but when I walked in with this Mohawk there was silence!

GARY MESKIL: We had some opportunities in New York City due to our friendship with Agnostic Front and Cause for Alarm. I'm pretty proud to say we were involved in the scene as early as when A7 was around. We played CBGB many, many times. We were starting to pick up some steam, but we were having some problems with Dave Brady. As a result of playing several gigs with our friends Krakdown, we thought we'd ask their singer Chris Notaro since he was great onstage and had a killer voice. This was around 1985, when we got Chuck Lenihan on second guitar.

PARRIS MAYHEW: After a Cro-Mags gig once, Chuck Lenihan asked me,

"Parris, that lead you do on 'Life of My Own,' what scale is that in?" I was like, "Scale? What's a scale? I'm sorry, I don't know what that is." He came over to my house and he showed me how to play the major scale, but it still didn't make any sense to me!

MIKE BULLSHIT: There was an older woman named Connie Barrett who was involved with this metal label's hardcore subsidiary, Combat Core. She tried to get some metal shows going at CBGB. There was one with Whiplash and all these other lousy metal bands. They called it the "hardcore metal matinee" or whatever. I swear there were maybe ten or twenty people there.

GARY MESKIL: Getting signed to a label was the furthest thing from our minds. We were basically a band that wanted to get together on weekends and have some fun. But we played once with Nuclear Assault at CBGB. Nuclear Assault had label reps there to see them from New Renaissance, Combat, and Roadrunner. Johnny Z from Megaforce was there. He showed up with some professional wrestlers, and they were stage diving and stuff. People were mortified! We just had a great show where everybody went crazy. As a result, these labels were coming up to us offering recording contracts. We didn't know what the fuck to do with that—or if that was something we even wanted to do! Around that time we were courted by Connie Barrett, a woman who was already managing Agnostic Front. She wanted to manage Pete Steele in Carnivore, and Whiplash, too. We asked her to help us out by representing us, and we went with the Combat Records contract.

PARRIS MAYHEW: The Crumbsuckers eventually went in the direction where they were embraced by the metalheads.

GARY MESKIL: Going into our deal with Combat, Chris was fresh in the band. He was still learning the lyrics and all that. I don't think he played a gig with us before signing that contract. After Chris joined the band, *Life of Dreams* was recorded in 1985 and released in 1986. That's when we started to get more recognized outside of the comfort zone of the tristate area, and things picked up from there.

MIKE BULLSHIT: The Crumbsuckers, Ludichrist, and all these bands in 1985 were totally awesome. I loved the Crumbsuckers. They used to do the "Inspector Gadget" theme song. Then when their records came out in 1986 or '87, they were kind of lame.

GARY MESKIL: There were certain aspects of the hardcore scene that started to bum us out. I think we made a conscious effort to go more in a thrash metal direction. We liked a lot of what that scene had to offer, and we were becoming fans of the bands that were playing that type of music. We didn't abandon our roots completely, but we went in a certain direction, and we polarized our audience in doing so. There's always this argument between fans. The more hardcore people like *Life of Dreams*, and the thrash metal people like the second one, *Beast on My Back*, from 1988.

JOE SONGCO: The second album by most of the crossover bands went further down the metal route. Bands like the Crumbsuckers and Ludichrist were too talented to keep playing minute-and-a-half-long songs about Tylenol.

HOWIE ABRAMS: It's hard to get past the cover of *Beast on My Back*. I don't know whose idea that was. I probably embraced a few songs from it here and there, but it deserved the hard time that it got. I always loved the musical aspect of the Crumbsuckers, so it wasn't like I thought there were too many guitar solos or anything like that. The record just strayed from any semblance of hardcore. All the aggression was gone.

GARY MESKIL: The hardcore scene is responsible for everything I've done in music. Those are great, unique roots to have as a musician. These days, it gets you immediate respect on a worldwide basis. That platform made it much easier for my next endeavor, Pro-Pain, to gain traction. We did that as a result of being in the Crumbsuckers, carrying a fan base over from one band to the next.

Above: *Baldwin, Long Island, teen guitar whiz Dave Wynn of the Crumbsuckers*
COURTESY DAVE BRADY

From top: *Murphy's Law rages at The Ritz* KEN SALERNO; *Early line-up of Murphy's Law with Russ Iglay on bass at the Jane Street Rock Hotel* GARY TSE TSE FLY

34. MURPHY'S LAW: FUN!

UNCLE AL MORRIS: The Dead Kennedys played a show on Staten Island one night during the summer of 1982, so our whole Lower East Side crew hopped the ferry and went. Afterwards, I talked with my friend Vinnie Stigma. We decided that punk was done, and hardcore was the way to go. Vinnie set out to create Agnostic Front. I held back and waited to create my band. I was working security at the A7 club on Avenue A in the East Village. Running the door was this crazy punk kid who had his own style of moshing and stage diving: Jimmy Gestapo, we called him.

DOUG HOLLAND: I first met Jimmy G on the CB radio. I would do this thing called "chucking." I'd play the Pistols and the Clash. If you got caught doing that, they'd yank your license and give you a fine. I didn't give a fuck! I did it, and Jimmy heard it. So he asked me what my 10-20 was—my location. I told him. There was a McDonald's on the corner, and he suggested we meet there. So that's how we became friends. We started going to parties and getting rip-roaring drunk.

MIKE JUDGE: Jimmy G was always on the dance floor and up against the stage. He was always in the pit. Before Murphy's Law, he started a band called the Cavity Creeps, and those shows were just crazy. They had a song called "The Pain Song." When they played it, everyone would make a wall of people and run over everybody.

BOBBY STEELE: Jimmy G is just the friendliest guy. Who could say anything bad about him? Jimmy was always a really, really nice guy. He's always been true and always been supportive of everyone. What else could you want?

GARY TSE TSE FLY: Jimmy G never repeated a joke twice. He was always funny. Somebody would come with a weird hat or something, and he would have a joke about it right on the spot. But at the same time, he was a tough guy in the pit.

RICHIE BIRKENHEAD: People don't give Murphy's Law their due. Jimmy is up there with Iggy Pop—he's the Iggy Pop of NYHC.

DOUG THOMPSON (DRUMMER, MURPHY'S LAW): Jimmy G is one of the best front men ever, and I'm not bullshitting you. I've been seeing live shows since I was ten years old. My first show was Queen. Freddie Mercury was unbelievable. I saw Van Halen fifteen times, and David Lee Roth was amazing. But Jimmy has something special. He knows how to work the crowd. He knows how to talk to the crowd.

UNCLE AL MORRIS: One night I asked Jimmy if he wanted to start a band, and he said, "Crucial!" We gathered up Adam Mucci, the bass player from Agnostic Front. We drove around looking for a drummer, and we spotted Harley Flanagan on the street. Jimmy yelled out the window, "Hey, Harley, we're starting a band, wanna come?" Harley said, "Crucial, man!" and hopped in the car.

We went back to my place on the west side, sat on amps, plugged in our guitars, drank beer and smoked herb, and started making up songs. Jimmy said, "I wanna make a fun song," so we wrote "Fun." After a while, we realized we had something going here. Jimmy said he could get us a show that night—this was New Year's Eve 1982—at the Plugg Club. We busted our brains thinking up a name. My refrigerator had a poster on describing Murphy's Law. We all looked at each other, and said, "Aggggggggh! *Murphy's Law!*"

VINNIE STIGMA: I was at Uncle Al's house the night they named Murphy's Law, with Uncle Al, Harley, Jimmy, and Adam. Uncle Al had an apartment at Father Flanagan's Square on Sixth Avenue. On his refrigerator, he had the poster that said "Murphy's Law" and listing all the things that can go wrong.

JESSE MALIN: That New Year's Eve, they tried to do a hardcore show at Irving Plaza and charge twenty dollars. So we were going to put on the opposition show at Giorgio Gomelsky's loft on Twenty-Fourth Street. It was Heart Attack, False Prophets, Misguided, and M.D.C. Then Jimmy G and Harley said they had a band. They jumped on Heart Attack's gear, and that was the first Murphy's Law gig.

CHRIS TSAKIS: There was a promoter, this lesbian with blond hair. She became friendly with Ron Rancid, and it was decided we were going to play this New Year's Eve gig. The show went south because someone held a competing show downtown with all these other bands. We ended up having almost nobody show up to our gig with D.O.A.

Jimmy G in his "Jah" jacket
GARY TSE TSE FLY

UNCLE AL MORRIS: We showed up at the gig and told the guy at the door we were one of the bands playing. We ran onstage, asked the band getting off if we could borrow their equipment—*nobody* said no to us, especially Jimmy—and Jimmy yelled into the mic, "Yo! Happy New Year! We're Murphy's Law and this song is called 'Fun'!" The place went nuts: People started ripping up chairs and attacking the stage. After two songs, the stage collapsed. The owner ran up to us—we thought he wanted to kill us. He pointed his finger at us and said, "Do you guys wanna play here next week?"

WENDY EAGER: The first Murphy's Law show was great. The Nihilistics were playing at Irving Plaza on New Year's Eve and it was expensive. Then this show was going on at the Plugg Club with all these bands, and it wasn't much money. Murphy's Law were amazing.

RUSS ISLAY: They just stuck out. They didn't adhere to the fast, slow, fast, slow formula of hardcore. They played a toss-up between punk and hardcore. They didn't do it purposefully—that's just how the music came out. Uncle Al was a ripping guitar player. When Harley was on the drums, it was great. Murphy's Law shows were a big party. There was always beer onstage and in the audience. Murphy's Law welcomed punks, skins, and longhairs: anybody who was cool. You could have fun without being picked on—unless you were an idiot who crossed the line, of course.

ALEXA POLI-SCHEIGERT: If you listen to some of the old live tapes of Murphy's Law, during "Bong" you'll hear Jimmy say, "Who's got the herb? Alexa's

Jimmy cools off the Ritz crowd KEN SALERNO

got the herb!" I was always rolling joints. I always had a big old spliff to get down on. I was a Murphy's Law kind of chick. I was all about partying and having a good time and balling. I'm still that way to a degree.

RUSS ISLAY: Uncle Al was in the band for quite a while. Harley split and this Queens dude Guzzy played drums for a while. Then they got Petey Hines. Shortly after that, Adam Mucci quit and I joined on bass. I had been the guitar player in Child Abuse. It was a toss-up between me and Johnny Waste to play bass. Johnny was a great guitar player; I looked up to him. But Urban Waste was his main thing, so Murphy's Law would have been his back-burner thing. I did a bunch of practices with them and all of a sudden, we were put on this Rock Against Racism show with Reagan Youth. It was stated that I was not in the band yet, but I was playing the show. I was excited, man. We went out to eat at Veselka afterwards, and they said, "Well, you're in the band now."

We had a whole U.S. tour booked without a record in '84. We played to small crowds, but it was a fun trip. It was the band and one roadie. I remember playing in Kent, Ohio, just being so young and hardcore being so fresh and new. But Petey Hines, our drummer got sick, which turned out to be mono. He kept getting sicker and sicker. We got as far as St. Louis, and he was just puking behind the drum set. He couldn't go any farther. We had to go back. I talk to Jimmy sometimes about that tour and wonder what would have happened if we made it out to California. Would things would have turned out different?

DOUG THOMPSON: I heard Murphy's Law needed a drummer. I went to the record store the next town over, bought their first record, and learned it. I remember thinking it was really something different. It wasn't heavy like *Victim in Pain* or *Age of Quarrel*. That was the NYHC I knew, but Murphy's Law fit my personality. I liked to drink and have fun.

RUSS ISLAY: I got kicked out, but if I didn't get kicked out of Murphy's Law, there wouldn't have been Underdog. When one door closes, another one opens.

JESSE MALIN: I remember Jimmy was the first one of us to get a tour bus, when he went on tour with the Beastie Boys. He pulled up on Avenue A with it, and I was like, "What the fuck?"

DOUG THOMPSON: They asked if I could go on the road in 1987, and I said sure. My dad had just died, and it was a perfect opportunity to get the hell away from here. Uncle Al was there when we were about to start the tour, but Todd Youth came in and took over guitar right before we left. I joined the band and next thing I know, I'm on a plane going to Seattle to tour with the Beastie Boys.

TODD YOUTH: The tour started out in clubs, then went to theaters, and then to arenas. Playing the Philadelphia Spectrum at sixteen years old was pretty fucking cool.

DOUG THOMPSON: At first, we were playing college shows, where they tolerated the slam dancing. But the Beastie Boys just kept blowing up due to MTV, so the shows started moved into arenas and things got crazy. People who knew of Murphy's Law were showing up and trying to stage dive. A typical arena show has a five-foot barrier in the front. I don't think they knew what to do with the kids who started slam dancing. Forget it. Kids started doing that and they were done. They were getting kicked out of the place by security. They thought they were starting a riot.

TODD YOUTH: This was pre-Lollapalooza and pre-–"alternative music." We were the first band to ever have a fucking pit in an arena. Public Enemy opened up for us on that tour.

DOUG THOMPSON: They didn't know what hit them. We threw beer, and we spit beer. People were throwing joints up, and we were lighting them up. The security was losing their minds. The South was not fun, because the cops were there due to the Beastie Boys. For punk rock to be on a stage like that and to hit people like that, we won over a lot of fans.

TODD YOUTH: After that, we made *Back with a Bong* in 1989. Dr. Know from the Bad Brains helped out on that. Jack from the Mob was managing us, and we had the guys from Fishbone playing on the record.

DOUG THOMPSON: We were tight. We knew that stuff frontwards and backwards. I did the drum tracks in one day. Chuck Valle was our bass player by then. He knew the studio and he prepped us. By that point, Chuck was engineering the early hip-hop stuff by Public Enemy and LL Cool J at Chung King, so he knew what to do. We didn't waste any time.

TODD YOUTH: While the touring really took off, we got on MTV with the video for "Panty Raid" from *Back with a Bong* and we were selling out the Ritz.

DOUG THOMPSON: The label had this guy follow us around with a camera when we went on tour with the Red Hot Chili Peppers, and that footage turned into the "Panty Raid" video. It was horrible. They had a video release party without us! We were on the road.

RUSS ISLAY: Then the lineups for Murphy's Law went crazy, with everyone coming and going. If you look at a list of Murphy's Law members, it's crazy. On Wikipedia I'm somewhere in there way at the bottom.

DOUG THOMPSON: I left the band sometime in 1991 or '92. We could play a festival with Sepultura, or we could go on tour with the Ramones or the Bosstones. We took the Bosstones out on their first tour. We could play with anybody. We opened up a lot of eyes to hardcore.

After I left the band, Chuck Valle was stabbed and murdered out in L.A. when the band was on tour. It threw us all for a loop. He was such a good person. That later album, *Dedicated*, is for Chuck.

The whole thing with Murphy's Law, though, is it's Jimmy. It's all Jimmy. When I was in the band, he'd always say this was our band, but we knew what people were coming out for. You could put anybody behind Jimmy, and it's still Murphy's Law. He's been through a million band members. He was a great representative of NYHC and still is to this day. He works it, and he continues to work it with the band. It's his band—end of story.

Clockwise from top: *Jimmy and his people*; *Murphy's Law bass player Chuck Valle—R.I.P.*;
Raybeez helps out Murphy's Law guitarist Todd Youth PHOTOS BY KEN SALERNO

35. THE BIRTH OF UNITY

GARY TSE TSE FLY: By the mid-'80s or so, Boston kind of fell on its face going overboard with the metal stuff. Washington, D.C., was dead, with pretty much every band breaking up before "Revolution Summer" in 1986. Those guys from the Midwest, like Die Kreuzen, and people from out west, like Meat Puppets and Black Flag, all decided that the hardcore thing was childish; they thought they needed to progress. Then you had a band like Youth Brigade, who started calling itself just the Brigade, and playing new wave rock. A lot of hardcore scenes were dying, but New York was in full force. New York was still firmly hardcore.

JOHN PORCELLY: When Ray Cappo and I moved to New York City, a whole second wave of bands had just started. We moved at the perfect time, because the rumor mill was exploding and all these great records were coming out. To most people, hardcore was already on its way out, but New York was just getting fired up.

TODD YOUTH: Around 1985 and 1986 is when New York was really taking off with Agnostic Front, the Cro-Mags, and Murphy's Law. Then you had new bands like Youth of Today and Bold. I guess a lot of people from my generation hated on them, but I always gave them props for keeping it going.

DAVE KOENIG: I look at 1986 as the beginning of the second wave of New York City hardcore. That was the year that Youth of Today exploded, Sick of It All released their demo, and the Cro-Mags, a band from New York City's earlier years, finally recorded their legendary debut LP, *The Age of Quarrel*. That was the year the crossover genre of music seemed to be coming to an end, and bands began to get back to basics.

WALTER SCHREIFELS: After Youth of Today put out their 7-inch, people would travel in from New Jersey and Connecticut to the matinees. The shows started to get full, and started to get a wider appeal. More bands started to form, because the kids who would come down would get into their own bands.

JOHN PORCELLY: That was such an exciting time in New York. Some Records was just opening. Warzone got back together and became a real band. Then you had Straight Ahead, and you had Gorilla Biscuits. With the whole second wave of new blood of New York Hardcore, the CBGB matinees would have a line down the frickin' Bowery.

RAY CAPPO: If anyone thinks hardcore stopped in 1985, maybe it's just because they personally weren't into hardcore anymore. Truthfully, that's when New York took off, thanks to Sick of It All, Youth of Today, Agnostic Front, and the Cro-Mags. That's when Agnostic Front became a global band. A big part of the New York scene happened after 1985.

MIKE JUDGE: The crowds were definitely bigger. That was the first time I went to a CB's matinee and saw a line. There were blue barricades, and lines around the block. Bands were popping up everywhere and it all revolved around Youth of Today. Straight edge was huge. Once upon a time, Johnny Stiff told Ray Cappo that there would never be a straight-edge scene. All of a sudden, some of the greatest bands were popping up, and everything was so fucking vibrant and new. Gorilla Biscuits and Straight Ahead were happening. The fanzines were going. It was a great time for music in the city. Anybody who thought it died in 1985 missed out on a cool part of New York musical history.

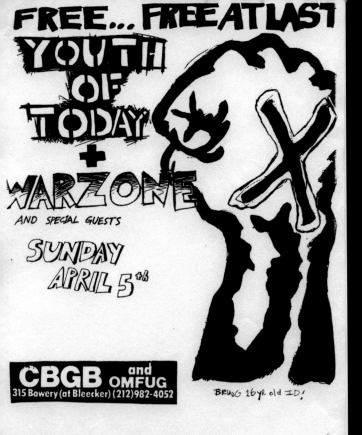

FREE... FREE AT LAST
YOUTH OF TODAY
+
WARZONE
AND SPECIAL GUESTS

SUNDAY APRIL 5th

CBGB and OMFUG
315 Bowery (at Bleecker) (212)982-4052

BRING 16yr old ID!

DOUBLE RECORD RELEASE PARTY

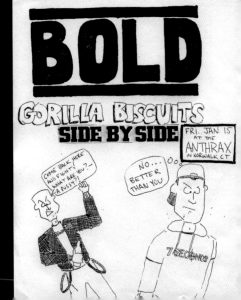

BOLD
GORILLA BISCUITS
SIDE BY SIDE

FRI..JAN. 15
AT THE
ANTHRAX
IN NORWALK CT

36. YOUTH OF TODAY: BREAK DOWN THE WALLS

TOMMY CARROLL: Violent Children from Connecticut played a lot of CBGB matinees. They were a great live band, really explosive.

RAY CAPPO: I lived in Danbury, Connecticut, an hour and fifteen minutes from New York City on the Metro North train. My parents were sort of New Yorkers, and my brothers and sisters were all older and lived in the city. I used to go to New York on weekends. My parents figured I'd stay with my brothers or sisters and everything would be cool. Little did they know! I would keep it pretty vague. I would just say, "I'm going to see some music." They had no idea I was hanging out on the Lower East Side all weekend. I liked alternative music. I wasn't quite sure what hardcore was. Then I stumbled into CBGB when the UK Subs were playing. The Young and the Useless were opening, which was Adam Horovitz from the Beastie Boys. I thought, "These are kids that are my age. I can do this."

When I got back to my typical American high school, I grabbed three of my friends who were the only other guys into alternative music, and we started Violent Children. I met John Porcelly at the Anthrax, and we asked him to join. Pretty soon, Violent Children pressed our own single. The cool thing about hardcore was if you wanted to make a record, you made a record. You made five hundred records, and after that—no more records.

JOHN PORCELLY: The end of Violent Children happened when Johnny Stiff called up Cappo and asked if we wanted to open up for the Circle Jerks at CBGB. Ray and I couldn't believe it, but the singer of Violent Children had a friggin' softball game that day and thought he would be too tired afterwards. He couldn't really be bothered with it. That's when we decided we had to break up the band.

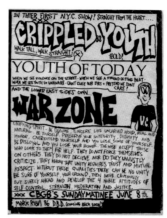

RAY CAPPO: In February 1985, the whole hardcore scene and everything that I loved was over. There was no such thing as straight edge anymore. I was completely made fun of for being straight edge. The other guys in Violent Children were straight edge, but they were really into heavy metal. The whole scene was crossing over. My dream was to establish the perfect hardcore band—as hard as Negative Approach but with the message of 7 Seconds.

JOHN PORCELLY: Youth of Today started in the summer of 1985. I was so into hardcore that I could barely concentrate on school. I met Dave Stein and Steve Reddy when they were putting on shows in Albany. I was going to SUNY Oswego, but spending all my book money taking trains to Albany every weekend to see shows. Dave Stein would take me to the cafeteria at his school to eat, because I was spending all my money on train fare. My head was not in my studies. My head was in being in a band and being a part of this whole thing.

GARY TSE TSE FLY: I think I saw the first Youth of Today show in New York City. It was at the Nameless Theatre in August of '85. The place was so stinky, I don't know if there were dead rats in there or what. Johnny Stiff was booking the shows there, and I think he opened it up after it being sealed for ten years. Youth of Today were great. Ray was speaking out. He was saying that Violent Children broke up because some of those guys wanted to go metal. He said he wanted to stick to his roots, and that was what the scene was all about. I swallowed all of it. I loved it. They played a set for ten people, and I was like, "Fuck! This is like 1983 again!" It brought me back. They rejuvenated the whole scene.

RICHIE BIRKENHEAD: There was a big shift toward metal going on in New York and I think that's what spawned bands like Youth of Today. Looking back, it's so weird; 1985 seemed *so* far away from 1982—it seemed like another era. But I remember watching Youth of Today and thinking, "This is very 1982."

WALTER SCHREIFELS: I felt all the good shit had already happened. I appreciated the heaviness of the metal stuff, but it wasn't what I wanted. Then Youth of Today came out and they sounded like Antidote. They had this image and expression of the old-school hardcore that was a relief to the whole crossover metal thing. That really attracted me.

ALEX BROWN: I think Youth of Today's first 7-inch, *Can't Close My Eyes*, came out the summer before I moved to New York City. It was just one of those records. It sounded like brutal early hardcore: Negative Approach meets early SSD and then thrown on Kevin Second's label, Positive Force. I was hooked, and hoping to meet those guys when I moved there. I was into the straight-edge thing and loved what they were about. Seeing Youth of Today live blew my mind. I had never seen a front man like Ray Cappo. Pure energy. Animal-growl vocals. He looked so cool onstage: It was really impressive.

JOHN PORCELL: We played a big show with Agnostic Front at CBGB in December of 1985. We were some tiny band from Connecticut, but there was a lot of hype about us. The place was packed, and this was way before straight edge got big in New York. Johnny Stiff told us, "Straight edge is so uncool in New York. If you come out on stage with an X on your hand, you're going to get your ass kicked!" I remember being backstage and asking Ray Cappo if we were going to put X's on our hands. As far as crazy-looking kids, New York had it back then. You had kids with shaved heads. People with their eyebrows shaved off. People messed up on drugs. It was intimidating! But we were like, "Fuck it! We're going out there with X's on our hands! We're going out there loud and proud!" We went out firing on all cylinders, and it was a great show. People loved us.

GARY TSE TSE FLY: You have to commend Youth of Today. They could have fallen on their faces. They could have come to New York, and people could have laughed at them. But that didn't happen.

RAY CAPPO: We played in New York in Agnostic Front and Damage right before our single came out. I'm a big-mouth, and I was really into straight edge. Back then no one was straight edge in New York, so we had a little bit of an attitude.

JOHN PORCELLY: After the show, Roger Miret came up to Cappo and said, "Yo, I really like that guitar player you got! That guy reminds me of Al from SSD!" What a compliment!

RAY CAPPO: After that show, we went to California and toured with 7 Seconds. They put out our single on their label, Positive Force. When we got back to New York, everybody was straight edge. It was unbelievable.

JOHN PORCELLY: Things started going really good for the band in New York, and we eventually moved there. When we started Youth of Today, we always had it in our minds that we would move there. I didn't even sign up for college the next year. At the end of that summer, I had to tell my dad I wasn't going back to college. I was spending all my money on guitar equipment and moving to New York City to be in a punk band.

MATT WARNKE: Ray and John moved into the city in 1986. Ray got an apartment on Fifteenth somewhere around Eighth and Ninth Avenues. That was a great location, because it was kind of off the beaten path, but just a twenty-minute walk from the action. We would always head down there from Katonah on the weekends and it became our launching pad and headquarters. Initially, our expanding circle hanging out downtown included Mark Ryan, Mark "Goober" McNeilly, Craig Setari, and Tommy Carroll. We would just hang out on Avenue A until the sun came up.

TODD YOUTH: When Ray and Porcell moved to New York, I used to skate with them and the guys from Token Entry. Those bands like Youth of Today and Crippled Youth had the spirit of that '82 thing that died when everything turned metal, so I was into it.

MIKE JUDGE: Mark Ryan called me up and said to go see Youth of Today. He said they were cool, and they played hardcore the way we used to do it. He talked me into driving him out down to Philly to see them. I was blown away. They sparked it up in me again. I wound up going to see live music again. I started going into New York again in 1986, and things were really happening.

RICHIE BIRKENHEAD: The straight-edge thing really took off in New York to the point that, all of a sudden, Raybeez was X'ing up, and Todd Youth was X'ing up. The biggest O.G.s of them all were being influenced by these kids from Connecticut and Westchester. It was kind of weird.

JOHN PORCELLY: It seemed like it happened overnight. At one point, we had Johnny Stiff saying we would get our asses kicked, and then suddenly straight edge was the biggest thing to ever hit CBGB. It happened so quickly. Frickin' Raybeez became straight edge! He reformed Warzone as a total straight-edge band!

From left: *Early Youth of Today gig at the Anthrax in Connecticut* JORDAN COOPER; *Youth of Today with Craig Setari on bass* GARY TSE TSE FLY

COME ROCK LOWER EAST SIDE STYLE WITH

WARZONE

AND YOUTH DEFENSE LEAGUE
TUESDAY NITE SEPT. 23RD
$5 AVE A AT 6TH ST. AT THE PYRAMID
SHOW STARTS AT 12:30

Warzone with the dearly departed Raybeez on vocals
GARY TSE TSE FLY

37. WARZONE: DON'T FORGET THE STREETS

RAY CAPPO: I knew Raybeez from hanging out. I remember coming back from California and seeing Todd Youth on the street. He grabbed me and said, "Check this out, Warzone is back and we're all straight edge now!" I thought he was kidding. When he told me Raybeez was straight edge, I was sure he was kidding! Sure enough, we went to hang out with Raybeez and he said, "We're all straight edge now!"

GARY TSE TSE FLY: Donny the Punk used to do the New York scene reports for *Maximum Rocknroll*, but he went to India or something like that. So I think me and Mike Bullshit wrote the scene report for him one month. I wrote that there was this straight-edge scene happening in New York. I mentioned Crippled Youth and Youth of Today. I was in Some Records, and this kid came up to me and asked if I was the guy who wrote the scene report in *Maximum Rocknroll* that month. I said yeah, and he said, "I'm Todd Youth from Warzone. Yo, why didn't you mention Warzone with all the other positive bands?"

TODD YOUTH: Skinhead Youth kind of morphed into Warzone. Warzone started out being called the Rat Poison Band. At one point, it was me on bass, Ray on drums, Sebastian "Tito" Perez on guitar, and Tommy Rat singing as Warzone. We did two shows in Virginia with Agnostic Front and after that Tommy quit. I went away for a little bit and when I came back Raybeez had Warzone going with him singing, and I came back into the band on guitar. I was probably in Warzone for two years, from the ages of fourteen to sixteen. I wrote almost all the music, including the lyrics to songs like "In the Mirror," "As One," and "We're the Crew."

JULES MASSE (VOCALIST, SIDE BY SIDE, ALONE IN A CROWD): The Warzone demo with all the vocal reverb—the one with Raybeez, Todd Youth, Batmite, and Charlie Ultra Violence—that was the best thing I ever heard. They were going to be the next big NYHC band, following Agnostic Front and the Cro-Mags.

RAY CAPPO: I don't think those early Warzone gigs were necessarily that great. It was just that Raybeez was such a great character. He was from the old scene where they did tons of drugs. When he went straight edge, it created that nice bridge between the two worlds. He was always a very positive, upbeat, welcoming person. Although he was hard, you never felt unwelcomed by the guy. He was a great ambassador for the old school.

ARTHUR SMILIOS: To know Raybeez was to love him. He was like an older brother. Walter and I were these skinny little working-class nerds from Queens, and he took care of us, especially once we joined Warzone. That was something. The scene was stratified: You had the top guys like Raybeez, Roger Miret, John Joseph, and Jimmy G. Walter and I were very far down that ladder. Once we were in Warzone, we became guys nobody would bother. As silly as that sounds, it was true. I am very proud to have been a part of that band.

WALTER SCHREIFELS: I think Arthur was asked to be in Warzone first and then he asked me to come in and play bass or second guitar. It's so long ago I can't really remember. Raybeez was the top scene guy, so I started to make more connections to the inside of the scene. It was really cool because Ray was this huge character. He was explaining a lot to me about what this shit was about. He told me about that real New York hardcore world that had happened a year and a half back. I had never been past Avenue A until I was in Warzone, but then I could go with him and it felt all right. It was just a weird scene, with angel dust flying around. Coming from Queens and Rockaway, it was a cool little peek inside.

MATT WARNKE: Warzone were integral to the Lower East Side at the time. The first time I saw Warzone at CB's, it was all just neighborhood people on the left side of the stage: women with big hair and leopard pants. Warzone had a smoke machine—they were fucking great.

WAR-ZONE
SxE UNDERDOG
SICK OF IT ALL SUPERTOUGH
KRACKDOWN RAW DEAL

JANUARY
30
7:00pm

& special guest
PROJECT X

$10

RITZ
11TH STREET BET. 3RD & 4TH AVENUES

WAR ZONE

$3.50 ppd.
REVELATION RECORDS
P.O. Box 1454
New Haven, CT 06506
NYC comp coming soon
with: Youth of Today,
Bold, etc.

Photos from top:
Warzone at CBGB
RANDY UNDERWOOD;
Warzone at CBGB
GARY TSE TSE FLY

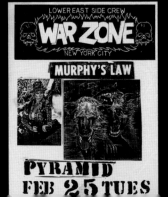

LOWER EAST SIDE CREW
WAR ZONE
NEW YORK CITY

MURPHY'S LAW

PYRAMID
FEB 25 TUES

WAR ZONE
YOUTH DEFENSE LEAGUE
SIDE BY SIDE BY SIDE
& special guest

SAT AUG 1st at the PYRAMID   2PM

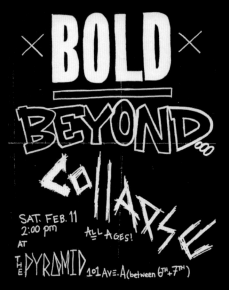

× BOLD ×

BEYOND...

COLLAPSE

SAT. FEB. 11
2:00 pm   ALL AGES!
AT
THE PYRAMID 101 AVE. A (between 6TH + 7TH)

From top: Bold vocalist Matt Warnke sporting the classic Youth Crew look on the CBGB stage; Youth of Today breaking down the walls at CBGB
PHOTOS BY GARY TSE TSE FLY

38. YOUTH CREW: BETTER THAN YOU!

TOMMY CARROLL: I got into that whole straight-edge thing. I grew up with a lot of alcohol and drugs. I did them at a young age, and got burnt out on drugs by the time I was fourteen years old. Straight edge was an easy choice for me. It was a better way of life.

ARTHUR SMILIOS: I wore X's on my hands and took it very seriously. My high school was filled with drugs and alcohol and I didn't partake. At that age, where you aren't yet secure with who you are, having something with which to identify was important. It gave me a sense of belonging, as well as pride that I was living in a way that was not the norm for my socioeconomic group.

RAY CAPPO: Youth of Today brought a suburban element to the scene and made it easier to not have to be a badass to hang out. You didn't have to be a criminal or a drug addict just to hang out. There was an influx of kids from the suburbs who would come up to the Lower East Side. They were kids who thought, "I can relate to hardcore, but I can't relate to the negative elements." Personally, that was a real deterrent to me. I wasn't into drugs or the "Live fast die young" thing. Straight edge let you become a part of the hardcore scene but still have ethics, morals, and self-integrity. Without a doubt, music was the common thread that brought all these different personalities all together.

WALTER SCHREIFELS: The one thing I liked about the straight-edge thing was the suburban imported fashion. Like, we're not going to have Mohawks and wear leather jackets: We're going to dress in Champion sweatshirts and look like kids from the suburbs. I thought that was cool. In New York, it was crazier because kids didn't dress like that anyway. There are no football teams in New York City!

ALEX BROWN: I didn't know that there was such a thing as the Youth Crew before going to New York, and I still don't really know what it was. Possibly it was just a convenient term to tag anyone who looked a certain way and hung with bands that weren't into the gutter drug scene.

MATT WARNKE: In New York, the skinhead vibe was there. But from day one— whether it was Ray and Porcell or Mark Ryan or Warzone or Richie Birkenhead— there was also the aesthetic of wearing high-tops, hooded sweatshirts, and baseball hats. Whether or not you want to say we co-opted the oncoming hip-hop scene and mixed it with existing skinhead trappings, eventually it led to what you would now define as Youth Crew.

LUKE ABBEY: I'm not sure there was any definitive meaning to the Youth Crew beyond the values and ideas of the bands that compromised it. The image has certainly developed over time to become somewhat iconic—hooded sweatshirts, football jerseys, and high-tops—but that was just a style. The power of the music and shows propelled all that and made it larger than life.

ARTHUR SMILIOS: For better or worse, my friends and I created the Youth Crew look. I went down to Orchard Street with Walter and Porcell, because we found a wholesaler who sold varsity jackets with fake leather sleeves. This was early on, and we were all vegetarian and trying not to wear leather. The hip-hop influence was huge. This was before *Yo! MTV Raps* and the hijacking of that scene by the mainstream. Hip-hop was very underground. The corporate music business wanted nothing to do with either of our scenes. That independent, underground aspect, as well as the geographical proximity, made hardcore and hip-hop into natural allies.

WALTER SCHREIFELS: We were all into the hip-hop shit. It was happening at the same time and was a big influence on us. You could probably hear it in the music—another reason why the mosh parts were better. Listen to "Break Down the Walls" and Ray's delivery. It sounds like a rap song!

MATT WARNKE: In some ways it was conscious, and in some ways it was just what we rocked every day. I was more inclined to go to Orchard Street or Rivington Street and try to pick up sneakers I saw Rakim wearing in the "I Ain't No Joke" video than I was to wear what someone was wearing on a record from England. That's even what I loved about bands from the Midwest who just got up onstage in flannel shirts and ripped jeans, or bands from California who wore Vans and looked like they just came from shredding a pool or a half-pipe. Represent who you are and where you come from!

RAY CAPPO: Nowadays, you have whole marketing and branding teams that are supposed to come up with the ideas. When you think about it, we were figuring out the concept of branding before we knew what it even was. There was a definitely a look from that period. I remember being in a club in East Germany and seeing all these kids wearing Revelation shirts. They looked they could have been from New York City circa 1986, but it was 1995. I realized, "Oh my God! We created a whole fashion and culture."

HOWIE ABRAMS: I never got into the fashion or making sure I had the newest Air Jordans. There was this look with the Champion sweatshirts with the cuffed jeans and the brand-new kicks, and I didn't get what that had to do with hardcore. I didn't adopt the uniform. Good for them, they looked great, but it wasn't me and wasn't what I recognize as the NYHC scene.

CRAIG SETARI: I ended up in Youth of Today. I was playing bass and Tommy Carroll was playing drums. I liked the band, and I liked Violent Children before that. I played with them for a year and I played on the first LP. That was the only band I ever quit just because I felt like it was getting trendy and it was corny. I felt like I was being pushed into something with that band. Don't get me wrong—not doing drugs is great. I used to be a burnout kid, so it helped me in a big way. But hardcore is grimy. I got into because I was a grimy kid. Some of that stuff started to come off way too clean for me.

WENDY EAGER: The skinheads made it the "good ol' boys" thing, but the straight-edge thing made it, "Hold my coat, I'm going into the pit." The whole youth crew ostracized women from hardcore. They wanted to be these jock guys who got into the pit. They wore their sports clothes and they thought the girls had a place. To me, hardcore and sports just don't mix.

TOMMY CARROLL: Let's face it, beyond the way people dressed and all that, straight edge was a good thing. People are a lot stronger the more unified they are. The straight-edge scene was a strength—the power of the movement made kids want to be a part of it. Everybody was trying to grasp that energy. I'm glad to have been a part of it. I'm a New York guy through and through. I'm cynical. I'm a pessimist. As much as I try to be positive and optimistic as an adult, that's the way I'll always be. Maybe it was because of the way I was brought up and the things I've seen and experienced. But it was nice to take a break from that as a kid, even for a small period of time. It was a very enjoyable part of my life.

"I'm for the people…" NYHC's "most tucked-under-the-rug incredible band," Straight Ahead. PHOTOS BY GARY TSE TSE FLY

39. STRAIGHT AHEAD: WE STAND

TOMMY CARROLL: I started working when I was fourteen. I saved up my money from my summer job at the boathouse on Ninetieth Street and First Avenue and I bought a drum set. I played with a few friends in the neighborhood. These guys Gordon Ancis and Tony Marc were taking lessons and they were pretty decent musicians. Metal was our thing: Sabbath, Priest, Maiden, and then Metallica. After going to see Adrenalin O.D. at CBGB, I got more into hardcore. We replaced Tony with Craig Setari and we started playing as NYC Mayhem.

ARMAND MAJIDI: Mayhem played a bunch of shows with Tommy playing the drums and singing, and it just didn't work.

TOMMY CARROLL: I played drums and sang, and those two things didn't really mix in hardcore. You couldn't get much crowd participation like that. My ego took over and I wanted to be a singer.

CRAIG SETARI: I started writing songs. Then Tommy wanted to sing. Gordon wanted to play metal, so he left and NYC Mayhem turned into Straight Ahead. I was in front of CBGB one day talking to Armand. He used to wear a silver-spray-painted trench coat. He was really creepy looking. I told him Tommy wanted to sing, so we needed a drummer. Armand had never played drums before, but he was willing to try. That's the way hardcore was—you just jumped right into things with no real training.

ARMAND MAJIDI: Right after I left high school, someone introduced me to the guys I would be in Rest in Pieces with. They were looking for a guitarist, so I just stepped into that band. After being in the band for a month or so, we recorded our first 7-inch. I ended up doing the vocals, even though my sense of timing was nonexistent.

PETE KOLLER: When I was a kid, I got an acoustic guitar and a book on how to read music. I could barely read fucking words, and you want me to read music? I said fuck that. But then I went to hardcore shows, and I realized I could do this. I could make a barre chord with my fingers. I wrote "My Life" and then "Friends like You" in the same day. I mean, they're basically the same fucking song! At first, Lou was learning how to play bass, and our friend David Lamb played drums. Then Lou started singing. My friend from high school Mark McNeilly played bass, and we wrote a couple of songs. That was the beginning of Sick of It All.

ARMAND MAJIDI: Rest in Pieces kept changing. I became sort of a musical dictator. I ended up being the front man, just to get Rob Echeverria on guitar. Later on, I kicked Joshua Barker out of the band to get Craig in on bass. I was familiar with Craig because he was playing in Mayhem. Everything was very incestuous in that way.

PETE KOLLER: Mark McNeilly was one of those guys who immediately went straight edge and he didn't want to hang out with anyone who wasn't straight edge. He left the band because he wanted to be down with Crippled Youth and Youth of Today. Armand said, "Well, I'm learning to play drums in Straight Ahead, why don't I play drums for you guys too?" Richie Cipriano was just hanging around with us, and he joined on bass.

ARMAND MAJIDI: I learned drums from joining Straight Ahead. I watched other drummers, so I had an understanding of what I had to do. Literally the fifth or sixth time I ever sat down behind a drum kit was the first Straight Ahead show, at February's on Long Island. The tenth time I sat down behind a drum kit was our first CB's gig. Looking back, I'm shocked at how quickly I picked it up.

JOHN PORCELLY: The band I love out of that time period is Straight Ahead. They are the most tucked-under-the-rug incredible band from New York. Tommy Carroll was one of the best front men ever!

ALEX BROWN: Straight Ahead! That band was a mindblower. Tommy Carroll was right there with Cappo as being the scene's best front man. Dude was scary, too. He was an amateur boxer: an Irish kid from way the fuck uptown who was not one to be messed with. They were fucking amazing live.

TOMMY CARROLL: When we did NYC Mayhem, we didn't give a fuck. We did whatever we wanted to do. With Straight Ahead, we consciously followed the blueprint to be a NYHC band. We started shaving our heads. I wanted to

Straight Ahead's Tommy Carroll GARY TSE TSE FLY

be accepted, so I lost some of my identity. I was definitely following a format to be accepted in the hardcore scene. I can't speak for all the other guys in the band, but, for me, I fell into that. I wanted to be accepted. Don't get me wrong—Straight Ahead was a good band. But I definitely toned it down to be accepted. I'm just being honest.

JOHN PORCELLY: I almost feel bad that I got Tommy Carroll and Craig to join Youth of Today, because it sort of broke up Straight Ahead and took away the momentum from them.

TOMMY CARROLL: Craig and I went on tour with Youth of Today. Even though people in that scene let us come into their houses and fed us and honestly cared and really took us in and embraced us, I couldn't take it. Our van broke down. Then I think we ended up just doing the tour in a car and that also broke down. We were starving and all that, a typical story for every hardcore band from that time. Craig still played with Youth of Today. Rob and I said, "Quit, and come back to Straight Ahead." So he did. We got back together for a little bit, but we didn't have enough steam to keep going.

CRAIG SETARI: After I left Youth of Today, Straight Ahead played this dismal show in Albany. We drove back as fast as we could to see Youth of Today at CBGB, and we got there just as they were finishing. The place was packed, and everyone was going nuts. I was like, "Shit, this sucks." I had a feeling in my stomach that I had let go of being part of a band that was so much fun.

TOMMY CARROLL: Eventually, I felt like there was nothing left for me in the band or the scene. There was nothing more that I could do, so I just lost interest. We weren't feeling it anymore. We couldn't write new songs. We just grew apart. I was always rolled a little tight and wanted things done my way, so that could be another reason the band broke up.

CRAIG SETARI: We were young kids, so there were disagreements between us, but nothing serious. One day something wasn't working out, and Tommy said he didn't want to do it anymore. Myself, Rob, and Armand much agreed we were done with this. I had quit Youth of Today to dedicate my time to Straight Ahead, and now, two months later, we broke up.

TOMMY CARROLL: Sometime after that, Sergio Vega asked me to join this band he was doing, Irate. Sergio was a real good kid. I just really liked him and he really had something going, but I was done by then. I tried to go through the motions, but it wasn't me anymore. I was washed up at twenty! I'm still just so glad to have had a part in it. You know how at CBGB everybody put their band's stickers up on the wall? Well, that's what we did. We put our sticker up on the wall of the NYHC scene, just like everybody else.

presents

KRAUT
MURPHY'S LAW

SAT. SEPT. 21

**REAGAN
YOUTH**
**SKINHEAD
YOUTH**

New York's Only
Doors Open
9pm
ROCK HOTEL
113 Jane St.
INFO.
279-1984

presents
The Exclusive Hardcore Reunion of

BAD
BRAINS

FRI. JULY 19
SAT. JULY 20

**RAW POWER
SCAB**
**CRO-MAGS
P.M.S.**

New York's Only
Doors Open
9pm
$10, Adm.
at door only
ROCK HOTEL
113 Jane St.
INFO.
279-1984

presents
A ONE TIME ONLY
STARTLING REUNION
of

MEATMEN

with

BORSCHT
and
OBSESSED

SAT. FEB 11

New York's Only
ROCK HOTEL
113 Jane St.
279-1986

Doors Open 9pm
Adm. $7.
For booking info:
Chase Park Prod.

40. ROCK HOTEL PRESENTS

JAMES KONTRA: To me, shit started going downhill in the scene when a gentleman by the name of Chris Williamson got wind of this shit. He ran the door at Mel's, an upscale dance club on Fourteenth Street where Prince and Jack Nicholson would go. He was the bringer of death to what was going on. He started putting on shows over in the West Village, calling it the Rock Hotel.

MIKE BULLSHIT: The original Rock Hotel was on Jane Street by the piers. It was the middle of nowhere. It was the type of place where you could play loud music until early in the morning.

WENDY EAGER: Chris Williamson had a lot to do with ruining the music. He created this big venue where he would pay bands money. That caused problems in the scene, because now people weren't content to play the smaller shows anymore. I've never said anything nice about Chris Williamson. I used to write bad stuff about him before it was cool to put him down.

PAUL CRIPPLE: The second time we played Rock Hotel, he wanted us go on before Murphy's Law and Kraut. We said no, because we had been around way before those bands. Fuck that shit. We went on after Murphy's Law, and the crowd left. Dave laughed in Chris' face. Chris Williamson wanted Dave to thank Andy Warhol for showing up. Right in the middle of him asking Dave to do that, I pointed and said, "Doesn't that faggot look like Andy Warhol?" Steam came out of Chris Williamson's ears.

NATALIE JACOBSON SHEARING (EMPLOYEE, THE RITZ; AUTHOR): Chris Williamson was predatory. He screwed over bands, manipulated the bookings, and started pushing speed metal and hardcore bands together. Williamson was a devil, but he saw a vacancy. He saw hardcore shows could draw more people than fit inside CBGB.

ALEXA POLI-SHEIBERT: I never had to pay to get into Rock Hotel shows because Big Charlie worked the door. I liked fucking over Chris Williamson. Anything to get over on that guy made me happy.

ERNIE PARADA: The best sneaking into a show that I can remember was at the Rock Hotel. We tried to crawl up a drainpipe to climb in a window: Wattie from the Exploited opened it and pulled us into the back room.

MICHAEL GIBBONS: Chris Williamson moved his shows over to the Ritz in 1985, and that's when it really blew up. The big Ritz shows were way more welcoming to kids who were maybe too intimidated to go down to CBGB on a Sunday. There were mixed bills with hardcore bands and metal bands like Exodus.

JAMES KONTRA: The shit he did at the Ritz became cliquish and real rock star–ish. It was all about guest lists, and who you knew, and all this name-dropping. I was really embarrassed. The system managed to infiltrate our scene.

WENDY EAGER: I think Rock Hotel screwed hardcore in a lot of ways. A big rock-star mentality entered the scene. All of a sudden, Chris Williamson took this scene and had a show every week. The out-of-town bands were making money, but the local bands weren't making shit.

RUSS ISLAY: I worked almost all of the Rock Hotel shows with Jimmy G and Raybeez as security. I had no problem coming to see the shows and getting paid. He put on good shows. He had local hardcore kids working the stage, and—most importantly—he paid us. Instead of hiring security goons, he got us. I thought that was cool. Those shows were great, and they wouldn't have happened if not for him.

NATALIE JACOBSON SHEARING: I was already working at the Ritz when Rock Hotel moved there from Jane Street. The shows got bigger, because the Ritz had a great location and an advertising budget. The shows were promoted better. More "outside" people started coming to the shows.

MICHAEL SCONDOTTO (VOCALIST, INHUMAN, THE LAST STAND): I went to the Ritz for my first hardcore show, and after that to CBGB four weeks later for my second hardcore show. Aside from the Ritz being far larger, I think the Ritz drew the punks and metalheads who liked hardcore but were hesitant about going to CBGB. There was more diversity at the Ritz, overall.

MICHAEL GIBBONS: I know a lot of purists will say they didn't want any big

Murphy's Law at the Ritz location of the Rock Hotel KEN SALERNO

business in the scene, and they wanted it to stay underground, but I thought it was great when the Rock Hotel shows started. The music was getting so big that it was bursting out of the underground. It couldn't be ignored anymore.

JORDAN COOPER (OWNER, REVELATION RECORDS): I guess you could complain that hardcore was getting too big, or bringing in too many kids who didn't get what it was about and were just there to pick fights. I'm not sure what effect that had on the scene in general. My take was that if people didn't like when bands got to the level where they could play at places that big, people didn't have to support those shows. There was just no stopping NYHC from getting bigger. Sick of It All, Agnostic Front, Cro-Mags, Youth of Today, Underdog, and Gorilla Biscuits were all getting to the level where they would be asked to play bigger venues. I guess that if it wasn't Rock Hotel and Chris Williamson, it would have been someone else.

EDDIE SUTTON: Chris was an asshole and definitely capitalized on everyone's naïveté, but if not for him, a lot of New York bands wouldn't have the place in history that they have today. The Cro-Mags would never have gone on tour with Motörhead. Leeway wouldn't have been able to say we were the only band that toured with the Bad Brains across the country for twelve weeks.

TOMMY CARROLL: I was never a fan of Chris Williamson. He was a money-hungry cheeseball, but I'm not going to lie: I did enjoy the shows he put on.

JOHN PORCELLY: They were great shows, but none of the bands got paid. The ticket prices were high, and they'd stuff the place to the rafters with two thousand people. Chris Williamson probably made a killing. Truth be told, he was a dick. It's one thing to put on big shows, but it's another thing to knowingly rip off every single band that plays. We'd go on tour and be ecstatic to get a meal and floor to sleep on. So it's not like we were expecting money, but you could at least be nice and kick a few dollars more to the local musicians who could barely afford their equipment. Instead, this one guy was taking the lion's share of the money home, and probably buying a ton of coke.

NATALIE JACOBSON SHEARING: At some point, Williamson started expanding his little empire and started signing bands to personal contracts. He began securing label deals for them and taking more money than he was entitled to.

JESSE MALIN: The closest New York got to have a big hardcore label was when there was the Rock Hotel label through Profile with Chris Williamson. I don't think that worked out too well. Those guys were real upset with him.

MICHAEL GIBBONS: Everyone was young, a little naïve, and desperate. Everyone thought this was the chance for hardcore to make a big splash on the map, since Profile had these big acts like Run-DMC and Special Ed on it.

EDDIE SUTTON: When we played our first show at CBGB, things started happening. At our fifth or sixth show at CB's, we opened for C.O.C. Chris Williamson saw us and put us on a Rock Hotel show in June of 1986. He was always looking at the dollar signs in things and was the premier promoter in New York at the time.

JOHN JOSEPH (VOCALIST, BLOODCLOT, M.O.I., CRO-MAGS): Chris Williamson came up to us after seeing us and was like, "You guys are fuckin' incredible! I want to work with you!" He booked this show for us at the Ritz and he tried to jerk us for the money. I was like, "Yo, motherfucker you better pay me!" He tried to put his hands on me, and I slammed him against the wall. I was like, "Yo, if you ever fuckin' touch me again, motherfucker, I'll bury you." He was a real pushy, physical dude. He worked out, and he ran. He actually liked that I got in his face, and then he *really* wanted to work with us! He got us a lot of great shows, and he did a lot of great shit. Profile Records wanted to sign us. Him being the manager, he set up his own record label called Rock Hotel Records as a subsidiary of Profile. All of a sudden, not only was he our manager, he was our record company dude too! Conflict of interest, you know?

RUSS ISLAY: People who have worked with him as a band manager, that's a different story. I heard the stories about him being an asshole, and not being honest with the money and shit like that. I didn't experience any of that.

MICHAEL GIBBONS: When I joined Leeway, the band was really breaking out. They were doing really well. I was in the band for a week, and A. J. Novello and Eddie had signed a contract with Rock Hotel through Profile. Doug Holland hooked us up with him. Doug totally had our best interests at heart, but no one really knew what a real scumbag Williamson was. When I read his managing contract, I didn't need a lawyer. My father and I read it together, and we were shocked. Sure, it was in fourteen-letter words and smoothly prepared by a big-shot entertainment lawyer, but if you had half a brain, everything was clear: "You work for me until the day you die."

JOHN JOSEPH: When we recorded *Age of Quarrel*, Chris Williamson made me sing that whole fuckin' album in one day, dude.

MICHAEL GIBBONS: Leeway recorded *Born to Expire* from November 16 to November 20 of '87. It was a grueling schedule. I think Chris Williamson was trying to save and pocket as much of the recording budget as possible. We were doing sixteen-hour days without eating anything. It was insane. When we got to the last track, "Unexpected," the drummer, Tony Fontão, physically couldn't play anymore. It was midnight, and we had started at six in the morning. I'll never forget that. Chris came into the room screaming, "I hope you have seven hundred dollars for this hour that you wasted." Profile gave us twenty-five thousand dollars to record both records. Chris wanted to keep the budget under ten grand for each record and pocket the rest.

JOHN JOSEPH: I started realizing Chris Willamson was fucking us over. He did some really grimy shit. I saw a Winterland merchandising contract on his desk and I called him on it. He said, "I'm going to get you out of this band." I was like, "Motherfucker, this is my band. You ain't getting me out of my band!" He said, "Watch!" He turned the band against me, talking about how I can't sing and how they could do better without me. He started patting Harley's ego, telling him he was the star of the band. He manipulated these dudes against me.

EDDIE SUTTON: The personalities in the Cro-Mags were just too volatile to stay together. They were too young to really understand what was going on. I think what happened was Chris realized he wasn't able to control John. He was finding a way to get everyone else in the band against John. It turned into a powder keg, and started to explode—but in a bad way, not in a good way.

TOMMY CARROLL: I thought the Cro-Mags hooking up with Chris Williamson did them a disservice. I thought the album was produced horribly. They could have been bigger. They got shortchanged, I think.

ALEXA POLI-SHEIGERT: He ruined that album. The tape was much better. The tape blew the album away. Chris Williamson had to stick his little fingers in there. ruined that album and ruined the Cro-Mags. That's my opinion. All this schism started with him.

EDDIE SUTTON: There was a lot of this silver-tongued, delusional talk going on and it started fucking with a lot of bands' heads. Individuals in bands stopped seeing each other eye to eye. The aspirations they started with were lost, because the band wasn't unified anymore. That's why New York never reached the level it could have reached.

ANTHONY DRAGO (DRUMMER, BREAKDOWN, RAW DEAL): Chris Williamson was looking at Raw Deal right off the bat. We actually went down to audition for him. We went to some high-end practice spot that I guess he took the Cro-Mags and Leeway to. We did five or six songs, and the whole time he read a magazine. He was acting uninterested. We'd start a song, and he would tell us to stop. Then he'd say anybody could write a song like that. He was a really unique type of person. We didn't think we impressed him at all. Then we heard horror stories about how long it took Leeway to get their record out.

EDDIE SUTTON: Not too long after we recorded *Born to Expire*, Chris Williamson's contract with Profile ended. Profile kicked him out and took over the whole game. They didn't know what the fuck to do with us.

MICHAEL GIBBONS: *Born to Expire* didn't get released until January 21, 1989. We were hounding him to just put it out already. The whole time Chris was shopping our album, the second Murphy's Law album, and the second Cro-Mags album as a package deal to major distributors. None of them were interested in taking the chance. Murphy's Law, Cro-Mags, and Leeway were guinea pigs for him. That's why our album took a year and two months to come out.

EDDIE SUTTON: Our label Profile kicked Chris out of the loop; then our bass player Zowie left the band for Circus of Power. He was on the road for a long time. Even to release the record, he had to sign a release, which took a lot of time.

MICHAEL GIBBONS: I remember Sob from Merauder said, "That better not happen with the next record!" I was like—no way! Of course, the same thing happened with *Desperate Measures*. Chris shopped it around, and it took about the same time frame. We recorded it in April of 1990, and it didn't come out until June of 1991.

ANTHONY DRAGO: Howie Abrams from In-Effect Records was sniffing around to sign the band, too, and he made an offer. There was a lot of energy behind In-Effect, and we didn't know where Chris Williamson wanted to go with us. He didn't really offer us anything. Finally, we all talked and we decided to go with In-Effect. Then I I got a phone call from Chris Willamson, and he was fuckin' livid. He was screaming at me, "If you fucking guys think you're going to go and record at the same studio I do my recording and think it's going to sound the same, you're fuckin' mistaken! It has nothing to do with where you go, it's how you sound. I make Leeway sound the way they do. I'm the one who makes those records sound good." I listened long enough and there was only so much shit I was going to take, so I fucking hung up on him.

MICHAEL GIBBONS: Chris had a vision, but the greed took over. It was all about him. He wanted his name on the map. He wanted to be the next Ron Delsener, the guy who promotes all the big stadium shows around New York.

TODD YOUTH: I don't hate on Chris Williamson and Rock Hotel as much as everyone else. It was just a fucking record label, and they are all the same. They gave us money, we made a record, and we went on tour. If it wasn't for them, who else was going do it? Record labels are a necessary evil. Someone's got to put the record out, because I'm definitely not going to. I'm not a businessman.

EDDIE SUTTON: He paid out of pocket for us to finish that tour with the Bad Brains. He might have kept us in the dark about some money here and some money there, but he earned his keep as far as I'm concerned. Obviously, after it was all said and done, I was bitter and upset and I didn't like him. But once I grew older, I realized he did his job. A lot of the people who continue to talk shit on him to this day, most of them don't even know the fucking guy. Everybody's got a little bit of asshole in them: It's just a matter of where and when it comes out.

MICHAEL GIBBONS: I heard Chris passed away awhile back, but I think that was just a rumor. The last time I saw Chris was in the fall of 1998, at that place Life on Bleecker Street. My friends' band, the Bullies, was playing. I walked up to him and asked if he recognized me. He said he did, but I could tell he didn't remember me. He was bullshitting me even then! I said, "You don't know who I am, do you? It's Mike Gibbons from Leeway!" Then he went on about how he wasted thousands and thousands of dollars on Leeway and the Cro-Mags. Time had passed, so I came right out and said, "Chris, you mismanaged everybody." I have no love for the guy.

EDDIE SUTTON: By the third Leeway album, *Adult Crash*, I was very depressed. I think what fueled my insecurities and drug problem was seeing other bands on MTV, and knowing we were doing something just as good as them. I didn't want to be a rock star or be rich, but I wanted public interest in the band. I wanted to tour, and I wanted the band on MTV. I wanted to be recognized for doing something valid. I was watching these shit bands get recognized, and they were nothing but long-haired gimmicks. New York should have been up against Seattle in competition. But the New York bands had a little bit more street in them and it fucked us up quicker. We didn't know how to handle the adulation and notoriety. It fueled my depression and I was self-medicating.

I had a ton of money at the time because I was bartending in the largest club in New York City. I had a ton of sex, and I started partying more to fuel that sensation. It's the same story with a lot of bands that went through the same shit I wasn't into picking some girl out from the crowd and having my way with her, and saying, "Peace out." But there were women that I desired who were regulars at the club, and I went for it. I was a growing boy, so I had my Maypo, you know? I never realized what I was doing. I didn't realize until I was in a jail cell. Even then, it took me another five years to get it all together.

I was lucky to survive opiate addiction. I volunteer now, and I might become a counselor. I'm still at a crossroads in my life. I wanted to make music my career, but it didn't happen that way. I was just being a forty-something-year-old kid for a long time. I still get by, and that's all that mattered to me for a long time, but now I'm getting ready to go back to school.

I feel lucky to not only still be on the planet, but to have all my facilities. It would be very easy for me to be a forty-nine-year-old kid now, but I was lucky to grow up, get my shit together, and slowly get myself on track while living a very quiet life.

DON'T BE BRAINWASHED!!!

By a few sad and envious people whose diminished importance in our scene have caused them to strike out unfairly and condemn Rock Hotel for the high ticket prices at the Ritz.

DON'T BE FOOLED !!!

By a certain few individuals who, I am told, live in one of the most expensive neighborhoods in N.J., and who instead of examining the situation and having the courtesy and respect to seek out a reasonable solution, chose to strike out blindly with propaganda and false information.

DON'T BE MISLED !!!

Into thinking that a $10.00 advance ticket price is so awfully high when the majority of hardcore-punk shows run anywhere from $10.00 to $15.00 all over the country and ESPECIALLY when N.Y.C and L.A. are always the shows WHICH MAKE OR BREAK A BAND'S TOUR!   AND MOST IMPORTANTLY-

DON'T BE DICKED !!!

Into thinking that our scene is something other than the BANDS, ~~BECAUSE~~

THE BANDS ARE THE SCENE

And without great shows with killer press,publicity,sound and lights and production which allows the bands to become great, they get pegged as nobodies, and get promoted by nobodies, in gigs which are nowhere,which keep them nowhere; and guess what?   THE SCENE STAYS NOWHERE

THE BANDS RULE

And as a musician,a producer, and a promoter- thats what I am all about. The whole idea of a killer show is not only to excite the hell out of an audience with the newest and the best, but also to do everything possible to help the bands get ahead. One of the great honors in my life is seeing a band I've helped build up,gain publicity,success,and in some cases, major record contracts. Don't you agree that a band whose worked hard for years on the road should have a chance to make it? Anyway, that's what my Rock Hotel shows have done for a great number of bands. And with the spectacular crowds and great production some of these bands are now becoming quite famous and commanding outrageous guarantees,and so,the whole deal begins to backfire on me a little- all of which brings us back to the high ticket price. So hell, we can't boycott the bands,can we?Or don't we boycott the real Scumbags; like the Promoters and Clubowners around the country who think they can get away with stiffing a band; or the Lowlife so-called 'bookers' who steer bands into clubs for a Needless and Dishonest Commission from the band, clubs which they could book themselves into with no cost or trouble; or the Agents who will suck every last penny out of you-usually to the point of hurting the show's production; or the Airlines whose trumped up prices make it harder for me to fly in these bands and put on these shows; or, why not the Hotels, or Equipment Rentals,or Vehicle Rentals, or Advertising Costs, or hell,why not Food and Beer prices I mean , Let's be real!! I really,really wish we could charge $5.00 at the door because if it were even remotely possible I would do it in a second. However, the harsh reality is that I can barely make a Rock Hotel at the Ritz show work with a $12. ticket! Every show I put on I'm at risk for $9000.00 and that's before adding in the cost for talent- which usually runs anywhere from $2000.00 to $7000.00. So it doesn't take much of a brain to figure out how many people I need to break evenfor a Circle Jerks show which cost more than $15000.00 or for a smaller show which runs around $10000.00. I would just love to have these scumbags who think through the door- hoping we can break even-especially after you've worked very hard putting the show together with production,posters and millions of phone calls. And so these bright people have the nerve to call me capitalistic, well listen up, cause no piece of trash literature is going to stop me. Anyway, I know that when I moved Rock Hotel to the Ritz there were a few problems with their staff and procedures, and I sincerely apologize for things that might have happened which I was unaware. But now, after all these shows, things have gotten totally cool, and the Ritz actually looks forward to our shows for their unique excitement. I still wish I could get it to be more like a club like the old Rock Hotel,but remember, the Ritz is a concert hall-they were good enough to take us in-it will always be there and not continually busted, like many places I've had to deal with, that this means is that we can have a steady flow of concerts put on in the most professional of ways. So yah, it costs a little more, and maybe some of these bands have been a little spoiled, but don't you think they Deserve a little bigger piece of the pie after busting their balls on the streets for so long, the bands do, they won't come in anymore and play for these sleaze-balls who think that it's great to throw a band in any place that will take them with shitty production and make a few bucks without the slightest notion of how to treat a band with class or the remotest care about planting seeds for the future. Yah, maybe I have spoiled them a little, and maybe the ticket price is a little high, but let me tell you, these bands are getting somewhere now and after 10 years of doing a million bands it feels pretty good. So anyway, I hope that all of you will continue to support Rock Hotel shows and remember to buy your $10.00 tickets in advance. And even though it seems kinda high, just think about your big bands on a bill- that's $2.50 per band- not so much to ask for shows which are difficult to produce and risky at best- not so much to ask for shows which put on the most amazing hardcore,punk and crunch bands anywhere in the world! Yes that's right PUNK AND HARDCORE ARE NOT DEAD but in fact, the greatest hardcore shows anywhere in the world happen right here at Rock Hotel and it's something the N.Y.C. scene should be PROUD OF. So please don't sacrifice seeing these shows for the sake of a few misdirected people who are unfairly trying to create a schism.

SUPPORT OUR SCENE AND BE PROUD OF OUR BANDS AND THE SHOWS WHICH ARE FINALLY HELPING THEM GET THE BREAKS THEY DESERVE

The whole idea of a killer show is not only to excite the hell out of an audience with the newest and the best, but also to do everything possible to help the bands get ahead. One of the great honors in my life is seeing a band I've helped build up,gain publicity,success,and in some cases, major record contracts. Don't you agree that a band whose worked hard for years on the road should have a chance to make it? Anyway, that's what my Rock Hotel shows have done for a great number of bands. And with the spectacular crowds and great production some of these bands are now becoming quite famous and commanding outrageous guarantees,and so,the whole deal begins to backfire on me a little- all of which brings us back to the high ticket price. So hell, we can't boycott the bands,can we?Or don't we boycott the real Scumbags; like the Promoters and Clubowners around the country who think they can get away with stiffing a band; or the Lowlife so-called'bookers' who steer bands into clubs for a Needless and Dishonest Commission from the band, clubs which they could book themselves into with no cost or trouble; or the Agents who will suck every last penny out of you-usually to the point of hurting the show's production; or the Airlines whose trumped up prices make it harder for me to fly in these bands and put on these shows; or, why not the Hotels, or Equipment Rentals,or Vehicle Rentals, or Advertising Costs, or hell,why not Food and Beer prices I mean , Let's be real!! I really,really wish we could charge $5.00 at the door because if it were even remotely possible I would do it in a second. However, the harsh reality is that I can barely make a Rock Hotel at the Ritz show work with a $12. ticket! Every show I put on I'm at risk for $9000.00 and that's before adding in the cost for talent- which usually runs anywhere from $2000.00 to $7000.00. So it doesn't take much of a brain to figure out how many people I need to break evenfor a Circle Jerks show which cost more than $15000.00 or for a smaller show which runs around $10000.00. I would just love to have these scumbags who think through the door- hoping we can break even-especially after you've worked very hard putting the show together with production,posters and millions of phone calls. And so these bright people have the nerve to call me capitalistic, well listen up, cause no piece of trash literature is going to stop me. Anyway, I know that when I moved Rock Hotel to the Ritz there were a few problems with their staff and procedures, and I sincerely apologize for things that might have happened which I was unaware. But now, after all these shows, things have gotten totally cool, and the Ritz actually looks forward to our shows for their unique excitement. I still wish I could get it to be more like a club like the old Rock Hotel,but remember, the Ritz is a concert hall-they were good enough to take us in-it will always be there and not continually busted, like many places I've had to deal with, that this means is that we can have a steady flow of concerts put on in the most professional of ways. So yah, it costs a little more, and maybe some of these bands have been a little spoiled, but don't you think they Deserve a little bigger piece of the pie after busting their balls on the streets for so long, the bands do, they won't come in anymore and play for these sleaze-balls who think that it's great to throw a band in any place that will take them with shitty production and make a few bucks without the slightest notion of how to treat a band with class or the remotest care about planting seeds for the future. Yah, maybe I have spoiled them a little, and maybe the ticket price is a little high, but let me tell you, these bands are getting somewhere now and after 10 years of doing a million bands it feels pretty good. So anyway, I hope that all of you will continue to support Rock Hotel shows and remember to buy your $10.00 tickets in advance. And even though it seems kinda high, just think about your big bands on a bill- that's $2.50 per band- not so much to ask for shows which are difficult to produce and risky at best- not so much to ask for shows which put on the most amazing hardcore,punk and crunch bands anywhere in the world! Yes that's right PUNK AND HARDCORE ARE NOT DEAD but in fact, the greatest hardcore shows anywhere in the world happen right here at Rock Hotel and it's something the N.Y.C. scene should be PROUD OF. So please don't sacrifice seeing these shows for the sake of a few misdirected people who are unfairly trying to create a schism.

SUPPORT OUR SCENE AND BE PROUD OF OUR BANDS AND THE SHOWS WHICH ARE FINALLY HELPING THEM GET THE BREAKS THEY DESERVE

Chris Williamson

41. UNDERDOG: NOT LIKE YOU!

ADAM NATHANSON: In the New York City scene, Underdog played the role that I imagine Minor Threat occupied several years earlier in D.C. They were the mutually agreed-upon and best-loved singalong band, and all of their songs were about growing up and having fun.

RICHIE BIRKENHEAD: Around 1983 I knew I only wanted to be playing this kind of music. My friend Scott and I started the Numskulls. We were a strange band. We had stuff that sounded like the Gun Club, and then we had stuff that sounded like JFA. The Numskulls had some sort of posi-core songs, but then we had songs with titles like "Teenage Bloodbath." Russ was playing bass for Murphy's Law, and I became friends with him through skateboarding.

RUSS ISLAY: I knew the Numskulls from skateboarding, and I got them on a couple bills opening up for Murphy's Law. I really liked the band, they had some good hard mosh parts, and they always needed someone to fill in for them on bass. After I got kicked out of Murphy's Law, and I immediately called Richie. That was it.

ALEXA POLI-SCHEIBERT: I don't know how I finagled it, but I got the Numskulls their first show at CB's. I used to sing "Nothing" by Negative Approach with the Numskulls. I had a good voice for it; I did the total John Brannon.

RUSS ISLAY: I liked the parts of the Numskulls songs that were a little harder, like the Cro-Mags. I also liked how the Cro-Mags weren't a goofy band. Murphy's Law was a party band, and I wanted to move to a band that was more serious. Richie decided he wanted to change the name of the band to something more serious. I came up with the name True Blue, because at that point there were people that were on the scene we thought were a little fake. We felt that we were "true blue"; we were real. But a week later, Underdog popped up in my head. We changed the name of the band and we became more serious.

RICHIE BIRKENHEAD: Our bass player was going away to college or something, so it was perfect timing. We retained some Numskulls songs, but with Underdog lyrically I was doing some sociopolitical commentary even if it was in allegory.

RUSS IGLAY: We were far from straight edge, but we got lumped in with that stuff. We put out our first 7-inch with New Beginning Records, which I think Ray Cappo had some involvement with at some point. Then Richie joined Youth of Today on second guitar, and that really roped us into that whole thing. We'd be on tour and show up in Lawrence, Kansas. We'd slide open the van door, and the cooler would be full of cold Budweisers. These kids would be so bummed out, expecting us to be straight edge! We were just dudes from Belmar, New Jersey.

RICHIE BIRKENHEAD: Joining Youth of Today came from my friendship with Ray and Porcell. Porcell moved into my apartment on Thompson Street between Prince and Spring Streets. We were roommates for a while. I joked about wanting to play guitar again, and he said, "Dude, join Youth of Today!" But I started feeling ambivalent toward the straight-edge scene. I loved the basic tenets of straight edge. The whole abstinence thing and the whole PMA thing—all that was great. For me, the big red flag was always the exclusionary attitude in a movement that's supposed to be nonconformist. With that straight-edge scene, once you got your membership card, you were better than anybody else. It was such bullshit, especially for a bunch of bourgeois fucking white kids. I was always on the fringes of that scene, though I loved a lot of straight-edge bands.

RUSS IGLAY: Richie was playing guitar in Youth of Today. There were a couple of times he blew us off. He was not making practices. It came to a point where we had a show booked, and he was going with Youth of Today to play somewhere else. We had a show booked on this date, so he had to be back by then. He said he would be back, but he didn't make it, so I was just like, "That's it, you're done."

We tried out a few people. Sean Taggart tried out and he didn't have the timing down. Carl Mosh was one of my good friends, and he nailed every song on the first try. We already knew he would be great on stage because he was such a great dancer. He danced like a fucking maniac. We didn't need to look any further. I couldn't think of a better fit.

Richie wasn't happy with the way Youth of Today was treating him. I think he didn't like being in the back of the spotlight on second guitar. We had been talking to all these record companies. Jem was interested. Caroline was interested. Richie wanted back in and we wanted him back in. Carl was great and all, but we knew the record would be better if Richie was singing. It was hard to do that to Carl, but it wasn't personal. It went amicably. Carl wasn't that pissed, but I remember his mom being pissed at me.

We had this deal going with the people that put out *Rock for Light* for the Bad Brains. We were going to go with them, but right before we did they fucking collapsed. Caroline Records were interested, so that was the way to go. We recorded the *The Vanishing Point* LP. I wish we didn't go to Caroline, because we did a one-off contract with them. I didn't realize that when you do something like that, they know you're not coming back, so how much are they going to put into you?

That record sounds like crap, because of a guitar effects unit called a GP8. It was a rack-mounted thing for recording that had just come out, and Richie heard it was the greatest thing. We took band money and bought one. We went into the studio and didn't really know how to use it. And that's why the guitar sounds like shit. If we just went through a Marshall cabinet with a Marshall head and a Les Paul guitar, we would have sounded great.

RICHIE BIRKENHEAD: We never liked anything that we recorded. We were definitely a live band. Underdog was a fairly major part of the NYHC scene, but I don't think you would know that from the recordings. We were a band that always had a chip on our shoulder, and we didn't want to choose between camps. We deliberately stayed off any of those NYHC compilations that came out while we were around like *The Way It Is* or *Where the Wild Things Are*. Looking back, that was a stupid choice. These days, I've noticed a lot of cognitive distortion when it comes to our place in history. It seems it's all about revisionist history; I guess since we didn't start our own Wikipedia page, or really promote ourselves in the new era, we've fallen into semi-obscurity.

TIM CHUNKS: Underdog was positive and melodic, and their spectrum was so wide. They covered so many different genres. Above and beyond anything else, it was Richie's voice. When I think of Underdog, I just think of one of the greatest singers ever.

IN NYC...
NEW US HARDCORE RECORDS
AT
SOME RECORDS

WAY BACK IN FLEA MARKET ON B'WAY,
BTWN. 3rd & 4th, NEXT TO TOWER RECORDS,
EVERY SATURDAY & SUNDAY, 11 - 7

LOCAL OR TOURING BANDS WITH PRODUCT (RECORDS/CASSETTES) STOP BY OR CONTACT DUANE 212·206·0558

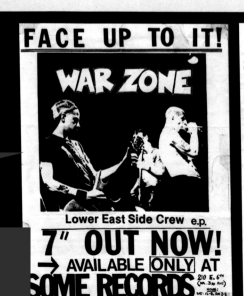

FACE UP TO IT!

WAR ZONE

Lower East Side Crew e.p.

7" OUT NOW!
→ AVAILABLE ONLY AT
SOME RECORDS

210 E. 6th
(nr. 3rd Ave)
HOURS:
SAT: 12-6, SUN 2-6
WED, THUR, FRI 4-8

NEW BREED!
TAPE COMPILATION

FEATURING: absolution, life's blood, raw deal, outburst, beyond and 13 more rocking N.Y.H.C. bands.

OUT SOON!
$5 ppd.
to: 31-80 51 st.
woodside
n.y. 11377
box: 4b

$5 ppd.
to: f. alva
35-18 93 st.
jck. hgts.
n.y. 11372

URBAN RECORDS

42. SOME RECORDS: U.S. HARDCORE AND NOT MUCH ELSE

JOHN PORCELLY: Any kind of scene—whether it's a music scene, an art scene, or a political scene—needs a hub where people can get together and exchange ideas. There's always a clubhouse where people meet. Some Records was that.

HOWIE ABRAMS: For the size of the city of New York, the community aspect of the hardcore scene here has been unbelievable. I think that came out of need early on. When the nucleus of the scene was A7, everybody had to try to get along and cooperate, because they had no choice. As it graduated and the bands started to get bigger, the clubhouse was CBGB. Kids did fanzines and sold them outside of the shows. Then bands started to make demos and sell them to Some Records, and that became the clubhouse away from the clubhouse.

WENDY EAGER: Some Records was sort of the descendant of Rat Cage. Rat Cage was a hangout and a place to go, and Some was like that too. That was the very last store like that in New York.

DAVE KOENIG: I'm pretty sure I heard about Some Records through *Maximum Rocknroll*. Since I was still very naïve about everything, I was kind of afraid to even go to this place. The ad promised "U.S. Hardcore and Not Much Else." I mean, being a new wave kid, I was thinking I was going to get my ass kicked by the people who ran the place. Some Records was the brainchild of Duane Rossignol. He initially was selling different types of records, along with a lot of hardcore and punk, at the Tower Records market on Fourth and Broadway.

DUANE ROSSIGNOL: The only reason the store happened was because of the woman I was involved with at the time, Gina Franklyn. She started Manic Panic with Tish and Snooky, and she was a part of the whole Danny Fields entourage. She left Manic Panic and started a store named 99 on MacDougal

Street in the summer of 1978. She talked Ed Baldwin into starting a record store there. So she was behind two of the more remembered record stores from that period, 99 and Some Records.

In the spring of 1984, Gina was sharing space at 99X on Sixth Street. I was looking at the wholesale prices in a supplement by the distributor Toxic Shock out in California, and I realized it would be feasible to bring these records in myself. Gina found me the place at the Tower Records flea market in the back. I only wanted to sell *some* records—that's where the name came from. I didn't want to sell all kinds of records, just some. We moved into the 99X space in September of 1985. That's the genesis of the store.

DAVE KOENIG: When he first opened, the store was upstairs in a long narrow storefront. There was a counter, with a bin of 12-inch and 7-inch records on the counter. In 1987, he moved the operation downstairs, and the rest is history. This is the location most everybody who has been there remembers with fondness.

RAY CAPPO: It was the most unassuming underground store, with one nerdy guy behind the counter. There were maybe two boxes of singles on the counter, and a very thin selection of hardcore, because Duane was such an epicurean of hardcore.

JASON O'TOOLE (VOCALIST, LIFE'S BLOOD): Some Records was to NYHC what Al's was to Happy Days. What would the Fonz be without his office? Just another greasy weirdo chasing after high school girls. I spent more time at Some Records than I did in my dorm room.

DUANE ROSSIGNOL: I wrote Tommy Carroll in the fall of 1985 because I read a review of the NYC Mayhem demo in *Maximum Rocknroll*. I asked if I could get copies for the store. Tommy started coming down to the store and hanging out. He had a whole crowd with him. The Sick of It All boys knew him and would come around.

TOMMY CARROLL: Duane was very knowledgeable about music. He was a big blues guy. Duane was out there, but his love for hardcore was incredible. He was a good man, and he treated me right. I think everything he did was for the love of the music and nothing else.

ALEX BROWN: Some was the place to go if you wanted to sell your demo. He would have any and every up-and-coming band's demo tape sitting on the counter when you stepped down into his little world from the street above.

BILL WILSON: Some was the place where you went to get the newest, coolest shit. Duane was such a lightning rod for that second generation of NYHC bands. I don't think there could have been a Sick of It All or a Breakdown or a Krakdown or a Raw Deal—or any of those bands that got huge off of shittily recorded demo tapes dubbed on multiple tape decks by girlfriends. Duane was instrumental to the NYHC scene in that era.

PETE KOLLER: Duane was the one who pushed us to our height. My brother Lou was really good friends with Duane. Lou would cut school and hang out down at the store. In between bands at CBGB, the whole crowd would go down to Some and back. As soon as people would walk in, Duane would just push things on people. "You got to buy this record. You got to buy this demo." When we had our demo—man, we were so psyched. We brought a box of fifteen cassettes down to the store. He really pushed that tape, and we sold fifteen or twenty cassettes in the first day. We had to keep making more and more. He pushed it to anyone who came in.

JEFF PERLIN: After we recorded the Breakdown demo in 1987, we brought it to Some Records for Duane to sell. He bought a couple boxes of cassettes and played it in the store right when we handed them to him. That was really cool. Immediately everyone in the store went to the counter and started buying it right in front of us. They were really into it. It was basically gone that day, and we had to bring more the next time we were around.

DUANE ROSSIGNOL: Tommy told me about a really great group up in Connecticut called Youth of Today. This was in December 1985. I met Ray Cappo and got totally converted. I was living on Horatio and Hudson at the time, and Ray's brother was living in a one-bedroom apartment on Fifteenth Street, further up Hudson. Ray lived there for the summer. He was a real doer, and a very smart fellow. Another turning point was when Raybeez and Todd Youth presented themselves at the store one day. Raybeez got into the straight-edge thing, so I pushed his band Warzone on Youth of Today. That was a big deal for me. I remember them leaving the store together, and they all had their painter hats on. I was impressed. A week later, Raybeez came by with a whole tape of a Warzone practice tape for me. The tape began, "This tape is for Duane, and for all you kids out there, never give in to society's bullshit!"

GAVIN VAN VLACK: I remember seeing the first Side by Side flyer at Some Records when they were looking for members. Porcell said, "I don't know what they're going to sound like, but their flyers are fuckin' awesome!"

DUANE ROSSIGNOL: Jules from Side by Side came into the store. He made up a flyer about looking for a band, put it up on the bulletin board, and proceeded to sit right by the bulletin board for the next three hours. Finally, I was like, "What gives, kid?" He was waiting to see if anyone would show up and join the band. New York is a fucking big town and everyone is welcome: That's the way I looked at it. As far as I was concerned, everyone was allowed inside. I never threw anyone out. The store wouldn't have existed without kids like him.

DAVE KOENIG: People used to post all sorts of flyers and trade lists on the bulletin board at Some Records. Adam Nathanson of Life's Blood made up a fake flyer: "WANTED: Black Sabbath LPs; Led Zeppelin LPs; Iron Maiden LPs. I HAVE: Agnostic Front *United Blood* 7-inch; Cause for Alarm 7-inch; Antidote 7-inch. If interested, call 555-DOPEY-SKIN." We all waited for some sucker to come by and read it. We wanted to see how long it took for them to figure out it was a gag. In walks Jason, the singer of Krakdown. He walks over to the bulletin board and starts reading the flyer out loud. "What the fuck? I have all those records. Hey Duane, give me a pen, I have to write this number down." Adam and a couple of others start laughing hard. Jason goes back and rereads the flyer, turns around, and just puts his hands around his throat in a joking manner. He knew he was fooled, and started laughing himself. That was a classic Some Records moment.

ADAM NATHANSON: I always thought it was a big deal when Duane would take a break and leave me sitting behind the counter for a while. I thought I was the king of the world because I was behind the counter at Some Records. I'd tell my mom when I got home that I was in charge of this store in Manhattan for thirty minutes. I don't have any stories about beatdowns or anything, but I have that.

JEFF PERLIN: After the demo had come out, Duane was all excited about the review in *Maximum Rocknroll*. I was all ready to laugh at how they'd torn it to shreds. *MRR* at the time hated NYHC, and gave tons of New York bands awful reviews. They'd say that there were loads of fascists in New York, which was definitely not the case. But the review came out and it was really, really good. They loved it. It was so weird. But the best part was how excited Duane was. He was really a big supporter of the band and did so much for us.

RAY CAPPO: Duane was such a fan of the music that he could not have a business brain in his head. I mean, the guy had a record store with no sign in front! Gina was more the businessperson. She would say, "Ray, you have to talk to him. He's going to go out of business! Every time a band comes down here to sell a demo tape, he buys ten of them!"

DUANE ROSSIGNOL: I am very proud of pushing that cassette business, because that's where the music was. The deal I had with kids is I would pay them two dollars for the cassette, and then charge three dollars for it. I never ran off extra copies. The most I ever sold was the Raw Deal demo. Two of the band members in Raw Deal and Breakdown had girlfriends who made the tapes and they made sure I had tapes. I ended up selling about four hundred copies of Raw Deal. I used to never take stuff out on consignment. You gave the kid the fucking money.

TOMMY CARROLL: Chuck Valle, rest his soul, got into the other side of music, and started working at Chung King Studios. He was a fan of Straight Ahead, and he played in Ludichrist. He wanted to start using Chung King to record hardcore. We had to come in there at three o'clock in the morning. We had no intentions of doing anything with it but seeing how it went on the twenty-four-track board, with Chuck producing. Then Duane approached me about putting in on vinyl.

DUANE ROSSIGNOL: I'm very proud of the record deal I did with Tommy Carroll. It was fifty-fifty, which was insane—who does a fifty-fifty record deal?

TOMMY CARROLL: Straight Ahead didn't last too much longer after that. We had already broken up by the time the record was pressed, I think.

DUANE ROSSIGNOL: About 1987 or so, a lot of the knives came out, and hardcore wasn't a united kind of thing anymore. Nothing lasts forever. People used to approach me a lot. Donny the Punk used to come around quite a bit. He wanted to use my store as a meeting place for some council he was doing. I was like, "What are you, fucking nuts?" A lot of those peace-punk people, I didn't care for those kids too much. They just seemed wishy-washy. A lot of people would be bitching about this faction or that faction, but I didn't want to hear it. The store never made any money. I was working seven days a week for about three years and I had brain seizures in March of '86 and another one in the fall of '87 and it just got to be a bit much. Also, in the fall of '87, a whole bunch of kids came in from Albany, all going to college. I don't like college kids. All the kids I was dealing with were sixteen or seventeen years old, and they had attitudes, but I started having these kids come in that were real know-it-alls. Gina told me we should sell Oi! records. So I had all these

Skrewdriver records, and I remember this college kid coming in and looking horrified. I found out after I closed that their whole faction decided to boycott my record store. I asked the guy afterwards, "How come you're boycotting me? Bleecker Bob's is selling this stuff." He was like, "We couldn't make any difference with Bleecker Bob's, but we could make a difference with you."

GAVIN VAN VLACK: I loved Some Records. Honestly, the scene closed that store down. I look back now on how people criticized Duane for certain products that he chose to sell, and harassed and shit-talked him so much. He basically threw up his hands in disgust and walked away from it.

DUANE ROSSIGNOL: I had spent two years pushing this fucking music, and when the records started coming out, every New York store started selling them. I wasn't Malcolm McLaren. I didn't put these kids under contract. I had spent two or three years promoting that music exclusively, and now anyone that could carry it was carrying it. I was not resentful, but I didn't see the point any longer.

ALEX BROWN: During the summer of 1988, all of the Sick of It All guys were in the store tagging shit. I think Duane was getting ready to close the shop, and was letting people graffiti whatever they wanted down there. I caught a big Judge tag: an X with the lyrics "You've . . . lost . . . my . . . respect." Duane asked me if I wrote that about him. Weird.

DUANE ROSSIGNOL: After I closed, I felt bad for a long time. I felt like I let everybody down. I had a girl come up to me a few years back at a hardware store on Broome Street and ask if I was the guy who ran Some Records. She started talking specifically about some New Jersey kids that used to come by. A lot of those kids came from unpleasant homes where the parents were abusive—not so much physically, but mentally—and how nice it was for them to have a place to come to in the city and feel good about themselves.

To have a scene where kids are involved, you have to have a fucking record store. There's got to be some kind of a circuit. There has to be some recognition of what they're doing. You've got to give them encouragement. The record store served that purpose for a little bit. All I did was open the place. It wouldn't have been possible without the kids.

SOME
RECORDS

AMERICAN HARDCORE and some Oi

210 E. 6th St. (btw. 2nd and 3rd Aves.)

PHONE: (212) 674-4065

VINYL, DEMOS, T-SHIRTS, FANZINES

OPEN FRI., SAT. AND SUN.

A RIGHTEOUS RECORD STORE

Above: *"Some Records closed for good"* PHOTO BY GARY TSE TSE

Breakdown are "safe in a crowd" at CBGB PHOTOS BY KEN SALERNO

43. BREAKDOWN: LIFE OF BULLSHIT— JUST ANOTHER RAW DEAL

CARL PORCARO (Guitarist, Breakdown, Raw Deal, Alone in a Crowd): Breakdown was started by me and my friend Don Angelilli. We started getting into hardcore in the mid-'80s. Back then, you could pretty much identify someone who was into hardcore by what they were wearing like patches or T-shirts or whatever. There was a small crew around Yonkers who found themselves that way, and through a record store called Mad Platters. Bill Wilson who started Blackout Records was a lifeguard at the public pool in Yonkers, and Don hung out there too. I think that's where they met Rich McLoughlin. That's pretty much how Breakdown came together. We started jamming in my parents' basement or Rich's garage, and then we settled into Drago's garage and spent decades there.

ANTHONY DRAGO: The early Breakdown lineup started in 1986 and lasted a year or even less than that. The drummer wasn't cutting it, so I slid in there. The next week, we had three songs down: "Your Problems," "Vengeance," and "Life of Bullshit." The lyrics Jeff was writing were real tough-guy shit. I guess that was different, because I think Breakdown is considered one of the first "tough guy" bands to come out of New York.

JEFF PERLIN: When Breakdown first started playing, the Sick of It All demo had just come out a few months earlier. Sheer Terror was still slogging it out with demos, trying to make a name for themselves. The Krakdown demo had just come out, along with Leeway's *Enforcer* demo, plus Rest in Pieces, and stuff like that. Some of the original NYHC bands were slowly disappearing, like Major Conflict, Reagan Youth, and Antidote. Around 1986 and 1987 a whole new wave of bands emerged that were influenced by all the original New York bands but also added something new.

ANTHONY DRAGO: We had the music together for that whole first demo within four weeks. We played in Connecticut and VFW halls in upstate New York, bingo halls, or whatever. We played a decent amount of shows in that small time. Rich made our shirts himself. He used to work at a T-shirt factory in White Plains. We paid for the ink, and his boss let us do the shirts there. It was some real do-it-yourself shit.

BILL WILSON: Carl Porcaro was my best friend and he's the founding member of Breakdown. I would go to all their practices. I drew a couple of the T-shirts and some of the stickers. That's how I got my start working with bands. I did that logo with the bricks, sitting at Carl's kitchen table with a Sharpie.

JEFF PERLIN: Bill was there from the first practice, and he went to every show, every practice. We'd hang out all the time, go to Fuddruckers to get huge burgers, then go to Don's house or my place. Bill really helped to get things going for us.

ANTHONY DRAGO: We had to get up enough songs to record, and then we had to get enough money to go somewhere and record a four-track demo. That was the only way people were going to hear us. The 1987 demo was recorded at this place called the Loft, a recording studio in Bronxville owned by Al Hemberger. It was more of a hippie scene there at the Loft, so we were one of the crazier bands they recorded there. After us, a lot of bands started finding out about it, so he got more of a punk rock clientele.

CARL PORCARO: We recorded everything live with one take. It worked out for us. There was this hippie guy behind the board who had no clue what we were doing. He seemed annoyed, but it all worked out. It was all about cheap guitars and cheap amps and a lot of energy and having all your boys in the studio singing background vocals. It was a free-for-all.

ANTHONY DRAGO: We copied all the demo tapes ourselves and brought them down to Duane at Some Records. Maybe we were one of the lucky ones, or maybe we were just good; I don't know. But he was selling it like crazy and we were getting good gigs right off the bat.

JEFF PERLIN: Any show at CBGB was great. I guess we were most excited about our first show there. They booked us with Uniform Choice, which was a really popular band at the time. The show was packed and we got a really good reaction. Our first shows there and at the Anthrax in Connecticut really made us feel like maybe we were doing something special, and that it was worth moving forward with the band.

Our first real show was a benefit at the Anthrax to keep the club open. This was our first show at a club that had hardcore shows on a regular basis and all of us were really nervous. We weren't sure if we were gonna be kicked off the stage. We had no idea if people would like us or not. But it was nuts. I don't want to sound like an egotistical asshole, but seriously—we kicked off with "Sick People" and the place just went berserk! I mean, the place was jam-packed, and the whole club turned into a giant pit. The kids went crazy for us for the whole set. It was like we were dreaming; it was unreal. Jim Gibson, who started Noiseville Records, was our roadie; he is this really big biker-looking dude with a heart of gold. When I came off the stage he was just beaming! He had tears in his eyes. It was a great night. I don't think any of us will forget that.

ANTHONY DRAGO: Everything with the first lineup of Breakdown happened within the first nine or ten months of knowing each other. Things all happened so quickly and then we ended up breaking up. The original beef was between Rich McLoughlin and Don Angelilli. It was girl thing. Somebody said they saw Rich with this girl. Don was pissed, and he talked to Jeff, who agreed that was fucked up. Then Rich talked to me, and I agreed that things were fucked up for him, and that split the band in two camps there.

CARL PORCARO: There was clearly other shit brewing and that was used as the excuse for the breakup to happen. Things are different at that age. People get on your fucking nerves really easily. When you all have different ideas on what to do with the music, and, all of a sudden, one band member is hanging out in the backseat of a car with another band member's girlfriend, things are set off. It all seems so silly in retrospect.

JEFF PERLIN: I didn't even remember the reason why we broke up until we got back together with the original lineup recently. Two members were arguing over this girl, the band members took sides, and then we started bickering. It was stupid. Supposedly the girl wasn't much to argue over, either. They called her "Rocky Dennis." Rocky Dennis from *Mask* was cool, but I don't think I'd date him.

CARL PORCARO: Me, Rich, and Drago just assumed we had just as much a right to play the songs as the other guys. There were three of us and only two of them! We had a show booked up at a VFW hall in Albany with Gorilla Biscuits. We asked Steve Reddy, who was in the band Wolfpack and went on to run Equal Vision Records, to sing for Breakdown at that show. We played one gig like that.

ANTHONY DRAGO: So Don and Jeff continued with Breakdown with Mark Sisto on bass and Larry Kaplan on drums. They already had the name, so Breakdown went and kept on doing shows. Me, Rich, and Carl went back to my father's garage. We had to start all over again. We just lost whatever fan base we had. From the beginning, all three of us really clicked together. We started writing music together, and it was so much better than what we were writing with Breakdown.

CARL PORCARO: We wondered what we going to do for a week or two and then we were down at Some Records and Duane said, "You should talk to Anthony Comunale, he's looking for a band." He came the day after Thanksgiving in 1987 to Drago's backyard. We did the first Raw Deal demo in 1988.

ANTHONY DRAGO: Anthony Comunale had been on the hardcore scene much longer than we were. He was there from the beginning. He had the connections. People who saw him sing for Token Entry and Gilligan's Revenge really wanted to see him in a new band. The first time we had him come down, he started singing "Telltale" and "One Other" and we had it together in seconds.

When Raw Deal first started, it was more of that tough-guy attitude. We looked at the dark side rather than the bright side. We weren't seeing anything great about life at that point. I was young and I was kind of pissed off about certain things. I didn't write about social issues or problems of the world. My issue was with *you*. You talk behind my back. You're stretching the truth. All those lyrics come from a very personal relationship I had with somebody who turned their back on me at one point in their life. There's a lot of stuff with our lyrics that people take as a tough-guy attitude, but the lyrics actually have more to do with girl problems.

The first Ritz show Raw Deal played, there was this great review: "They came out onstage, and three of them looked like little preppy kids, and the other two guys looked like two greasy jamokes you wouldn't want to sit next to on the bus." I thought that was a good start.

SiDE BY SiDE

AFTERCATION

SATURDAY
JULY 11
3PM
PYRAMID
CLUB

AVE A
BET 6&7
$5
ALL AGES

FREE SHIRTS
AND
STICKERS

NO
POSERS

BREAKDOWN

CROSSROAD PRODS. PRESENTS LIVE FROM NYC
UNDERDOG SUPERTOUCH
RAW DEAL
STRANGE FLESH
ROCKET
73 Richmond st.
Providence
SUN. MAR 20. 2 PM

Limited Edition
BREAKDOWN

Dissed + Dismissed
All I Ask
What It Is
BreakDown
Down For the Count

All Songs Copyright © 1989
Dirty Sock Music

17 of 100

BREAKDOWN
Runnin' Scared
BREAKDOWN

From top: *Token Entry with a pre-Raw Deal Anthony Comunale on vocals.* GARY TSE TSE FLY; *Jeff Perlin of Breakdown.* KEN SALERNO

44. REVELATION RECORDS AND GORILLA BISCUITS: TOGETHER

JORDAN COOPER: Ray Cappo was always looking for something to do, and I was also getting more involved with hardcore. Finally we just decided to go ahead and try to put out a record for Warzone. Their singer Raybeez had been in Agnostic Front, and was looked at as kind of a godfather of the scene along with the other guys in Agnostic Front, Murphy's Law, Cro-Mags, and other bands. In the mid-'80s, it seemed like hardcore was disappearing, or at least changing from the sound that we liked. Youth of Today were an intentional agent to counter that. We saw Warzone as a band that embodied the original sound of hardcore. I think the band might have been talking about splitting up, and the record was going to be just something to document their existence. Somehow the band stuck around and went on to do a lot after that. Ray Cappo was definitely the brains and the spokesperson for what we started doing.

RAY CAPPO: Jordan and I admired Raybeez as an ambassador of the old school. We thought Warzone was breaking up after doing so many demos, why shouldn't we put out some of their demos on a record? We almost laughed to ourselves about it. Then I said it would be really cool if we put posters inside the singles. Warzone was a band filled with characters. Todd Youth was a crazy character. Tito was another colorful character. We thought we should put a different poster for each band member. We might have done that for a few limited copies of the record. At first, we just wanted to document Warzone. Then it grew into wanting to document this band and that band. The second thing we put out was the *Together* compilation. Then we started releasing a whole new wave of bands that no one had ever heard of. We never thought it was going to be popular outside of New York. Then it became this sick phenomenon that spread internationally.

WALTER SCHREIFELS: With the first Revelation compilation 7-inch in 1987, *Together*, and the *The Way It Is* LP, too, Ray really was reaching out to all aspects of the scene. He gave certain bands a voice, and those compilations also had Sick of It All and Nausea on them. Those weren't Youth Crew bands. People might have had shit to say about Ray, but at the same time they couldn't fully dis him either, because they were kind of benefiting from it.

JORDAN COOPER: Youth of Today was Ray's band, and a lot of people didn't like straight edge and didn't think a positive message was punk, so a lot of that sentiment flowed through to Revelation, even though we put out bands like Sick of It All and No for an Answer who weren't at all trying to promote those ideas. Ray definitely had his group of friends and bands who had similar tastes and opinions, but when we did the *The Way It Is* compilation, we tried to cover as much of the scene as we could.

JOHN BELLO: When Ray and Jordan started Revelation, they were just putting out 7-inches, but they were a force. They were doing some stuff that I was jealous of in a competitive way. I was working with budgets, and I was courting bands, but they had it all built in. That's what the rest of the country saw as NYHC. But I'm happy they did it, because it brought bands to light and showed it was not about the money but the reinforcements you had. A band like Gorilla Biscuits really benefited from being on that label.

WALTER SCHREIFELS: When I lived in Rockaway I had a punk band called the Rodents. We played Ramones-y punk type of stuff. Then I moved to Astoria. Even though it was another part of Queens, it was so different. The Rockaways was so far from the city while Astoria was right next to it. In Astoria, I became close with the guys in Token Entry. Arthur Smilios is a guy I met while working at a Waldbaums. He would become the bass player for Gorilla Biscuits. He went to school in Jackson Heights and knew all these punk kids there.

ARTHUR SMILIOS: I met Walter Schreifels at my first job. We became fast friends; whether it was because we looked exactly the same or because we both had ridiculous names, I don't know. He had the idea for what eventually became Gorilla Biscuits. I wanted to be a part of it because he was my closest friend—at the time, we were pretty much inseparable—and I wanted the opportunity to play bass, which was always my preferred instrument.

WALTER SCHREIFELS: We went to a party in Jackson Heights, and I met Civ and all these other dudes from Jackson Heights who are among my best

AVAILABLE NOW ON LP, CASSETTE, & CD FROM
REVELATION RECORDS, P.O. BOX 1454, NEW HAVEN, CT 06506-1454
SEND S.A.S.E. FOR CATALOG. ©1989 REVELATION RECORDS

friends to this day. Civ was a super-cool guy and we hit it off. I found it hard to sing and play guitar at the same time, so I thought it would be better to have a lead singer, and someone suggested we get Civ. So that was our band. I would call CBGB every single Wednesday to try to get a gig. They would never give us a gig. Finally Token Entry put us on a bill opening. Our people from Jackson Heights showed up. A good way to get popular back then was to be tough, or at least be perceived to be that way, but we were named Gorilla Biscuits! Did you want to tell your tough friends you really liked a band called Gorilla Biscuits? Somehow we got in with Youth of Today and got on Ray's radar, and he asked us to make a 7-inch with Revelation.

DON FURY: The Gorilla Biscuits 7-inch was groundbreaking. For years afterward, bands would ask to record to sound like the Biscuits' EP.

WALTER SCHREIFELS: The lyrics were inviting to everyone, and the music had elements of pop, you could still mosh to it. Unintentionally, we found a center in the scene. You could be in either camp in hardcore and be into it. We just wanted people to mosh and have a good time. We weren't running for class president of hardcore or anything.

JORDAN COOPER: Gorilla Biscuits were great, had a lot of personality, and were doing something different. People loved the 7-inch, and when they played it was kind of a bigger deal than a lot of bands at the time. They weren't obviously more popular than other bands at first, but I think there was extra excitement when they were playing. What set them apart on the lyric side is that the ideas had a more subdued anger, some humor, and a kind of sane perspective that a lot of people related to. On the music side, they're great musicians and their songs took influences that most bands ignored and integrated them into hardcore.

ALEX BROWN: I didn't think they were all that memorable until I saw them open for Youth of Today at the Anthrax after Youth of Today's summer tour. This must have been 1987. Civ had roadied that tour, and Ray had become a big influence on him. Previously, I thought they were a goofy band with a goofy name, sort of an Adrenalin O.D.–type deal, but they were awesome at that show. They were tight, they looked cool, and they had catchy songs. They were definitely not in sync with the NYHC tradition of street kids, drugs, and violence. That certainly set them apart from both the older New York bands and a lot of their contemporaries.

TOBY MORSE (VOCALIST, H2O; ROADIE, SICK OF IT ALL): They were kids from Queens who were straight edge, but not preaching about it. They had songs that everybody could relate to. Civ's vocals were so pure and filled with melody. They were just themselves. They could be funny, or they could be serious. They stood out, but they also fit in. It was a breath of fresh air to what was coming out at that time.

DON FURY: The most well known eight-track session from my studio was the Gorilla Biscuits LP *Start Today*. The vocal recording on that record is meticulous. I worked hard with Civ and Walt Schreifels. *Start Today* had a huge worldwide impact, like Agnostic Front's *Victim in Pain*.

TOBY MORSE: To see how important a record like *Start Today* is to me and to the world is overwhelming. I was just singing backups on that album because those dudes were my friends. The impact that record had is awesome. Thirty years later people are still buying that record and loving that band. The inspiration was friends just doing something that they loved and believed in; and look where it went from generation to generation.

RAY CAPPO: We never thought Revelation Records was going to become as huge as it did. We did the label because it was a cool time with cool music and people. We always felt almost like historians who were documenting the scene. We wanted to capture something that would be over in the wink of an eye. For me, each record is like a yearbook to me as an adult. I look through my record collection and hit upon the ones released on Revelation, and I remember everything; what I was thinking when I made it, and where I was living, and who I was hanging out with. It reminds me of what a great place New York was to be at that time.

UNDERDOG
gorilla biscuits
Good Humor!

Token Entry

BACK FROM 86 TOUR...

Jody Foster's Army

THE NEW YORK HOODS AND THE gorilla biscuits!

CB-GB's AUG 31 HARDCORE MATINEE 2:00 5$

*Yet more commanding
stage action from Civ*
KEN SALERNO

YOUTH
OF
TODAY
SIDE BY SIDE
gorilla biscuits

sun oct. 18 cb's

EDGE ON YOU!

Above: *Sheer Terror's Paul Bearer at CBGB:*
"Don't hate me 'cause I'm beautiful"
PHOTOS BY GARY TSE TSE FLY

45. BLACKOUT: JUST CAN'T HATE ENOUGH

BILL WILSON: I went to junior high with Paul Bearer from Sheer Terror. On my first day of seventh grade, and there was this pudgy kid holding a copy of the Plasmatics' *No Hope for the Wretched* record, saying, "This is the best band I've ever seen." Here he was waving around a record cover with a chick with a Mohawk sitting in a swimming pool, and I had just gotten done listening to Pink Floyd's "Another Brick in the Wall." That was my first inkling of ever knowing about anything like punk rock, and it was through Paul Bearer. After he showed me the record, he proceeded to go punch another kid in the face. I guess that was the foreshadowing for the rest of my adolescent life.

All I wanted to do was design record covers: I wanted that to be my career. I figured if I wanted to design a record cover, I should put out a record. There were no labels putting out the bands I liked in New York. Revelation was so focused on Youth Crew. The bands that I liked were a little bit angrier and a little bit darker. That's why I chose the name Blackout. Revelation is this bright idea of happy kids jumping. My opinion of the world was darker, and I wanted to have something with a bit more of a "fuck you" attitude. I had friends in popular bands, so my friend Jim Gibson and I pooled our money. I collected the master tapes from the bands, and then I designed a record cover. That became the *Where the Wild Things Are* compilation. That's how the Blackout label got started in 1989.

JOE SONGCO: When Bill asked us to be on *Where the Wild Things Are*, he said he wanted to do a compilation of the harder bands. He achieved it with that record, with bands like Raw Deal and Breakdown, and some really, really angry songs.

BILL WILSON: I loved Sheer Terror before I knew Paul was in the band. Bar none, the lyrics that he wrote make him the poet laureate of NYHC. His lyrics

surpassed any from any other band. The music was heavy and the attitude was "fuck everything." I would go see them play this biker joint in Brooklyn.

PAUL BEARER: When the metal thing came in, I really didn't want to go out to shows. Then the Youth Crew thing happened and that didn't appeal to me. I'll admit it—I was a fucking lunkhead. I liked to get drunk and do stupid shit like smash windows. A lot of people didn't like what I did, and that's understandable, but a lot of my friends were troublemakers too. It was what it was. It's around then that the Sheer Terror thing started and I tried to concentrate on that.

JEFF PERLIN: I really identified with Paul's lyrics. Alan Blake had a big Celtic Frost influence, and Celtic Frost were the shit! Sheer Terror really had their own thing going—no one sounded like them. Their attitude was so great, basically "Fuck everyone, I'm gonna do what I like and be honest about how I feel about everything." Paul had balls. He'd write lyrics about really personal shit, about depression and stuff. I was going through that, too. So I really got into them.

BILL WILSON: I got to be friendly with Mark Neuman from Sheer Terror, and that nurtured our relationship. Sheer Terror released their first LP on a label called Starving Missile from Germany. I was able to get the record from there to release in America, which started my long-lasting relationship with Sheer Terror. Then I think Anthony from Raw Deal turned me onto Outburst. Joe Songco, their drummer, was a cool kid, and that song "The Hard Way" was fucking awesome. The singer had a lot of energy, so why not put out a record by them?

JOE SONGCO: Bill really liked our stuff and wanted to sign us to Blackout. He was doing the label out of his basement in White Plains. We liked Bill a lot, and we knew we weren't going to be looked at by any other labels at the time. Revelation wouldn't put us out; we weren't their flavor. We recorded at the Power Station in Long Island. Rock Jay did the logo—which everyone cops these days—and we did that ridiculous pose for the cover. To this day, people still say we look like a bunch of guidos. We just didn't look like all the other NYHC bands at the time. Our singer, Brian Donohue, looked like Kurt Cobain. George D'Errico, our guitarist was kind of *GQ*. He still dresses nice! I've got a Def Jam shirt on in that picture. We weren't wearing black Adidas and making hip-hop poses like other bands at that time. We were the exact opposite of that. Also, there were two Asian kids in the band.

BILL WILSON: I put out the Outburst 7-inch, and they broke up on the day that it came out. Then I released the Uppercut 12-inch, and likewise those guys broke up right when the record came out. Story of my life! But who cares? This was the hardcore that I believed in.

ANTHONY DRAGO: Bill's been in the music business his entire life, all because once we were talking in the car and he said, "I'm going to put out a fuckin' record." I was like, "You should." It's amazing how all this shit changed everybody's lives.

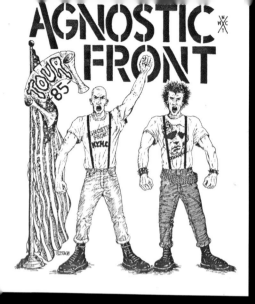

AGNOSTIC FRONT

TOUR 85

C.B.G.B's
THE CRO-MAGS

the Age of Quarrel
LAST NYC GIG BEFORE MISFITS TOUR
SAT JULY 5 TOUR
3PM

LOVE HALL

DC's IRON CROSS

MAY 21
8:00pm

BROAD
&
SOUTH

with
2 New York
Bands

ALL
AGES
$4.

URBAN WASTE
MURPHYS LAW
PLUS PHILLY GUESTS
YDI

FRIDAY AUG. 4th
YOUTH OF TODAY
LAST L.A. APPEARANCE

BOLD
GORILLA
BISCUITS
UNDER DOG
INSTED
JUDGE
CHAIN OF STRENGTH

XXX

FRIDAY AUGUST 4TH
8:00 PM
Fender's

46. NYHC ON THE ROAD: REPRESENT NEW YORK CITY AND DANCE HARD

RUSS IGLAY: New York was our hometown, so we didn't realize we were constantly playing the best place in the world. We would get so excited to go on tour, but we soon realized we were leaving New York to play worse shows. We would drive one thousand miles to play a show where we would draw nobody and nobody really knew us. Once you wrapped your head around it and put it into that context, it was kind of weird.

VINNIE STIGMA: We were the first national skinhead band ever, just four bald guys with boots and braces on going across America! I'm not saying I'm the first skinhead, but we were the first national American skinhead band, and that's a fact! When we did the 1984 tour by ourselves, that put us on the map. There were a lot of fights. We're talking Texas in 1984. Here were these New York guys. Tattoos. Bald. Skinhead. You know what I mean? We're talking *beef*!

JOHN PORCELLY: NYHC was definitely on everybody's radar by the time we made it outside of the area in 1986. It was considered dangerous. People thought we were all nuts. The very first time Youth of Today went out to California with 7 Seconds, we played at Fender's Ballroom, which was a gang hangout. The whole California hardcore scene was all gangs: Circle One, the Suicidals, the L.A. Death Squad, and that was it—nothing but gangs. I didn't know anything. That was my first time in California. I was used to playing the Anthrax in Connecticut, where people were playing frickin' Twister in between bands! When we started playing, this small, little kid Murphy was on stage with us, and the L.A.D.S. were bouncing. They were a gang, above and beyond the punk scene. I didn't know that. Murphy got onstage to dive: The bouncer grabbed him and, for no good reason, threw him right into the metal barrier. The bouncer was right in front of the stage sort of flexing after doing that, and I came up behind him and kicked him as hard as I could in the back. He went flying into the crowd. Dan O'Mahony from No for an Answer came up a few seconds later and screamed in my ear, "We have to get you out of here!" I was still playing, and he dragged me off the stage. He unplugs my guitar, grabs my arm, and he's pushing me down this corridor, going, "You don't understand! That guy's in the L.A.D.S.! They're going to fucking kill you! They're going to shoot you! They're going to knife you!" I still had my guitar on me. Before we got to the back door, I looked down that corridor and saw that bouncer. I'm thinking, "This guy's going to shoot me, I'm fucking dead!" The guy was huge. But he came up to me and said, "We don't have no beef with New York! We don't have no beef with the Cro-Mags!" It was almost like he thought I was in a gang, and I was going to kick his ass! He gave me all this mad respect. He shook my hand and apologized. I realized that New York's reputation preceded us.

WALTER SCHREIFELS: Going on tour in Youth of Today was amazing. We came from New York with a message. We had such a cool counterargument to what was going on at the time—which was either metal crossover or just waiting for punk dinosaurs like GBH to come around. Every night would be the fucking best show, you could just hear people in the audience thinking, "I'm going to write a fanzine!" or, "Fuck, I'm going to start a band!" Every night! It was awesome. I guess the main resistance we would get would be from the drunk crowd—older punks thinking we were fucking assholes. But we were so sure of our message and what we were doing that we didn't give a shit about that. We played the whole country; some of these people didn't know the story, but we knew the story, and we were spreading it.

ALEX BROWN: My first road trip with Youth of Today was going down to Philly in a 1970 Econoline with no seats in the back and leaking floorboards. The club was upstairs and you had to lug all the gear up two or three flights of stairs. It also had this rickety balcony right over the stage, which gave you a really great vantage point over what was happening. Mark Goober and Mark Ryan came along to represent. Everybody was wearing New York Rangers hockey jerseys. As we got out of the van, Mark Ryan said something about how we had to represent New York City and dance hard, or something like that. It sounded kind of funny to me, but it felt cool to be included and part of the inside of such an amazing band as Youth of Today. I often think about playing those shows in Jersey, Philly, D.C., and anywhere south of New York.

We'd know we were almost home when we saw the Twin Towers on the horizon over the Jersey Turnpike. After driving to that Philly show, Ray just parked the van on Fourteenth Street, took the plates off, and wrote it off. I thought that was pretty irresponsible, but punk and cool at the same time.

MIKE JUDGE: I toured the whole country with Youth of Today. I didn't really know about the preconceptions of the band that people had. All I knew was that I dug them. I knew nothing about the whole PMA and positive thing. I was from more of a violent background.

In the beginning, I was always getting reprimanded, especially by Ray. Like, we were selling the 7-inch, and this guy didn't want to pay full price. Ray told him he couldn't sell it for cheaper. The guy started talking shit, so I pushed Ray aside. I was just going to fight the guy. Ray was like, "Whoa! Whoa! We talk things out." I was like, "I'm not good at that." I never got fully used to that. How are you supposed to sit there and let some guy say shit, and you're the better man by walking away? I'd rather be the better man who's stepping over his body. That's why I wound up wanting to quit Youth of Today. I couldn't deal with having to turn the other cheek.

I was always asking Ray, "So what exactly does a guy have to do to get his ass beat? Is there a set of rules? Do I have to get hit first? Because I hate getting hit first!" I was always taught, "If there's any doubt, lay him out!" Ray's answer to everything with me was, "Listen to more 7 Seconds."

Then, in Detroit, there was a band called Boom and the Legion of Doom. They were throwing fucking deer meat at us; I guess because of Ray's vegetarian thing. I was behind the drums, seething. Man, I just want to kill these fucking guys. Richie felt the same way. We got offstage and I was ready to tear those guys apart. At first, Ray wasn't into it, but then he said, "All right, but let me lead us into it." I thought he was leading us into battle and we were going to get bloody together. But Ray went up, recited 7 Seconds lyrics in the guys' faces, and then walked out of the club! I was so confused. In my mind, someone should have been laid out. They had gone too far! Even the guys in the other band were confused. We were all looking at each other, confused about whether we were still going to get a fight.

CRAIG SETARI: Agnostic Front played a show in Savannah, Georgia. We pulled up at the club, and Vinnie and Roger were like, "Oh no, it's Bo." This guy was blowing stuff up with a twelve-gauge pump shotgun. He was blowing out windows and shooting at people's feet. A guy would come out of the bar, and this Bo would shoot at him. Roger and I looked at each other; we had to do something, because this guy was crazy. We called the police, and they totally didn't care. They just patted his back and told him, "No shooting if you're drinking. Put the gun back in your car."

PETE KOLLER: We played Gilman Street in Berkeley. The people who ran the club had an issue with us immediately. There were sixty fucking people there, and we were getting paid one hundred dollars. The guys who were supposed to be bouncers in front of the stage kept calling the kids and us "these straight-edge faggots." We didn't understand. Did being on Revelation make us a straight-edge band? Maybe the kids who came to see us were the local straight-edge guys—who knows? People started throwing shit at the bouncers, and they would throw kids out who were into the band. As I was playing, a bouncer's girlfriend literally grabbed the neck of my guitar and started trying to pull the strings off it while yelling, "Get the fuck out of here, you straight-edge faggot!" I soccer kicked her in the face and she fell down. Her boyfriend came toward me, and our roadie Squirm jumped over me and started beating the fucking shit out of the guy. Then things got crazier! From the right side door, forty Nazis came charging in and started beating everybody up! We just stopped playing and stood there. All the Nazis were just waiting outside for something to happen, because they already hated the people who ran the club. They were just looking for a reason to start a fight. Years later, I talked to Tim Armstrong from Rancid, who was there. Even he couldn't explain what happened. He was a lifelong local, and even he had no idea why the Gilman Street people were fucking with us New Yorkers at that show.

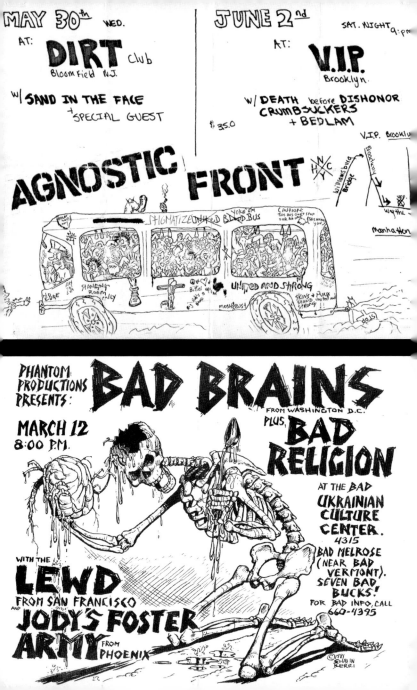

NIGHT!
+ the
ANTHRAX ←
JECT "X"!
UDGE ...

SURE RELEAS

18 [X]

s Blood. ✝
FA

THE KIDS ON THE STREET
AND THE KIDS EVERYWHERE
ALL I GOTTA SAY
IS THE KIDS DON'T CARE
– BLITZ

JECT X

LISMAR
LOUNGE

LOWER EAST SIDE
CREW

WAR-ZONE

FRI.
MAY
27TH

H N C
X
N Y

PROJECT X
LIFES BLOOD!
BEYOND

7:00 PM

JUDGE
New York Crew

WITH
BEYOND

LIVE AT THE
PYRAMID CLUB
AT 2:30 SHARP
ONLY 5 BUCKS
NO SAPS!

GORILLA

47. JUDGE: NEW YORK CREW

JOHN PORCELLY: The "shutdown" show at CBGB was a real milestone as far as the end of that era. The innocence of thinking we were all in this together wasn't there anymore.

ALEX BROWN: The lineup that day was the Pagan Babies from Philly, Side by Side, Gorilla Biscuits, and Youth of Today. Hilly Kristal had enacted a no-stagediving policy after being sued by someone who got injured at a show there. The gigantic bouncers were in force and instructed to keep shit in order. I don't think there was any sort of conspiracy to sandbag Hilly's wish for there to be a calm show, but it was just too much of a good opportunity to let go to waste.

RAY CAPPO: CBGB wasn't allowing stagediving anymore, because they were getting sued. Now, as an adult, I get it. Imagine an insurance company asking, "What goes on in your club?" and you say, "We allow people to get up onstage and jump off onto other people's heads." But stage diving was such a part of the culture, there was no way of not coming off like a bad guy when Hilly asked people not to do it. The whole hardcore scene was built on the fact that there was no difference between band and audience. There was nothing where the band members were rock stars and the people in the audience were puny and sitting in chairs. It was just as important to be in the crowd as it was to be in the band. That was the thing people loved most about hardcore.

ALEX BROWN: Ray took that energy like a judo master and flipped it back on itself. My most vivid memory of that show is a pile of bodies pushed up against the ceiling above the stage. It was like some weird creature from a Japanese horror movie or Bosch painting; really primal dude stuff.

RAY CAPPO: That show was sensationalized into more than what it was. It was your typical, ordinary show, where everybody wanted to stage dive—only they couldn't. I got eighty-sixed from CBGB for some time due to that show, and I was pissed off. What could you do? Not stage dive? But that's what we do!

JOHN PORCELLY: After that, CBGB stopped having hardcore matinees for a few weeks. There was a huge backlash against straight edge, and we got lumped into it. Then we formed bands like Judge and Project X, and that was sort of the backlash against the backlash.

ALEX BROWN: Project X was a direct response to the people who were talking shit. I don't know if it was actually tongue-in-cheek, but it was really fun to put something so polemical out there and wait for people to take the bait.

WALTER SCHREIFELS: There was definitely a sense of humor to Project X. We wanted to give these people the monster that they actually thought we were. We created that monster for them.

JOHN PORCELLY: No one caught more shit for being straight edge than Ray or me. I had more beer bottles thrown at me than anybody. I've had beer poured on my head, and I've been threatened. Project X was just that feeling where you just can't take any more and you say, "Fuck you!" As much as Project X was tongue-in-cheek, our song "Straight Edge Revenge" still strikes a chord in anyone who ever tried to be straight edge in an American high school; especially in the 1980s. I think the reason anyone remembers Project X is because of that song.

I loved singing for Project X. I was strapped to a guitar for years, you know? I played a Les Paul, the heaviest guitar in the world. I had to play, stay tight, and concentrate. But singing bypasses any of the thought processes required in playing guitar. You just take what's in your heart and pour it out your mouth. It's such a release. I wish I sang for a more serious band than Project X!

MIKE JUDGE: On the last tour I did with Youth of Today, the van broke down in Florida. We parked it in a junkyard while it was being repaired. We talked these girls into letting us stay in their apartment, but someone had to sleep in the van with the equipment. We'd take turns. On my night to watch the van, I was lying there in the middle of this Florida junkyard. I had ideas in my head, and I started writing words down for a band. It was painfully obvious that these words would never be a Youth of Today song. They wouldn't have it. So I thought when I got back to New York I would start my own band. I couldn't keep muzzling myself.

Judge brings the storm in the live setting KEN SALERNO

Porcell came out to keep me company one night, and we started talking about this band that didn't exist yet. We had so much fun just talking about it. Basically, we were starting Judge right then and there, and we didn't know it.

JOHN PORCELLY: Mike really wanted to do a band and he wanted to sing. At first, I was very skeptical. Mike can be a hothead, but he's a pretty shy, anti-social kind of dude. I couldn't picture him as a front man whatsoever. I could picture him getting onstage and staring at his shoes.

MIKE JUDGE: Let me tell you something: I loved Youth of Today. I love Ray. We spent many nights on tour in a fucking van pouring our hearts out to each other. I love him as a person. I love Porcell too, but we come from different places. The end game for each of us was different. There were so many times when I was in that band where I just knew I would never be like those guys. I was getting way too frustrated, and it wasn't worth it to me.

JOHN PORCELLY: I was a Westchester kid who was popular in high school. I was on the football team. Mike Judge was this troubled guy from New Jersey who was picked on in school.

MIKE JUDGE: When we got back to New York, we started rehearsals for a new Youth of Today record. I told Ray that I was going to go my own way. A week later, I came up with the name of the band and asked Porcell if he was interested in helping out. I was living with Porcell, Al Brown, and Ray in Brooklyn. While those guys went to work during the day, I would just sit there

Judge bassist Matt Pincus takes the plunge while Mike works the crowd KEN SALERNO

with a bass and write songs. I had Al Brown's record collection, Porcell's record collection, and Cappo's record collection; it was a punk rock library. I sat listening to SSD, Negative Approach, Last Rights, and a little bit of Slapshot, then I'd go and play bass.

JOHN PORCELLY: Mike's original lyrics were way more militant and violent than what's on that EP, let me tell you! That's the "edited by Porcell" version! There was stuff in there about killing motherfuckers or something.

MIKE JUDGE: One night, I read him Porcell the lyrics to "New York Crew" over the phone. He said, "Great song, but you have to change the words. You can't fucking say that shit. You're copping to crimes in some of this shit." I sat back and read it, and I sort of realized he was right about that.

JOHN PORCELLY: The music came together really quickly; probably in less than a month. We were practicing in our apartment, and at Giant Studios. Sometimes Mike would grab the mic and try to sing without drums. The sound at Giant was the worst, so I couldn't tell what his voice was going to sound like. Before we went into the studio to record, I was thinking, "This music is awesome, but if Mike can't pull it off, maybe we'll just find someone else to sing."

When Mike walked up to that microphone at Don Fury's studio and started singing, it was incredible! I was shocked! The roar that came out of that guy's mouth! You should have seen the look on his face; it was just knotted, and he was filled with pure rage. It was glorious! We were just planning to make a demo, but then I felt like this was going to be the best band ever! I went all the way to Walter Schreifels' apartment in Queens and played him the tape. His

HALF PAGE AD

JUDGE
BRINGS IT DOWN
WITH THEIR
HARD-HITTING DEBUT

JUDGE 'BRINGIN' IT DOWN'

AVAILABLE ON LP, CASSETTE, CD
FROM REVELATION RECORDS

P.O. BOX 1454, NEW HAVEN, CT 06506-1454
SEND S.A.S.E. FOR CATALOG

DIST. BY VENUS NYC, CAROLINE NYC, IMPORTANT NYC

REVELATION
© 1989 REVELATION RECORDS

reaction was, "Holy shit! I've been working on Gorilla Biscuits for years, and you guys worked on this for two weeks?"

MIKE JUDGE: After the first Judge EP came out in 1988, there was this demand to see it live. Porcell wanted to put a band together and play a show. We got Drew from Bold to play drums, and Jimmy Yu to play bass. We played the Anthrax, and it was fucking awesome. We never stopped after that. Judge went straight on into 1990.

ALEX BROWN: Bold were great, too, by the way. I always wish their *Speak Out* LP on Revelation from back in 1987 had been recorded properly. I think their legacy is a bit overlooked due to that substandard recording, along with the fact that they lived in Westchester and not New York City, and thus were seen as outsiders by the people who cared about that sort of stuff.

JOHN PORCELLY: I got a lot of satisfaction seeing the transformation of Mike Ferraro into Mike Judge. He grabbed that mic and came into his own. It was remarkable. I'm so proud of the guy. He wrote these incredible lyrics that connected with a lot of people; that was both the glory of Judge and the downfall of Judge. Youth of Today championed a higher cause. It was more positive. Mike was troubled, and he sang about it in a very sincere way, so we attracted a troubled crowd. People could connect with the songs because they had fucked-up lives, fucked-up families, and fucked-up childhoods. If you put one hundred people like that in a room, something's going to happen. All the violence we saw on our first tour of the country was too much. We eventually broke up. The second Judge record would have been awesome. I had a lot of ideas for some incredible songs—really slow and pounding.

48. ABC NO RIO: NO RACIST, SEXIST OR HOMOPHOBIC BANDS WILL BE BOOKED

BRENDAN RAFFERTY: In mid-1989, Connie Hall at CBGB gave us the heads-up that, for insurance reasons, CBGB was going to stop doing matinees. They were still going to do the ones that were booked, but no more booking new shows. We knew November was going to be the end there. Some of us started looking for new venues. Mike Bullshit suggested ABC No Rio as an option, since we had done a couple shows there in the spring.

MIKE BULLSHIT: There was a show at ABC No Rio with S.F.A. and Bugout Society in the middle of 1989. I was there and thought it was kind of cool. Thanks to an introduction by Gavin Van Vlack from Absolution and Burn, I started booking shows there. The space was available and CB's had stopped doing matinees.

CHARLES MAGGIO (VOCALIST, RORSCHACH): Around November of 1989, there was a show at a bar on Houston Street called Downtown Beirut with Born Against and Citizens Arrest, both part of a new group of bands. At the time, due to all the rumors of CB's being shut down for hardcore, there was a push to find an alternative space. There was talk of this other club that the guy from S.F.A. was going to be booking, and someone was handing out flyers for a show at ABC No Rio.

WALTER SCHREIFELS: ABC No Rio was more interesting than what was left of the straight-edge scene or what was left of the CB's scene. I loved bands like Killing Time; they have fucking sick riffs. I would go see them because they were a good band, but I didn't want to be part of that tough scene. The ABC No Rio scene was more just nerds into music. They didn't want to get beat up. I related to that.

NICK FORTE (GUITARIST, RORSCHACH): ABC No Rio was pretty crucial in my hardcore existence. I remember that Rorschach really couldn't find a gig anywhere in New York City. We dropped off demos, and nobody called us back. We went to one of the first hardcore shows at ABC No Rio, and gave a tape to Mike Bullshit. We were leaving and he asked if we could play the next Saturday. So the first Rorschach show in New York City was at ABC No Rio in December of 1989 with Citizens Arrest.

DARYL KAHAN (VOCALIST, CITIZENS ARREST, TRUE COLORS): Our band Citizens Arrest was lucky enough to be one of the first hardcore bands to play ABC No Rio. We took an active role in helping to build the scene there, which was great in the beginning.

CHARLES MAGGIO: When we arrived to play, the flyer at the front said, "Rorschach and whoever else wants to play: Five dollars." We played to all of Citizens Arrest, half of Born Against, Mike Bullshit, Neil Robinson maybe, and Gavin from Burn.

NICK FORTE: It was an extremely cold day and freezing inside, and the steps were covered in ice. I played guitar with gloves on. There were maybe ten people there. For us, it was a huge thing. It felt to us like something was happening.

MIKE BULLSHIT: For the first six months, we mic'd the vocals literally just by plugging a microphone into this tiny, rudimentary, kindergarten-level amp. We had shit money and I was broke. It was fantastic. I felt so bad for one band. They were from Long Island, I don't remember their name. They had two singers. Since we only had one mic, they had to pass the mic back and forth.

BRENDAN RAFFERTY: When Gavin and I both got caught up in the world of working two jobs to support pregnant girlfriends, we had to step back. Later, Mike took off on another journey. For a while, there were a bunch of people booking shows there. By mid-1990, it was mostly Freddy Alva.

FREDDY ALVA: I was one of the original volunteers who got together with Mike Bullshit to help put on shows at ABC No Rio during the first eight months of 1990. Then Mike decided to do a cross-country bike trip for an undetermined amount of time. I took over the bookings for about a year. There was a joyous feeling in the air of making it up as we went along. I don't think I've ever seen so many people with smiles on their faces at hardcore shows. It was quite a difference from the macho-driven, violence-prone shows that were the regular thing back then.

CHARLES MAGGIO: When CB's matinees ended, there were still two distinct groups of people going there. Some people loved the music. CBGB was their equivalent of the high school kegger they weren't invited to, and this was the place where they felt they belonged. Then there was a group of people who wanted to beat all those people up. I think the people who ended up at ABC No Rio were the ones standing to the side with their arms folded, not making eye contact. Previously, there became this constant struggle of thinking, "I really want to see this band, but I really don't want to get beat up." I think ABC No Rio took away the second part of that statement, because the violent part of the scene didn't go there. Beating up people at ABC No Rio would have been like shooting fish in a barrel. It was almost like a fresh start to me. It was like someone hit the reset button and said, "Take everything you like from CB's and bring it here, and take everything you hated about CB's and leave it there."

FREDDY ALVA: From the beginning, our stated aim was to get away from the violence that had grown out of proportion at the CBGB matinees by late 1989. We refused to book bands that attracted violent cliques, and we wanted to provide a space for newer bands that didn't fit into the stereotypical NYHC sound, with mosh parts, tough-guy vocals, and a gang-like mentality. Eventually, as within any tightly knit group, infighting and nitpicking started to tear apart the original group of volunteers. My decision to include members from the crust punk scene received a less-than-favorable reaction in certain quarters. The subsequent displays of drunken behavior by some of these crusties made people say to me, "I told you so."

BRENDAN RAFFERTY: ABC No Rio was such a major disappointment. It was a monument to arrogance and ego. Between two jobs, and my baby twins born May 1990, I didn't have the free time to promote ABC. I remember arguing with a bunch of people at a meeting. Outside of ABC No Rio, the only other hardcore shows in the city during those years were at the bigger venues with the bigger bands. A decision was made at the meeting that flyers for ABC No Rio would not be handed out at these shows and that only select kids be given flyers. A bunch of the people running ABC No Rio decided to demonize the CBGB hardcore scene that had just ended. They patted themselves on the back and were so proud of themselves for having created a scene at ABC that was free of the knuckleheads and the elitist cliques. Of course, they wound up creating an even more elitist clique themselves. I begged people to hand out flyers for upcoming ABC shows at some big Sick of It All show coming up. The response was a resounding *no*. Someone actually said that they didn't want those people to know about ABC. Everybody agreed. I was incensed. I was thinking about the kids who were just discovering this music and would fit in just fine. Those kids only knew about the big shows uptown. Without flyers, they would never find ABC No Rio. Nope. The people running ABC wanted to be an exclusive club and that's what they got.

FREDDY ALVA: Even though the early days were great, and it saddens me that I'll never see that group of people in the same room ever again, the risk of becoming yet another exclusive in-group was not what I was about—or what I think most the people involved were about.

DARYL KAHAN: If any band slightly disagreed or didn't completely adhere to the organizers' guidelines, they were banned for life. From what I've heard, they became like fascists, scanning band lyric sheets for potential political offenses. After a while, I lost interest in the scene at ABC. The whole thing became an over-the-top drunken PC nightmare covered in vomit.

CHARLES MAGGIO: There was no line in the sand where there was a certain show that made me stop going to ABC No Rio. I didn't stop going there. I just wasn't going there as often. I went there in mid-1994 for a show and my car got stolen. Then I couldn't go even if I wanted to. Still, it's a great club. I went there more recently and had a great time.

DARYL KAHAN: Years later, I went back to good old ABC to check out a show, which was filled with really young kids wearing brand-new punk patches on their intentionally dirtied pants. Most of these kids were passed out drunk in the backyard. They had no interest in seeing the bands or taking part in what was happening. They were there to drink, smoke, and look like authentic, elitist PC punks. Whatever the case, they are keeping the place alive, which is the most important and surprising part.

FREDDY ALVA: Creating an alternative to the alternative scene, and sticking to DIY principles became the extra reasons for ABC No Rio to exist. I'm happy to say it continues to thrive till this day.

THE MATINEE AT
ABC NO RIO
156 RIVINGTON NYC

ABC No Rio was started as an alternative to the few clubs in NYC who's only concern was in making money off punk/HC bands. We are NYC's only non-profit, volunteer-run, all-ages venue. Background: Mike Bullshit first got access to the space at No Rio in the Winter of '89 and began booking shows. A collective took over when Mike left this summer. The shows take place in the basement of the No Rio building. We have recently renovated the basement, adding a stage and sound equipment. The space holds 100-150 people. We have a record and fanzine table and a recycling center regularly during the Saturday matinees. We have always had the policy of booking only independent and alternative music — no sexist, racist or homophobic bands are booked. Oi Polloi, MDC, Neurosis,

Poison Idea, Filth, Nausea, Jawbreaker, Econochrist, and Christ On A Crutch are just a few of the bands which have appeared at the No Rio matinee in recent months. Most shows have 4-5 bands, both touring and local, for $5 admission. We are considerate of the financial situation of the out-of-town bands. We also do benefit shows for local and national organizations such as Food Not Bombs, ALF, Greenpeace, etc. Groups or bands wishing to do benefits are encouraged to contact us. For the future, we would like to start a record/literature cafe and meeting place. We are also discussing the possibility of a rehearsal space. The matinee at ABC No Rio is an alternative to the rip-off commercial clubs in NYC. It's a damn good time, too.

BOOKING: FREDDY 718-672-2507(9-11 PM) / NEIL 718-782-6448/F. ALVA 35-18 93RD ST. JCK. HGTS. NY 11372

CITIZENS ARREST
RORSCHACH
SFA
NEW YORK CITY HATE-CORE
GO!
QUICKSAND (SERIOUSLY WILD) YUPPIECIDE

..AS THE BEAST ONCE AGAIN REARS ITS UGLY HEAD!!

FRIDAY MAY 4 8:00PM

At
ABC-NO-RIO
156 Rivington St.
$5

WORD OF GOD

UP FRONT
PLUS FACE UP!

POSITIVE RELAXED FLANNEL
ANGRY MOSH LOOK
STRONG TEETH FROM DRINKING LOTS OF MILK
X EDGE
"PARENT APPROVED"
XXL POSI-T-SHIRT
MOSH TAT
"WHAT A POSITIVE FEELINGS"

A FAUX BENEFIT FOR S.A.Dx STRAIGHTEDGERS AGAINST DRUGS

PLUS THESE DRUGGIE-LOSER UN POSITIVE BANDS TOO...
STICKS AND STONES
THE WRETCHED ONES

AT GOOD OL'
ABC-NO-RIO
56 Rivington St.
2 Blocks South of Houston (near Ave B)

"WATCHA GONNA DO WHEN POSIMANIA RUSHES ALL OVER U ARMA"

SEASON'S BEATINGS
with:
RORSCHACH
Born Against

Fri. dec. 28 7 pm.

t: CASTILLO CULTURAL CENTER • 500 GREENWICH ST. 2nd FLR
TWN SPRING AND CANAL 1 BLOCK W. OF HUDSON. FOR INFO:
NDREW · (212-233-3606) AFTER 12/17. ALSO-SUBZERO, EYE FOR AN EYE
nd DEGREE, BAD TRIP $6 DAMAGES

THE MATINEE

ABC NO RIO
NEW YORK CITY'S ONLY NON-PROFIT, VOLUNTEER-RUN, ALL-AGES VENUE
SATURDAYS / 3PM / $5 / 156 RIVINGTON ST

09/29 - KRACK (MD) / STICKS & STONES (NJ) / NUTJOB / RON'S BETTER HALF
10-06 - SEIZURE (CT) / WUSSIES (CT) / DISRUPT (MA) / CASUALTIES
10/13 - SFA / HECRACEDIA (PA) / 23 MORE MINUTES (CA) / ANTIEM WORLD DISCRIMINATION (NJ) / STUPID AMERICANZ (TN)
10/27 - AFFIRMATIVE ACTION / WORD MADE FLESH / WRETCHED ONES (NJ) / +?

BOOKING: NEIL-718-782-6448 / FREDDY 718-672-2507(9-11 PM) / F. ALVA 35-18 93RD ST. JCK. HGTS. NY 11372
NO RACIST, SEXIST, OR HOMOPHOBIC BANDS WILL BE BOOKED

Photo: Citizens Arrest

WHERE MAN ONCE STOOD SUPREME—NOW RULE THE APES

'ALL AGES 3:00 PM

AT:
A·B·C NO RIO
156 RIVINGTON STREET

WHEN:
SATURDAY FEBRUARY 24th
$5.00 MATINEE

SWIZ
BEGINNING THIS ISSUE!

HARDCORE SHOWS ON THE PLANET OF THE APES!

RORSCHACH

FACE THE FACTS

BOSTON'S
EYE FOR AN EYE

SQUAT OR ROT PRESENTS...

FIGHT BACK
WHILE YOU STILL CAN

POLICE
LOWER EAST SIDE

cult of rage
RADICTS

KRAKDOWN
TOMP. SQ. PK.
FRI. AUG. 4

FREE

slaughter

6PM — 10PM

SQUAT OR ROT
AND
THE DIRECT CRIME CHANNEL
PRESENTS
A BENEFIT FOR
5TH ST SQUAT

$5.00

FRIDAY AUG. 9 7 P.M.

BRING A FRIEND

SMELL COMP. AVAILABLE TOO

RECORDS

JESUS CHRUST
WÜRST (FROM R.I.)
S.F.A. ∘ PIG PEN
BREAKDOWN
RADICTS
AND MORE
ABC NO RIO 156 RIVINGTON

Squat or Rot
April 14th
5
with

the Insurgence
World Discrimination

Citizens Arrest

E. 13th ST
Lucky 13
N.Y.C.

Support SPAR

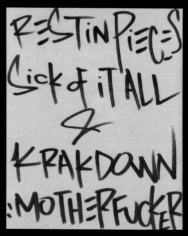

Sick of It All live and dangerous ADAM TANNER

49. SICK OF IT ALL: HARDER THAN YOU

PETE KOLLER: I think the first Sick of It All show was with Straight Ahead and Youth of Today at the Right Track Inn on Long Island. I could not tune a guitar at all, and I didn't have money for a tuner, so Craig or Armand would tune the guitar for me between songs. But the cool thing about hardcore is, who gives a fuck? Maybe that even gave us some cred, you know? "Hey, it's the guy from Straight Ahead helping him out!" At our first show, we were really generic and really sloppy, but all our friends were there, so they all went nuts. We covered a Cause for Alarm song, so that made everybody go crazy—even though we probably fucked it up big-time. There was a pile-on with Tommy Carroll, Craig, Armand, and Rob; basically, that was the pit, all of our friends!

After that, every show that Straight Ahead or Rest in Pieces would play, we would be on the bill with them, because everybody was in the same band! Armand would drum for us, drum for Straight Ahead, and then sing for Rest in Pieces. That was our little crew. But we seemed to pick up steam pretty quickly. Ray Cappo was really into us, and he was starting a label with his friend Jordan and he did a 7-inch with us in 1987. We were being asked to record a record, so that was great.

JORDAN COOPER: Sick of It All was a solid band from the first time they played. I don't remember how we got to work with them, but through the 7-inch compilation we did we got to know them a bit. We liked the same stuff about them that everyone does. They have great songs and great lyrics. They were sometimes funny but mostly just played a unique kind of hardcore that gave an outlet and a voice to aggression and anger. I'm not great at describing music, but to me Sick of It All was pretty different from a lot of other bands at the time. No formula at all; they just wrote the songs they wanted to play without trying to sound like any other band. Somehow they came up with a variation on hardcore that ended up influencing a lot of other bands.

TODD YOUTH: Sick of It All became the holders of the crown, so to speak. My generation was kind of gone, so it was time for these other kids to have their band.

HOWIE ABRAMS: The thing I liked about hardcore was that you never felt like you were just watching; you always felt a part of it. It wasn't a big arena concert experience where you were miles away from the band, and you felt lucky just to be in the building. There were kids selling fanzines and demos outside of the show. Bands always needed help carrying their gear in. By 1985, I was doing a fanzine called *Occasional Irregularity* with a good friend of mine. Through that, I met a lot of people involved in the scene. Unbeknownst to me, I was networking. I was offered job as a salesperson at Important Record Distributors in Jamaica, Queens. When I went for the interview, the owner realized I was only sixteen. He didn't want to be responsible for me quitting high school, so he gently suggested that I graduate high school and then give him a call. I graduated and went to college for a year, just taking classes for the hell of it before I called Important back. Then I became the salesperson dealing with the mom-and-pops: everyone from Bleecker Bob's to Zed in L.A., all the good indie stores.

Across the hall from my desk was Combat Records, a metal label that also had their hardcore side label, Combat Core, with Agnostic Front, the Circle Jerks, Ludichrist, and the Crumbsuckers. I discovered that these bands were wildly underserved. Agnostic Front would go on tour and the shows would be packed, but they'd get paid dirt. Because the metal bands were dealing with a more sophisticated industry, they were getting larger guarantees to play to just twenty percent of the people the hardcore bands could draw. I started thinking about helping to promote these bands. My idea basically revolved around taking Agnostic Front off of Combat and putting them on another label that would focus on promoting them in a respectful way.

PETE KOLLER: I remember our first headlining CBGB matinee. Our friend John drove us to CB's—seven or eight of us packed into his car coming from Queens. We pulled up and there was a line that went around and around the block. It was insane. It was sold out. To us, that was like selling ten million records. In early 1988, Rest in Pieces was asked to play the Ritz to open for

Exodus, which we thought was weird. Rest in Pieces was going to open for a metal band? That was fucking crazy! We thought Rest in Pieces was on the way to being a huge band. The next day, we got a phone call from the promoter, Chris Williamson. He and Raybeez were setting up the Superbowl of Hardcore together. We were so psyched that we were going to play the Ritz, too! We played in front of twelve hundred people on an all-hardcore bill. That was crazy.

HOWIE ABRAMS: We came up with the name In-Effect. We were based out of Hollis, so I can't say that hip-hop wasn't an influence. We started in 1989 with some Prong and Agnostic Front records, and soon we signed Sick of It All and Raw Deal.

CARL PORCARO: When we got the contracts from In-Effect, they recommended a lawyer. We were these hardcore kids sitting in some music industry lawyer's Midtown office where there was a gold record from Salt-N-Pepa on the wall. The guy had no clue what we were talking about, and we had no idea what he was talking about. It was bizarre shit at the time.

PETE KOLLER: When we heard that someone would want to pay us money to make a record, it was great. Not putting it down, but the labels that were being run out of some guy's mom's basement weren't prepared to do that. This was a step in a different direction for this type of music. We signed a contract to make ten albums, which is ridiculous. But we didn't give a shit. They gave us ten grand. I didn't even know what one hundred dollars was.

ADAM NATHANSON: Let's see, the war in Central America, the AIDS crisis, homelessness, increasing racial tension, gentrification . . . All these issues raged seemingly without end during that time. So what did Born Against decide to focus on? Whether In-Effect Records bands self-censored the word *shit* from their lyrics sheets. Talk about a lack of perspective!

When we started Born Against in 1989, our vocalist, Sam McPheeters, was doing a lot of work for the Committee in Solidarity with People of El Salvador and Nicaragua and Guatemala. They had an office at the War Resisters League on Lafayette Street. The very first song Born Against put on a record was "The Good Father," about the war in Central America. I had always been concerned about that. When I first got into punk five years earlier I would send away for stuff from the addresses on the back of the M.D.C. record. I don't know why we fixated on fratricidal weird scene politics things instead of dealing with real issues. There was stuff that was right up in our face that was really important, like poor and homeless people getting kicked out of Manhattan, or tax dollars going to the war in El Salvador. I don't know what was up with us wanting to scrutinize other bands and their business dealings.

FREDDY ALVA: On one hand, you had kids who had grown up in a working-class neighborhood with an outer-borough mentality, like Sick of It All, versus kids who came from a middle-class background, like Born Against. One side saw this type of music as a possible career path that would allow them to make a living doing something they loved. The others viewed hardcore as a protest against the well-fed privilege that they'd been raised to believe in.

ADAM NATHANSON: I had this crazy Stalinist type of view with hardcore that you were either with us or against us. If I didn't see you at Some Records or at Sunday matinees every week, then you weren't dedicated to hardcore. That was my teenage interpretation. If there were people in my high school who liked that kind of music, but I didn't see them every Sunday on the Bowery, then I thought they were clearly not dedicated. I had no time for these people. I had an extreme view. Some of the craziness that our band Born Against got to be known for started in my first band, Life's Blood. There was some vandalism of Venus Records related to them selling collectible punk records for a lot of money.

CRAIG SETARI: It's not like In-Effect was some guy we didn't know in a cheap suit telling us we were going to be stars. It was Howie Abrams. We used to go out and get pizza with him every week.

ANTHONY DRAGO: When we signed with In-Effect, we found out there was another band called Raw Deal out of the United Kingdom. They were approached by In-Effect with a heavy hand, saying, "You guys have to change your name." Their attorneys came back and said, "No, we don't. You guys actually have to change your name. We've had this name for years." Then In-Effect told us we needed a new name. That was the worst. We had gone through through Breakdown breaking up, and then this happened. It was ridiculous. That's when we changed our name to Killing Time. After that, there was this big issue that we changed our name. People were saying, "You let someone define you."

HOWIE ABRAMS: The idea that we were in any way corporate or that we were manipulating anyone is laughable. I kept asking if someone could please tell me respectfully what we were doing that was wrong. I got that ABC No Rio was trying to have this alternative scene, and that was fine. But the self-righteousness was insane, and people were also making shit up. Kids were listening to half a conversation and repeating the thing as fact. That was offensive. I thought, "You're looking in my pockets. You don't know me. You've never spoken to me, and yet you have an awful lot to say." Kids were complaining when they saw Sick of It All records at the mall in 1989. Listen to the first Sick of It All LP, *Blood, Sweat, and No Tears*, and tell me that was a safe thing to sell in record stores in the rest of the country in early 1989. One complaint from one parent out in the middle of nowhere and we were all done.

ANTHONY DRAGO: I had plenty of talks with people outside of different shows. Their idea of what hardcore should be was really threatened by me having a good time. They were calling the band sellouts. I didn't understand what they meant by sellout. If we were flying around in jets, then I'd get calling us sellouts. We got the opportunity to get someone else to pay to put our record out and we were sellouts. That's not selling out. That's just being smart.

HOWIE ABRAMS: This was the hardcore scene. These weren't people hiding in motel rooms. These were people who were out and about and at other people's shows all the time. These people were approachable and you could ask them questions. When you're dealing with people like that, and then you go and spew a bunch of bullshit about them, it's pretty transparent.

CARL PORCARO: They would pass out flyers at shows protesting us and shit. If there was one thing on any of those flyers that was true, it is that we got new gear. In terms of anything else, it was bullshit. We weren't on a rock-star trip, and we didn't have our own bouncers beating anyone up or anything like that.

ADAM NATHANSON: We never had a plan to be as crazy as we ended up acting. We obviously didn't comprehend these were typical social relationships that we should respect and maintain. We were like children acting out on every impulse, basically. We might have developed big platforms to justify particular things we ranted and raved about, but there was no filter. As I went further and further with my extremes and increasingly defined everything narrowly, I just thought everybody else through telepathy was going to come with me in that pursuit.

PETE KOLLER: Plenty of people came to our shows who didn't give a shit about anything else but having fun and going to a great hardcore show. But the people who were acting holier-than-thou and came from well-off families all had the loudest mouths. Where are they today? Everything in my life is hardcore. These guys were trying to shut us down because we were on a label that they thought was corporate. Where the fuck do you get your electricity from? Do you have a bicycle with a generator on it or something? Where do you get the gasoline for your fucking car? Shut the fuck up! You can be whatever you want to be. Eat vegan. Eat raw. Grow your own vegetables. But you always have to pay somebody for something.

HOWIE ABRAMS: I was flabbergasted by it all. Then in 1990 there was a debate on WNYU between the Born Against guys and Sick of It All, which I thought was totally retarded. These kids felt the hardcore thing became too tough-guy and they couldn't relate to that anymore. And that's fine. I just couldn't understand why they couldn't just do that without knocking someone else. They knocked people who were the most hardworking, honest motherfuckers I ever met.

MARLENE GOLDMAN (RADIO HOST, WNYU *Crucial Chaos*): I hosted the event. It seems so dated now, with everything being available digitally. At the time, it was a huge issue; hardcore on major labels, and whether compromising printed lyrics for mainstream distribution was selling out, and whether Sick of It All was kowtowing to their label for fame and money. Born Against and Sick of It All went at it, with Steve Martin representing the label side. At the time, I was more idealistic, so I tended to side with the Born Against guys, though I don't think the presented their case as well as they could have. In retrospect, Sick of It All's decision didn't undermine the whole scene all that much. They did what they felt they needed to do in order to keep playing and make a living. That night got pretty heated, and I could tell nobody was going to budge on their beliefs. I tried a couple of times to point specific questions at them, but it kept ending up in a shouting match. I don't think anyone swayed anyone else's opinion, but I am glad the issue got some airtime.

CHARLES MAGGIO: It had nothing to do with Sick of It All being on a major label. The entire concept of that thing was about censorship. It was about the lyrics sheet on the Sick of It All record being censored. We did not say Sick of It All sucked. We had no ill will toward them. It was a question of whether or not this was a dangerous precedent to set. Here we are, punk rockers and hardcore kids telling the record label we are willing to censor our lyrics in order to "gain sales." That's what it was all about for me.

NICK FORTE: I was present at the infamous Born Against versus Sick of It All debate. That was just silly. I was on the Born Against side, thinking major labels are bullshit, but our beef with these guys was so much deeper than the major-label thing. In the end, there was the snarky hardcore intelligentsia versus the meat-and-potatoes hardcore dudes. What we just really wanted to say to Sick of It All was, "You guys suck and you need to stop making music." But we had to be clever and wrap it up in some silly agenda that had a lot of holes in it. Also they would have killed us if we told them they sucked. They almost killed us anyway.

CHARLES MAGGIO: We were in a confined room with three guys who we watched onstage, and we knew were physically bigger and stronger than us. Plus they had other people around who were physically stronger than us. We felt threatened, so anything we said, we said under duress. Years later, I can understand their side of it. Their side of it was "Fuck you for criticizing us. We've been doing this for years." I totally get it and I appreciate it and respect it. I apologize to everyone completely on both sides.

ADAM NATHANSON: I really liked doing Born Against because I really liked the songs we were coming up with and it was a lot of fun. I just wanted to be known more for being a really good band, but I think we sabotaged ourselves on that one after all we did. I realized things were wacky when a lot of people at ABC No Rio and that micro-scene had taken our cue and turned on Born Against and started to call us out on things. They were biting the hand that feeds, in a way. We were a bunch of little monsters, and then we created a bunch of other little monsters who rejected us.

PETE KOLLER: Sometime around when all that shit was going on, Exodus was on Combat, and they wanted to take a new band on tour with them. Howie Abrams wanted them to take Sick of It All, since our record was just coming out. We did five shows with them to a crowd who had no idea what we were at all. There were all these big-hair metal guys and girls staring at us with our shaved heads and goatees and tattoos. After two songs, everybody was into it. It was a really great thing. It was our turn to cross over to a different audience.

After that, we went on tour with D.R.I. We got paid fifty dollars a night for two months straight. That was pretty rough, but we were kids. In our minds, this was going to be the last time we were ever going to see Florida or Texas. We thought we were going to go home, get jobs, and that would be it. We never thought we were going to be hardcore and make a living from it. We knew it wasn't metal or regular rock music, where people would sell hundreds of thousands of records. But we were wrong! Thank God for that, or I would have killed myself a long time ago.

ANTHONY DRAGO: When we changed our name to Killing Time and our *Brightside* LP came out in 1989, In-Effect wanted to send us out on tour. We couldn't go because our singer, Anthony Comunale, was already working a sheet-metal job with the union. All we could do were local shows around the East Coast on the weekends. In-Effect was not happy about that. It pissed them off like you wouldn't believe. They had just put a lot of money into putting that record out. Not only that, but we gave them a record that was under the normal running time, for them to sell for the full price of an LP! We just didn't have any more material. All the other bands really went to work for In-Effect and pushed the product. Sick of It All from that first fuckin' record onward was out on the road. If we had taken off on tour with Sick of It All and played all those clubs, I might be a totally different person today in a different place in life.

JOHN BELLO: These bands went to the next level at a time that people didn't want them to go there. But that was probably the best thing for them, because if Agnostic Front kept putting out records on Rat Cage every two or three years, would they have survived thirty years? Probably not! Same thing goes for Sick of It All. Without that major push, who knows? They might have disbanded after three years. So looking back on it, God bless them. They've been surviving for thirty years on hardcore. Not many people can do that.

Killing Time taking its toll KEN SALERNO

John Porcelly attaining the supreme in Shelter ADAM TANNER

50. SHELTER: PERFECTION OF DESIRE

JOHN PORCELLY: By 1988 or '89, I can see why people got pissed off with straight edge. The kids coming in who were just getting into straight edge were shitting on every other band. We came from that Agnostic Front thing where we were all in this together. The Youth of Today song "Break Down the Walls" was about the people who put an X on their hand and then thought they were better than everybody else. People had legitimate gripes against the cliché straight-edge kid. Things became factionalized and splintered. You'd have straight-edge kids who would only go to straight-edge shows. Just a few years before, straight-edge kids went to see Sick of It All, and Tommy Carroll moshed to Agnostic Front. We were all in it together. When I think of the early days of Youth of Today, there was so much scene unity and it was such a creative time.

RAY CAPPO: I didn't grow up in the straight-edge scene. If anything, we created that scene. But at a point, I could see where some people were coming from. The straight-edge scene seemed kind of dumbed down. It bummed me out. Straight edge created a bubble, was a scene within a scene, and it wasn't really interested in anything that wasn't straight edge. That made me sad. I loved the Buzzcocks, PiL, and other things. Newer kids were exclusively getting into Youth of Today or Uniform Choice. They would buy any record by these straight-edge bands like Wide Awake and Aware, but if some other punk band put out a record, they wouldn't care. Their whole view of hardcore was narrow.

JOHN PORCELLY: For the first time, a lot of bands on the scene started to become cookie-cutter to me. With Youth of Today, we loved Minor Threat, we loved SSD, we loved DYS, but I don't think we sounded like any of those bands. There was this punk mentality that you would find your own style and sound. When you just had bands aping shit, it got weird—especially the bands that were aping Youth of Today. I didn't like it! I was a punk, and I was into the idea of everyone being themselves.

WALTER SCHREIFELS: Everyone wanted to think like us and be like us, so our dream sort of backfired. We would go to shows and everyone would look the same. I started feeling like maybe this wasn't that cool. It just became so much about the T-shirts, and the Swatch watches with the X's on them.

RICHIE BIRKENHEAD: Here's a non sequitur: I lived around the corner from the Swatch flagship store, and I saw some piece of literature about the X Swatch coming out. Of course, it wasn't intended to be a straight-edge thing by them. I asked the girl in the shop to let me know when they were going to become available. It was many months to a year before I saw anyone else on the scene rockin' it. I will go to my grave swearing I owned the first X Swatch out of the whole New York scene.

JOHN PORCELLY: In 1988, after Youth of Today's second LP, *We're Not in This Alone*, we felt we had said everything we wanted to say. We had taken straight-up hardcore to its limit. We were all going in different directions. Walter wanted to get serious about Gorilla Biscuits. I was totally into Judge. Ray was on his spiritual trip.

RAY CAPPO: I began to read books by yogis and Buddhists and Christian mystics. All the things about the material world that all these great yogis and mystics wrote about, I felt, "I'm over that shit. I'm not greedy. I'm not envious. I'm not competitive. I know the material world is temporary." But I was immersed in the success of this micro-world that was filled with greed, envy, lust, and ignorance. I thought I was above it, but I was immersed in it. My success had made me suffer even more. I was really burnt out. Then my father died unexpectedly. That's when I understood the temporality of the material world.

ALEX BROWN: I was living with Ray in Williamsburg, Brooklyn. I woke up to him making weird noises in the next room. He was chanting!

RAY CAPPO: In the straight-edge scene, everybody was looking up to me. Truthfully, I didn't know what I was talking about. There were tenets of the straight-edge thing, like you should strive to be a better person, and be forgiving, and not kill animals. But, you know, my mom could tell you that! It's not like I was some Dali Lama for saying something as simple as that. The straight-edge scene became too much of this thing where kids just thought they were perfect. They didn't use straight edge as a stepping-stone to do greater things in life. There was arrogance in the straight-edge scene that you find in religion, or anything people do for their self-betterment. Instead of doing it for yourself; you end up doing it to lord over other people. It defeats the whole idea of self-betterment. I was watching this happen, and it was super bumming me out. I got to thinking about what I wanted. Would getting ten times bigger in hardcore make me a happier person? I realized nothing would make me happy except for some sort of God quest. So I quit music.

When I recorded the first Shelter record, it was supposed to me my final record ever. I did that with Tom Capone from Beyond and Quicksand, and some older guys I knew from Connecticut. They helped me record what was supposed to be my goodbye to hardcore. Then I became a monk.

JOHN PORCELLY: After Judge broke up was a very hard time for me. I had dedicated my life to Youth of Today and Judge. I had dropped out of college and left my home to live in a crappy apartment on the Lower East Side of New York City to play in these bands. I was still straight edge, but no one else was anymore. Around that time, I think I saw Gus "Straight Edge" Peña smoking a cigar. So that's where the Youth Crew was at that point! The new thing to do was hang around in bars. I didn't want to go to bars. But I wasn't a kid anymore, I was twenty-two. I couldn't fuck around on the Lower East Side until four in the morning forever. I had to get my life together. I really got into fitness and being healthy. I was a raw-foodist and a vegan before anyone knew what vegan was. I went through a real spiritual crisis. I was always wondering what life was about. People kind of looked up to me and I had an easy life. I had all these things that people were knocking themselves out to get, and I was completely unsatisfied with them. It was a dark, soul-searching time for me, and I spent a lot of the time alone. There was a bookstore on Sixth Avenue called East West Books, and I spent all my money on books there. I would sit in my apartment and read. I sold everything that I owned except for my guitar and my amp. I moved into the Krishna Farm upstate with nothing. I tried to start my life in a totally new direction.

RAY CAPPO: The more I studied Indian philosophy, I noticed that a big part of that philosophy is that you don't quit what you were born to do. You take what you do and do it in a spiritual way instead of the material way. That's how Shelter became a full-fledged band. It took me to give it up to get me to refine it.

JOHN PORCELLY: I had very little contact with Ray during the time that Shelter had started. He didn't know that I was going to the Brooklyn temple every week and that I eventually moved to the farm. Vic DiCara, the guitarist for Shelter, quit the band Ray was in India, and when he came back he went right to the farm and tried to talk me into joining Shelter. No way. I was happy at the farm. Eventually I gave in and joined Shelter. If anything, going to that farm was a detox from living on the Lower East Side for so long. But in the end—me being on a farm for the rest of my life milking cows? It wasn't going to happen. I'm not a farmer; I'm a musician.

Raghunath, aka Ray Cappo, vocalist for Shelter ADAM TANNER

51. CLEAN SLATE

JOHN PORCELLY: Just when everything became so generic in hardcore, the 1990s came in, and everyone wanted to become something different. That was a really cool thing.

ALEX BROWN: I got kicked out of Gorilla Biscuits late 1990 or so. There was really not much happening in the hardcore world that kept my interest. Shows were often violent and not much fun unless you were looking for a fight. The great thing to come out of that scene was all the bands that went on to try and break out of the box. Quicksand is the most obvious example of taking the hardcore vibe, ethos, heaviness, and whatever other adjective you want to ascribe to it, and throwing in more esoteric influences.

RICHIE BIRKENHEAD: The time when bands like Into Another, Quicksand, and Orange 9mm started is just like the early hardcore scene in a way. All these bands were wonderfully disparate in sound, spirit, and aesthetic. All of us were not exactly a scene per se; we all sounded different, but we all sprang out of the same thing for similar reasons.

WALTER SCHREIFELS: For a few years or so, I wasn't listening to anything other than hardcore. I didn't think I was going to be interested in anything else, but that wore off.

RICHIE BIRKENHEAD: I was becoming disgruntled with Underdog. We were all going in different directions. In my estimation, the hardcore scene didn't resemble what it had been to me anymore.

WALTER SCHREIFELS: I didn't like the Krishna consciousness thing that was coming into the hardcore scene. Maybe it's just being from Queens, but I think my root reaction to Hare Krishna was that it was a cult. Not to discredit the people that get a lot out of it, like Ray and Porcell, but that was just my impression at the time. On the other side of it you had the violence. Hardcore had been discovered by too many bullies, smart ones and dumb ones. People were going to hardcore shows just to beat people up. They weren't into the music. It was either a bunch of clowns or bullies, so I grew less interested.

JORDAN COOPER: The two big factors that seemed to end an era for me in 1989 were Ray getting into Krishna and Nirvana's *Bleach* coming out. Those two things did really change a lot of things for quite a few people, me included.

WALTER SCHREIFELS: I remember touring with Gorilla Biscuits in Europe. Someone gave me Nirvana's *Bleach*, and I was like, "Wow!" Fugazi was happening at the same time, and that was more interesting to me, too. There was something there that seemed more adult that I wanted to grab onto. I wanted to write lyrics that were more inwardly focused, more pondering. I was no longer in high school, so I wondered what was next for me.

I started a project in the spring of 1989 named Moondog with Luke, the drummer of Gorilla Biscuits, and Tom Capone from Beyond. That was kind of a step on the way to Quicksand. That came along because a tape got out of me singing the new Gorilla Biscuits stuff to show Civ how the words fit. We got a lot of compliments, even though I didn't think it was very good, but I thought maybe I should sing something, too. I wanted to do something scary but also poppy.

TOM CAPONE (GUITARIST, BEYOND, BOLD, GORILLA BISCUITS, QUICKSAND): Walter called me up and told me he had this idea to do a band called Moondog. He wanted Moondog to be a darker version of Gorilla Biscuits. That sounded cool to me, and that led us into Quicksand. We played a show at ABC No Rio when I don't think we even had a name yet.

ALEX BROWN: I saw their first show at ABC No Rio, and I was so psyched to see the potential that lay beyond the horizon of four-chord, verse and chorus, mosh-style hardcore.

TOM CAPONE: We approached Quicksand differently than we did Moondog. I just think Walter said he wanted to do a rock band. We both didn't want to play straight-up hardcore anymore.

WALTER SCHREIFELS: Forming Quicksand in 1990 was sort of my reaction to the monster I helped create in hardcore.

RICHIE BIRKENHEAD: Drew from Bold and I were good friends; we were always talking about making music together. The single criterion for our music was we wouldn't subscribe to any genre on any level. We were huge fans of Bowie, Queen, the Beatles, Black Sabbath, and Syd Barrett, and we were even huger Kiss fans. That's where Into Another sprang from.

WALTER SCHREIFELS: In Quicksand, everyone was a real musician and really had a voice with their instrument. Everybody who was in Youth of Today and Gorilla Biscuits was good, but there was something about Quicksand where the dudes I was playing with were just on another level musically.

RICHIE BIRKENHEAD: When we started Into Another in 1990, we almost intentionally tried to alienate ourselves from hardcore kids. I was like, "I'm going to sing long fucking high notes like Rob Halford and I don't give a rat's ass!" We wanted to express ourselves musically, whether it was an acoustic ballad or a heavy metal song.

TOM CAPONE: We were trying to step away from hardcore, but not in a snotty way. We definitely weren't trying to push the people we knew from hardcore away from us at all. We were just trying to create a new sound for ourselves. Our efforts went into just being Quicksand.

RICHIE BIRKENHEAD: When we first started playing, we knew there were going to be people who fucking hated us, but there might be some people who would get it. After playing our first show, I was almost in tears. I was so grateful and so humbled. I also felt like such an asshole for totally underestimating the scope of acceptance and taste of these kids. I was being elitist.

TOM CAPONE: We weren't looking to sign to a major label. Fugazi was a huge inspiration in how they dealt with their band; just being sincere in how you approach your music. We were still thinking about this stuff in hardcore terms. We thought that if we could be as big as Bad Religion were in Europe at the time, that would be making it. Then when Nirvana got signed, all these other bands got signed and we were being looked at by major labels. Eventually, a contract came our way. It was a hard decision. But I think for the most part, people supported our choice to sign with a major. All the people we knew from hardcore were digging what we were doing. We believed in what we were doing.

JOHN PORCELLY: We had all been in a box for so long and all of a sudden, it felt like it was okay to do something different. We hit a point where we said, "Fuck it, let's experiment." Don't get me wrong, people made mistakes. Look at the drum machine on the Ray and Porcell 7-inch!

TIM CHUNKS: On that cusp of the '80s going into the '90s, it seemed everybody was trying to do something new. When Token Entry recorded our last record, *Weight of the World*, in 1990, we definitely made a conscious effort to try something different and outside of our realm. The Red Hot Chili Peppers were just blowing up and we thought their stuff was awesome. When that record came out, we still had a core group of people who would come to our shows. We didn't really lose that many people. After we broke up, I listened to that record and wondered what the fuck we were thinking. After enough time passed, people felt comfortable telling me what they thought about that last record. I just shake my head and say, "Yeah, I know!"

52. THE LEGACY: SET IT OFF

HOWIE ABRAMS: One day around 1988 Roger Miret walked into In-Effect with this cassette of like three or four minutes of a little kid singing in front of what could be Agnostic Front's "United Blood, Part Two." It was a recording of his little brother, what was to become Madball's *Ball of Destruction* EP. We released that as a 7-inch in 1989.

Fast-forward a few years, and Madball started to gain some interest. They were getting invited to play places like South America, because Agnostic Front was touring there. The 7-inch had traveled, and people were asking about Madball. The band had become a myth. So that's when Hoya Roc came in on bass, Willie Shepler on drums, and Matt Henderson was on guitar. Stigma was a part of that lineup as well. They didn't have serious intentions of being a band.

By 1993, they made it known that they wanted to be a real band. I ended up sitting down with Freddy, who was seventeen at that time, and Hoya. They wanted to make an actual album and become one of those bands that did albums and tour cycles. So we went and did *Set It Off*. Madball took the old version of the NYHC formula and presented it in a new package and it worked. People really connected with it.

TOBY MORSE: I started going to South America and Europe with Sick of It All. I wasn't the best roadie in the world. I would help break down the drums and do a bunch of stage dives. I was just a friend they brought on tour. They brought me around the world as a kid. That was pretty much my college. When I came back, the scene was really driving with V.O.D., Madball, Sub-zero, and Crown of Thornz. It was a whole new generation of NYHC, and it was awesome.

HOWIE ABRAMS: The '90s era of bands like H20 and Crown of Thornz were made up of roadies and fans and scenester kids. All the kids you would see on the road with Sick of It All or Madball or Killing Time started their own bands.

TOBY MORSE: I ended up starting H20 because I would sing with Sick of It All as a joke. H20 did their first show in Queens opening for Murphy's Law. When we came out, there was so much of the tough-guy chugga-chugga stuff. People were like, "Oh shit, what's this?" To some people, it was a breath of fresh air because we had melody.

HOWIE ABRAMS: Ezec and Toby had been around the scene for quite a while, and both were super-charismatic guys. They decided they wanted to have bands, but both of them went in two totally different ways musically. H20 had the NYHC vibe but also had a West Coast punk vibe with influences like Descendents and Bad Religion. They didn't just play mosh parts. But Crown of Thornz had been influenced by the crossover era of Agnostic Front. Both bands also paid a shitload of respect to the Cro-Mags and Murphy's Law, but each band had an identity of its own.

MICHAEL SCONDOTTO: Around that time, Brooklyn exploded with new bands too. In 1990 alone Merauder, Patterns, my band Confusion, Lament, and Life of Agony all formed. Other bands from that era were Nobody's Perfect and Social Disorder. L'Amour and the Crazy Country Club were both were having hardcore shows. A lot of the members of these Brooklyn bands were going to CB's in the late '80s, but didn't get to play there due to being too young. This was all happening simultaneously to Biohazard making the rounds. Carnivore was the beginning point for all of the bands in Brooklyn, really.

DREW STONE: I saw Biohazard at a hardcore matinee in the late '80s. I remember watching two songs and thinking, "Two skinheads, two longhairs. Half hardcore, half metal. I get the gimmick." But things worked out well for them later on, and they got better and better. Biohazard opened the doors for a lot of the bands that came in toward the 1990s. A lot of guys saw what was going on with Biohazard and got inspired. Look at the Biohazard video I shot for "Punishment." Most of those guys in the video ended up in that next wave of bands. There are guys from Merauder and Sub Zero, plus Ezec and the guys from Madball. That's what most people know as NYHC today.

TOBY MORSE: When CB's got shut down, there were shows going on at Coney Island High. Oh my God, Coney Island High! Another wave of amazing shows were put on by Jimmy G and Steve Poss, who were doing Creepy Crawl Productions, and a whole new wave of kids went to those shows.

HOWIE ABRAMS: During the '90s era, none of the hardcore bands that influenced the NYHC thing sounded like NYHC when it first came out. Everything was all stripped away and started anew. Of course, everyone still gave respect to the people who started it: Crown of Thornz carried on the influence of Agnostic Front throughout their career. But hardcore as a separate thing from metal, the kind of hardcore that still recognized punk as a distant cousin, that stuff was pretty much wiped away. The genuine community aspect of the scene remained. That was still undoubtedly NYHC. That spirit will always be there, and I think that's fascinating. In fact, for that to survive in a city this big and this diverse, with kids coming from so many different places, not only is it fascinating—it's almost a miracle.

VINNIE STIGMA: The early NYHC thing was a true moment in time. It was where the worlds of music crossed: punk, hardcore, Oi!, and metal. These days, people try to tweet themselves to fame. They have no idea that you have to earn your bones. You have to write good music. You have to be there for the people.

JESSE MALIN: People like us think of hardcore as this great part of American culture, but, in reality, it's a small little blip. But it influenced so much. Without it, you wouldn't have Nirvana. You wouldn't have the way people tour. You wouldn't have South by Southwest. In New York, we had kids into the peace-punk shit. We had kids into the skinhead shit. We had kids into angel dust. NYHC was all over the map and it was diverse.

WENDY EAGER: We could sit here forever and I still think we wouldn't cover all the bands from that time. There's so many other bands that are going be left out, like Anti-Warfare and Rapid Deployment Force. It just seemed like every week, a new band was starting. There were the Agnostic Fronts and the Murphy's Laws, but there was a band like Ultra Violence who started before A7 and lasted through to the mid-'80s.

TOMMY CARROLL: I thought NYHC was the only thing on earth. Over the years, people look in and idolize the people involved, and I guess I can see why. It made history—it made a wave. To me, it was just about being young, being from New York, our personalities, and being who we were as people. I thought L.A. was soft and I still think they are. I'm not a big fan of the West Coast and I never will be. New York *is* hardcore, period! Why is NYHC great? Because New York's great!

Freddy Cricien sets it off in 1994. CHRIS MINICUCCI

HOWIE ABRAMS: At the end of the day, you're doing a book about NYHC because it's still relevant. We have the Black N' Blue Bowl, and there are hardcore festivals all over the world where NYHC bands play. These bands are constantly on tour in Europe, Japan, Asia, and Australia. Who the fuck ever saw that happening? At the end of the day, nobody thought they would tour the world and make a living. It's amazing how widespread it's become.

TOBY MORSE: People live this life forever. Not everybody lives in New York still, but everybody is still a part of that scene. Sick of It All, Madball, and Agnostic Front still tour. How far it has come from little CBGB to massive tours where all these bands still kill it. It's so inspiring.

PETE KOLLER: It's really crazy to think I wouldn't own the house I live in if I didn't go to CBGB to see an Agnostic Front show. Armand wouldn't have met his wife if it wasn't for this band. I wouldn't be living where I live with my wife and a beautiful baby. This is our lives.

GARY TSE TSE FLY: There are so many guys married to this lifestyle. The band is their wife, their kids, maybe even their mother-in-law. Jimmy G and Paul Bearer still hang out in New York City. They didn't come here to squat for the summer. NYHC was real and it stayed real. Murphy's Law never went away.

Agnostic Front never went away. The Nihilistics never went away. They never cashed in on a reunion or anything, because they stayed in the scene, for better or for worse.

TIM CHUNKS: For me, it was about who was there. All my peers were making music. It was guys I went to school with and guys I hung out with. We hung out and laughed and joked. We talked about serious shit and fought together. It was so important to me, because it was people I respected and held dear in my heart; and I still do. For me, it was important about *who* it was, and not so much *what* it was.

ALEXA POLI-SCHEIBERT: The poverty and the squalor was the most influential thing on the NYHC scene. It made us hard, and maybe a little bitter for our age, but we were pissed off. Reaganomics wasn't working for our situation and we bonded. We were a family. To this day, I consider Jimmy, Vinnie, and Roger family. When I got badly burned, nobody I knew from Albany came to the hospital. B. J. Papas flew from Hollywood to be by my side. Melissa Kabula showed up with a DVD player and a whole bunch of DVDs. I hadn't seen her in twenty-two years. I used to defend her because everyone would fuck with her because she was this nice girl who was marrying Rob. She remembered that. We were coming from really fucked-up homes and we needed a family. I have a lot of love for these people because they're special to me. They're my family because I never really had one. Being a girl and a part of it and not sleeping around crazily was special. Being a sister to the guys was more important to me.

VINNIE STIGMA: Look at someone like Todd Youth. Here's this kid who ended up playing for Ace Frehley, Motörhead, and Glenn Campbell. You name them and he played with them. This kid is kind of like my legacy. Look at Sindi from the Lunachicks. I taught her guitar when she was a little, little girl, and she ended up being in this great all-girl band.

As you get older, you find out life is too important and there's things you should stay true to. That's why I've got mixed feelings about these bands who haven't played in twenty years and all of a sudden, they come back. I got two ways of looking at them. One: Welcome back, brother. We missed you. Two: Where the fuck were ya? Now go fuck yourself! I'm funny like that because there's other bands that have been out there doing the struggle for the last twenty years and you think you're just going to come waltzing in after you left us flat? I take it personal. I'm mixed up on it because they're all my friends. I just don't want them to think they can come waltzing in here and think they're better than these kids in bands today because these kids are here and they deserve the respect. That's me looking out for the new kids. When punk turned into hardcore, you had guys who were always asking kids, "Where were you?" My thing has always been, hey, they're here now and that's what matters. Now you look around, and you ask where are these guys who said that twenty years ago to all those kids? You understand where I'm coming from here?

JIMMY G: People don't realize how important our scene is and how much we put into the music community of New York. It's sort of good and sort of bad. If we had gotten a lot of attention, we would be done by now. Everyone can toot their own horn and all that, and that's fine. That's just pride—but I'll put it this way—Agnostic Front and Murphy's Law still do it and we never stopped doing it. My existence is a tribute to A7. Me carrying the torch, and Vinnie carrying the torch, and Roger carrying the torch, and Harley still doing it: That's a tribute. I understand that some people have to go off and grow up and start a family. Roger has three kids, and he's still a major part of the scene. I have no reason to go off and grow up and start a family and a new life. This is my life.

Sick of It All, With Full Force Festival, Roitzschjora Airfield, Germany, July 2, 2010. DIRK BEHLAU / THE PIXELEYE

RANDY UNDERWOOD

CAST OF CHARACTERS

LUKE ABBEY: Drummer, Loud & Boisterous, Gorilla Biscuits, Warzone, Judge; bass player, Moondog

HOWIE ABRAMS: A&R, In-Effect Records; editor *Occasional Irregularity* fanzine

UNCLE AL MORRIS: Guitarist, the Attack, Murphy's Law, Unholy Alliance

FREDDY ALVA: Editor, *New Breed* fanzine; show promoter, ABC No Rio; owner, Wardance Records; coowner Urban Style Records

PAUL BEARER: Vocalist, Fathead Suburbia, Sheer Terror

JOHN BELLO: A&R, Hawker Records

CHARLIE BENANTE: Drummer, Anthrax, S.O.D.

RICHIE BIRKENHEAD: Vocalist, Numskulls, Underdog, Into Another; guitarist, Youth of Today

DAVE BRADY: Vocalist, Crumbsuckers;

ALEX BROWN: Guitarist, Side by Side, Gorilla Biscuits; coeditor, *Schism* fanzine

MIKE BULLSHIT: Vocalist, SFA, Go!; editor, *Bullshit Monthly* fanzine

KEITH BURKHARDT: Vocalist, Agnostic Front, Cause for Alarm

TOM CAPONE: Guitarist, Beyond, Bold, Gorilla Biscuits, Quicksand

RAY CAPPO: Drummer, Violent Children; vocalist, Youth of Today, Shelter, Reflex From Pain

JOHNNY CARCO: Bassist, the Misguided

TOMMY CARROLL: Vocalist/drummer, NYC Mayhem; drummer, Youth of Today; vocalist, Straight Ahead, Irate

TIM CHUNKS: Vocalist, Token Entry

JORDAN COOPER: Owner, Revelation Records

PAUL CRIPPLE: Guitarist, Reagan Youth

KEVIN CROWLEY: Vocalist, the Abused

PETER CROWLEY: Talent booker, Max's Kansas City

ROBBIE CRYPTCRASH: Drummer, Cryptcrashers, Agnostic Front, Cause for Alarm

DONNA DAMAGE: Vocalist, No Thanks

PAUL DORDAL: NYHC scenester; writer of Murphy's Law songs "Skinhead Rebel" and "California Pipeline"

ANTHONY DRAGO: Drummer, Breakdown, Raw Deal

KIT E. HAWK: Bassist, the Eliminators, Killer Instinct, XKI, P.M.S.

WENDY EAGER: Editor, *Guillotine* fanzine

HARLEY FLANAGAN: Drummer, the Stimulators, M.O.I.; bassist and later vocalist, Cro-Mags

JACK FLANAGAN: Guitarist, Heart Attack, the Mob

NICK FORTE: Guitarist, Rorschach; coeditor, *Mindset* fanzine

DON FURY: Owner, Fury Studios; responsible for all crucial NYHC recordings

JIMMY G: Vocalist, Cavity Creeps, Murphy's Law

RALPHIE G: Vocalist, the Mob

SCREAMING MAD GEORGE: Vocalist, the Mad

MICHAEL GIBBONS: Guitarist, Leeway

MARLENE GOODMAN: Radio Host, WNYU *Crucial Chaos*

DAVEY GUNNER: Vocalist, Kraut

DOUG HOLLAND: Guitarist, Apprehended, Kraut, Cro-Mags

MERYL HURWICH: Guitarist, XKI

LYLE HYSEN: Drummer, Misguided; editor, *Damaged Goods* fanzine

DEAN ISLAY: Drummer, Child Abuse, Murphy's Law, Underdog

RUSS ISLAY: Guitarist, Child Abuse; bassist, Murphy's Law, Underdog

DARRYL JENIFER: Bassist, Bad Brains

JOHN JOHN JESSE: Bassist, Nausea

JOHN JOSEPH: Vocalist, Bloodclot, M.O.I., Cro-Mags

MIKE JUDGE: Vocalist and drummer, Death Before Dishonor, Youth of To-day; vocalist, Judge

ROB KABULA: Bassist, Cause for Alarm, Agnostic Front

DARYL KAHAN: Vocalist, Citizens Arrest, True Colors

JOHN KELLY: Guitarist, Urban Waste, Major Conflict

ALEX KINON: Guitarist, Cause for Alarm, Agnostic Front, Skinhead Youth

DAVE KOENIG: Editor, *In Memory Of . . .* fanzine; coeditor, *Hardware* fanzine

PETE KOLLER: Guitarist, Sick of It All

JAMES KONTRA: Vocalist, Agnostic Front, Virus

REBECCA KORBET: Vocalist, Even Worse

CAROLYN LENGEL: Vocalist, Killer Instinct, XKI

DANNY LILKER: Bassist, Anthrax, Nuclear Assault, S.O.D.

CHARLES MAGGIO: Vocalist, Rorschach; coeditor, *Mindset* fanzine

ARMAND MAJIDI: Vocalist/drummer, Rest in Pieces; drummer, Straight Ahead, Sick of It All

JESSE MALIN: Guitarist/vocalist, Heart Attack, D-Generation

NICK MARDEN: Bassist, Even Worse, the Stimulators

JULES MASSE: Vocalist, Side by Side, Alone in a Crowd

PARRIS MAYHEW: Guitarist, Cro-Mags

DENISE MERCEDES: Guitarist, the Stimulators

GARY MESKIL: Bassist, Crumbsuckers, Pro-Pain

ROGER MIRET: Vocalist, Agnostic Front; bassist, the Psychos

JAE MONROE: Vocalist, A.P.P.L.E.

PITO MONTIEL: Guitarist, Major Conflict; film director

TOBY MORSE: Vocalist, H2O; roadie, Sick of It All

ADAM MUCCI: Bassist, Agnostic Front, Murphy's Law, Sacrilege

ADAM NATHANSON: Guitarist, Life's Blood, Mister Softy, Born Against; coeditor, *Constructive Rebellion* fanzine

ROBB NUNZIO: Guitar, Antidote, M.O.I.

TOM O'HARA: Coeditor, *Combat Stance* fanzine

JASON O'TOOLE: Vocalist, Life's Blood

ERNIE PARADA: Drummer, Gilligan's Revenge, Token Entry, Underdog

JEFF PERLIN: Vocalist, Breakdown

DAVE PARSONS: Owner, Rat Cage Records; editor, *Mouth of the Rat* fanzine

MIKE PERILLO: Guitarist, Savage Circle; editor, *Yet Another Rag* fanzine

BILLY PHILLIPS: Vocalist, Urban Waste, Major Conflict

AL PIKE: Bassist, Reagan Youth; coeditor, *Straight Edge* fanzine

ALEXA POLI-SCHEIGERT: NYHC scenester

CARL PORCARO: Guitarist, Breakdown, Raw Deal, Alone in a Crowd

JOHN PORCELLY: Guitarist, Violent Children, Youth of Today, Bold, Judge, Gorilla Biscuits, Shelter; vocalist, Project X; coeditor, *Schism* fanzine

STEVE POSS: Drummer, Cavity Creeps; NYHC legend

JACK RABID: Editor, *Big Takeover* fanzine; drummer, Even Worse

BRENDAN RAFFERTY: Vocalist, SFA; bouncer, CBGB

RON RANCID: Vocalist, the Nihilistics

TOMMY RAT: Vocalist, Agnostic Front, Warzone, Life's Blood, Trip 6, Rejuvenate; NYHC legend

LOUIE RIVERA: Vocalist, Antidote

JULIE H. ROSE: Guitarist, the Mad, the Cramps

DANNY SAGE: Guitarist, the Possessed, Heart Attack, D-Generation

WALTER SCHREIFELS: Guitairst, Gorilla Biscuits; guitarist/vocalist, Quicksand; bassist, Youth of Today, Project X, Warzone, Supertouch

MICHAEL SCONDOTTO: Vocalist, Inhuman, the Last Stand

DAVE SCOTT: Drummer, Adrenalin O.D.; vocalist, Pleased Youth

CRAIG SETARI: Bassist, NYC Mayhem, Straight Ahead, Agnostic Front, Youth of Today, Sick of It All

NATALIE JACOBSON SHEARING: Employee, the Ritz; author

ARTHUR SMILIOS: Guitarist/bassist, Token Entry, Underdog, Gorilla Biscuits, Warzone

TIM SOMMER: Radio host, WNYU *Noise the Show*; guitarist, Even Worse

JOE SONGCO: Drummer, Outburst

BOBBY STEELE: Guitarist, the Misfits; guitarist/vocalist, the Undead

VINNIE STIGMA: Guitarist, the Eliminators, Agnostic Front, Madball; vocalist, Stigma

DREW STONE: Vocalist, the High and the Mighty, Antidote; filmmaker

EDDIE SUTTON: Vocalist, Leeway

TONY T-SHIRT: Vocalist, Ultra Violence; screen-printer of many classic NYHC shirts (hence the name)

SEAN TAGGART: Vocalist, Shok; artist (Cro-Mags, Crumbsuckers)

DOUG THOMPSON: Drummer, Murphy's Law

CHRIS TSAKIS: Guitarist, the Nihilistics, Missing Foundation

GARY TSE TSE FLY: Editor, *Tse Tse Fly* fanzine

GAVIN VAN VLACK: Guitarist, NY Hoods, Suburban Uprise, Side by Side, Absolution, Burn, Die 116

VICTOR VENOM: Guitarist, Reagan Youth, Sacrilege, Nausea

KEN WAGNER: NYHC scenester

MATT WARNKE: Vocalist, Bold

JOHN WATSON: Vocalist, Agnostic Front

JERRY WILLIAMS: Owner, 171A; NYHC producer/engineer

BILL WILSON: Owner, Blackout Records

STEVE WISHNIA: Bassist, False Prophets

DAVE WYNN: Guitarist, Crumbsuckers

TODD YOUTH: Bassist, Agnostic Front, Skinhead Youth; guitarist, Warzone, Murphy's Law, D-Generation

SOURCE INDEX

CHAPTER ONE: LOUD FAST RULES!

All Nick Marden and Denise Mercedes quotes from an interview conducted by Diane Farris.

Quotes from Tommy Rat, Robbie Cryptcrash and Rebecca Korbet from unpublished interviews conducted by Scott Horton.

Quote from Harley Flanagan from Vista Fanzine Blog

CHAPTER THREE: I HATE MUSIC : THE MAD

Quote from Robbie Cryptcrash from an unpublished interview conducted by Scott Horton.

CHAPTER FOUR: THE BIG TAKE-OVER: BAD BRAINS

Quote from Denise Mercedes from an interview conducted by Diane Farris.

CHAPTER FIVE: EVEN WORSE: WE SUCK!

Quote from Rebecca Korbet from an unpublished interview conducted by Scott Horton.

CHAPTER SIX: AVENUE A: 171 A

Nick Marden quotes from an interview conducted by Diane Farris.

Quotes from Donna Damage, Rebecca Korbet and Carolyn Lengel from unpublished interviews conducted by Scott Horton.

Quote from Dave Parson from an interview conducted by Lyle Hysen and published in Maximum Rock N Roll. Used with the permission of Lyle Hysen.

CHAPTER TEN: NOISE THE SHOW

Quote from James Kontra from an interview conducted by Scott Horton and published on the In Effect website.

CHAPTER FOURTEEN: THE 'ZINE SCENE: GIVE 'EM THE AXE!

Quotes from Mike Perillo from an unpublished interview conducted by Scott Horton.

CHAPTER FIFTEEN: NO ONE RULES : DC VS BOSTON VS NY

Quotes from Tommy Rat and Tony T-Shirt from an unpublished interview conducted by Scott Horton.

CHAPTER SEVENTEEN: EAST VILLAGE NIGHTS A7 AND 2 +2

Quote from Donna Damage "It was total mayhem…' from an unpublished interview conducted by Scott Horton.

Quote from Nick Marden from an interview conducted by Diane Farris.

Quote from Meryl Hurwich from an unpublished interview conducted by Scott Horton.

CHAPTER 18. URBAN WASTE AND MAJOR CONFLICT: HOW DO YOU FEEL?

Quotes from Billy Phillips from an interview conducted by Dan Skirba and published on the Mad at the World blog.

CHAPTER 19. THE ABUSED DRUG FREE YOUTH

Quote from Robbie Cryptcrash from an unpublished interview conducted by Scott Horton.

CHAPTER 22. CAUSE FOR ALARM: STAND AS ONE!

Quote from Robbie Cryptcrash from an unpublished interview conducted by Scott Horton.

CHAPTER 23. APARTMENT X

Quotes from Tony T-Shirt and Robbie Robbie Cryptcrash from unpublished interviews conducted by Scott Horton.

CHAPTER 25. ANTIDOTE

Quotes from Robb Nunzio from an interview conducted by Brian Jordan for the Double Cross website.

CHAPTER 26 MATINEE

Quote from Gary Tse Tse Fly 'We made it down to a matinee…' from an unpublished interview conducted by Scott Horton.

Quotes from Brendan Rafferty, Gavin Van Vlack and Tom O'Hara from unpublished interviews conducted by David Koenig

Quotes from Mike Bullshit from an unpublished interview conducted by Scott Horton.

CHAPTER 28: SKANK YOURSELF TO DEATH

Quotes from John Porcelly about John Watson and Jay Krakdown from 'Porcell's Top 10 Best Moshers' published on the Double Cross site.

CHAPTER 30: THE CRO-MAGS

Gavin Van Vlack quote from an interview conducted by James Damion for the United By Rocket Science website.

John Joseph quote 'Bloodclot was all..' from an interview conducted by Brett Beach published in Hardware Fanzine #7.

Gary Tse Tse Fly quote 'I think the Cro-Mags…' from an from an unpublished interview conducted by Scott Horton.

CHAPTER 31: PEACE PUNKS

All quotes from Victor Venom and Adam Mucci from interviews conducted by Freddy Alva for the liner notes of the Sacrilege LP.

Quote from John John Jesse from an unpublished interview conducted by Scott Horton.

CHAPTER 32: UNITED FORCES

Mike Bullshit quote from an unpublished interview conducted by Scott Horton.

Quote from Luke Abbey from an interview conducted by Tim McMahon and Brian Jordan for the Double Cross website.

CHAPTER 33: CRUMBSUCKERS

Quotes from Mike Bullshit from an unpublished interview conducted by Scott Horton.

CHAPTER 34: FUN!

All Uncle Al Morris quotes are from an interview published on the Swnk website.

CHAPTER 36: YOUTH OF TODAY

Ray Cappo quote, 'In February 1985...' from an interview conducted by Ron Guardipee that appeared in Bringin' It Back Fanzine #2

CHAPTER 37: WARZONE

Quote from Jules Massee from an interview conducted by Tim McMahon and Brian Jordan for the Double Cross website.

CHAPTER 38: YOUTH CREW

Quote from Luke Abbey from an interview conducted by Tim McMahon and Brian Jordan for the Double Cross website.

CHAPTER 39: STRAIGHT AHEAD

All Craig Setari quotes from an interview conducted by Lenny Zimkus for the Double Cross Website.

CHAPTER 40: ROCK HOTEL

Mike Bullshit quote from an unpublished interview conducted by Scott Horton.

CHAPTER 41: UNDERDOG

Adam Nathanson quote from an unpublished interview conducted by Dave Koenig.

CHAPTER 42: SOME RECORDS

Jason O'Toole and Gavin Van Vlack quotes from an unpublished interview conducted by Dave Koenig.

CHAPTER 46: DANCE HARD

Craig Setari quote from an interview conducted by Lenny Zimkus for the Double Cross Website.

CHAPTER 48: ABC NO RIO

Quotes from Brendan Rafferty, Mike Bullshit, Nick Forte and Daryl Kahan are from an unpublished interview conducted by Dave Koenig.

CHAPTER 49: HARDER THAN YOU

Quote from Adam Nathanson 'Let's see...' from an unpublished interview conducted by Dave Koenig.

Quote from Marlene Goldman from an unpublished interview conducted by Dave Koenig.

Quote from Nick Forte an unpublished interview conducted by Dave Koenig.

NYHC ESSENTIALS

FIFTY ESSENTIAL NYHC 7" RECORDS

STIMULATORS "Loud Fast Rules" 7" (self-released)

THE MAD "Eyeball" (Disgusting)

THE MAD "Fried Egg" (Disgusting)

EVEN WORSE "Mouse or Rat?" (Worse Than You)

THE MOB "Upset the System" (Mob Style)

THE MOB "Step Forward" (Mob Style)

HEART ATTACK "God Is Dead" (Damaged Goods)

MISGUIDED "Bringing It Down" (Reality)

MISGUIDED "Options" (Reality)

FALSE PROPHETS "Blind Obedience" (Worn out Brothers)

FALSE PROPHETS "Good Clean Fun" (Worn Out Brothers)

UNDEAD "Nine Toes Later" (Stiff)

UNDEAD "Verbal Abuse" (Post Mortem)

NIHILISTICS s/t (Visionary)

KRAUT "Kill for Cash" (Cabbage)

KRAUT "Unemployed" (Cabbage)

CRUCIAL T "Darkened Days" (Rat Cage)

URBAN WASTE (Mob Style)

THE ABUSED "Loud and Clear" (Abused Music)

AGNOSTIC FRONT "United Blood" (self-released)

CAUSE FOR ALARM (self-released)

ANTIDOTE "Thou Shall Not Kill" (self-released)

MAJOR CONFLICT (Silent Scream)

NO THANKS "Are You Ready To Die?" (Dead Space)

BEASTIE BOYS "Pollywog Stew" (Rat Cage)

TOKEN ENTRY "Ready or Not, Here We Come!" (Turnstyle Tunes)

YOUTH OF TODAY "Can't Close My Eyes" (Positive Force)

CRIPPLED YOUTH "Join the Fight" (New Beginning)

WARZONE "Lower East Side Crew" (Revelation)

UNDERDOG s/t (New Beginning)

SICK OF IT ALL s/t (Revelation)

PROJECT X s/t (Schism)

SIDE BY SIDE "You're Only Yong Once..." (Revelation)

GORILLA BISCUITS s/t (Revelation)

JUDGE "New York Crew" (Schism)

LIFES BLOOD "Defiance" (Combined Effort)

KRAKDOWN s/t (Common Cause)

YOUTH OF TODAY "Disengage" (Revealtion)

OUTBURST "Miles to Go" (Blackout)

BOLD s/t (Revelation)

BAD TRIP "Positively Bad" (Bell Bottom)

ALONE IN A CROWD s/t (Flux)

YOUTH DEFENSE LEAGUE "American Pride" (Oi! Core)

SUPERTOUCH (Combined Effort)

TRIP 6 "No Defeat! No Submission!" (Inner Strength)

GO! "Your Power Means Nothing" (King Fish)

CITIZENS ARREST "A Light in The Darkness" (Wardance)

BORN AGAINST s/t (Vermiform)

MADBALL "Ball of Destruction" (In-Effect)

QUICKSAND s/t (Revelation)

50 ESSENTIAL NYHC FULL LENGTHS

STIMULATORS *Loud Fast Rules* (ROIR)

BAD BRAINS s/t (ROIR)

NIHILISTICS s/t (Braineater)

KRAUT *An Adjustment to Society* (Cabbage)

HEART ATTACK *Keep Your Distance* (99)

ISM *Diet for the Worms* (S.I.N)

BAD BRAINS *Rock for Light* (PVC)

AGNOSTIC FRONT *Victim in Pain* (Ratcage)

STARK RAVING MAD s/t (Slob)

HEART ATTACK *Subliminal Seduction* (Rat Cage)

VIRUS *Dark Ages* (Rat Cage)

KRAUT *Whetting the Scythe* (Cabbage)

DAMAGE *Sins of our Fathers* (Gnarl)

BAD BRAINS *I Against I* (SST)

REAGAN YOUTH *Youth Anthems for the New Order* (R Radical)

FALSE PROPHETS s/t (Alternative Tentacles)

CRO-MAGS *The Age of Quarrel* (Rock Hotel/Profile)

MENTAL ABUSE *Streets of Filth* (Urinal)

STORMTROOPERS OF DEATH (S.O.D.) *Speak English or Die* (Megaforce)
MURPHYS LAW s/t (Rock Hotel/Profile)
AGNOSTIC FRONT *Cause for Alarm* (Combat Core)
CRUMBSUCKERS *Life of Dreams* (Combat Core)
REST IN PIECES *My Rage* (One Step Ahead)
CARNIVORE s/t (Roadrunner)
YOUTH OF TODAY *Break Down The Walls* (Wishingwell)
STRAIGHT AHEAD *Breakaway* (I Risk)
TOKEN ENTRY *From Beneath the Streets* (Positive Force)
REAGAN YOUTH *Volume Two* (New Red Archives)
WARZONE *Don't Forget the Struggle, Don't Forget the Streets* (Fist)
AGNOSTIC FRONT *Liberty and Justice For...* (Combat Core)
TOKEN ENTRY *Jaybird* (Hawker)
YOUTH OF TODAY *We're Not In This Alone* (Caroline)
BOLD *Speak Out* (Revelation)
WARZONE *Open Your Eyes* (Caroline)
LEEWAY *Born to Expire* (Profile)
CRO-MAGS *Best Wishes* (Profile)
MURPHYS LAW *Back With a Bong!* (Profile)
PRONG *Force Fed* (In-Effect)
AGNOSTIC FRONT *Live at CBGB* (In-Effect)
GORILLA BISCUITS *Start Today* (Revelation)
UNDERDOG *The Vanishing Point* (Caroline)
BAD BRAINS *Quickness* (Caroline)
JUDGE *Bringing It Down* (Revelation)
SICK OF IT ALL *Blood, Sweat and No Tears* (In-Effect)
KILLING TIME *Brightside* (In-Effect)
SHEER TERROR *Just Can't Hate Enough* (Starving Missile)
NAUSEA *Extinction* (Profane Existence)
BEYOND *No Longer at Ease* (Combined Effort)
RORSCHACH *Remain Sedate* (Vermiform)
SHELTER *Perfection of Desire* (Revelation)

15 ESSENTIAL NYHC COMPILATIONS

New York Thrash cassette (ROIR)
Big Apple : Rotten To the Core LP (S.I.N.)
Big City: Ain't Too Pretty 7" (Big City)
Big City: Nice 'N' Loud 7" (Big City)

Big City: Don't Want No Pity 7" (Big City)

Big City: One Big Crowd LP (Big City)

United Scene cassette (Guillotine Fanzine)

New York City Hardcore: Together 7" (Revelation)

New York City Hardcore: The Way It Is LP (Revelation)

New York Hardcore: Where The Wild Things Are LP (Blackout)

Squat or Rot 7" (Squat Or Rot)

Squat or Rot 2 7" (Squat Or Rot)

New Breed cassette (Urban Style)

Murders Among Us 7" (Vermiform)

Look at All the Children Now LP (Evacuate)

ESSENTIAL NYHC DEMO CASSETTES

THE ABUSED "1982 Demo"

MURPHYS LAW "Bong Blast"

CRO-MAGS "The Age of Quarrel"

THE PSYCHOS s/t

WARZONE "Street Kids"

LEEWAY "Enforcer"

SHEER TERROR "No Grounds for Pity…"

BREAKDOWN "'87 Demo"

BREAKDOWN "Running Scared"

SICK OF IT ALL s/t

UNDERDOG "True Blue"

UNDERDOG "Over the Edge"

RAW DEAL s/t

NY HOODS "Neutral"

OUTBURST "'87 Demo"

KRAKDOWN "'88 Demo"

YOUTH DEFENSE LEAGUE "Skins for Skins"

BEYOND "Dew It!"

ABOMINATION s/t

ABSOLUTION s/t

OUR GANG "Uprising"

MAXIMUM PENALTY "89 Demo"

PRESSURE RELEASE s/t

TRIP 6 "Back With A Vengeance"

BORN AGAINST "My Country Tis of Thee, Enemy of All Tribes"

TOMMY CARROLL

ACKNOWLEDGMENTS

THANKS TO: Howie Abrams, Jordan Cooper, Freddy Cricien, Steven Dilodovico, Mike D'elia, Tim McMahon, Freddy Alva, Diane Farris, Mike Gitter, Pete Talbot, Jack Rabid, and Roger Miret for contacts and leads for interviews.

Scott "Scoot' Horton, Diane Farris, Dave Koenig, Lyle Hysen, Dan Skibra, Freddy Alva, Lenny Zimkus, James Damion, Brett Beach, Tim McMahon, Brian "Gordo" Jordan for use of interviews they conducted.

Justine Demetrick, Greg Licht, Adam Tanner, Randy Underwood, Jordan Cooper, Gary Tse Tse Fly, Ken Salerno, and all the other photographers for use of the images they captured.

Dave Brady, Dave Scott, John Kelly, Tim Mcmahon, Freddy Alva, and Joe Songco for the use of their archives.

Steve Poss, Geoff D'agostino, Paul Bearer, Jonathan Buske, Doug Holland, Chris Zusi, Drew Stone, John Watson, Wendy Eager, Don Fury, Tim Mcmahon, Russ Iglay, Mike Judge, Jack Rabid, and Michael Scondotto for the support and help with checking facts.

EXTRA SPECIAL THANKS TO: Chris Minicucci and Rich Warwick from Radio Raheem Records for the use of their extensive NYHC archives.

M.V.P. AWARD GOES TO: Freddy Cricien for the continous encouragement and support throughout the project.

AND, OF COURSE, THANKS TO: Danielle, Carlin, Sandy, and my family for the support and understanding.